The Bible Handbook

The Bible Handbook

Revised Edition

W.P. Ball
G.W. Foote
John Bowden
Richard M. Smith
and others

American Atheist Press   Austin, Texas   1986

American Atheist Press, P.O. Box 2117, Austin, Texas 78768-2117.

ISBN 0-910309-26-4

Contents

ii

INTRODUCTION

It has long been the opinion of the officers and directors of the American Atheist Center that biblical criticism is not an appropriate exercise for Atheists. Atheism's *weltanschauung* is entirely too positive, too inspiring, too enlightening to be held back in its soaring flight by the need to peck at the entangled web of absurdities known as the "Holy Bible." The officials of the Center feel that it is usually demeaning to an Atheist to argue with a theist over his "holy" book no matter which idiotic "holy" book is proposed for discussion. Desperately, the theist does nothing with the Atheist's arguments and evidences but attempt to rationalize them in order to reinforce his religious ideology. Thus the exercise usually ends in futility.

Recently however, the culture of the Untied States has been infested anew by the vermin of religion to the point that on April 5, 1982, the United States Congress passed a resolution that the president of the nation should designate 1983 as "The Year of The Bible." In the early part of that year, on February 3rd, the President did so. Both the resolution of the Congress and the statement of designation of the President are herein reproduced, immediately following this introduction. With this kind of challenge flung into the face of American Atheists it became apparent that the challenge must have a reply.

Looking around for an appropriate reply, those of us who staff the Center found several small booklets and pamphlets written along the way by hopeful critics of the Bible. In addition, there was the old-time classic — Foote & Ball's *Bible Handbook* — which had once before been issued by the American Atheist Press. It was felt that if all of them were put under one cover, this would be the source that Atheists would need for "Letters to The Editor," for general argument, or to call in on television and talk-back radio programs to show the citizenry of the United States just exactly what the Bible was and why it should not be so exalted. Excerpts from the *Bible Handbook* would be the best of all material to send to a congressman or a senator who had voted for this noxious resolution.

Meanwhile, the American Atheist Center continues to point out to good Atheists everywhere that they should not, really, get their feet stuck in the flypaper. To enter into debates concerned with the Bible is to take a stand *on the grounds of the religionists.* This is *their* territory

— not ours. Also, it puts the Atheist into a negative position. It is, after all, not the logical position to attempt to affirm the negative in any proposition. It is the burden on the affirmative side to prove — not the burden of the Atheist to disprove, especially when he is challenged to disprove the nonsense of the entire Bible.

Despite our reluctance to get into this position, logic, reason, history and the scientific method are all on the side of the Atheist. To make a laughingstock of the Bible is a simple enough task.

In this edition Foote & Ball's *Bible Handbook* is set first, naturally. At the time that their book was first published in England, it was only necessary to give biblical references with chapter and verse since most people of that time era knew the Bible, often by rote. Such is not the situation today, and so it became necessary to look up each citation and copy the text in full for that citation. It was also decided that the King James version of the Bible should be used for these citations, since Foote and Ball had originally relied upon that version. There has, however, been much tampering with the King James version since their time.

When necessary, words, phrases, dates, numbers and places were italicized to make the references obvious.

It must be remembered that the Old Testament was originally written in Hebrew in what is called an "unpointed" system. Theologians and rabbis mean that it was written without vowels. Later "points" were added as vowels were guessed. There were no spaces between words, no punctuation, no sentences, and the verb "to be" was generally omitted. This short ensuing example of a very famous speech by an American president will suffice to show the problem. Where would you, dear reader, put vowels in order to interrupt the following flow of letters.

FRSCRNDSVNYRSGRFTHRSBR
GHTFRTHNTHSCNTNNTNWNT
NCNCVDNLBRTNDDDCTDTTH
PRPSTNTHTLLMNRCRTDQL

If you guessed that this was Abraham Lincoln's first sentence in the Gettysburg Address, you were right. But what would a German or Frenchman, a Palestinian or Egyptian guess? The above should be translated as:

Four score and seven years ago our fathers brought forth on this continent a new nation, conceived in liberty and dedicated to the proposition that all men are created equal.

Almost all biblical contradiction booklets which were issued in the United States — or for that matter anywhere in the world — are and have been based on Foote & Ball. The second section of this book presents two of these — one from the United States titled *Self-Contradictions of The Bible, 144 Propositions,* of which the author is unknown, and another from Australia titled *The Bible Contradicts Itself* by John Bowden. The latter was assembled by the author to attack one particular church (Herbert Armstrong's Worldwide Church of God) which is now about defunct. When Richard Smith of the American Atheist Center staff was typesetting this compilation, he took care to delete redundancies of these two booklets with Foote & Ball, as well as to correct erroneous citations, of which there were several. In the process he discovered several more absurdities and contradictions, and these were also inserted in a section which is titled "American Atheist Addenda."

It is the position of the American Atheist Center that almost all of the characters and some of the geographical locations of the Bible, both Old and New Testament, are completely mythological. However, spellings have been double checked and the text hews to the current, accepted, King James translation.

Since *The Bible Handbook* has been undertaken, albeit reluctantly, American Atheists will enlarge upon it in subsequent editions, if necessary. If you have even one more Bible contradiction, absurdity, atrocity, or indecency that you have found in your research, please forward it to the address given for the American Atheist Press in the first pages of this book.

It appears to me that this particular *Bible Handbook* is much more needed by the religious community in our nation than by any Atheist. We, therefore, exhort you to purchase copies to send to your congressmen, your senators, and perhaps one for the president of the United States. You may be interested in sending a copy to each member of your family who is religious, because *The Bible Handbook* is really "Good News for Modern Man."

Jon G. Murray

Senate Joint Resolution 165

97th Congress   2nd Session
IN THE HOUSE OF REPRESENTATIVES
April 5, 1982

Passed the Senate March 31 (legislative day, February 22), 1982.
Attest: William F. Hildebrand, Secretary.
Authorizing and requesting the President to proclaim 1983 as
the "Year of the Bible."

5527

Federal Register   **Presidential Documents**

Vol. 48, No. 26

Monday, February 7, 1983

Title 3 —   Proclamation 5018 of February 3, 1983
The President   **YEAR OF THE BIBLE, 1983**
By the President of the United States of America
A Proclamation

Of the many influences that have shaped the United States of
America into a distinctive nation and people, none may be said to be
more fundamental and enduring than the Bible.

Deep religious beliefs stemming from the Old and New Testaments
of the Bible inspired many of the early settlers of our country, providing
them with the strength, character, convictions, and faith necessary to
withstand great hardship and danger in this new and rugged land.
These shared beliefs helped forge a sense of common purpose among
the widely dispersed colonies — a sense of community which laid the
foundation for the spirit of nationhood that was to develop in later
decades.

The Bible and its teachings helped form the basis for the Founding
Fathers' abiding belief in the inalienable rights of the individual, rights
which they found implicit in the Bible's teachings of the inherent worth
and dignity of each individual. This same sense of man patterned the
convictions of those who framed the English system of law inherited by

our own nation, as well as the ideals set forth in the Declaration of Independence and the Constitution.

For centuries the Bible's emphasis on compassion and love for our neighbor has inspired institutional and governmental expressions of benevolent outreach such as private charity, the establishment of schools and hospitals, and the abolition of slavery.

Many of our greatest national leaders — among them Presidents Washington, Jackson, Lincoln, and Wilson — have recognized the influence of the Bible on our country's development. The plainspoken Andrew Jackson referred to the Bible as no less than "the rock on which our Republic rests." Today our beloved America and, indeed, the world, is facing a decade of enormous challenge. As a people we may well be tested as we have seldom, if ever, been tested before. We will need resources of spirit even more than resources of technology, education, and armaments. There could be no more fitting moment than now to reflect with gratitude, humility, and urgency upon the wisdom revealed to us in the writing that Abraham Lincoln called "the best gift God has ever given to man . . . But for it we could not know right from wrong."

The Congress of the United States, in recognition of the unique contribution of the Bible in shaping the history and character of this nation, and so many of its citizens, has by Senate Joint Resolution 165 authorized and requested the President to designate the year 1983 as the "Year of the Bible."

Federal Register / Vol. 48, No. 26 / Monday, February 7, 1983

5528

NOW, THEREFORE, I, RONALD REAGAN, President of the United States of America, in recognition of the contributions and influence of the Bible on our Republic and our people, do hereby proclaim 1983 the Year of the Bible in the United States. I encourage all citizens, each in his or her own way, to reexamine and rediscover its priceless and timeless message.

IN WITNESS WHEREOF, I have hereunto set my hand this third day of February, in the year of our Lord nineteen hundred and eighty-three, and of the Independence of the United States of America the two hundred and seventh.

[FR Doc. 82-31372
Filed 11-12-82; 11:15 am]
Billing code 3195-01-M

FOREWORD
TO
THE FIRST AMERICAN EDITION

Citizens of the United States are, by and large, religious illiterates. They know little, often nothing, of the religions of the world and even less of the distinctions, obvious or subtle, which set apart the sects of Christianity. They slip easily from one creed to another. Born into the Methodist faith, a casual encounter with a Presbyterian can lead to adherence to that schemata of Christianity. The tender whisper of love can later hand the same person to the Episcopalian faith, the Baptists, or the Lutheran church.

Rock groups have led our young to salvation through gurus, saffron robes, shaved heads, religious communes, and the sale of flowers on street corners.

A political campaign can send Christians of our nation in stampedes into the arms of evangelicals of every stripe, obvious charlatans, phony faith healers, screamers, tiny tot preachers or Bible thumpers. Black, white, yellow, or brown, the Elmer Gantrys stand poised to lead the flock and to fleece them.

Gifts pour into religious coffers at the rate of over $30 billion a year, approximately $80 million a day. City, county, state, and federal governments vie each one with the other to offer stipends to religion as politicians see in the malleable religious mass certain victory in the next political test for office. Corporations and foundations spread their largess to the increase of this bizarre commitment to irrationality.

The Bible and religious books continue as all-time best sellers. At any hour of the day or night religion can be heard from half a dozen radio stations in any city or town. Television bogs down with it. Christmas and Easter become nightmares of repetititous religious drivel.

This is all reinforced by the resurrection of religion's counterpart: Satanism, witchcraft and demon possession. Cinema exploits the fear of evil and hell to herd the faithful and the not-so-faithful into compliance with the idea of a "Christian America."

From this we see a massive attack on the scientific process, a contempt for education, and a reliance, in a technological age, on "human instinct." Religious leaders are voted as "most admired" of all in the United States and their access is into the center of political, business, and educational power. The highest courts in the states, the federal court system, and even the United States Supreme Court cringe before the power of organized religion. The scientific community is so cowed it dares not challenge. Educators, especially college and university professors, are paralyzed in fear, not even hoping to confront the great beast of religion.

Yet, our citizens, by and large, remain religious illiterates. The Bible is accepted, but not read — critically or religiously. Yet, on this book, as the alleged word of god, rests the entire superstructure of religion in our nation and, particularly, the peculiar, wholly American phenomenon of "evangelism."

It is at this time that we can dip into history to the thoughts of Robert G. Ingersoll, writing even before Foote and Ball produced this *Bible Handbook*. Incredibly, in the United States, well over a hundred years ago, he was saying what needs to be repeated today:

> Somebody ought to tell the truth about the Bible. The preachers dare not, because they would be driven from their pulpits. Professors in colleges dare not, because they would lose their salaries. Politicians dare not. They would be defeated. Editors dare not. They would lose subscribers. Merchants dare not, because they might lose customers. Men of fashion dare not, fearing that they would lose caste. Even clerks dare not, because they might be discharged. And so I thought I would do it myself.

> There are many millions of people who believe the Bible to be the inspired word of God — millions who think that this book is staff and guide, counselor and consoler; that it fills the present with peace and the future with hope — millions who believe that it is the fountain of law, justice and mercy, and that to its wise and benign teachings the world is indebted for its liberty, wealth and civilization — millions who imagine that the book is a revelation from the wisdom and love of God to the brain and heart of man — millions who regard this book as a torch that conquers the darkness of death, and pours its radiance on another world — a world without a tear.

> They forget its ignorance and savagery, its hatred of liberty, its religious persecution; they remember heaven, but they forget the dungeon of eternal pain.

> They forget that it imprisons the brain and corrupts the heart. They forget that it is the enemy of intellectual freedom.

I attack this book because it is the enemy of human liberty — the greatest obstruction across the highway of human progress.

Let us free ourselves from the tyranny of a book, from the slavery of dead ignorance, from the aristocracy of the air.

* * *

After all, the real question is not whether the Bible is inspired, but whether it is true. If it is true, it does not need to be inspired. If it is true, it makes no difference whether it was written by a man or a god. The multiplication table is just as useful, just as true as though God had arranged the figures himself. If the Bible is really true, the claim of inspiration need not be urged; if it is not true, its inspiration can hardly be established. As a matter of fact, the truth does not need to be inspired. Nothing needs inspiration except a falsehood or a mistake. Where truth ends, where probability stops, inspiration begins. A fact never went into partnership with a miracle. Truth does not need the assistance of a miracle. A fact will fit every other fact in the universe, because it is the product of all other facts. A lie will fit nothing except another lie made for the express purpose of fitting it.

If the Bible is really the work of God, it should contain the grandest and sublimest truths. It should, in all respects, excel the works of man. Within that book should be found the best and loftiest definitions of justice; the truest conceptions of human liberty; the clearest outlines of duty; the tenderest, the highest, and the noblest thoughts — not that the human mind has produced, but that the human mind is capable of receiving. Upon every page should be found the luminous evidence of its divine origin. Unless it contains grander and more wonderful things than man has written, we say that it was written by no being superior to man. It may be said that it is unfair to call attention to certain bad things in the Bible, while the good are not so much as mentioned. To this may be replied that a divine being would not put bad things in a book. Certainly a being of infinite intelligence, power, and goodness could never fall below the ideal of depraved and barbarous man. It will not do, after we find that the Bible upholds what we now call crimes, to say that it is not verbally inspired.

If there is one uninspired word — that is, one word in the wrong place, or a word that ought not to be there — to that extent the Bible is not an inspired book.

Either God should have written a book to fit my brain, or should have made my brain to fit his book. The inspiration of the Bible depends on the credulity of him who reads.

Why should men, in the name of religion, try to harmonize the contradictions that exist between nature and a book? Why should philosophers be denounced for placing more reliance upon what they know than upon what they are told?

Why indeed? Because, in the culture of our times, if a large dose of nonsense is repeated with great solemnity time after time, it comes to be accepted and believed. The truth of this is demonstrated in television commercials daily. Nothing can be more patently absurd than the canonization of Mother Seton and Cardinal Neumann, who — although both dead for many scores of years — have been documented to have interceded with god for the cure of cancer of several persons suffering therefrom. These saints of the Roman Catholic Church, given the opportunity to such an intercession, chose to halt the progress of the disease in several good Roman Catholic adherents, but did not choose to overcome cancer by the total eradication of it.

The fewer persons who read the Bible, the more powerful it becomes in symbolism. Left to interpretation by the clergy, it can mean anything that it is desired to mean. We, thus, come full cycle back to the Church dominance prior to the Protestant Revolution. Although our inward screaming is heard in our heads, too many simply rejoin with "We can't have slipped back to the Dark Ages." Ah, but indeed we have.

It is for this reason that we bring out the first American edition of this extraordinary book — a clear, precise assault upon the basis of Judeo-Christianity, a review of the contradictions and irrationalities of the Old and the New Testaments. You need the knowledge to face, again, your "brothers and sisters in Christ" and to rescue them from the mental stultification which they see as "salvation."

Madalyn O'Hair
May 1977

(*This introduction by Dr. O'Hair was written when the first U. S. issue of the* Bible Handbook *was released by American Atheist Press.*)

ORIGINAL PREFACE
to
BIBLE HANDBOOK
by
G. W. FOOTE

The Bible is a volume of miscellaneous character. It was written by many authors, some of whose names are known and others unknown. It contains poetry, history, legends, myths, philosophy, ethics, prophecy, parable, and superstition. Good and bad, beautiful and ugly, savage and tender, are wonderfully mixed up in its pages. It is also a very large book, and therefore it is easily read in an uncritical spirit. There is not even an index to help the reader, although the deficiency is to some extent supplied by concordances. But who, except a student in search of a half-remembered passage, or a parson picking out texts for a sermon, ever thinks of working in those dreary mines? Hence the necessity for this *Bible Handbook*, which is chiefly designed for freethinkers, but should also be of service to inquiring Christians.

The object of this compilation is certainly not orthodox, and the general body of Christians will doubtless object to its methods. They will probably deny the fairness of pulling the Bible to pieces in this fashion. But the apologists of the Christian scriptures are constantly occupied in belauding them, and there is no necessity to duplicate their performance; on the contrary, there is room for something of an opposite description, and this is what is here produced. Not the best, but the worst things in the Bible are selected; its self-contradictions, its absurdities, immoralities, its indecencies, and its brutalities. Unquestionably it would be grossly unfair to disembowel an ordinary book in this way. One would not so treat Shakespeare, or any other great classic, either of modern times or of antiquity. But the Bible is not an ordinary book. It is stamped as "god's word" by act of Parliament; it is forced into the hands of children in our private and public schools; it is used as a kind of fetish for swearing upon in our Courts of Law and our Houses of Legislation. People have been robbed of their children in its name, or excluded from public positions to which they were elected by their fellow-citizens. Men are still liable, at law, to imprisonment for bringing it into "disbelief and contempt." Surely, then, a book which makes, or has made for it, such extraordinary pretensions should be subjected to extraordinary tests. We may admit a mirror to be a good one, although we observe some blemishes; but we are entitled to point out its flaws when it is declared to be perfect.

When the Bible takes its place beside the other Sacred Books of the East, it will call for no exposure. But that time is far distant, in spite of the great advances of what is called the Higher Criticism; and in the meantime it is a requisite, even if a thankless, task to accentuate the false, foolish, and wicked features of the Bible, as an antidote to the reckless adulation of its bigoted devotees and mercenary flatterers.

With regard to our Bible Contradictions, it may be observed that most of them are printed in a chronological order, but those relating to the deity are massed together. It would have been easy to include a great many more, but these would have been less obvious, and would have required elucidation. Being printed in parallel columns, the Contradictions strike the eye as well as the mind; and it seems surprising that such a useful arrangement was not adopted before.

In the subsequent parts of this Handbook the various extracts are printed under headlines; but this is not exactly an innovation, for headings are given to all the chapters in the authorized version. Editorial notes are also appended in brackets, wherever they appeared to be necessary, either for explication or for emphasis. But there has been no tampering with the Bible text, and text and comment have always been kept well apart, so that the Bible might speak for itself and tell its own tale.

Such is our general rule, but an exception was necessary in the case of Bible Obscenities. Whether it were advisable, if it were safe, to print a collection of inspired filth, is a question we need not argue. Such a course is *not* safe. The courts have decided that to publish the obscene parts of *any* volume, for *whatever* purpose, is a criminal offence, punishable with heavy fine or long imprisonment. We refrain, therefore, from printing the libidinous and bestial parts* of the Bible, and rest satisfied with giving the fullest references. Thorough-going students can easily copy out the loathsome texts for themselves, and every sensible

---

*The American Atheist Press felt no such compunction and the texts are quoted in full throughout this edition.

man will excuse us from martyrdom in such a cause. But the very fact that we *dare* not print a multitude of Bible texts is a sufficient refutation of its claim to be considered as the Word of God.

It is only common courtesy to mention our predecessors in this field. We have derived some help from *The Scripturian's Creed*, by J. Davies, which was first printed in 1807, and reprinted in 1822, by Richard Carlile. Henry Hetherington also published a voluminous work on the discrepancies of the Bible, by an anonymous writer who must have had uncommon patience and uncommon leisure. Half the Bible is flung pell-mell over its pages, and text and comment are jumbled together. Far more workmanlike and useful was the *Few Self-Contradictions of The Bible*, published and possibly compiled by Thomas Scott, of Ramsgate. This was sold at a shilling, and only circulated through the post. Robert Cooper's *Holy Scriptures Analysed* was long in use, but it must have been in default of a better. It seems a very hasty compilation done in the scanty leisure of a busy life. Twelve pages are devoted to Contradictions, but many of them were only discrepancies of expression, while a number of striking contradictions in fact were omitted.

The compilation of our Bible Handbook involved a great expenditure of time and trouble. Most of the drudgery was done by Mr. Ball, who went through the Bible again and again, with more than the patience of Job. For the sake of accuracy the texts were cut out of "Holy Writ" with a penknife. This necessitated the merciless mutilation of several Bibles; a deed which, in orthodox eyes, will be probably not the least of our offences.

The labour bestowed on this volume must give it some merit. Still, we are prepared to find it has imperfections. Such as it is, however, we send it forth, hoping it will assist Freethinkers, suggest fresh thoughts to inquiring Christians, and startle others out of their superstitious sleep. To the Freethinker, especially, it should prove very useful. Unless he keeps a Common-place Book, he will often be puzzled to find a text that he remembers. Sometimes he has forgotten the text, and only retains a dim recollection of its character. But with this little volume by him he need never be at a loss. Should he, as is very probable, get into discussion with a Christian, he has only to open our Handbook, and in five minutes he will be able to advance more arguments against the Bible than his opponent will be able to answer in a lifetime.

G. W. Foote
July, 1900

BIBLE CONTRADICTIONS

I. THE OLD TESTAMENT — HISTORICAL, ETC.

But of the tree of the knowledge of good and evil, thou shalt not eat of it: for in the day that thou eatest thereof thou shalt surely die. Gen. 2:17.

And all the days that Adam lived were nine hundred and thirty years: and he died. Gen. 5:5.

And God made the beast of the earth after his kind, and cattle after their kind, and every thing that creepeth upon the earth after his kind: and God saw that it was good. And God said, "Let us make man in our image, after our likeness." Gen. 1:25, 26. [Man was made *after* the beasts.]

And the LORD God said, "It is not good that the man should be alone; I will make him an help meet for him." And out of the ground the LORD God formed every beast of the field, and every fowl of the air; and brought them unto Adam . . . .but for Adam there was not found an help meet for him. Gen. 2:18-20. [Man was made *before* the beasts.]

And Arphaxad lived five and thirty years, and begat Salah. Gen. 11:12.

Sala, which was the son of Cainan, which was the son of Arphaxad. Luke 3:35, 36.

Of every clean beast thou shalt take to thee by sevens, the male and his female. Gen. 7:2.

Of every living thing of all flesh, two of every sort shalt thou bring into the ark. Gen. 6:19.

Of clean beasts, and of beasts that are not clean, and of fowls. . . . There went in two and two unto Noah into the ark, the male and the female, as God had commanded Noah. Gen. 7:8, 9.

1

And Abraham called the name of that place Jehovah-jireh: as it is said to this day, In the mount of the LORD it shall be seen. Gen. 22: 14. ["The LORD" in the Old Testament always represents the Hebrew "Jehovah." See Gen. 2:4: The LORD God made the earth and the heavens.]

And God spake unto Moses and said unto him, "I am the LORD: and I appeared unto Abraham, unto Isaac, and unto Jacob, by the name of God Almighty, but by my name JEHOVAH was I not known to them." Exod. 6:2, 3.

And Terah lived seventy years, and begat Abraham, Nahor, and Haran. . . . And the days of Terah were two hundred and five years: and Terah died in Haran. Gen. 11: 26, 32.

And Abram was seventy and five years old when he departed out of Haran. Gen. 12:4. (Then came he out of the land of the Chaldeans, and dwelt in Haran: and from thence, when his father was dead, he removed him into this land, wherein ye now dwell.) Acts 7:4. [After living 135 years Abraham was only 75 years old.]

By faith Abraham, when he was tried, offered up Isaac; and he that had received the promises offered up his only begotten son. Heb. 11:17.

For it is written, that Abraham had two sons, the one by a bondmaid, the other by a freewoman. Gal. 4:22. And Hagar bare Abram a son. Gen. 16:15.

Then again Abraham took a wife, and her name was Keturah. Gen. 25:1.

Keturah, Abraham's concubine. 1 Chron. 1:32.

And I will give unto thee [Abraham] and to thy seed after thee . . . all the land of Canaan, for an everlasting possession. Gen. 17: 8.

And he gave him none inheritance in it, no, not so much as to set his foot on. Acts 7:5.
By faith he sojourned in the land of promise . . . with Isaac and Jacob. . . . These all died in faith, not having received the promises. Heb. 11:9, 13.

All the souls that came with Jacob into Egypt, which came out of his loins, besides Jacob's sons' wives, all the souls were threescore and six; and the sons of Joseph, which were born him in Egypt, were two souls: all the souls of the house of Jacob, which came into Egypt, were threescore and ten. Gen. 46:26, 27.

For his sons carried him into the land of Canaan, and buried him in the cave of the field of Machpelah, which Abraham bought with the field for a possession of a burying-place of Ephron the Hittite, before Mamre. Gen. 50: 13.

Now the sojourning of the children of Israel, who dwelt in Egypt, was four hundred and thirty years. Exod. 12:40. Now to Abraham and his seed were the promises made . . . the covenant . . . the law . . . was four hundred and thirty years after. Gal. 3:16, 17.

And those that died in the plague were twenty and four thousand. Num. 25:9.

And they removed from Kadesh, and pitched in mount Hor, in the edge of the land of Edom. And Aaron the priest went up into

Then sent Joseph, and called his father Jacob to him, and all his kindred, threescore and fifteen souls. Acts 7:14.

And all the souls that came out of the loins of Jacob were seventy souls: for Joseph was in Egypt already. Exod. 1:5.

So Jacob went down into Egypt, and died, he, and our fathers, and were carried over into Sychem, and laid in the sepulchre that Abraham bought for a sum of money of the sons of Emmor the father of Sychem. Acts 7:15, 16.

And God spake on this wise, That his seed should sojourn in a strange land; and that they should bring them into bondage, and entreat them evil four hundred years. Acts 7:6. [Jacob and his sons did not enter Egypt till 215 years after the call of Abraham (and 112 years after Abraham's death); so that the Israelites could not have suffered in Egypt for more than 215 years.]

Neither let us commit fornication, as some of them committed, and fell in one day three and twenty thousand. 1 Cor. 10:8.

And the children of Israel took their journey from Beeroth of the children of Jaakan to Mosera: there Aaron died, and there he

mount Hor at the commandment of the LORD, and died there. . . . And they departed from mount Hor, and pitched in Zalmonah. And they departed from Zalmonah, and pitched in Punon. Num. 33:37-42.

And God spake all these words, saying . . . "the seventh day is the sabbath of the LORD thy god; in it thou shalt not do any work, thou, nor thy son, nor thy daughter, thy manservant, nor thy maidservant, nor thy cattle, nor thy stranger that is within thy gates: For in six days the LORD made heaven and earth, the sea, and all that in them is, and rested the seventh day; wherefore the LORD blessed the sabbath day, and hallowed it." Exod. 20:1, 10, 11.

It shall be a statute for ever. Lev. 23:14, 21, 31, 41.

Thou shalt not kill. Exod. 20:13.

Now the man Moses was very meek, above all the men which were upon the face of the earth. Num. 12:3.

was buried, and Eleazar his son ministered in the priest's office in his stead. From thence they journeyed unto Gudgodah; and from Gudgodah to Jotbath. Deut. 10: 6, 7.

The LORD talked with you face to face in the mount out of the midst of the fire . . . saying, "the seventh day is the sabbath of the LORD thy God: in it thou shalt not do any work . . . And remember that thou wast a servant in the land of Egypt, and that the LORD thy God brought thee out thence through a mighty hand and by a stretched out arm: therefore the LORD thy God commanded thee to keep the sabbath day." Deut. 5:4, 5, 14, 15.

But now we are delivered from the law. Rom. 7:6.

Thus saith the LORD God of Israel, "Put every man his sword by his side, and go in and out from gate to gate throughout the camp, and slay every man his brother, and every man his companion, and every man his neighbour." Exod. 32:27.

And Moses was wroth . . . And Moses said unto them, "Have ye saved all the women alive? . . . Now therefore kill every male among the little ones, and kill every woman. . . . But all the women children . . . keep alive for yourselves." Num. 31:14, 17, 18.

4

And it came to pass in the *four hundred and eightieth* year after the children of Israel were come out of the land of Egypt, in the fourth year of Solomon's reign over Israel in the month Zif, which is the second month, that he began to build the house of the LORD. 1 Kings 6:1. [By Paul's reckoning this should be the 595th year after the Exodus; 40 plus 450 plus 21 (Samuel's rule) plus 40 (Saul's reign) plus 40 (David's reign) plus 4 equals 595.]

And about the time of forty years suffered he their manners in the wilderness. . . . And after that he gave unto them judges about the space of four hundred and fifty years, until Samuel the prophet. And afterward they desired a king; and God gave unto them Saul the son of Cis, a man of the tribe of Benjamin, by the space of forty years. And when he had removed him, he raised up unto them David to be their king. Acts 13:18-22.

And the Spirit of the LORD came upon him, and he went down to Ashkelon, and slew thirty men of them, and took their spoil. Judg. 14:19.

But the fruit of the Spirit is love, joy, peace, longsuffering, gentleness, goodness, faith, meekness, temperance. Gal. 5:22, 23.

And when Saul enquired of the LORD, the LORD answered him not, neither by dreams nor by Urim, nor by prophets. 1 Sam. 28:6.

Saul . . . enquired not of the LORD: therefore he slew him, and turned the kingdom unto David, the son of Jesse. 1 Chron. 10:13, 14.

Again, Jesse made seven of his sons to pass before Samuel. And Samuel said unto Jesse, "The Lord hath not chosen these." And Samuel said unto Jesse, "Are here all thy children?" And he said, "There remaineth yet the youngest, and, and, behold, he keepeth the sheep." 1 Sam. 16:10, 11

And Jesse begat his first-born, Eliab, and Abinadab the second, and Shimma the third, Nethaneel the fourth, Raddai the fifth, Ozem the sixth, David the seventh. 1 Chron. 2:13-15.

Wherefore Saul sent messengers unto Jesse, and said, "Send me David thy son." . . . And David came to Saul, and stood before him: and he loved him greatly; and

And when Saul saw David go forth against the Philistine, he said unto Abner, the captain of the host, "Abner, whose son is this youth?" and Abner said, "As thy

5

he became his armourbearer. And Saul sent to Jesse, saying, "Let David, I pray thee, stand before me; for he hath found favour in my sight." 1 Sam. 16:19-22.

And there went out a champion out of the camp of the Philistines, named Goliath, of Gath, whose height was six cubits and a span . . . and the staff of his spear was like a weaver's beam. . . . So David prevailed over the Philistine with a sling and with a stone, and smote the Philistine and slew him. 1 Sam. 17:4, 7, 50.

And when they came to Nachon's threshingfloor, Uzzah put forth his hand to the ark of God, and took hold of it; for the oxen shook it. 2 Sam. 6:6.

And David took from him a thousand chariots, and *seven hundred* horsemen, and twenty thousand footmen. 2 Sam. 8:4.

And the Syrians fled before Israel; and David slew the men of *seven hundred* chariots of the Syrians, and *forty thousand horsemen*, and smote Shobach the captain of their host, who died there. 2 Sam. 10:18.

And Satan stood up against Israel, and provoked David to number Israel. 1. Chron. 21:1.

soul liveth, O king, I cannot tell." And the king said, "Inquire thou whose son the stripling is." 1 Sam. 17:55, 56.

Elhanan the son of Jaareoregim, a Bethlehemite, slew Goliath, the Gittite, the staff of whose spear was like a weaver's beam. 2 Sam. 21:19. (Revised Version) [Gittite, equal to "of Gath." The words "the brother of" are inserted in the Authorized Version to avoid the contradiction. Verse 22 (These four were born to the giant in Gath . . .) would seem to necessitate the words "son of."]

And when they came unto the threshingfloor of Chidon, Uzza put forth his hand to hold the ark; for the oxen stumbled. 1 Chron. 13:9.

And David took from him a thousand chariots, and *seven thousand* horsemen, and twenty thousand footmen. 1 Chron. 18:4.

But the Syrians fled before Israel; and David slew of the Syrians *seven thousand* men which fought in chariots, and forty thousand *footmen*, and killed Shophach the captain of the host. 1 Chron. 19:18.

And again the anger of the LORD was kindled against Israel, and he moved David against them to say, "Go, number Israel and Judah." 2 Sam. 24:1.

And Joab gave up the sum of the number of the people unto the king: and there were in Israel eight hundred thousand valiant men that drew the sword; and the men of Judah were five hundred thousand men. 2 Sam. 24:9.

And the king said unto Araunah, "Nay; but I will surely buy it of thee at a price: neither will I offer burnt offerings unto the LORD my God of that which doth cost me nothing." So David bought the threshingfloor and the oxen for fifty shekels of silver. 2 Sam. 24:24.

So Gad came to David, and told him, and said unto him, "Shall *seven years of famine* come unto thee in thy land? or wilt thou flee three months before thine enemies, while they pursue thee? or that there be three days' pestilence in thy land?" 2 Sam. 24:13.

I will give you the sure mercies of David. Acts 13:34.

And Joab gave the sum of the number of the people unto David. And all they of Israel were a thousand thousand and an hundred thousand men that drew sword: and Judah was four hundred threescore and ten thousand men that drew sword. But Levi and Benjamin counted he not among them: for the king's word was abominable to Joab. 1 Chron. 21:5, 6.

So David gave to Ornan for the place six hundred shekels of gold by weight. 1 Chron. 21:25.

So Gad came to David, and said unto him, "Thus saith the LORD Choose thee either *three years' famine*; or three months to be destroyed before thy foes, while that the sword of thine enemies overtaketh thee; or else three days the sword of the LORD, even the pestilence.' " 1 Chron. 21:11, 12.

And he brought out the people that were in it, and cut them with saws, and with harrows of iron, and with axes. Even so dealt David with all the cities of the children of Ammon. 1 Chron. 20:3.

And he brought forth the people that were therein, and he put them under saws, and under harrows of iron, and under axes of

7

For I have kept the ways of the LORD, and have not wickedly departed from my God. For all his judgments were before me: and as for his statutes, I did not depart from them. I was also upright before him, and have kept myself from mine iniquity. 2 Sam. 22:22-24; Ps. 18:21-23.

David did that which was right in the eyes of the LORD, and turned not aside from anything that he commanded him all the days of his life, save only in the matter of Uriah the Hittite. 1 Kings 15:5.

Therefore Michal the daughter of Saul had no child unto the day of her death. 2 Sam. 6:23.

iron, and made them pass through the brickkiln: and thus did he unto all the cities of the children of Ammon. 2 Sam. 12:31.

Remember not the sins of my youth, nor my transgressions: according to thy mercy remember thou me for thy goodness sake, O LORD. Ps. 25:7.

Mine iniquities have taken hold upon me. Ps. 40:12; 38:3, 4.

The five sons of Michal the daughter of Saul, whom she bare for Adriel. 2 Sam. 21:8. (Revised Version). [The Authorized Version attempts to cover the contradiction by substituting "brought up" for "bare." See also verses 4-6:

And the Gibeonites said unto him, "We will have no silver nor gold of Saul, nor of his house; neither for us shalt thou kill any man in Israel." And he said, "What ye shall say, that will I do for you."

And they answered the king, "That man that consumed us, and that devised against us that we should be destroyed from remaining in any of the coasts of Israel.

[Let seven men of *his sons* be delivered unto us, and we will hang them up unto the LORD in Gibeah of Saul, whom the LORD did choose." And the king said, "I will give them."]

And Solomon had forty thousand stalls of horses for his chariots, and twelve thousand horsemen. 1 Kings 4:26.

And Solomon had four thousand stalls for horses and chariots, and twelve thousand horsemen. 2 Chron. 9:25.

For he cast two pillars of brass, of eighteen cubits high apiece: and a line of twelve cubits did compass either of them about. . . . And he set up the pillars in the porch of the temple: and he set up the right pillar, and called the name thereof Jachin: and he set up the left pillar, and called the name thereof Boaz. 1 Kings 7:15, 21.

Also he made before the house two pillars of thirty and five cubits high, and the chapiter that was on the top of each of them was five cubits . . . . And he reared up the pillars before the temple, one on the right hand, and the other on the left; and called the name of that on the right hand Jachin, and the name of that on the left Boaz. 2 Chron. 3:15, 17.

And he made a molten sea . . . . it contained two thousand baths. 1 Kings 7:23, 26.

Also he made a molten sea . . . . and it received and held three thousand baths. 2 Chron. 4:2, 5.

Wisdom is the principal thing; therefore get wisdom: and with all thy getting get understanding. Prov. 4:7.

For it is written, I will destroy the wisdom of the wise, and will bring to nothing the understanding of the prudent. 1 Cor. 1:19.

Happy is the man that findeth wisdom, and the man that getteth understanding. Prov. 3:13.

For in much wisdom is much grief: and he that increaseth knowledge increaseth sorrow. Eccles. 1:18.

The righteous shall flourish like the palm tree. Ps. 92:12.

The righteous perisheth, and no man layeth it to heart. Isa. 57:1.

All things come alike to all: there is one event to the righteous, and to the wicked. Eccles. 9:2.

There shall no evil happen to the just. Prov. 12:21.

For whom the Lord loveth he chasteneth, and scourgeth every son whom he receiveth. Heb. 12:6.

The years of the wicked shall be shortened. Prov. 10:27.
Bloody and deceitful men shall not live out half their days. Ps. 55: 23.

Wherefore do the wicked live, become old, yea, are mighty in power? Their seed is established in their sight with them, and their offspring before their eyes. Their houses are safe from fear, neither is the rod of God upon them. Job 21:7, 8, 9.

Yea, the light of the wicked shall be put out, and the spark of his fire shall not shine. . . . Terrors shall make him afraid on every side. . . . He shall be driven from light into darkness, and chased out of the world. He shall neither have son nor nephew among his people, nor any remaining in his dwellings. Job 18:5, 11, 18, 19.

For I was envious at the foolish, when I saw the prosperity of the wicked. For there are no bands in their death: but their strength is firm. They are not in trouble as other men; neither are they plagued like other men. . . . Behold, these are the ungodly, who prosper in the world; they increase in riches. Ps. 73:3-5, 12.

Who shall not fear thee, O Lord, and glorify thy name? for thou only art holy. Rev. 15:4.

Preserve my soul; for I am holy. Ps. 86:2.

The dead know not any thing, neither have they any more reward. Eccles. 9:5.

These shall go away into everlasting punishment: but the righteous unto life eternal. Matt. 25:46.

Look not thou upon the wine when it is red, when it giveth his colour in the cup, when it moveth itself aright. At the last it biteth like

And thou shalt bestow that money for whatsoever thy soul lusteth after, for oxen, or for sheep, or for wine, or for strong

a serpent, and stingeth like an adder. Prov. 23:31, 32.

Wine is a mocker, strong drink is raging: and whosoever is deceived thereby is not wise. Prov. 20:1.

drink, or for whatsoever thy soul desireth: and thou shalt eat there before the LORD thy God, and thou shalt rejoice, thou, and thine household. Deut. 14:26.

After the same manner also he took the cup, when he had supped, saying, "This cup is the new testament in my blood: this do ye, as oft as ye drink it, in remembrance of me." 1 Cor. 11:25.

And Jehoram [the son of Ahab] reigned in his stead in the second year of Jehoram the son of Jehoshaphat king of Judah. 2 Kings 1:17.

And in the fifth year of Joram [Jehoram] the son of Ahab king of Israel, Jehoshaphat being then king of Judah, Jehoram the son of Jehoshaphat king of Judah began to reign. 2 Kings 8:16.

And Rehoboam loved Maachah the daughter of Absalom above all his wives. . . . And Rehoboam made Abijah the son of Maachah the chief, to be ruler among his brethren. 2 Chron. 11:21, 22.

Now in the eighteenth year of king Jeroboam began Abijah to reign over Judah. He reigned three years in Jerusalem. His mother's name also was Michaiah the daughter of Uriel of Gibeah. 2 Chron. 13:1, 20.

And out of the city he took an officer that was set over the men of war, and *five men* of them that were in the king's presence, which were found in the city. 2 Kings 25:19.

He took also out of the city an eunuch, which had the charge of the men of war; and *seven men* of them that were near the king's person, which were found in the city. Jer. 52:25.

Jehoiachin was eight years old when he began to reign, and he reigned three months and ten days in Jerusalem. 2 Chron. 36:9.

Jehoiachin was eighteen years old when he began to reign, and he reigned in Jerusalem three months. 2 Kings 24:8.

So Baasha slept with his fathers, and was buried in Tirzah: and Elah

In the six and thirtieth year of the reign of Asa Baasha king of his son reigned in his stead. . . . In the twenty and sixth year of Asa king of Judah began Elah the son of Baasha to reign over Israel. 1 Kings 16:6, 8.

Two and twenty years old was Ahaziah when he began to reign. 2 Kings 8:26.
So he [Jehoram, the father of Ahaziah] died of sore diseases. . . . Thirty and two years old was he when he began to reign, and he reigned in Jerusalem eight years, and departed. . . . And the inhabitants of Jerusalem made Ahaziah his youngest son king in his stead. 2 Chron. 21:19, 20; 22:1.

Israel came up against Judah, and built Ramah. 2 Chron. 16:1. [Thus Baasha built a city ten years after his death.]

Forty and two years old was Ahaziah when he began to reign. 2 Chron. 22:2. [The verses here given will show that Ahaziah was forty-two when he came to the throne on his father's death at the age of forty. The son was thus two years older than his father!]

II. THE NEW TESTAMENT — HISTORICAL, ETC.

God sent his only begotten Son into the world. 1 John 4:9.

The sons of God came to present themselves before the LORD, and Satan came also among them. Job 1:6.

The sons of God saw the daughters of men that they were fair. Gen. 6:2.

Jesus . . . the son of Joseph, which was the son of Heli. Luke 3: 23.

And Jacob begat Joseph the husband of Mary, of whom was born Jesus. Matt. 1:16.

God had sworn with an oath to him [David], that of the fruit of his loins, according to the flesh, he would raise up Christ to sit on his throne. Acts 2:30.

Now the birth of Jesus Christ was on this wise: When as his mother Mary was espoused to Joseph, before they came together, she was found with child of the Holy Ghost. Matt. 1:18.

And when they had performed all things according to the law of the Lord, they returned into Galilee, to their own city Nazareth. Luke 2:39.

When he arose, he took the young child and his mother by night, and departed into Egypt: And was there until the death of Herod. Matt. 2:14, 15.

Now *after that John was put in prison*, Jesus came into Galilee, preaching the gospel of the kingdom of God. Mark 1:14. [This was followed by the conversion of Peter and Andrew: (Now as he walked by the sea of Galilee, he saw Simon and Andrew his brother casting a net into the sea: for they were fishers. And Jesus said unto

After these things came Jesus and his disciples into the land of Judaea; and there he tarried with them, and baptized. And John also was baptizing. . . . For John was not yet cast into prison. John 3:22-24. [Peter and Andrew had already been converted: (One of the two which heard John speak, and followed him, was Andrew,

13

them, "Come ye after me, and I will make you to become fishers of men." And straightway they forsook their nets, and followed him. Mark 1:16-18.)].

Simon Peter's brother. He first findeth his own brother Simon, and saith unto him, "We have found the Messias," which is, being interpreted, the Christ. And he brought him to Jesus. And when Jesus beheld him, he said, "Thou art Simon the son of Jona: thou shalt be called Cephas," which is by interpretation, A stone. John 1:40-42.].

Jesus came from Nazareth of Galilee, and was baptized of John in Jordan. And straightway coming up out of the water, he saw the heavens opened, and the Spirit like a dove descending upon him. . . . And immediately the spirit driveth him into the wilderness. And he was there in the wilderness forty days, tempted of Satan. Mark 1:9-13.

And the third day [after Christ's baptism and the descent of the Holy Ghost in the shape of a dove] there was a marriage in Cana of Galilee. . . . And both Jesus was called, and his disciples, to the marriage. John 2:1, 2.

And there was in their synagogue a man with an unclean spirit; and he cried out, saying, "Let us alone; what have we to do with thee, thou Jesus of Nazareth? art thou come to destroy us? I know thee who thou art, the Holy One of God." Mark 1:23, 24.

Beloved, believe not every spirit, but try the spirits whether they are of God; because many false prophets are gone out into the world. Hereby know ye the Spirit of God: Every spirit that confesseth that Jesus Christ is come in the flesh is of God. 1 John 4:1, 2.

And they came over unto the other side of the sea, into the country of the Gadarenes. And when he was come out of the ship, immediately there met him out of the tombs a man with an unclean spirit. . . . And the unclean spirits

And when he was come to the other side into the country of the Gergesenes, there met him two possessed with devils, coming out of the tombs, exceeding fierce. . . . And he said unto them, "Go." And when they were come out, they

14

went out, and entered into the swine: and the herd ran violently down a steep place into the sea (they were about two thousand), and were choked in the sea. Mark 5:1, 2, 13.

went into the herd of swine: and, behold, the whole herd of swine ran violently down a steep place into the sea, and perished in the waters. Matt. 8:28, 32.

And when he went forth to land, there met him *out of the city* a certain man, which had devils long time. Luke 8:27.

And as he went out of Jericho with his disciples and a great number of people, blind Bartimaeus, the son of Timaeus, sat by the highway side begging. And when he heard that it was Jesus of Nazareth, he began to cry out, and say, "Jesus, thou son of David, have mercy on me." Mark 10:46-47.

And as they departed from Jericho, a great multitude followed him. And, behold, two blind men sitting by the way side, when they heard that Jesus passed by, cried out, saying, "Have mercy on us, O Lord, thou son of David." Matt. 20:29, 30.

Except a man be born of water and of the Spirit, he cannot enter into the kingdom of God. John 3:5.

Every one that loveth is born of God, and knoweth God. 1 John 4:7.

No man hath ascended up to heaven, but he that came down from heaven, even the Son of man which is in heaven. John 3:13.

And Elijah went up by a whirlwind into heaven. 2 Kings 2:11.

By faith Enoch was translated that he should not see death. Heb. 11:5

And Enoch walked with God: and he was not; for God took him. Gen. 5:24

And ye will not come to me, that ye might have life. John 5:40.

No man can come to me, except the Father which hath sent me draw him: and I will raise him up at the last day. John 6:44.

For the Father judgeth no man, but hath committed all judgement unto the Son. John 5:22.

I judge no man. John 8:15.

And if any man hear my words, and believe not, I judge him not; for I came not to judge the world, but to save the world. John 12:47.

Think not that I am come to send peace on earth: I came not to send peace, but a sword. Matt. 10:34.

I am come to send fire on the earth; and what will I, if it be already kindled: . . . Suppose ye that I am come to give peace on earth? I tell you, Nay; but rather division: for from henceforth there shall be five in one house divided, three against two, and two against three. The father shall be divided against the son, and the son against the father; the mother against the daughter, and the daughter against the mother; the mother in law against the daughter in law and the daughter in law against her mother in law. Luke 12:49-53.

The word which God sent unto the children of Israel, preaching peace by Jesus Christ. Acts 10:36.

On earth peace, good will toward men. Luke 2:14.

If any man come to me, and hate not his father, and mother, and wife, and children, and brethren, and sisters, yea, and his own life also, he cannot be my disciple. Luke 14:26.

Whosoever hateth his brother is a murderer: and ye know that no murderer hath eternal life abiding in him. 1 John 3:15.

Ask, and it shall be given you; seek, and ye shall find; knock, and it shall be opened unto you. For everyone that asketh receiveth; and he that seeketh findeth; and

Strive to enter in at the strait gate: for many, I say unto you, will seek to enter in, and shall not be able. Luke 13:24.

16

to him that knocketh it shall be opened. Matt. 7:7, 8.

And he sighed deeply in his spirit, and saith, "Why does this generation seek after a sign? Verily I say unto you, There shall no sign be given unto this generation." And he left them. Mark 8:12-13.

Jesus of Nazareth, a man approved of God among you by miracles and wonders and signs which God did by him in the midst of you, as ye yourselves also know. Acts 2:22.

Then certain of the scribes and of the Pharisees answered, saying "Master, we would see a sign from thee." But he answered and said unto them, "An evil and adulterous generation seeketh after a sign; and there shall no sign be given to it, but the sign of the prophet Jonas." Matt. 12:38, 39.

And many other signs truly did Jesus in the presence of his disciples. John 20:30.

We know that thou art a teacher come from God; for no man can do these miracles that thou doest, except God be with him. John 3:2.

Jesus saith unto him, "I am the way, the truth, and the life: no man cometh unto the Father, but by me." John 14:6.

There is none other name under heaven given among men, whereby we must be saved. Acts 4:12.

In every nation he that feareth him, and worketh righteousness, is accepted with him. Acts 10:35.

Of them which thou gavest me have I lost none. John 18:9.

And I appoint unto you a kingdom, as my Father hath appointed unto me; that ye may eat and drink at my table in my kingdom, and sit on thrones judging the twelve tribes of Israel. Luke 22:29, 30.

Those that thou gavest me I have kept, and none of them is lost, but the son of perdition. John 17:12.

And when he had dipped the sop, he gave it Judas Iscariot, the son of Simon. And after the sop Satan entered into him. John 13:26, 27.

The Lord God shall give unto him the throne of his father David: And he shall reign over the house of Jacob for ever. Luke 1:32, 33.

And I give unto them eternal life; and they shall never perish, neither shall any man pluck them out of my hand. John 10:28.

And he said unto them, "Have ye never read what David did, when he had need, and was an hungred, he, and they that were with him? How he went into the house of God *in the days of Abiathar the high priest*, and did eat the shewbread, which is not lawful to eat but for the priests, and gave also to them which were with him?" Mark 2:25, 26.

And commanded them that they should take nothing for their journey, save a staff only. Mark 6:8.

Take therefore no thought for the morrow: for the morrow shall take thought for the things of itself. Matt. 6:34.

Jesus answered, and said unto them, "Though I bear record of myself, yet my record is true. . . . I am one that bear witness of myself." John 8:14, 18.
There is another that beareth witness of me; and I know that the

Jesus answered, "My kingdom is not of this world." John 18:36.
He came unto his own, and his own received him not. John 1:11.

Now the Spirit speaketh expressly, that in the latter times some shall depart from the faith. 1 Tim. 4:1.

Then came David to Nob to Ahimelech the priest. . . . So the priest gave him hallowed bread: for there was no bread there but the shewbread, that was taken from before the LORD. . . . And one of the sons of Ahimelech the son of Ahitub, named Abiathar, escaped, and fled after David. 1 Sam. 21:1, 6; 22:20.

Provide neither gold, nor silver, nor brass in your purses, nor scrip for your journey, neither two coats, neither shoes, nor yet staves. Matt. 10:9, 10.

But if any provide not for his own, and specially for those of his own house, he hath denied the faith, and is worse than an infidel. 1 Tim. 5:8.

If I bear witness of myself, my witness is not true. John 5:31.
And ye also shall bear witness, because ye have been with me from the beginning. John 15:27.

18

witness which he witnesseth of me is true. Ye sent unto John, and he bare witness unto the truth. But I receive not testimony from man. John 5:32-34.

Think not that I am come to destroy the law, or the prophets: I am come not to destroy, but to fulfil. For verily I say unto you, Till heaven and earth pass, one jot or one tittle shall in no wise pass from the law, till all be fulfilled. Whosoever therefore shall break one of these least commandments, and shall teach men so, he shall be called the least in the kingdom of heaven; but whosoever shall do and teach them, the same shall be called great in the kingdom of heaven. Matt. 5:17-19.

The Father loveth the Son, and hath given all things into his hand. John 3:35.

When the Son of man shall sit in the throne of his glory, ye also shall sit upon twelve thrones judging the twelve tribes of Israel. Matt. 19:28.

There is no man which sinneth not. 2 Chron. 6:36.

For there is not a just man upon earth, that doeth good, and sinneth not. Eccles. 7:20.

Wherefore, my brethren, ye also are become dead to the law by the body of Christ. Rom. 7:4.

Having abolished in his flesh the enmity, even the law of commandments contained in ordinances. Eph. 2:15.

All that ever came before me are thieves and robbers. John 10:8.

To sit on my right hand, and on my left, is not mine to give, but it shall be given to them for whom it is prepared of my Father. Matt. 20:23.

Have I not chosen you twelve, and one of you is a devil? John 6:70.

Woe to that man . . . good were it for that man if he had never been born. Mark 14:21.

Whosoever is born of God doth not commit sin; for his seed remaineth in him: and he cannot sin, because he is born of God. 1 John 3:9.

Who, being in the form of God, thought it not robbery to be equal with God. Phil. 2:6.

All things that the Father hath are mine. John 16:15.

My Father is greater than I. John 14:28.

But of that day and that hour knoweth no man, no, not the angels which are in heaven, neither the Son, but the Father. Mark 13:32.

Then came the day of unleavened bread, when the passover must be killed. And he sent Peter and John, saying, "Go and prepare us the passover, that we may eat.". . . And they went, and found as he had said unto them: and they made ready the passover. And when the hour was come, he sat down, and the twelve apostles with him. And he said unto them, "With desire I have desired to eat this passover with you before I suffer." Luke 22:7-8, 13-15.

Now before the feast of the passover, when Jesus knew that his hour was come . . . supper being ended. John 13:1, 2.

And it was the preparation of the passover, and about the sixth hour: and he saith unto the Jews, "Behold your king!" But they cried out, "Away with him, away with him, crucify him." John 19:14-15.

Then all the disciples forsook him, and fled. Matt. 26:56.

That the saying might be fulfilled, which he spake, "Of them which thou gavest me have I lost none." John 18:9.

And he said, "I tell thee, Peter, the cock shall not crow this day, before that thou shalt thrice deny that thou knowest me." Luke 22:34.

Jesus answered him, "Wilt thou lay down thy life for my sake? Verily, verily, I say unto thee, The cock shall not crow, till thou hast denied me thrice." John 13:38.

And he went out into the porch; and the cock crew. And a maid saw him again, and began to say to them that stood by, "This is one of them." And he denied it again. And a little after, they that stood by said again to Peter, "Surely thou art one of them: for thou art a Galilean, and thy speech agreeth thereto." But he began to curse and to swear, saying, "I know not this man of whom ye speak." And the second time the cock crew.

And Peter called to mind the word that Jesus said unto him. "Before the cock crow twice, thou shalt deny me thrice." Mark 14:68-72.

And it was the third hour, and they crucified him. Mark 15:25.

About the sixth hour . . . they cried out, "Away with him, away with him, crucify him." John 19:14, 15.

And many women were there beholding afar off, which followed Jesus from Galilee, ministering unto him: Among which was Mary Magdalene, and Mary the mother of James and Joses, and the mother of Zebedee's children. Matt. 27:55, 56.

Now there stood by the cross of Jesus his mother, and his mother's sister, Mary the wife of Cleophas, and Mary Magdalene. John 19:25.

And Jesus said unto him, "Verily I say unto thee, Today shalt thou be with me in paradise." Luke 23:43.

Jesus saith unto her, "Touch me not: for I am not yet ascended to my Father." John 20:17.

And at the ninth hour Jesus cried . . . "My God, my God, why hast thou forsaken me?" Mark 15:34

I and my Father are one. John 10:30
For in him dwelleth all the fulness of the Godhead bodily. Col. 2:9

The Jews, therefore, because it was the preparation, that the bodies should not remain upon the cross on the sabbath day (for that sabbath day was an high day), besought Pilate that their legs might be broken, and that they might be taken away. Then came the soldiers, and brake the legs of the first, and of the other which was crucified with him. John 19:31, 32.

And now when the even was come, because it was the preparation, that is, the day before the sabbath, Joseph of Arimathea, an honourable counsellor, which also waited for the kingdom of God, came, and went in boldly unto Pilate, and craved the body of Jesus. And Pilate *marvelled if he were already dead.* Mark 15: 42-44.

21

For as Jonas was three days and three nights in the whale's belly; so shall the Son of man be three days and three nights in the heart of the earth. Matt. 12:40

In the end of the Sabbath, as it began to dawn toward the first day of the week, came Mary Magdalene and the other Mary to see the sepulchre. . . . "He is not here: for he is risen, as he said." Matt. 28:1, 6.

The first day of the week cometh Mary Magdalene early, when it was yet dark, unto the sepulchre, and seeth the stone taken away from the sepulchre. John 20:1. [This gives only one night and the part of a night, and one day and part of a day.]

Christ . . . the first that should rise from the dead. Acts 26:23.

The first begotten of the dead. Rev. 1:5.

And when he had thus spoken, he cried with a loud voice, "Lazarus, come forth." And he that was dead came forth, bound hand and foot with graveclothes. John 11:43, 44.

And when Elisha was come into the house, behold, the child was dead, and laid upon his bed. . . . Then he returned, and walked in the house to and fro; and went up, and stretched himself upon him: and the child sneezed seven times, and the child opened his eyes. 2 Kings 4:32, 35.

Now when he [Jesus] came nigh to the gate of the city, behold, there was a dead man carried out, the only son of his mother, and she was a widow: . . . And when the Lord saw her, he had compassion on her, and said unto her, "Weep not." And he came and touched the bier: and they that bare him stood still. And he said,

"Young man. I say unto thee, Arise." And he that was dead sat up, and began to speak. Luke 7:12-15.

Then the same day [the Sunday succeeding the crucifixion] . . . Jesus . . . breathed on them, and saith unto them, "Receive ye the Holy Ghost." John 20:19-22.

He shewed himself alive after his passion by many infallible proofs, being seen of them forty days. . . . [Jesus said] ye shall be baptized with the Holy Ghost not many days hence. Acts 1:3, 5.

And when the day of Pentecost was fully come, they were all with one accord in one place. . . . there came a sound from heaven as of a rushing mighty wind. . . . And there appeared unto them cloven tongues like as of fire. . . . And they were all filled with the Holy Ghost, and began to speak with other tongues. . . . Acts 2:1-4.

And when they bring you unto the synagogues, and unto magistrates, and powers, take ye no thought how or what thing ye shall answer, or what ye shall say: For the Holy Ghost shall teach you in the same hour what ye ought to say. Luke 12:11, 12.

Nevertheless, I tell you the truth: It is expedient for you that I go away: for if I go not away, the Comforter will not come unto you; but if I depart, I will send him unto you. John 16:7.

And he [John the Baptist] shall be filled with the Holy Ghost, even from his mother's womb. Luke 1:15.

And Elizabeth was filled with the Holy Ghost. Luke 1:41.

And his father, Zacharias, was filled with the Holy Ghost, and prophesied. Luke 1:67.

But this spake he of the Spirit, which they that believe on him should receive: for the Holy Ghost was not yet given; because that Jesus was not yet glorified. John 7:39.

And, behold, there was a man in Jerusalem, whose name was Simeon; and the same man was just and devout, waiting for the consolation of Israel: and the Holy Ghost was upon him. And it was revealed unto him by the Holy Ghost, that he should not see death, before he had seen the Lord's Christ. And he came by the Spirit [of the Holy Ghost] into the temple: and when the parents brought in the child Jesus, to do for him after the custom of the law. . . . . Luke 2:25-27.

Now this man [Judas] purchased a field with the reward of iniquity; and falling headlong, he burst asunder in the midst, and all his bowels gushed out. Acts 1:18.

And he [Judas] cast down the pieces of silver in the temple, and departed, and went and hanged himself. And the chief priests . . . bought with them the potter's field. Matt. 27:5-7.

Tarry ye in the city of Jerusalem. Luke 24:49.
[Jesus] commanded them that they should not depart from Jerusalem, but wait for the promise of the Father. Acts 1:4.
Christ ascended:
[1] from Bethany (And he led them out as far as to Bethany, and he lifted up his hands, and blessed them. And it came to pass, while he blessed them, he was parted from them, and carried up into heaven. Luke 24:50, 51);
[2] from mount Olivet. (And when he had spoken these things, while they beheld, he was taken up; and a cloud received him out

He goeth before you into Galilee: there shall ye see him, as he said unto you. Mark 16:7
Then the eleven disciples went away into Galilee, into a mountain where Jesus had appointed them. Matt. 28:16.

of their sight. . . . Then returned they unto Jerusalem from the mount called Olivet, which is from Jerusalem a sabbath day's journey. Acts 1:9, 12);

[3] from a house in Jerusalem. (Afterward he appeared unto the eleven as they sat at meat, and upbraided them with their unbelief and hardness of heart, because they believed not them which had seen him after he was risen. . . . So then after the Lord had spoken unto them, he was received up into heaven, and sat on the right hand of God. Mark 16:14, 19); and

[4] from Galilee also. (Then the eleven disciples went away into Galilee, into a mountain where Jesus had appointed them. And when they saw him, they worshipped him: but some doubted. And Jesus came and spake unto them, saying, "All power is given unto me in heaven and in earth. Go ye therefore, and teach all nations, baptizing them in the name of the Father, and of the Son, and of the Holy Ghost: Teaching them to observe all things whatsoever I have commanded you: and, lo, I am with you always even unto the end of the world. Amen." Matt. 28:16-20.)

And they went out quickly, and fled from the sepulchre; for they trembled and were amazed: neither said they any thing to any man; for they were afraid. Mark 16:8.

And they remembered his words, and returned from the sepulchre, and told all these things unto the eleven, and to all the rest. Luke 24:8, 9.

25

Then went in also that other disciple, which came first to the sepulchre, and he saw, and believed. For as yet they knew not the scripture, that he must rise again from the dead. John 20:8, 9.

Now when Jesus was risen early the first day of the week, he appeared first to Mary Magdalene, out of whom he had cast seven devils. And she went and told them that had been with him, as they mourned and wept. Mark 16:9, 10.

Remember how he spake unto you when he was yet in Galilee, saying, "The Son of man must be delivered into the hands of sinful men, and be crucified, and the third day rise again." And they remembered his words. Luke 24:6-8.

And Jesus going up to Jerusalem took the twelve disciples apart in the way, and said unto them. "Behold, we go up to Jerusalem; and the Son of man shall be betrayed unto the chief priests and unto the scribes, and they shall condemn him to death. And shall deliver him to the gentiles to mock, and to scourge, and to crucify him; and the third day he shall rise again." Matt. 20:17-19.

The chief priests and Pharisees came together unto Pilate, Saying, "Sir, we remember that deceiver said, while he was yet alive, 'After three days I will rise again.' Command therefore that the sepulchre be made sure until the third day, lest his disciples come by night, and steal him away, and say unto the people, 'He is risen from the dead': so the last error shall be worse than the first." Matt. 27:63, 64.

And he began to teach them, that the Son of man must suffer many things, and be rejected of the elders, and of the chief priests, and scribes, and be killed, and after three days rise again. Mark 8:31.

And they shall mock him, and shall scourge him, and shall spit upon him, and shall kill him: and the third day he shall rise again. Mark 10:34.

For he shall be delivered unto the Gentiles, and shall be mocked, and spitefully entreated, and spitted on: And they shall scourge him, and put him to death: and the third day he shall rise again. Luke 18:32-34.

Jesus saith unto her, "Touch me not; for I am not yet ascended unto my Father." John 20:17.

In the end of the sabbath, as it began to dawn toward the first day of the week, came Mary Magdalene and the other Mary to see the sepulchre. . . . And as they went to tell his disciples, behold Jesus met them, saying, "All hail." And they came and held him by the feet, and worshipped him. Matt. 28:1, 9.

After these things Jesus shewed himself again to the disciples at the sea of Tiberias. . . . This is now the third time that Jesus shewed himself to his disciples, after that he was risen from the dead. John 21:1, 14.

Jesus had already shown himself:

[1] to Mary Magdalene;

[2] to the two Marys;

[3] to the two disciples going to Emmaus (And, behold, two of them went that same day to a village called Emmaus, which was from Jerusalem about threescore furlongs. . . . And it came to pass, that, while they communed to-

gether and reasoned, Jesus himself drew near, and went with them. Luke 24:13, 15.);

[4] to Peter (Saying, "The Lord is risen indeed, and hath appeared to Simon." Luke 24:34.);

[5] to the eleven (And they rose up the same hour, and returned to Jerusalem, and found the eleven gathered together, and them that were with them, . . . And as they thus spake, Jesus himself stood in the midst of them, and saith unto them, "Peace be unto you." Luke 24:33, 36.);

[6] to the ten (But Thomas, one of the twelve called Didymus, was not with them when Jesus came. John 20:24.);

[7] again, to the eleven (And after eight days again his disciples were within, and Thomas with them: then came Jesus, the doors being shut, and stood in the midst, and said, "Peace be unto you." John 20:26.);

[8] to "the twelve" [!] '(And that he was seen of Cephas, then of the twelve." 1 Cor. 15:5.);

[9] to the "five hundred brethren at once";

[10] to James; and

[11] to all the apostles ("After that, he was seen of above five hundred brethren at once; of whom the greater part remain unto this present, but some are fallen asleep. After that he was seen of James; then of all the apostles." 1 Cor. 15:6, 7.).

All power is given unto me [Jesus] in heaven and in earth. Matt. 28:18.

To him who alone doeth great wonders: for his mercy endureth for ever. Ps. 136:4.

The number of names [of the disciples] together were about an hundred and twenty. Acts 1:15. [This was after Christ's ascension.]

And the men which journeyed with him stood speechless, hearing a voice, but seeing no man. Acts 9:7.

God is no respecter of persons. Acts 10:34.

For there is no respect of persons with God. Rom. 2:11.

The working of Satan with all power and signs and lying wonders. 2 Thess. 2:9.

He was seen of above five hundred brethren at once. 1 Cor. 15:6.

But they heard not the voice. Acts 22:9.

And when we were all fallen to the earth, I heard a voice. Acts 26:14.

For the children being not yet born, neither having done any good or evil . . . it was said unto her, "The elder shall serve the younger. As it is written, Jacob have I loved, but Esau have I hated." Rom. 9:11-13.

"I have loved you," saith the LORD. Yet ye say, "Wherein hast thou loved us?" "Was not Esau Jacob's brother?" saith the LORD: "yet I loved Jacob, And I hated Esau, and laid his mountains and his heritage waste for the dragons of the wilderness." Mal. 1:2-3.

And Abel, he also brought of the firstlings of his flock and of the fat thereof. And the LORD had respect unto Abel and to his offering: But unto Cain and to his offering he had not respect. And Cain was very wroth, and his countenance fell. Gen. 4:4, 5.

And they watched the gates day and night to kill him. Then the disciples took him by night, and let him down by the wall in a basket. And when Saul was come to Jerusalem, he assayed to join himself to the disciples: but they were all afraid of him, and believed not that he was a disciple. But Barnabas took him, and brought him to the apostles, and declared unto them how he had seen the Lord in the way, and that he had spoken to him, and how he had preached boldly at Damascus in the name of Jesus. And he was with them coming in and going out at Jerusalem. Acts 9:24-28.

But when it pleased God . . . to reveal his Son in me, that I might preach him among the heathen; immediately I conferred not with flesh and blood: Neither went I up to Jerusalem to them which were apostles before me; but I went into Arabia, and returned again unto Damascus. Then after three years I went up to Jerusalem to see Peter, and abode with him fifteen days. But other of the apostles saw I none, save James the Lord's brother. Now the things which I write unto you, behold, before God, I lie not. Gal. 1:15-20.

But to him that worketh not, but believeth on him that justifieth the ungodly, his faith is counted for righteousness. Even as David also describeth the blessedness of the man, unto whom God imputeth righteousness without works. Rom. 4:5, 6.

For by grace are ye saved through faith; and that not of yourselves: it is the gift of God: Not of works, lest any man should boast. Eph. 2:8, 9.

What doth it profit, my brethren, though a man say he hath faith, and have not works? can faith save him? . . . Even so faith, if it hath not works, is dead, being alone . . . Ye see then how that by works a man is justified, and not by faith only. . . . For as the body without the spirit is dead, so faith without works is dead also. James 2:14, 17, 24, 26.

For as many as have sinned without law shall also perish without law. Rom. 2:12.

For where no law is, there is no trangression. Rom 4:15.

For many are called, but few are chosen. Matt. 22:14.

For it is written, "As I live," saith the Lord, "every knee shall bow to me, and every tongue shall confess to God." Rom. 14:11.

Your adversary the devil, as a roaring lion, walketh about, seeking whom he may devour. 1 Pet. 5:8.

Whosoever is born of God doth not commit sin; for his seed remaineth in him: and he cannot sin, because he is born of God. 1 John 3:9.

The effectual fervent prayer of a righteous man availeth much. James 5:16.

But he that shall blaspheme against the Holy Ghost hath never forgiveness. Mark 3:29.

My brethren, count it all joy when ye fall into divers temptations. James 1:2.

Though I have all faith, so that I could remove mountains, and have not charity, I am nothing. 1 Cor. 13:2.

For if the dead rise not, then is not Christ raised. . . . For the trumpet shall sound, and the dead shall be raised. 1 Cor. 15:16, 52.

Marvel not at this: for the hour is coming, in the which all that are in the graves shall hear his voice, and shall come forth. John 5:28, 29.

And I saw the dead, small and

And the angels which kept not their first estate, but left their own habitation, he hath reserved in everlasting chains under darkness unto the judgment of the great day. Jude 6.

If we say that we have no sin, we deceive ourselves, and the truth is not in us. 1 John 1:8.

There is none righteous, no, not one. Rom. 3:10.

And by him all that believe are justified from all things. Acts 13:39.

Lead us not into temptation. Matt. 6:13.

If any man preach any other gospel unto you than that ye have received, let him be accursed. Gal. 1:9.

As the cloud is consumed and vanisheth away: so he that goeth down to the grave shall come up no more. Job 7:9.

The dead know not any thing, neither have they any more a reward. Eccles. 9:5.

For that which befalleth the sons of men befalleth beasts; even one thing befalleth them: as the

31

great, stand before God . . . and they were judged every man according to their works. Rev. 20:12, 13.

One generation passeth away, and another generation cometh: but the earth abideth for ever. Eccles. 1:4.

Who laid the foundations of the earth, that it should not be removed for ever. Ps. 104:5.

one dieth, so dieth the other; yea, they have all one breath; so that a man hath no preeminence above a beast: for all is vanity. All go unto one place; all are of the dust, and all turn to dust again. Who knoweth the spirit of man that goeth upward, and the spirit of the beast that goeth downward to the earth? Wherefore I perceive that there is nothing better, than that a man should rejoice in his own works; for that is his portion: for who shall bring him to see what shall be after him? Eccles. 3:19-22.

The heavens shall pass away with a great noise, and the elements shall melt with fervent heat, the earth also and the works that are therein shall be burned up. 2 Pet. 3:10.

Thou, Lord, in the beginning hast laid the foundation of the earth; and the heavens are the works of thine hands; They shall perish; but thou remainest. Heb. 1:10, 11.

III. DIVINE ATTRIBUTES

No man hath seen God at any time. John 1:18.

Whom no man hath seen, nor can see. 1 Tim. 6:16.

God is a Spirit. John 4:24.

Then went up Moses, and Aaron, Nadab, and Abihu, and seventy of the elders of Israel: And they saw the God of Israel: and there was under his feet as it were a paved work of a sapphire stone. Exod. 24:9, 10.

I will put thee in a clift of the rock, and will cover thee with my hand while I pass by: And I will take away mine hand, and thou shalt see my back parts; but my face shall not be seen. Exod. 33:22, 23.

I saw the Lord standing upon the altar. Amos 9:1.

And the LORD appeared unto him [Isaac]. Gen. 26:2.

Jesus saith unto him, "Have I been so long time with you, and yet hast thou not known me, Philip? He that hath seen me hath seen the Father; and how sayest thou then, 'Shew us the Father'? " John 14:9.

Thou canst not see my face: for there shall no man see me, and live. Exod. 33:20.

And the Lord spake unto Moses face to face, as a man speaketh unto his friend. Exod. 33:11.

And Jacob called the name of the place Peniel: for I have seen God face to face, and my life is preserved. Gen. 32:30.

God is not the author of confusion. 1 Cor. 14:33.

I form the light, and create darkness: I make peace and create evil:

I the LORD do all these things. Isa. 45:7.

Then God sent an evil spirit between Abimelech and the men of Shechem; and the men of Shechem dealt treacherously with Abimelech. Judg. 9:23.

But the Spirit of the LORD departed from Saul, and an evil spirit from the LORD troubled him. 1 Sam. 16:14.

And for this cause God shall send them strong delusion, that they should believe a lie. 2 Thess. 2:11.

I have sworn by myself . . . That unto me every knee shall bow, every tongue shall swear. Isa. 45:23.

Swear not at all. Matt. 5:34.

With God all things are possible. Mark 10:27; Matt. 19:26.

The Lord God omnipotent. Rev. 19:6.

I am the Almighty God. Gen. 17:1.

The Father loveth the Son, and hath given all things into his hand. John 3:35.

And the LORD was with Judah: and he drave out the inhabitants of the mountain; but could not drive out the inhabitants of the valley, because they had chariots of iron. Judges 1:19.

And he could there do no mighty work. Mark 6:5.

The Lord is . . . not willing that any should perish. 2 Peter 3:9.

The Lord hath made all things for himself: yea, even the wicked for the day of evil. Prov. 16:4.

Who will have all men to be saved. 1 Tim. 2:4.

Whom he will he hardeneth. Rom. 9:18.

His anger endureth but a moment. Ps. 30:5.

And the LORD's anger was kindled against Israel, and he made them wander in the wilderness forty years. Num. 32:13.

34

Lying lips are abomination to the LORD. Prov. 12:22.

God is not a man, that he should lie; neither the son of man, that he should repent. Num. 23:19.

The Strength of Israel will not lie nor repent: for he is not a man, that he should repent. 1 Sam. 15:29.

I am the LORD, I change not. Mal. 3:6.

With whom is no variableness, neither shadow of turning. James 1:17.

Let no man say when he is tempted, I am tempted of God: for God cannot be tempted with evil, neither tempteth he any man. James 1:13.

The anger of the LORD was kindled against Israel, and he moved David against them to say, "Go, number Israel and Judah." 2 Sam. 24:1.

He stretcheth out the north

Now therefore, behold, the LORD hath put a lying spirit in the mouth of all these thy prophets, and the LORD hath spoken evil concerning thee. 1 Kings 22:23.

And it repented the LORD that he had made man on the earth, and it grieved him at his heart. Gen. 6:6. Also: For the LORD shall judge his people, and repent himself for his servants, when he seeth that their power is gone, and there is none shut up, or left. Deut. 32:36; For the LORD will judge his people, and he will repent himself concerning his servants. Ps. 135:14.

The LORD repented that he had made Saul king over Israel. 1 Sam. 15:35.

And the LORD repented of the evil which he thought to do unto his people. Exod. 32:14.

And God repented of the evil, that he had said that he would do unto them; and he did it not. Jon. 3:10.

And it came to pass after these things, that God did tempt Abraham. Gen. 22:1.

And Satan stood up against Israel, and provoked David to number Israel. 1 Chron. 21:1.

The pillars of the earth are the

over the empty place, and hangeth the earth upon nothing. Job 26:7.

LORD's, and he hath set the world upon them. 1 Sam. 2:8.

Who laid the foundation, of the earth, that it should not be removed for ever. Ps. 104:5.

Hear, O Israel: the LORD our God is one LORD. Deut. 6:4.

For there are three that bear record in heaven, the Father, the Word, and the Holy Ghost; and these three are one. 1 John 5:7.

But to us there is but one God, the Father, of whom are all things, and we in him; and one Lord Jesus Christ, by whom are all things, and we by him. 1 Cor. 8:6.

The LORD is righteous in all his ways, and holy in all his works. Ps. 145:17.

The LORD is merciful and gracious, slow to anger, and plenteous in mercy. Ps. 103:8.

For the LORD is good; his mercy is everlasting. Ps. 100:5.

A just God. Isa. 45:21.

Thus said the LORD of hosts, "I remember that which Amalek did to Israel, how he laid wait for him in the way, when he came up from Egypt. Now go and smite Amalek, and utterly destroy all that they have, and spare them not; but slay both man and woman, infant and suckling, ox and sheep, camel and ass." 1 Sam. 15:2, 3. [The offence preceded the punishment by some four hundred years.]

The eyes of all wait upon thee; and thou givest them their meat in due season. Thou openest thine hand, and satisfiest the desire of every living thing. Ps. 145:15, 16.

For we know that the whole creation groaneth and travaileth in pain together until now. Rom. 8:22.

And we know that all things work together for good to them that love God. Rom. 8:28.

For whom the Lord loveth he chasteneth, and scourgeth every son whom he receiveth. Heb. 12:6.

Now the God of peace be with you all. Amen. Rom. 15:33.

The LORD is a man of war. Exod. 15:3.

God is love. 1 John 4:8.

God is a consuming fire. Heb. 12:29.

Who will have all men to be saved, and to come unto the knowledge of the truth. 1 Tim. 2:4.

He hath blinded their eyes, and hardened their heart; that they should not see with their eyes, nor understand with their heart, and be converted, and I should heal them. John 12:40.

Every word of God is pure. Prov. 30:5.

And the LORD said to Hosea, "Go, take unto thee a wife of whoredoms and children of whoredoms." Hos. 1:2; Also Hos. 3:1-3. Then said the LORD, "Go yet, love a woman beloved of her friend, yet an adulteress. . . . " So I bought her to me for fifteen pieces of silver. . . . And I said, "Thou shalt abide for me many days; thou shalt not play the harlot."

And God saw every thing that he had made, and, behold, it was very good. Gen. 1:31.

Behold, he putteth no trust in his saints; yea, the heavens are not clean in his sight. Job 15:15.

Forgiving iniquity and transgression and sin, and that will by no means clear the guilty; visiting the iniquity of the fathers upon the children, and upon the children's children, unto the third and to the fourth generation. Exod. 34:7.

The soul that sinneth, it shall die. The son shall not bear the iniquity of the father, neither shall the father bear the iniquity of the son; the righteousness of the righteous shall be upon him, and the wickedness of the wicked shall be upon him. Ezek. 18:20.

Prepare slaughter for his children for the iniquity of their fathers. Isa. 14:21.

The fathers shall not be put to death for the children, neither shall the children be put to death for the fathers: every man shall be put to death for his own sin. Deut. 24:16.

Thou shalt not defraud thy neighbour, neither rob him. Lev. 19:13.

But every woman shall borrow of her neighbour, and of her that sojourneth in her house, jewels of silver, and jewels of gold, and raiment: and ye shall put them upon your sons, and upon your daughters; and ye shall spoil the Egyptians. Exod. 3:22.

Thou shalt not make unto thee any graven image, or any likeness of any thing that is in heaven above, or that is in the earth beneath, or that is in the water under the earth. Exod. 20:4.

And thou shalt make two cherubims of gold, of beaten work shalt thou make them, in the two ends of the mercy seat. Exod. 25:18.

And these shall go away into everlasting punishment. Matt. 25:46.

He retaineth not his anger for ever, because he delighteth in mercy. Mic. 7:18.

The earth is the Lord's, and the fulness thereof. 1 Cor. 10:26.
The earth is the LORD's, and the fulness thereof; the world, and they that dwell therein. Ps. 24:1.
Jesus Christ who is . . . the prince of the kings of the earth. Rev. 1:5.

Again, the devil taketh him up into an exceeding high mountain, and sheweth him all the kingdoms of the world, and the glory of them; and saith unto him, "All these things will I give thee, if thou wilt fall down and worship me." Matt. 4:8,9.
Now shall the prince of this world [the Devil] be cast out. John 12:31.

Dwelling in the light which no man can approach unto. 1 Tim. 6:16.

He made darkness his secret place; his pavilion round about him were dark waters and thick clouds of the skies. Ps. 18:11.
Then spake Solomon, "The LORD said that he would dwell in the thick darkness." 1 Kings 8:12.

The LORD is gracious, and full

And he smote the men of Beth-

38

of compassion: slow to anger, and of great mercy. The LORD is good to all: and his tender mercies are over all his works. Ps. 145:8,9.

A just weight and balance are the LORD's. Prov. 16:11.

He is gracious and merciful, slow to anger, and of great kindness, and repenteth him of the evil. Joel 2:13.

For he doth not afflict willingly nor grieve the children of men. Lam. 3:33.

O give thanks unto the LORD; for he is good: for his mercy endureth for ever. O give thanks unto the God of gods: for his mercy endureth for ever. Ps. 136:1, 2.

And the LORD passed by before him, and proclaimed, "The LORD, the LORD God, merciful and gracious, longsuffering, and abundant in goodness and truth." Exod. 34:6.

Thou art of purer eyes than to behold evil, and canst not look on iniquity. Hab. 1:13.

shemesh, because they had looked into the ark of the LORD, even he smote of the people fifty thousand and threescore and ten men: and the people lamented, because the LORD had smitten many of the people with a great slaughter. 1 Sam. 6:19.

God is jealous, and the LORD revengeth; the LORD revengeth, and is furious; the LORD will take vengeance on his adversaries, and he reserveth wrath for his enemies. Nah. 1:2.

And when the LORD thy God shall deliver them before thee; thou shalt smite them, and utterly destroy them; thou shalt make no covenant with them, nor shew mercy unto them. . . . And thou shalt consume all the people which the LORD thy God shall deliver thee; thine eye shall have no pity upon them. Deut. 7:2,16.

Thou shalt save alive nothing that breatheth. Deut. 20:16.

But the fearful and unbelieving. . . shall have their part in the lake which burneth with fire and brimstone. Rev. 21:8.

Wherefore I gave them also statutes that were not good, and judgments whereby they should not live. Ezek. 20:25.

Shall there be evil in a city, and the LORD hath not done it? Amos 3:6.

He loveth righteousness and judgment: the earth is full of the goodness of the LORD. Ps. 33:5.

He is the Rock, his work is perfect: for all his ways are judgment: a God of truth and without iniquity, just and right is he. Deut. 32.4.

The eyes of the LORD are in every place, beholding the evil and the good. Prov. 15:3.
"Can any hide himself in secret places that I shall not see him?" saith the LORD. "Do not I fill heaven and earth?" saith the LORD. Jer. 23:24.
For mine eyes are upon all their ways: they are not hid from my face, neither is their iniquity hid from mine eyes. Jer. 16:17.

Howbeit the most High dwelleth not in temples made with hands; as saith the prophet. Acts 7:48.

The LORD is nigh unto all them that call upon him, to all that call upon him in truth. Ps. 145:18.

God is our refuge and strength, a very present help in trouble. Ps. 46:1.

Therefore hath he mercy on whom he will have mercy, and whom he will he hardeneth. Rom. 9:18.

Jacob have I loved, but Esau have I hated. Rom. 9:13.
And the smoke of their torment ascendeth up for ever and ever. Rev. 14:11.
He that believeth not shall be damned. Mark 16:16.

And the LORD came down to see the city and the tower, which the children of men builded. Gen. 11:5.
And the LORD said, "Because the cry of Sodom and Gomorrah is great, and because their sin is very grievous; I will go down now, and see whether they have done altogether according to the cry of it, which is come unto me; and if not, I will know." Gen. 18:20, 21.

I have surely built thee an house to dwell in, a settled place for thee to abide in for ever. 1 Kings 8:13.

Why standest thou afar off, O LORD? Why hidest thou thyself in times of trouble? Ps. 10:1.

My God, my God, why hast thou forsaken me? why art thou so far from helping me, and from the words of my roaring? Ps. 22:1.

ADDENDA — MISCELLANEOUS

And God said, "Let the *waters* bring forth abundantly the moving creature that hath life, and *fowl that may fly above the earth* in the open firmament of heaven." Gen. 1:20.

And *out of the ground* the LORD God formed every beast of the field, and *every fowl of the air*. Gen. 2:19.

The doers of the law shall be justified. Rom. 2:13.

By the deeds of the law there shall no flesh be justified. Rom. 3:20.

And when he was accused of the chief priests and elders, he answered nothing. Matt. 27:12.

The high priest then asked Jesus of his disciples, and of his doctrine. Jesus answered him, "I spake openly to the world; I ever taught in the synagogue, and in the temple, whither the Jews always resort; and in secret have I said nothing." John 18:19, 20; also John 18: 21-23: "Ask them which heard me. . . ." One of the officers which stood by struck Jesus with the palm of his hand, saying, "Answerest thou the high priest so?" Jesus answered him, "If I have spoken evil, bear witness of the evil."

Then said Pilate unto him, "Hearest thou not how many things they witness against thee?" And he answered him to never a word; insomuch that the governor marvelled greatly. Matt. 27:13, 14.

Then Pilate entered into the judgment hall again, and called Jesus, and said unto him, "Art thou the King of the Jews?" Jesus answered him, "Sayest thou this thing of thyself, or did others tell it thee of me?" John 18:33, 34; also

41

John 18:35-38: Pilate answered . . . "Thine own nation and the chief priest have delivered thee unto me; what hast thou done?" Jesus answered, "My kingdom is not of this world. . . ." Pilate therefore said unto him, "Art thou a king then?" Jesus answered, "Thou sayeth that I am a king. . . ." Pilate . . . went out again . . . and said, "I find in him no fault at all."

Some of you shall they cause to be put to death. Luke 21:16.

But there shall not an hair of your head perish. Luke 21:18.

Submit yourselves to every ordinance of man. 1 Pet. 2:13; Rom. 13:1, 2: Let every soul be subject unto the higher powers. . . . Whosoever therefore resisteth the power, resisteth the ordinance of God.

Then Peter and the other apostles answered and said, "We ought to obey God rather than men." Acts 5:29.

Then he called his twelve disciples together, and gave them power and authority over all devils, and to cure diseases. Luke 9:1; also Matt. 10:1, 8: He gave them power . . . to cast them [unclean spirits] out . . . and to heal all manner of sickness. . . . "Heal the sick, cleanse the lepers, raise the dead, cast out devils."

And Jesus rebuked the devil; and he departed out of him: and the child was cured from that very hour. Then came the disciples to Jesus apart, and said, "Why could not we cast him out?" And Jesus said unto them, "Because of your unbelief." Matt. 17:18-20.

"Verily I say unto you, If ye have faith as a grain of mustard seed . . . nothing shall be impossible unto you." Matt. 17:20.

And when he was come into the house, his disciples asked him privately, "Why could not we cast him out?" And he said unto them, "This kind can come forth by

42

nothing, but by prayer and fasting." Mark 9:28, 29.

And when Jesus was entered into Capernaum, there came unto him a centurion, beseeching him. Matt. 8:5.

He sent unto him the elders of the Jews, beseeching him that he would come and heal his servant. . . . The centurion sent friends to him. Luke 7:3, 6.

And they that were crucified with him reviled him. Mark 15:32.

The thieves also, which were crucified with him, cast the same in his teeth. Matt. 27:44.

And one of the malefactors which were hanged railed on him. . . . But the other answering rebuked him. Luke 23:39, 40.

BIBLE ABSURDITIES
I. OLD TESTAMENT

The globe shapeless.
And the earth was without form. . . . And the Spirit of God moved upon the face of the waters. Gen. 1:2.

Day and night made, and vegetation created, before the sun.
And God said, "Let there be light." . . . And God called the light Day, and the darkness he called Night. And the evening and the morning were the first day. Gen. 1:3, 5.

And the earth brought forth grass, and herb yielding seed after his kind, and the tree yielding fruit, whose seed was in itself, after his kind: and God saw that it was good. And the evening and the morning were the third day. Gen. 1:12, 13.

And God made two great lights; the greater light to rule the day, and the lesser light to rule the night; he made the stars also. And God set them in the firmament of the heaven. . . . And the evening and the morning were the fourth day. Gen. 1:16-19.

Heaven a solid roof supporting reservoirs of water.
And God said, "Let there be a firmament in the midst of the waters, and let it divide the waters from the waters." And God made the firmament, and divided the waters which were under the firmament from the waters which were above the firmament: and it was so. And God called the firmament Heaven. Gen. 1:6-8.

And the windows of heaven were opened. Gen. 7:11.

Hast thou with him spread out the sky, which is strong, and as a molten looking glass? Job 37:18.

Heaven has foundations and pillars.
The foundations of heaven moved and shook. 2 Sam. 22:8.

The pillars of heaven tremble and are astonished at his reproof. Job 26:11.

The ocean brings forth the birds of the air simultaneously with fishes and whales.

And God said, "Let the waters bring forth abundantly the moving creature that hath life, and fowl that may fly above the earth in the open firmament of heaven." Gen. 1:20.

Whales, etc., are created before the mammals from which they are descended.

And God created great whales, and every living creature that moveth, which the waters brought forth abundantly, after their kind. . . . And the evening and the morning were the fifth day. Gen. 1:21, 23.

And God said, "Let the earth bring forth the living creature after his kind, cattle, and creeping thing, and beast of the earth after his kind": and it was so. . . . And the evening and the morning were the sixth day. Gen. 1:24, 31.

Beasts of prey, serpents, sharks, parasites, internal worms, volcanoes, etc., are excellent things.

God saw every thing that he had made, and, behold, it was very good. Gen. 1:31.

The carnivora are fed on grass.

To every beast of the earth, and to every fowl of the air, and to every thing that creepeth upon the earth, wherein there is life, I have given every green herb for meat: and it was so. Gen. 1:30.

Man is a copy of God (science reverses this), and God is of both sexes.

So God created man in his own image, in the image of God created he him; male and female created he them. Gen. 1:27.

Man made out of dust.

And the LORD God formed man of the dust of the ground, and breathed into his nostrils the breath of life; and man became a living soul. Gen. 2:7.

Science contradicted.

And the evening and the morning were the first day. Gen. 1:5. And on the seventh day God ended his work. Gen. 2:2.

[Geology shows that the formation of the earth and the evolution of species must have taken vast ages.]

46

God the omnipotent is tired.

In six days the LORD made heaven and earth, and on the seventh day he rested, and was refreshed. Exod. 31:17.

Magic trees.

The tree of life also in the midst of the garden, and the tree of knowledge of good and evil. Gen. 2:9.

Adam being lonely, God makes the animals and brings them all before him to name and to choose a partner from.

And the LORD God said, "It is not good that the man should be alone; I will make him an help meet for him." And out of the ground the LORD God formed every beast of the field, and every fowl of the air; and brought them unto Adam to see what he would call them; and whatsoever Adam called every living creature, that was the name thereof. And Adam gave names to all cattle, and to the fowl of the air, and to every beast of the field; but for Adam there was not found an help meet for him. Gen. 2:18-20.

The rib story.

And the Lord God caused a deep sleep to fall upon Adam, and he slept: and he took one of his ribs, and closed up the flesh instead thereof; and the rib, which the LORD God had taken from man, made he a woman, and brought her unto the man. And Adam said, "This is now bone of my bone, and flesh of my flesh: she shall be called Woman, because she was taken out of man." Gen. 2:21-23.

A talking serpent.

Now the serpent was more subtil than any beast of the field which the LORD God had made. And he said unto the woman, "Yea, hath God said, 'Ye shall not eat of every tree of the garden?' " Gen. 3:1.

The fall of man.

And when the woman saw that the tree was good for food, and that it was pleasant to the eyes, and a tree to be desired to make one wise, she took of the fruit thereof, and did eat, and gave also unto her husband with her; and he did eat. Gen. 3:6.

By the offence of one judgment came upon all men to condemnation. Rom. 5:18.

[Why should eating an apple condemn all mankind? How could Adam and Eve be morally responsible and commit sin when they were ignorant of the distinction between good and evil till they had acquired the knowledge by eating the magic fruit? Science shows that man has risen from a low condition, not fallen from a high one.]

Death unknown in the world before Adam sinned.

For since by man came death, by man came also the resurrection of the dead. 1 Cor. 15:21.

Wherefore, as by one man sin entered into the world, and death by sin; and so death passed upon all men, for that all have sinned. Rom. 5:12.

[Did carnivora originally live upon grass, refusing to kill their prey till Adam ate an apple? Are the ample proofs of geology that death was in the world long before man only a delusion and a snare designed by God to entrap the wise and thoughtful?]

The infinite God, who has neither parts nor passions, walks and talks.

And they heard the voice of the LORD God walking in the garden in the cool of the day: and Adam and his wife hid themselves from the presence of the LORD God amongst the trees of the garden. And the LORD God called unto Adam, and said unto him, "Where art thou?" And he said, "I heard thy voice in the garden, and I was afraid, because I was naked; and I hid myself." Gen. 3:8-10.

A stupid curse.

And the LORD God said unto the serpent, "Because thou hast done this, thou art cursed above all cattle, and above every beast of the field; upon thy belly shalt thou go, and dust shalt thou eat all the days of thy life." Gen. 3:14.

[Why should all serpents be cursed because Satan assumed the shape of one? How did serpents move before they went on their bellies? Why don't serpents eat dust in fulfilment of the curse? Isaiah (65:25) prophesies that they will do so when the lion eats straw like the bullock, and the wolf and the lamb eat together.]

God a tailor.

Unto Adam also and to his wife did the LORD God make coats of skin, and clothed them. Gen. 3:21.

Divine precautions against an evicted rival.

And the LORD God said, "Behold, the man is become as one of us, to know good and evil: and now, lest he put forth his hand, and take also of

48

the tree of life, and eat, and live for ever": therefore the LORD God sent him forth from the garden of Eden, to till the ground from whence he was taken. So he drove out the man; and he placed at the east of the garden of Eden Cherubims, and a flaming sword which turned every way, to keep the way of the tree of life. Gen. 3:22-24.

The Lord likes hot roast meat better than cold vegetables.
Cain brought of the fruit of the ground an offering unto the Lord. And Abel, he also brought of the firstlings of his flock and of the fat thereof. And the Lord had respect unto Abel and to his offering: but unto Cain and to his offering he had not respect. Gen. 4:3-5.
Jacob have I loved, but Esau have I hated. Rom. 9:13.

The Lord protects Cain, but not Abel.
And the LORD said unto him, "Therefore whosoever slayeth Cain, vengeance shall be taken on him sevenfold." And the LORD set a mark upon Cain, lest any finding him should kill him. Gen. 4:15.

The oldest inhabitant.
And all the days of Methuselah were nine hundred sixty and nine years: and he died. Gen. 5:27.

Angels courting women.
There were giants in the earth in those days: and also after that, when the sons of God came in unto the daughters of men, and they bare children to them, the same became mighty men which were of old, men of renown. Gen. 6:4.

Alleged total depravity of man, and consequent destruction of beasts.
And God saw that the wickedness of man was great in the earth, and that every imagination of the thoughts of his heart was only evil continually. . . . And the LORD said, "I will destroy man whom I have created from the face of the earth; both man, and beast, and the creeping thing, and the fowls of the air; for it repenteth me that I have made them." Gen. 6:5, 7.

Man's depravity is equally a reason for not destroying living things.
And the LORD said in his heart, "I will not again curse the ground any more for man's sake; for the imagination of man's heart is evil from his youth; neither will I again smite any more every thing living, as I have done." Gen. 8:21.

Noah's menagerie.

The length of the ark shall be three hundred cubits, the breadth of it fifty cubits, and the height of it thirty cubits. Gen. 6:15.

And of every living thing of all flesh, two of every sort shalt thou bring into the ark. . . . Of fowls after their kind, and of cattle after their kind, of every creeping thing of the earth after his kind, two of every sort shall come unto thee. Gen. 6:19, 20. ["Sevens" according to Gen. 7:2, 3: Of every clean beast thou shalt take to thee by sevens, the male and his female: and of beasts that are not clean by two, the male and his female. Of fowls also of the air by sevens, the male and the female.]

In the selfsame day entered Noah, and Shem, and Ham, and Japheth, the sons of Noah, and Noah's wife, and the three wives of his sons with them, into the ark; they, and every beast after his kind, and all the cattle after their kind, and every creeping thing that creepeth upon the earth after his kind, and every fowl after his kind, every bird of every sort. And they went in unto Noah into the ark, two and two of all flesh, wherein is the breath of life. Gen. 7:13-15.

[Noah's ark, 150 yards long by 25 wide and 15 high, has pairs or sevens or fourteen of every living thing crammed into it. There are already known at least 1,600 species of mammalia, 12,500 of birds, 600 of reptiles, and of insects and other inferior creatures at least 1,000,000, besides animalculae. (The first edition of this work was published in 1900.) These came from all parts of the world. The South American sloths, it is calculated, must have started several years before the creation.]

Noah has to find food for them all.

And take thou unto thee of all food that is eaten, and thou shalt gather it to thee; and it shall be food for thee, and for them. Thus did Noah; according to all that God commanded him, so did he. Gen. 6:21, 22.

[The voyage lasted over a year (compare Gen. 7:11 and Gen. 8:14: In the six hundredth year of Noah's life, in the second month, the seventeenth day of the month, the same day were all the fountains of the great deep broken up. . . . And it came to pass in the six hundredth and first year, in the first month, the first day of the month, the waters were dried up from off the earth). Eight persons attended to the wants of some two million living creatures.]

The ark has three stories, but only one twenty-two inch window for ventilation and one door for exit and drainage.

A window shalt thou make to the ark, and in a cubit shalt thou finish it above; and the door of the ark shalt thou set in the side thereof, with lower, second, and third stories shalt thou make it. Gen. 6:16.

The whole earth covered with water to a depth of five miles and a half. Where did all this water come from?
And the waters prevailed exceedingly upon the earth; and all the high hills, that were under the whole heaven, were covered. Gen. 7:19.

God has a keen scent for roast meat.
Noah builded an altar unto the LORD; and took of every clean beast, and of every clean fowl, and offered burnt offerings on the altar. And the LORD smelled a sweet savour. Gen. 8:20, 21.

Tigers and sharks delivered into Noah's hands.
God blessed Noah and his sons, and said unto them . . . "The fear of you and the dread of you shall be upon every beast of the earth . . . and upon all the fishes of the sea; into your hand are they delivered." Gen. 9:1, 2.

God allots man a rather extensive diet, including insects, worms, poisonous fishes, etc., but he takes care to prohibit the eating of meat with blood in it.
Every moving thing that liveth shall be meat for you. . . . but flesh with the life thereof, which is the blood thereof, shall ye not eat. Gen. 9:3, 4.

Beasts have hands, and are morally responsible.
And surely your blood of your lives will I require; at the hand of every beast will I require it, and at the hand of man. Gen. 9:5.

The Infinite and Omniscient has to make inquiries.
And the LORD came down to see the city and the tower, which the children of men builded. Gen. 11:5.
[The top of the tower was to "reach unto heaven." Gen. 11:4.]

Unscientific account of the origin of languages.
And the LORD said, "Behold, the people is one, and they have all one language; and this they begin to do: and now nothing will be restrained from them, which they have imagined to do. Go to, let us go down, and there confound their language, that they may not understand one another's speech." . . . Therefore is the name of it called Babel; because the LORD did there confound the language of all the earth: and from

thence did the LORD scatter them abroad upon the face of all the earth. Gen. 11:6-9.

Fetishism, incantation, or holy sacrifice?

And he believed in the LORD; and he counted it to him for righteousness. And he said unto him, "I am the LORD. . . . Take me an heifer of three years old, and a she goat of three years old, and a ram of three years old, and a turtledove, and a young pigeon." And he took unto him all these, and divided them in the midst, and laid each piece one against another, but the birds divided he not. . . . And it came to pass, that, when the sun went down, and it was dark, behold a smoking furnace, and a burning lamp that passed between those pieces. In the same day the LORD made a covenant with Abram. Gen. 15:6-7, 9-10, 17-18.

An indecent rite.

And God said unto Abraham. . . . "This is my covenant, which ye shall keep, between me and you and thy seed after thee; Every man child among you shall be circumcised. And ye shall circumcise the flesh of your foreskin; and it shall be a token of the covenant betwixt me and you. And he that is eight days old shall be circumcised among you, every man child in your generations, he that is born in the house, or bought with money of any stranger, which is not of thy seed. He that is born in thy house, and he that is bought with thy money, must needs be circumcised: and my covenant shall be in your flesh for an everlasting covenant. And the uncircumcised man child whose flesh of his foreskin is not circumcised, that soul shall be cut off from his people; he hath broken my covenant." Gen. 17:9-14.

Pharaoh in love with an old woman of seventy.

And it came to pass, when he was come near to enter into Egypt, that he said unto Sarai his wife, "Behold now, I know that thou art a fair woman to look upon: therefore it shall come to pass, when the Egyptians shall see thee, that they shall say, 'This is his wife:' and they will kill me, but they will save thee alive. Say, I pray thee, thou art my sister: that it may be well with me for thy sake; and my soul shall live because of thee." And it came to pass, that, when Abram was come into Egypt, the Egyptians beheld the woman that she was very fair. The princes also of Pharaoh saw her, and commended her before Pharaoh: and the woman was taken into Pharaoh's house. And he entreated Abram well for her sake: and he had sheep, and oxen, and he asses, and menservants, and maidservants, and she asses, and camels. And the LORD plagued

Pharaoh and his house with great plagues because of Sarai Abram's wife. And Pharaoh called Abram, and said, "What is this that thou hast done unto me? . . . Why saidst thou, 'She is my sister?' so I might have taken her to me to wife: now therefore behold thy wife, take her, and go thy way." Gen. 12:11-19.

[Abraham was 75 when he left Haran (Gen. 12:4: And Abram was seventy and five years old when he departed out of Haran.), and Sarah was ten years younger (Gen. 17:17: "Shall a child be born unto him that is an hundred years old? and shall Sarah, that is ninety years old, bear?").]

King Abimelech in love with Sarah at the age of ninety.

And Abraham said of Sarah his wife, "She is my sister": and Abimelech king of Gerar sent, and took Sarah. But God came to Abimelech in a dream by night, and said to him, "Behold, thou art but a dead man, for the woman which thou hast taken; for she is a man's wife." . . . And Abimelech took sheep, and oxen, and menservants, and womenservants, and gave them unto Abraham, and . . . a thousand pieces of silver. . . . So Abraham prayed unto God; and God healed Abimelech, and his wife, and his maidservants; and they bare children. For the LORD had fast closed up all the wombs of the house of Abimelech, because of Sarah, Abraham's wife. Gen. 20:2-3, 14, 16, 17-18.

Abraham feeds God and three angels.

And the LORD appeared unto him in the plains of Mamre: and he sat in the tent door in the heat of the day; and he lift up his eyes and looked, and, lo, three men stood by him. . . . And Abraham ran unto the herd, and fetcht a calf tender and good, and gave it unto a young man; and he hasted to dress it. And he took butter, and milk, and the calf which he had dressed, and set it before them; and he stood by them under the tree, and they did eat. Gen. 18: 1-2, 7-8.

God's tiff with Sarah.

And he said . . . "Lo, Sarah thy wife shall have a son." And Sarah heard it in the tent door, which was behind him. Now Abraham and Sarah were old and well stricken in age, and it ceased to be with Sarah after the manner of women. Therefore Sarah laughed within herself, saying, "After I am waxed old shall I have pleasure, my lord being old also?" And the LORD said unto Abraham, "Wherefore did Sarah laugh, saying, 'Shall I of a surety bear a child, which am old?' Is any thing too hard for the LORD? At the time appointed I will return unto thee, according to the time of life, and Sarah shall have a son." Then Sarah denied, saying, "I laughed not": for she was afraid. And he said, "Nay; but thou didst laugh." Gen. 18:10-15.

[Sarah was then ninety years old and Abraham ninety-nine or one hundred. See Gen. 17:17, 24: "Shall a child be born unto him that is an hundred years old? and shall Sarah, that is ninety years old, bear?" ... And Abraham was ninety years old and nine, when he was circumcised.]

A far cry — or a near heaven.

The angel of God called to Hagar out of heaven, and said unto her, "What aileth thee, Hagar?" Gen. 21:17.

And the angel of the LORD called unto him out of heaven, and said, "Abraham, Abraham": and he said, "Here am I." And he said, "Lay not thine hand upon the lad, neither do thou any thing unto him: for now I know that thou fearest God, seeing thou hast not withheld thy son, thine only son, from me." Gen. 22:11, 12.

And the angel of the Lord called unto Abraham out of heaven the second time. Gen. 22:15.

Lot's wife changed into chloride of sodium.

But his wife looked back from behind him, and she became a pillar of salt. Gen. 19:26.

Jacob's miraculous method of swindling his uncle.

And Jacob took him rods of green poplar, and of the hazel and chestnut tree; and pilled white strakes in them, and made the white appear which was in the rods. And he set the rods which he had pilled before the flocks in the gutters in the watering troughs when the flocks came to drink, that they should conceive when they came to drink. And the flocks conceived before the rods, and brought forth cattle ringstraked, speckled, and spotted. . . . But when the cattle were feeble, he put them not in: so the feebler were Laban's, and the stronger Jacob's. Gen. 30:37-39, 42.

Joseph interprets dreams.

And they dreamed a dream both of them, each man his dream in one night, each man according to the interpretation of his dream, the butler and the baker of the king of Egypt, which were bound in the prison. . . . And he restored the chief butler unto his butlership again, and he gave the cup into Pharaoh's hand: but he hanged the chief baker: as Joseph had interpreted to them. Gen. 40:5, 21, 22.

And Joseph said unto Pharaoh, "The dream of Pharaoh is one: God hath shewed Pharaoh what he is about to do. The seven good kine are seven years; and the seven good ears are seven years; the dream is one. And the seven thin and ill favoured kine that came up after them are seven years; and the seven empty ears blasted with the east wind shall be seven years of famine." Gen. 41:25-27.

Miraculous multiplication of the Israelites in Egypt.

And all the souls that came out of the loins of Jacob were seventy souls: for Joseph was in Egypt already. . . . And the children of Israel were fruitful and increased abundantly, and multiplied, and waxed exceeding mighty; and the land was filled with them. Exod. 1:5,7.

And the children of Israel journeyed from Rameses to Succoth, about six hundred thousand on foot that were men, besides children. Exod. 12:37.

From twenty years old and upward, all that were able to go forth to war in Israel; even all they that were numbered were six hundred thousand and three thousand and five hundred and fifty. But the Levites after the tribe of their fathers were not numbered among them. Num. 1:45-47.

[With women and children added to the fighting men there must have been a total population of over three millions, a tremendous increase in 215 years. (Compare Gal. 3:16 — Now to Abraham and his seed were the promises made. He saith not, "And to seeds," as of many; but as of one, "And to thy seed," which is Christ . . . — with Gen. 12:2 — "And I will make of thee a great nation, and I will bless thee, and make thy name great; and thou shalt be a blessing.") If they had doubled every 25 years, they would have been fewer than 20,000. As the firstborn males only numbered 22,273 (Num. 3:40-43: "Take the number of their [the firstborn] names. . . . And all the firstborn males . . . from a month old and upward . . . were twenty and two thousand two hundred and threescore and thirteen.), it has been calculated that the mothers must have had on an average sixty-six children apiece!]

Enormous population of Palestine.

The Hittites, and the Girgashites, and the Amorites, and the Canaanites, and the Perizzites, and the Hivites, and the Jebusites, seven nations greater and mightier than thou. Deut. 7:1.

[The "holy land," which only contains about twelve thousand square miles, thus sustained a population of at least twenty-one millions! That sterile province was far more densely peopled than England at the present day.]

God in a bonfire.

And the angel of the LORD appeared unto him in a flame of fire out of the midst of a bush: and he looked, and, behold the bush burned with fire, and the bush was not consumed. . . . And when the LORD saw that he turned aside to see, God called unto him out of the midst of the bush, and said, "Moses, Moses." And he said, "Here am I." And he said, "Draw not nigh hither: put off thy shoes from off thy feet, for the place whereon thou standest is holy ground." Exod. 3:2, 4-5.

Conjuring feats a proof of a divine mission.

And Moses answered and said, "But, behold, they will not believe me, nor hearken unto my voice: for they will say, 'The LORD hath not appeared unto thee.'" And the LORD said unto him, "What is that in thy hand?" And he said, "A rod." And he said, "Cast it on the ground." And he cast it on the ground, and it became a serpent; and Moses fled from before it. And the LORD said unto Moses, "Put forth thine hand, and take it by the tail." And he put forth his hand, and caught it, and it became a rod in his hand: "That they may believe that the LORD God of their fathers, the God of Abraham, the God of Isaac, and the God of Jacob, hath appeared unto thee." Exod. 4:1-5.

And Moses and Aaron went in unto Pharaoh, and they did so as the LORD had commanded: and Aaron cast down his rod before Pharaoh, and before his servants, and it became a serpent. Then Pharaoh also called the wise men and the sorcerers: now the magicians of Egypt, they also did in like manner with their enchantments. For they cast down every man his rod, and they became serpents: but Aaron's rod swallowed up their rods. Exod. 7:10-12.

The Lord, perhaps mad with drink, tries to murder his own emissary, and is conciliated with a curious offering.

And the LORD said unto Moses in Midian, "Go, return into Egypt. . . ." And it came to pass by the way in the inn, that the LORD met him, and sought to kill him. Then Zipporah took a sharp stone, and cut off the foreskin of her son, and cast it at his feet, and said, "Surely a bloody husband art thou to me." So he let him go: then she said, "A bloody husband thou art, because of the circumcision." Exod. 4:19, 24-26.

Water converted into blood twice over.

And Moses and Aaron did so, as the LORD commanded; and he lifted up the rod, and smote the waters that were in the river . . . and all the waters that were in the river were turned to blood. . . . And the magicians of Egypt did so with their enchantments. Exod. 7:20, 22.

[Moses transmuted all the water there was, but his opponents, still more cleverly, transmuted all the water there wasn't.]

Two strata of frogs (a) religious, and (b) magical, cover the whole country.

And Aaron stretched out his hand over the waters of Egypt; and the frogs came up, and covered the land of Egypt. And the magicians did so with their enchantments, and brought up frogs upon the land of Egypt. Exod. 8:6,7.

Evidently a divine miracle.

And the LORD said unto Moses, "Say unto Aaron, 'Stretch out thy rod, and smite the dust of the land, that it may become lice throughout all the land of Egypt.'" And they did so; for Aaron stretched out his hand with his rod, and smote the dust of the earth, and it became lice in man, and in beast; all the dust of the land became lice throughout all the land of Egypt. . . . Then the magicians said unto Pharaoh, "This is the finger of God." Exod. 8:16-17, 19.

"All the cattle," etc., are killed with murrain, and then afflicted with boils and blains; then most of them are killed once more with hail; after which the first-born among them are again killed by the destroying angel. Tough cattle these.

Behold, the hand of the LORD is upon thy cattle which is in the field, upon the horses, upon the asses, upon the camels, upon the oxen, and upon the sheep; there shall be a very grievous murrain. . . . And the LORD did that thing on the morrow, and all the cattle of Egypt died; but of the cattle of the children of Israel died not one. Exod. 9:3,6.

And the LORD said unto Moses and unto Aaron, "Take to you handfuls of ashes of the furnace, and let Moses sprinkle it towards the heaven in the sight of Pharaoh. And it shall become small dust in all the land of Egypt, and shall be a boil breaking forth with blains upon man, and upon beast, throughout all the land of Egypt." And they took ashes of the furnace, and stood before Pharaoh; and Moses sprinkled it up toward heaven; and it became a boil breaking forth with blains upon man, and upon beast. Exod. 9:8-10.

Upon every man and beast which shall be found in the field, and shall not be brought home, the hail shall come down upon them, and they shall die. . . . And Moses stretched forth his rod towards heaven: and the LORD sent thunder and hail, and the fire ran along upon the ground . . .

57

and the hail smote throughout all the land of Egypt all that was in the field, both man and beast. Exod. 9:19, 22-23, 25.

And it came to pass, that at midnight the LORD smote all the firstborn in the land of Egypt . . . and all the firstborn of cattle (Exod. 12:29). The LORD slew all the firstborn in the land of Egypt, both the firstborn of man, and the firstborn of beast: therefore I sacrifice to the LORD all that openeth the matrix, being males. Exod. 13:15.

The horses revive and are killed a third (or fourth) time.

But the Egyptians pursued after them, all the horses and chariots of Pharaoh, and his horsemen, and his army. . . . And Moses stretched forth his hand over the sea. . . . And the waters returned, and covered the chariots, and the horsemen, and all the host of Pharaoh that came into the sea after them; there remained not so much as one of them. Exod. 14:9, 27, 28.

Solid darkness, distributed in patches over Egypt like the black squares of a chessboard.

And the LORD said unto Moses, "Stretch out thine hand towards heaven, that there may be darkness over the land of Egypt, even darkness which may be felt." And Moses stretched forth his hand towards heaven; and there was a thick darkness in all the land of Egypt three days: they saw not one another, neither rose any from his place for three days: but all the children of Israel had light in their dwellings. Exod. 10:21-23.

God as a fiery cloud.

And the LORD went before them by day in a pillar of a cloud, to lead them the way; and by night in a pillar of fire, to give them light; to go by day and night: he took not away the pillar of the cloud by day, nor the pillar of fire by night, from before the people. Exod. 13:21, 22. (See also Num. 9:17-23: When the cloud was taken up from the tabernacle . . . the children of Israel journeyed. . . . As long as the cloud abode upon the tabernacle they rested in their tents. And when the cloud tarried long upon the tabernacle . . . the children of Israel kept the charge of the LORD.)

A talking cloud.

And it came to pass, as Moses entered into the tabernacle, the cloudy pillar descended, and stood at the door of the tabernacle, and the LORD talked with Moses. And all the people saw the cloudy pillar stand at the tabernacle door.... And the LORD spake unto Moses face to face, as a man speaketh unto his friend. Exod. 33:9-11. (See also Num. 12:5, 6: And the LORD came down in the pillar of the cloud ... and called Aaron and Miriam.... And he said, "Hear now my words: If there be a prophet among you, I the LORD will make myself known unto him ... and will speak unto him in a dream.")

Moses with his "rod of God" drives back and dries up the waters of the Red Sea, and at the same time makes them stand upright in heaps at each side of the narrow roadway along which the three million Israelites pass.

And Moses stretched out his hand over the sea; and the LORD caused the sea to go back by a strong east wind all that night, and made the sea dry land, and the waters were divided. And the children of Israel went into the midst of the sea upon the dry ground: and the waters were a wall unto them on their right hand, and on their left. Exod. 14:21, 22.

With the blast of thy nostrils the waters were gathered together, the floods stood upright as an heap, and the depths were congealed in the heart of the sea. Exod. 15:8.

The cloudy God as a mischievous wheelwright.

And it came to pass, that in the morning watch the LORD looked unto the host of the Egyptians through the pillar of fire and of the cloud, and troubled the host of the Egyptians, and took off their chariot wheels, that they drave them heavily. Exod. 14:24, 25.

During the forty years' wanderings in the desert the Israelites are fed with bread from heaven, or "angels' food" (Ps. 78:25: Man did eat angels' food. . . .), which possesses peculiar qualities.

Then said the LORD unto Moses, "Behold, I will rain bread from heaven for you." ... And when the dew that lay was gone up, behold, upon the face of the wilderness there lay a small round thing, as small as the hoar frost on the ground. And when the children of Israel saw it, they said one to another, "It is manna"; for they wist not what it was. ... And when they did mete it with an omer, he that gathered much had nothing over, and he that gathered little had no lack; they gathered every man according to his eating. And Moses said, "Let no man leave of it till the morning." Notwithstanding they hearkened not unto Moses; but some of them left of it until the morning, and it bred worms, and stank: and Moses was wroth with them. And they gathered it every morning, every man according to his eating: and when the sun waxeth hot, it melted. And it came to pass, that on the sixth day they gathered twice as much bread, two omers for one man. . . . And they laid it up till the morning, as Moses bade: and it did not stink, neither was there any worm therein. . . . And it came to pass, that there went out some of the people on the seventh day for to gather, and they found none. . . . And the children of Israel did eat manna forty years. Exod. 16:4, 14-15, 18-22, 24, 27, 35.

Everlasting clothing.

And I have led you forty years in the wilderness: your clothes are not waxen old upon you, and thy shoe is not waxen old upon thy foot. Deut. 29:5.

Victory dependent on lifting the hand.

Then came Amalek, and fought with Israel in Rephidim. . . . And it came to pass, when Moses held up his hand, that Israel prevailed: and when he let down his hand, Amalek prevailed. But Moses' hands were heavy; and they took a stone, and put it under him, and he sat thereon; and Aaron and Hur stayed up his hands, the one on the one side, and the other on the other side; and his hands were steady until the going down of the sun. And Joshua discomfited Amalek and his people with the edge of the sword. Exod. 17:8, 11-13.

Visible noises.

And all the people saw the thunderings, and the lightnings, and the noise of the trumpet. Exod. 20:18.

Enormous flocks survive during the forty years' wanderings in the desert; about 150,000 firstborn male lambs being slain at a time for the annual passover.

Speak ye unto all the congregation of Israel, saying . . . "They shall take to them every man a lamb, acording to the house of their fathers, a lamb for an house. . . . Your lamb shall be without blemish, a male of the first year. . . . and ye shall eat it in haste: it is the LORD's passover. . . . ye shall keep it a feast of the LORD throughout your generations." Exod. 12:3, 5, 11, 14.

And they kept the passover on the fourteenth day of the first month at even in the wilderness of Sinai: according to all that the LORD commanded Moses, so did the children of Israel. Num. 9:5.

Three million people assemble in front of a tent twenty-two feet wide, and Moses addresses them. The 600,000 men alone would have made a column of twenty-four miles or a dense square mass of a quarter of a mile across. The whole width of the outer court was only seventy-five feet (Exod. 27:18: The length of the court shall be an hundred cubits, and the breadth fifty every where.).

And gather thou all the congregation together unto the door of the tabernacle of the congregation. And Moses did as the LORD commanded him; and the assembly was gathered together unto the door of the tabernacle of the congregation. And Moses said unto the congregation: "This is the thing which the LORD commanded to be done." Lev. 8:3-5.

Three million people stoning one man to death.

Bring forth him that hath cursed without the camp . . . let all the congregation stone him. . . . And he that blasphemeth the name of the LORD, he shall surely be put to death, and all the congregation shall certainly stone him. Lev. 24:14, 16.

And the LORD said unto Moses, "The man shall be surely put to death: all the congregation shall stone him with stones without the camp." And all the congregation brought him without the camp, and stoned him with stones, and he died; as the LORD commanded Moses. Num. 15:35, 36.

Sculpture, painting, etc., forbidden as unpardonable religious crimes.

Thou shalt not make thee any graven image, or any likeness of anything that is in heaven above, or that is in the earth beneath, or that is in the waters beneath the earth. Deut. 5:8.

Lest ye corrupt yourselves, and make you a graven image, the similitude of any figure, the likeness of male or female, the likeness of any beast that is on the earth, the likeness of any winged fowl that flieth in the air, the likeness of any thing that creepeth on the ground, the likeness of any fish that is in the waters beneath the earth: . . . Take heed unto yourselves, lest ye forget the covenant of the LORD your God, which he made with you, and make you a graven image, or the likeness of any thing, which the LORD thy God hath forbidden thee. Deut. 4:16-18, 23.

Thou shalt not make unto thee any graven image, or any likeness of any thing that is in heaven above, or that is in the earth beneath, or that is in the water under the earth. Exod. 20:4.

The Invisible is visible, and the Infinite has feet.

Then went up Moses, and Aaron, Nadab, and Abihu, and seventy of

61

the elders of Israel: and they saw the God of Israel: and there was under his feet as it were a paved work of a sapphire stone, and as it were the body of heaven in his clearness. And upon the nobles of the children of Israel he laid not his hand: also they saw God, and did eat and drink. Exod. 24:9-11.

God shows his back parts.

And the LORD said, "Behold, there is a place by me, and thou shalt stand upon a rock: and it shall come to pass while my glory passeth by that I will put thee in a clift of the rock, and will cover thee with my hand while I pass by: and I will take away mine hand, and thou shalt see my back parts; but my face shall not be seen." Exod. 33:21-23.

Many chapters of God's revealed word are taken up with his trumpery instructions for making a holy box, a tent, a candlestick, snuffers, snuff-dishes, wash-basins, curtains, lamps, etc.

See Exodus, chapters 25 to 30, as follows:

And the LORD spake unto Moses, saying, . . . And let them make me a sanctuary; that I may dwell among them. . . . And they shall make an ark of shittim wood: two cubits and a half shall be the length thereof, and a cubit and a half the breadth thereof, and a cubit and a half the height thereof. And thou shalt overlay it with pure gold, within and without shalt thou overlay it, and shalt make upon it a crown of gold round about. And thou shalt cast four rings of gold for it, and put them in the four corners thereof; and two rings shall be in the one side of it, and two rings in the other side of it. And thou shalt make staves of shittim wood, and overlay them with gold. And thou shalt put the staves into the rings by the sides of the ark, that the ark may be borne with them. The staves shall be in the rings of the ark: they shall not be taken from it. And thou shalt put into the ark the testimony which I shall give thee. . . . And there I will meet with thee, and I will commune with thee. . . . Thou shalt also make a table of shittim wood: two cubits shall be the length thereof, and a cubit the breadth thereof, and a cubit and a half the height thereof. And thou shalt overlay it with pure gold, and make thereto a crown of gold round about. And thou shalt make unto it a border of an hand breadth round about, and thou shalt make a golden crown to the border thereof round about. . . . And thou shalt make the dishes thereof, and spoons thereof, and covers thereof, and bowls thereof, to cover withal: of pure gold shalt thou make them. And thou shalt set upon the table shewbread before me alway. And thou shalt make a candlestick of pure gold: of beaten work shall the candlestick be made: his shaft, and his branches, his bowls, his knops, and his flowers, shall be of the same. . . . And the tongs thereof, and the snuffdishes thereof, shall be of pure gold. Exod. 25:1, 8, 10-16, 22-25, 29-31, 38.

Moreover thou shalt make the tabernacle with ten curtains of fine twined linen, and blue, and purple, and scarlet: with cherubims of cunning work shalt thou make them. The length of one curtain shall be eight and twenty cubits, and the breadth of one curtain four cubits: and every one of the curtains shall have one measure. The five curtains shall be coupled together one to another; and other five curtains shall be coupled one to another. And thou shalt make loops of blue upon the edge of the one curtain from the selvedge in the coupling; and likewise shalt thou make in the uttermost edge of another curtain, in the coupling of the second. Fifty loops shalt thou make in the one curtain, and fifty loops shalt thou make in the edge of the curtain that is in the coupling of the second; that the loops may take hold one of another. And thou shalt make fifty taches of gold, and couple the curtains together with the taches: and it shall be one tabernacle. And thou shalt make curtains of goats' hair to be a covering upon the tabernacle: eleven curtains shalt thou make. . . . And thou shalt make a covering for the tent of rams' skins dyed red, and a covering above of badgers' skins . . . . And thou shalt set the table without the veil, and the candlestick over against the table on the side of the tabernacle toward the south: and thou shalt put the table on the north side. Exod. 26:1-7, 14, 35.

All the vessels of the tabernacle in all the service thereof, and all the pins thereof, and all the pins of the court, shall be of brass. And thou shalt command the children of Israel, that they bring thee pure oil olive beaten for the light, to cause the lamp to burn always. Exod. 27:19-20.

And thou shalt make holy garments for Aaron thy brother for glory and for beauty. . . . And these are the garments which they shall make; a breastplate, and an ephod, and a robe, and a broidered coat, a mitre, and a girdle: and they shall make holy garments for Aaron thy brother, and his sons, that he may minister unto me in the priest's office. . . . And thou shalt take two onyx stones, and grave on them the names of the children of Israel: Six of their names on one stone, and the other six names on the rest of the other stone, according to their birth. . . . And thou shalt put in the breastplate of judgment the Urim and the Thummim; and they shall be upon Aaron's heart, when he goeth in before the LORD: and Aaron shall bear the judgment of the children of Israel upon his heart before the LORD continually. And thou shalt make the robe of the ephod all of blue. And there shall be an hole in the top of it, in the midst thereof: it shall have a binding of woven work round about the hole of it, as it were the hole of an habergeon, that it be not rent. And beneath upon the hem of it thou shalt make pomegranates of blue, and of purple, and of scarlet, round about the hem thereof; and bells of gold between them round about: A golden bell and a pomegranate, upon the hem of the robe round about. And it shall be upon Aaron to minister: and his sound shall be heard when he goeth in unto the holy place before the LORD, and when he cometh out, that he die not. And thou shalt make a plate of pure gold, and grave upon it, like the engravings of a signet, HOLINESS TO THE LORD. And thou shalt put it on a blue lace, that it may be upon the mitre; upon the forefront of the mitre it shall be. And it shall be upon Aaron's forehead, that Aaron may bear the iniquity of the holy things, which the children of Israel shall hallow in all their holy gifts; and it shall be always upon his forehead, that they may be accepted before the LORD. . . . And for Aaron's sons thou shalt make coats, and thou shalt make for them girdles, and bonnets shalt thou make for them, for glory and for beauty. . . . And thou shalt make them linen breeches to cover their nakedness; from the loins even unto the thighs they shall reach: and they shall be upon Aaron, and upon his sons, when they come in unto the tabernacle of the congregation, or when they come near unto the altar to minister in the holy place; that they bear not iniquity, and die: it shall be a statute for ever unto him and his seed after him. Exod. 28:2, 4, 9-10, 30-38, 40, 42-43.

And thou shalt kill the bullock before the LORD, by the door of the tabernacle of the congregation. And thou shalt take of the blood of the bullock, and put it upon the horns of the altar with thy finger, and pour all the blood beside the bottom of the altar. And thou shalt take all the fat that covereth the inwards, and the caul that is above the liver, and the two kidneys, and the fat that is upon them, and burn them upon the altar. But the flesh of the bullock, and his skin, and his dung, shalt thou burn with fire without the camp: it is a sin offering. Thou shalt also take one ram; and Aaron and his sons shall put their hands upon the head of the ram: And thou shalt slay the ram, and thou shalt take his blood, and sprinkle it round about upon the altar. . . . And thou shalt take of the ram the fat and the rump, and the fat that covereth the inwards, and the caul above the liver, and the two kidneys, and the fat that is upon them, and the right shoulder; for it is a ram of consecration: And one loaf of bread, and one cake of oiled bread, and one wafer out of the casket of the unleavened bread that is before the LORD: And thou shalt put all in the hands of Aaron, and in the hands of his sons; and shalt wave them for a wave offering before the LORD. And thou shalt receive them of their hands, and burn them upon the altar for a burnt offering, for a sweet savour before the LORD: it is an offering made by fire unto the LORD. . . . And thou shalt sanctify the breast of the wave offering, and the shoulder of the heave offering, which is waved, and which is heaved up, of the ram of the consecration, even of that which is for Aaron, and of that which is for his sons. . . . Now this is that which thou shalt offer upon the altar; two lambs of the first year day by day continually. The one lamb thou shalt offer in the morning; and the other lamb thou shalt offer at even: And with the one lamb a tenth deal of flour mingled with the fourth part of an hin of beaten oil; and the fourth part of an hin of wine for a drink offering. And the other lamb thou shalt offer at even, and shalt do thereto according to the meat offering of the morning, and according to the drink offering thereof, for a sweet savour, an offering made by fire unto the LORD. This shall be a continual burnt offering throughout your generations at the door of the tabernacle of the congregation before the LORD: where I will meet you, to speak there unto thee. And there I will meet with the children of Israel, and the tabernacle shall be sanctified by my glory. And I will sanctify the tabernacle of the congregation, and the altar: I will sanctify also both Aaron and his sons, to minister to me in the priest's office. And I will dwell among the children of Israel, and will be their God. And they shall know that I am the LORD their God, that brought them forth out of the land of Egypt, that I may dwell among them: I am the LORD their God. Ex. 29:11-16, 22-27, 38-46.

And thou shalt make an altar to burn incense upon: of shittim wood shalt thou make it. A cubit shall be the length thereof, and a cubit the breadth thereof; foursquare shall it be; and two cubits shall be the height thereof: the horns thereof shall be of the same. And thou shalt overlay it with pure gold, the top thereof, and the sides thereof round about, and the horns thereof; and thou shalt make unto it a crown of gold round about. And two golden rings shalt thou make to it under the crown of it, by the two corners thereof, upon the two sides of it shalt thou make it; and they shall be for places for the staves to bear withal. . . . Thou shalt also make a laver of brass, and his foot also of brass, to wash withal: and thou shalt put it between the tabernacle of the congregation and the altar, and thou shalt put water therein. For Aaron and his sons shall wash their hands and their feet thereat: When they go into the tabernacle of the congregation, they shall wash with water, that they die not; or when they come near to the altar to minister, to burn offering made by fire unto the LORD: So they shall wash their hands and their feet, that they die not: and it shall be a statute for ever to them, even to him and to his seed throughout their generations. . . . Take thou also unto thee principal spices, of pure myrrh five hundred shekels, and of sweet cinnamon half so much, even two hundred and fifty shekels, and of sweet calamus two hundred and fifty shekels, and of cassia five hundred shekels, after the shekel of the sanctuary, and of oil olive an hin: And thou shalt make it an oil of holy ointment, an ointment compound after the art of the apothecary: it shall be an holy anointing oil. . . . Take unto thee sweet spices, stacte, and onycha, and galbanum; these sweet spices with pure frankincense: of each shall there be a like weight: And thou shalt make it a perfume, a confection after the art of the apothecary, tempered together, pure and holy. And thou shalt beat some of it very small, and put of it before the testimony in the tabernacle of the congregation, where I will meet with thee: it shall be unto you most holy. Exod. 30:1-4, 18-21, 23-25, 34-36.

God's idea of glory and beauty.
And thou shalt make holy garments for Aaron thy brother for glory and for beauty. . . . And bonnets shalt thou make for them, for glory and for beauty. Exod. 28:2, 40.

God regulates the priests' breeches.
And thou shalt make them linen breeches to cover their nakedness; from the loins even unto the thighs they shall reach. Exod. 28:42.

Gory garments sanctify the soul. [The Hindu religion attributes similarly sanctifying virtues to cow-dung.]
Then shalt thou kill the ram, and take of his blood, and put it upon the tip of the right ear of Aaron, and upon the tip of the right ear of his sons, and upon the thumb of their right hand, and upon the great toe of their right foot, and sprinkle the blood upon the altar round about. And thou shalt take of the blood that is upon the altar, and of the anointing oil, and sprinkle it upon Aaron, and upon his garments, and upon his sons, and upon the garments of his sons with him: and he shall be hallowed, and his garments, and his sons, and his sons' garments with him. Exod. 29:20, 21.

And Moses took the blood, and sprinkled it on the people. Exod. 24:8.

Shedding blood wipes away wickedness. (See also Lev. 9:8-22; 4:13-35; 8:19-24; 16:15-19; 14:25.)

And if the whole congregation of Israel sin through ignorance, and the thing be hid from the eyes of the assembly, and they have done somewhat against any of the commandments of the LORD concerning things which should not be done, and are guilty; When the sin, which they have sinned against it, is known, then the congregation shall offer a young bullock for the sin, and bring him before the tabernacle of the congregation. And the elders of the congregation shall lay their hands upon the head of the bullock before the LORD: and the bullock shall be killed before the LORD. And the priest that is anointed shall bring of the bullock's blood to the tabernacle of the congregation; and the priest shall dip his finger in some of the blood, and sprinkle it seven times before the LORD, even before the vail. And he shall put some of the blood upon the horns of the altar which is before the LORD, that is in the tabernacle of the congregation, and shall pour out all the blood at the bottom of the altar of the burnt offering, which is at the door of the tabernacle of the congregation. And he shall take all his fat from him, and burn it upon the altar. Lev. 4:13-19.

And if a soul sin, and hear the voice of swearing, and is a witness, whether he hath seen or known of it; if he do not utter it, then he shall bear his iniquity. Or if a soul touch any unclean thing, whether it be a carcase of an unclean beast, or a carcase of unclean cattle or the carcase of unclean creeping things, and if it be hidden from him; he also shall be unclean, and guilty. . . . And he shall bring his trespass offering unto the LORD for his sin which he hath sinned, a female from the flock, a lamb or a kid of the goats, for a sin offering; and the priest shall make an atonement for him concerning his sin. And if he be not able to bring a lamb, then he shall bring for his trespass, which he hath committed, two turtledoves, or two young pigeons, unto the LORD; one for a sin offering, and the other for a burnt offering. And he shall bring them unto the priest, who shall offer that which is for the sin offering first, and wring off his head from his neck, but shall not divide it asunder: and he shall sprinkle of the blood of the sin offering upon the side of the altar; and the rest of the blood shall be wrung out at the bottom of the altar: it is a sin offering. . . . But if he be not able to bring two turtledoves, or two young pigeons, then he that sinned shall bring for his offering the tenth part of an ephah of fine flour for a sin offering; he shall put no oil upon it, neither shall he put any frankincense thereon: for it is a sin offering. Then shall he bring it to the priest, and the priest shall take his handful of it, even a memorial thereof, and burn it on the altar, according to the offerings made by fire unto the LORD: it is a sin offering. And the priest shall make an atonement for him as touching his sin that he hath sinned in one of these, and it shall be forgiven him: and the remnant shall be the priest's, as a meat offering. Lev. 5:1, 2, 6-9, 11-13.

And he killed it; and Moses sprinkled the blood upon the altar round about. . . . And he brought the other ram, the ram of consecration. . . . And he slew it; and Moses took of the blood of it, and put it upon the tip of Aaron's right ear, and upon the thumb of his right hand, and upon the great toe of his right foot. . . . And Moses sprinkled the blood upon the altar round about. Lev. 8:19, 22-24.

And he cut the ram into pieces; and Moses burnt the head, and the pieces, and the fat. And he washed the inwards and the legs in water; and Moses burnt the whole ram upon the altar: it was a burnt sacrifice for a sweet savour, and an offering made by fire unto the Lord. Lev. 8:20-21.

He slew also the bullock and the ram for a sacrifice of peace offerings, which was for the people: and Aaron's sons presented unto him the blood, which he sprinkled upon the altar round about, and the fat of the bullock and of the ram, the rump, and that which covereth the inwards, and the kidneys, and the caul above the liver: and they put the fat upon the breasts, and he burnt the fat upon the altar: and the breasts and the right shoulder Aaron waved for a wave offering before the LORD; as Moses commanded. And Aaron lifted up his hand toward the people, and blessed them, and came down from offering of the sin offering, and the burnt offering, and peace offerings. And Moses and Aaron went into the tabernacle of the congregation, and came out, and blessed the people: and the glory of the LORD appeared unto all the people. And there came a fire out from before the LORD, and consumed upon the altar the burnt offering and the fat: which when all the people saw, they shouted, and fell on their faces. Lev. 9:18-24.

And he shall kill the lamb of the trespass offering, and the priest shall take some of the blood of the trespass offering, and put it upon the tip of the right ear of him that is to be cleansed, and upon the thumb of his right hand, and upon the great toe of his right foot. Lev. 14:25.

Then shall he kill the goat of the sin offering, that is for the people, and bring his blood within the vail, and do with that blood as he did with the blood of the bullock, and sprinkle it upon the mercy seat, and before the mercy seat: And he shall make an atonement for the holy place, because of the uncleanness of the children of Israel, and because of their transgressions in all their sins: and so shall he do for the tabernacle of the congregation, that remaineth among them in the midst of their uncleanness. Lev. 16:15,16.

And almost all things are by the law purged with blood: and without shedding of blood is no remission. Heb. 9:22.

For if the blood of bulls and of goats, and the ashes of an heifer sprinkling the unclean, sanctifieth to the purifying of the flesh: how much more shall the blood of Christ, who through the eternal Spirit offered himself without spot to God, purge your conscience from dead works to serve the living God? Heb. 9:13, 14.

The blood of Jesus Christ his Son cleanseth us from all sin. 1 John 1:7.

A nation's sins carried by a goat.

And Aaron shall lay both his hands upon the head of the live goat, and confess over him all the iniquities of the children of Israel, and all their transgressions in all their sins, putting them upon the head of the goat, and shall send him away by the hand of a fit man into the wilderness: And the goat shall bear upon him all their iniquities unto a land not inhabited. Lev. 16:21, 22.

Holy oil.

Take thou also unto thee principal spices, of pure myrrh five hundred shekels, and of sweet cinnamon half so much, even two hundred and fifty shekels, and of sweet calamus two hundred and fifty shekels, and of cassia five hundred shekels, after the shekel of the sanctuary, and of olive oil an hin: And thou shalt make it an oil of holy ointment, an ointment compound after the art of the apothecary: it shall be a holy anointing oil. Exod. 30:23-25.

And Moses took of the anointing oil, and of the blood which was upon the altar, and sprinkled it upon Aaron and upon his garments, and upon his sons, and upon his sons' garments with him; and sanctified Aaron, and his garments, and his sons, and his sons' garments with him. Lev. 8:30.

Sacred scent.

And the LORD said unto Moses, "Take unto thee sweet spices, stacte, and onycha, and galbanum; these sweet spices with pure frankincense: of each shall there be a like weight. . . . And as for the perfume which thou shalt make, ye shall not make to yourselves according to the composition thereof: it shall be unto thee holy for the LORD. Whosoever shall make like unto that, to smell thereto, shall even be cut off from his people." Exod. 30:37-38.

Cold sabbaths.

Ye shall kindle no fire throughout your habitations upon the sabbath day. Exod. 35:3.

The finger of God.

And he gave unto Moses, when he had made an end of communing with him upon mount Sinai, two tables of testimony, tables of stone, written with the finger of God. Exod. 31:18.

An old man of eighty fasts for forty days on a bleak mountain top.

And he was there with the LORD forty days and forty nights; he did neither eat bread nor drink water. Exod. 34:28.

A shining prophet.

And when Aaron and all the children of Israel saw Moses, behold, the skin of his face shone; and they were afraid to come nigh him. . . . And till Moses had done speaking with them, he put a vail on his face. But when Moses went in before the LORD to speak with him, he took the vail off, until he came out. Exod. 30:33-34.

A curious disinfectant.

And he shall take to cleanse the house two birds, and cedar wood, and scarlet, and hyssop: and he shall kill the one of the birds in an earthen vessel over running water: and he shall take the cedar wood, and the hyssop, and the scarlet, and the living bird, and dip them in the blood of the slain bird, and in the running water, and sprinkle the house seven times: and he shall cleanse the house with the blood of the bird, and with the running water, and with the living bird, and with the cedar wood, and with the hyssop, and with the scarlet. Lev. 14:49-52.

Witchcraft.

The sin of witchcraft. 1 Sam. 15:23.

Thou shalt not suffer a witch to live. Exod. 22:18.

[Manasseh] used enchantments, and dealt with familiar spirits and wizards. 2 Kings 21:6.

Regard not them that have familiar spirits, neither seek after wizards. Lev. 19:31.

Divination by Urim and Thummim, cups, ephods, etc.

And he shall stand before Eleazar the priest, who shall ask counsel for him after the judgment of Urim before the LORD. Num. 27:21.

Is not this it in which my lord drinketh, and whereby indeed he divineth? Gen. 44:5.

A certain damsel possessed with a spirit of divination met us, which brought her masters much gain by soothsaying. Acts 16:16.

And David knew that Saul secretly practised mischief against him; and he said to Abiathar the priest, "Bring hither the ephod." Then said David, "O LORD God of Israel, thy servant hath certainly heard that Saul seeketh to come to Keilah, to destroy the city for my sake. Will the men of Keilah deliver me up into his hand? Will Saul come down, as thy servant hath heard?" . . . And the LORD said, "He will come down." 1 Sam. 23:9-11.

And when Saul inquired of the LORD, the LORD answered him not, neither by dreams, nor by Urim, nor by prophets. Then said Saul unto his servants, "Seek me a woman that hath a familiar spirit, that I may go to her, and enquire of her." And his servants said to him, "Behold, there is a woman that hath a familiar spirit at Endor." 1 Sam. 28:6, 7.

And David said to Abiathar the priest, Ahimelech's son, "I pray thee, bring me hither the ephod." And Abiathar brought thither the ephod to David. And David inquired at the LORD, saying, "Shall I pursue after this troop? shall I overtake them?" And he answered him, "Pursue: for thou shalt surely overtake them, and without fail recover all." 1 Sam. 30:7, 8.

Divination by casting lots.

So they cast lots, and the lot fell upon Jonah. Jonah 1:7.

And they gave forth their lots; and the lot fell upon Matthias; and he was numbered with the eleven apostles. Acts 1:26.

The lot is cast into the lap; but the whole disposing thereof is of the LORD. Prov. 16:33.

Therefore Saul said unto the LORD God of Israel, "Give a perfect lot." And Saul and Jonathan were taken: but the people escaped. And Saul said, "Cast lots between me and Jonathan my son." And Jonathan was taken. 1 Sam. 14:41-42.

Hare chewing the cud.
And the hare, because he cheweth the cud, but divideth not the hoof; he is unclean unto you. Lev. 11:6.

Four-footed birds.
All fowls that creep, going upon all fours, shall be an abomination unto you. Lev. 11:20.

Four-footed beetles, etc.
Yet these may ye eat of every flying creeping thing that goeth upon all four, which have legs upon their feet, to leap withal upon the earth; . . . the locust . . . and the beetle after his kind, and the grasshopper after his kind. But all other flying creeping things, which have four feet, shall be an abomination unto you. Lev. 11:21-23.

It is twice as wicked for a woman to bear a daughter as a son.
And the LORD spake unto Moses, saying, "Speak unto the children of Israel, saying, 'If a woman have . . . born a man child: then she shall be unclean seven days. . . . But if she bear a maid child, then she shall be unclean two weeks.' " Lev. 12:1-2, 5.

Voracious priests.
And Aaron and his sons shall eat the flesh of the ram, and the bread that is in the basket, by the door of the tabernacle of the congregation. And they shall eat those things wherewith the atonement was made, to consecrate and to sanctify them. Exod. 29:32, 33.

The remnant shall be the priest's, as a meat offering. Lev. 5:13.

And the remainder thereof shall Aaron and his sons eat: with unleavened bread shall it be eaten in the holy place; in the court of the tabernacle of the congregation they shall eat it. Lev. 6:16.

And Moses said unto Aaron and to his sons, "Boil the flesh at the door of the tabernacle of the congregation: and there eat it with the bread that is in the basket of consecrations, as I commanded, saying, 'Aaron and his sons shall eat it.' " Lev. 8:31.

And ye shall eat it in the holy place, because it is thy due, and thy sons' due, of the sacrifices of the LORD made by fire: for so I am commanded. Lev. 10:13.

And when the days of her purifying are fulfilled, for a son, or for a daughter, she shall bring a lamb of the first year for a burnt offering, and a young pigeon, or a turtledove, for a sin offering, unto the door of the tabernacle of the congregation, unto the priest. . . . And if she be not able to bring a lamb, then she shall bring two turtles, or two young pigeons; the one for the burnt offering, and the other for a sin offering; and the priest shall make an atonement for her, and she shall be clean. Lev. 12:6, 8.

[There were then only three priests ("Aaron, Nadab and Abihu, Eleazar and Ithamar, Aaron's sons." Exod. 28:1; but "Nadab and Abihu . . . offered strange fire before the LORD, which he commanded them not. . . . And they died before the LORD." Lev. 10:1, 2) to three million people, among whom there would be at least three hundred births daily, so that these three priests should have devoured some six hundred pigeons a day. See Exod. 29:33 (And they shall eat those things wherewith the atonement was made, to consecrate and to sanctify them.).]

Trial by ordeal: the magic waters of jealousy.

If . . . the spirit of jealousy come upon him, and he be jealous of his wife . . . . then shall the man bring his wife unto the priest. . . . And the priest shall take holy water in an earthen vessel; and of the dust that is in the floor of the tabernacle the priest shall take, and put it into the water. . . . And the priest shall write these curses in a book, and he shall blot them out with the bitter water. . . . And when he hath made her to drink the water, then it shall come to pass, that, if she be defiled, and have done trespass against her husband, that the water that causeth the curse shall enter into her, and become bitter, and her belly shall swell, and her thigh shall rot: and the woman shall be a curse among her people. Num. 5:14-15, 17, 23, 27.

Military hornets.

And I will send hornets before thee, which shall drive out the Hivite, the Canaanite, and the Hittite, from before thee. Exod. 23:28.

A magic brass serpent.

And Moses made a serpent of brass, and put it upon a pole, and it came to pass, that if a serpent had bitten any man, when he beheld the serpent of brass, he lived. Num. 21:9.

A talking ass.

And when the ass saw the angel of the LORD, she fell down under Balaam: and Balaam's anger was kindled, and he smote the ass with a staff. And the LORD opened the mouth of the ass, and she said unto Balaam, "What have I done unto thee, that thou has smitten me these three times?" Num. 22:27-28.

Sold without being bought.

And the LORD shall bring thee into Egypt again with ships, by the way whereof I spake unto thee, "Thou shalt see it no more again; and there ye shall be sold unto your enemies for bondmen and bondwomen, and no man shall buy you." Deut. 28:68.

Moses describes his own death and burial.

So Moses the servant of the LORD died there in the land of Moab, according to the word of the LORD. And he buried him in a valley in the land of Moab, over against Bethpeor: but no man knoweth of his sepulchre unto this day. Deut. 34:5, 6.

Fighting for a corpse.

Michael the archangel, when contending with the devil he disputed about the body of Moses, durst not bring against him a railing accusation. Jude 9.

A docile river.

And as they that bare the ark were come unto Jordan, and the feet of the priests that bare the ark were dipped in the brim of the water . . . the waters which came down from above stood and rose up upon an heap . . . . . And the priests that bare the ark of the covenant of the LORD stood firm on dry ground in the midst of Jordan, and all the Israelites passed over on dry ground. Joshua 3:15-17.

Joshua stops the sun and moon.

Then spake Joshua to the LORD . . . and he said in the sight of Israel, "Sun, stand thou still upon Gibeon; and thou, Moon, in the valley of Ajalon." And the sun stood still, and the moon stayed, until the people had avenged themselves upon their enemies. Is not this written in the book of Jasher? So the sun stood still in the midst of heaven, and hasted not to go down about a whole day. Josh. 10:12, 13.

Omnipotence is easily defeated.

And the LORD was with Judah; and he drave out the inhabitants of the mountain; but could not drive out the inhabitants of the valley, because they had chariots of iron. Judg. 1:19.

Three hundred men under Gideon defeat a huge army.

And the three hundred blew the trumpets, and the LORD set every man's sword against his fellow, even throughout all the host: and the

74

host fled. . . . Judg. 7:22.

For there fell an hundred and twenty thousand men that drew sword. Judg. 8:10.

Wonderful slaughter with a spiked stick.

And after him was Shamgar the son of Anath, which slew of the Philistines six hundred men with an ox goad. Judg. 3:31.

A salamandrine angel.

And the angel did wondrously; and Manoah and his wife looked on. For it came to pass, when the flame went up toward heaven from off the altar, that the angel of the LORD ascended in the flame of the altar. Judg. 13:19, 20.

A wonderful jawbone.

And he found a new jawbone of an ass, and put forth his hand, and took it, and slew a thousand men therewith. And Samson said: "With the jawbone of an ass, heaps upon heaps, with the jaw of an ass have I slain a thousand men." Judg. 15:15, 16.

A surprising acrobat.

And Samson lay till midnight, and arose at midnight, and took the doors of the gate of the city, and the two posts and went away with them, bar and all, and put them upon his shoulders, and carried them up to the top of an hill that is before Hebron. Judg. 16:3.

Long hair a source of enormous muscular strength.

And Delilah said to Samson, "Tell me, I pray thee, wherein thy great strength lieth, and wherewith thou mightest be bound to afflict thee." And Samson said unto her . . . "There hath not come a razor upon mine head; for I have been a Nazarite unto God from my mother's womb: if I be shaven, then my strength will go from me, and I shall become weak, and be like any other man." And when Delilah saw that he had told her all his heart . . . she made him sleep upon her knees; and she called for a man, and she caused him to shave off the seven locks of his head; and she began to afflict him, and his strength went from him. . . . The Philistines took him, and put out his eyes, and brought him down to Gaza, and bound him with fetters of brass; and he did grind in the prison house. Howbeit the hair of his head began to grow again after he was shaven. . . . And Samson took hold of the two middle pillars upon which the house stood. . . . And he bowed himself with all his might: and the house fell upon the lords, and upon all the people that were therein. So the dead which he slew at his death were more than they which he slew in his life. Judg. 16:6-7, 17-19, 21-22, 29-30.

Rival gods.

When the Philistines took the ark of God, they brought it into the house of Dagon, and set it by Dagon. And when they of Ashdod arose early on the morrow, behold, Dagon was fallen upon his face to the earth before the ark of the LORD. And they took Dagon, and set him in his place again. And when they arose early on the morrow morning, behold, Dagon was fallen upon his face to the ground before the ark of the LORD; and the head of Dagon and both the palms of his hands were cut off upon the threshold; only the stump of Dagon was left to him. 1 Sam. 5:2-4.

Disgusting effect of the proximity of "God in a box."

And they carried the ark of the God of Israel about thither. And it was so, that, after they had carried it about, the hand of the LORD was against the city with a very great destruction; and he smote the men of the city, both small and great, and they had emerods [hemorrhoids] in their secret parts. 1 Sam. 5:8, 9.

Forty years a favourite period.

Moses was forty years in Egypt, forty years in Midian, and forty years in the desert. Acts 7:23, 30, 36.

Othniel judged Israel forty years. Judg. 3:11.

Ehud and Shamgar judged consecutively for a double period of eighty years. Judg. 3:30.

Barak gave Israel peace for forty years Judg. 5:31.

Gideon gave Israel peace for forty years. Judg. 8:28.

The Philistines oppressed Israel forty years. Judg. 13:1.

Eli judged Israel forty years. 1 Sam. 4:18.

Saul reigned forty years. Acts 13:21.

David reigned forty years. 2 Sam. 5:4.

Solomon reigned forty years. 1 Kings 11:42.

And Moses was learned in all the wisdom of the Egyptians, and was mighty in words and in deeds. And when he was full *forty* years old, it came into his heart to visit his brethren the children of Israel. . . . And when *forty* years were expired, there appeared to him in the wilderness of mount Sina an angel of the Lord in a flame of fire in a bush. . . . He brought them out, after that he had shewed wonders and signs in the land of Egypt, and in the Red sea, and in the wilderness *forty* years. Acts 7:22, 23, 30, 36.

And the spirit of the LORD came upon him, and he judged Israel, and went out to war: and the LORD delivered Chushanrishathaim king of Mesopotamia into his hand; . . . And the land had rest *forty* years. And Othniel the son of Kenaz died Judg 3:10, 11.

But when the children of Israel cried unto the LORD, the LORD raised them up a deliverer, Ehud the son of Gera, a Benjamite, a man lefthanded: and by him the children of Israel sent a present unto Eglon the king of Moab. . . . So Moab was subdued that day under the hand of Israel. And the land had rest fourscore (*forty and forty*) years. And after him was Shamgar the son of Anath, which slew of the Philistines six hundred men with an ox goad: and he also delivered Israel. Judg 3:10, 30, 31.

Then sang Deborah and Barak the son of Abinoam on that day, saying, . . . "So let all thine enemies perish, O lord: but let them that love him be as the sun when he goeth forth in his might." And the land had rest *forty* years. Judg 5:1, 31.

Thus was Midian subdued before the children of Israel, so that they lifted up their heads no more. And the country was in quietness *forty* years in the days of Gideon. Judg 8:28.

And the children of Israel did evil again in the sight of the LORD; and the LORD delivered them into the hand of the Philistines *forty* years. Judg 13:1.

And the man said unto Eli, "I am he that came out of the army, and I fled today out of the army." And he said, "What is there done, my son?" . . . And it came to pass, when he made mention of the ark of God, that he fell from off the seat backward by the side of the gate, and his neck brake, and he died: for he was an old man, and heavy. And he had judged Israel *forty* years. 1 Sam. 4:16, 18.

And afterward they desired a king: and God gave unto them Saul the son of Cis, a man of the tribe of Benjamin, by the space of *forty* years. Acts 13:21.

David was thirty years old when he began to reign, and he reigned *forty* years. 2 Sam. 5:4.

And the time that Solomon reigned in Jerusalem over all Israel was *forty* years 1 Kings 11:42.

[The frequent recurrence of this period of years shows the mythical nature of the biblical story.]

A many-lived people.

And Saul smote the Amalekites . . . and utterly destroyed all the people with the edge of the sword . . . utterly destroyed the Amalekites. 1 Sam. 15:7, 8, 20.

And David and his men went up and invaded . . . the Amalekites . . . and David smote the land, and left neither man nor woman alive. 1 Sam. 27:8, 9.

The Amalekites had invaded the south, and Ziklag, and smitten Ziklag, and burned it with fire; and had taken the women captives that were therein: they slew not any, either great or small, but carried them away, and went on their way. . . . And David smote them from the twilight even unto the evening of the next day; and there escaped not a man of them, save four hundred young men, which rode upon camels, and fled. 1 Sam. 30:1, 2, 17.

[Later on in the days of Hezekiah the Amalekites were exterminated positively for the last time. (1 Chron. 4:43: And they smote the rest of the Amalekites that were escaped.)]

The Midianites also flourish despite extermination.

And they warred against the Midianites, as the LORD commanded Moses; and they slew all the males. . . . And the children of Israel took all the women of Midian captives. . . . And Moses said unto them, . . . "Now therefore kill every male among the little ones, and kill every woman that hath known man by lying with him. But all the women children, that have not known a man by lying with him, keep alive for yourselves." Num. 31:7, 9, 15, 17, 18.

And the children of Israel did evil in the sight of the LORD: and the LORD delivered them into the hand of Midian seven years. . . . For they came up with their cattle and their tents, and they came as grasshoppers for multitude. Judg. 6:1, 5.

The Edomites are also a tough race.

Six months did Joab remain there with all Israel, until he had cut off every male in Edom. 1 Kings 11:16.

Yet Edom revolted from under the hand of Judah unto this day. 2 Kings 8:22.

Raising the spirits of the dead.

There is a woman that hath a familiar spirit at Endor. And Saul disguised himself, and put on other raiment, and he went, and two men with him, and they came to the woman by night: and he said, "I pray thee, divine unto me by the familiar spirit, and bring me him up, whom I shall name unto thee." And the woman said unto him, "Behold, thou knowest what Saul hath done, how he hath cut off those that have familiar spirits, and the wizards, out of the land: wherefore, then, layest thou a snare for my life, to cause me to die?" . . . Then said the woman, "Whom shall I bring up unto thee?" And he said, "Bring me up Samuel." And when the woman saw Samuel, she cried with a loud voice. . . . "An old man cometh up; and he is covered with a mantle." And Saul perceived that it was Samuel. . . . And Samuel said to Saul, "Why hast thou disquieted me, to bring me up?" 1 Sam. 28:7-9, 11-15.

Census-taking is an awful crime.
And David said to Joab and to the elders of the people, "Go, number Israel." . . . And God was displeased with this thing; therefore he smote Israel. . . . So the LORD sent pestilence upon Israel: and there fell of Israel seventy thousand men. 1 Chron. 21:2, 7, 14.

Plagues are caused by destroying angels.
And God sent an angel unto Jerusalem to destroy it: and as he was destroying, the LORD beheld, and he repented him of the evil, and said to the angel that destroyed, "It is enough, stay now thine hand." And the angel of the LORD stood by the threshingfloor of Ornan the Jebusite. And David lifted up his eyes, and saw the angel of the LORD stand between the earth and the heaven, having a drawn sword in his hand stretched out over Jerusalem. 1 Chron. 21:15, 16.

Wisdom equals polygamy.
And God gave Solomon wisdom and understanding exceedingly much, and largeness of heart, even as the sand that is on the sea shore. 1 Kings 4:29.
And he had seven hundred wives, princesses, and three hundred concubines. 1 Kings 11:3.
For he was wiser than all men. 1 Kings 4:31.

The wisest of men is fooled by sexual partners.
For it came to pass, when Solomon was old, that his wives turned away his heart after other gods. 1 Kings 11:4.

A magnificent temple about the size of a small chapel.
And the house which king Solomon built for the LORD, the length thereof was threescore cubits, and the breadth thereof twenty cubits,

and the height thereof thirty cubits. And the porch before the temple of the house, twenty cubits was the length thereof, according to the breadth of the house; and ten cubits was the breadth thereof before the house. . . . And then he built chambers against all the house, five cubits high: and they rested on the house with timber of cedar. 1 Kings 6:2-5, 10.

[A cubit equals the length of the forearm from elbow to fingertip — twenty-two inches. Solomon's great temple was thus only one hundred and ten feet long by thirty-six feet wide by fifty-five feet high, or about the size of a small chapel. A good, but small, town hall of these dimensions could easily be built by forty men at a cost of about £6,000. (This is a figure from the year 1900, at the time of the original publication of the book.)]

A disproportionate porch, thirty-six feet long and two hundred and twenty feet high.

And the porch that was in front of the house, the length of it was according to the breadth of the house, twenty cubits, and the height was an hundred and twenty: and he overlaid it within with pure gold. 2 Chron. 3:4.

Enormous preparations for so small a task. Over 180,000 men employed for eleven years in all.

So Hiram gave Solomon cedar trees and fir trees according to all his desire. And Solomon gave Hiram twenty thousand measures of wheat for food to his household, and twenty measures of pure oil: thus gave Solomon to Hiram year by year. . . . And king Solomon raised a levy out of all Israel, and the levy was thirty thousand men. And he sent them to Lebanon, ten thousand a month by courses. 1 Kings 5:10-11, 13-14.

And Solomon told out threescore and ten thousand men to bear burdens, and fourscore thousand to hew in the mountain, and three thousand and six hundred to oversee them. 2 Chron. 2:2.

So was he seven years in building it. 1 Kings 6:38.

[Commentators assume that four years had been previously spent in getting materials together.]

Solomon's wealth.

Now the weight of gold that came to Solomon in one year was six hundred threescore and six talents of gold. . . . So king Solomon exceeded all the kings of the earth for riches and for wisdom. 1 Kings 10:14, 23.

[The chief of a petty barren district of Asia Minor, without arts, manufactures, or civilization, thus received £4,000,000 (*Am. Atheist Ed. — value based on the year 1900*) a year in gold besides "great plenty" of precious stones, etc. The Romans only received £4,500,000 from the whole of their Asiatic provinces. Cruden makes a talent of gold equal £7,200, and a talent of silver equal £450.]*

The queen of Sheba (an unknown country) presents Solomon with nearly £1,000,000 out of sheer admiration for his "wisdom" and finery.
And when the queen of Sheba heard of the fame of Solomon, she came to prove Solomon with hard questions. . . . and Solomon told her all her questions: and there was nothing hid from Solomon which he told her not. And when the queen of Sheba had seen the wisdom of Solomon, and the house that he had built, and the meat of his table, and the sitting of his servants, and the attendance of his ministers, and their apparel; his cup-bearers also, and their apparel; and his ascent by which he went up into the house of the LORD; there was no more spirit in her. . . . And she gave the king an hundred and twenty talents of gold, and of spices great abundance, and precious stones. 2 Chron. 9:1-4, 9.

Every king on earth (!) visits Solomon and sends annual tribute.
And all the kings of the earth sought the presence of Solomon, to hear his wisdom, that God had put in his heart. And they brought every man his present, vessels of silver, and vessels of gold, and raiment, harness, and spices, horses, and mules, a rate year by year. 2 Chron. 9:23, 24.

David and his chiefs subscribed over £65,000,000 in gold and silver for the temple.
David the King. . . prepared for the holy house, even three thousand talents of gold, of the gold of Ophir, and seven thousand talents of

---

* Because of fluctuations in valuation of currency, the weight of the metals might be considered. Rev. Owen C. Whitehouse, as quoted in the Abradale Press version of the Bible used here, states that a gold talent weighed about 131 pounds, 8 ounces troy (1,580 oz. avoirdupois, or 98.75 pounds), while a silver talent weighed 177 pounds troy (1404 oz. avoirdupois, or 87.75 pounds). Thus, Solomon's 666 gold talents (one year's income) equalled 65,767.5 pounds. This is nearly one-seventh of the world gold production between 1492 and 1600 (*Encyclopedia Britannica*, 15th edition, 1980, Vol. 8, p. 237).

refined silver, to overlay the walls of the houses withal. . . . Then the chief of the fathers and princes of the tribe of Israel . . . offered willingly, and gave for the service of the house of God of gold five thousand talents and ten thousand drams, and of silver ten thousand talents, and of brass eighteen thousand talents, and one hundred thousand talents of iron. 1 Chron. 29:1, 3-4, 6-7.

David prepared £720,000,000 in gold and £450,000,000 in silver for the temple.

Now, behold, in my trouble I have prepared for the house of the LORD an hundred thousand talents of gold,* and a thousand thousand talents of silver;** and of brass and iron without weight. 1 Chron. 22:14.

[Mongredien estimates that the total value of gold and silver of every sort in the British Isles barely amounts to £143,000,000. A barbarous chieftain of an obscure Syrian tribe thus possessed eight times as much gold and silver as the richest country in the civilised world at a time when the precious metals have been poured into Europe in unprecedented abundance from the vast stores of America and Australia. He must have had more bullion than all the civilised world now possesses.]

Ravens bring sandwiches to Elijah.

And the ravens brought him bread and flesh in the morning, and the bread and flesh in the evening: and he drank of the brook. 1 Kings 17:6.

Inexhaustible food.

And she said, "As the LORD thy God liveth, I have not a cake but an handful of meal in a barrel, and a little oil in a cruse: and, behold, I am gathering two sticks, that I may go in and dress it for me and my son, that we may eat it, and die." And Elijah said unto her, "Fear not; go and do as thou hast said: but make me thereof a little cake first, and bring it unto me, and after make for thee and for thy son." . . . And she went and did according to the saying of Elijah: and she, and he, and her house, did

---

*One hundred thousand talents of gold is equal to 9,875,000 pounds avoirdupois of gold metal. This is nearly three times the total amount of gold produced worldwide beween 1492 and 1700 (*Encylopedia Britannica*, 15th Edition, 1980, Vol. 8, p. 237).

**One thousand thousand (1,000,000) talents of silver would weigh 87,750,000 pounds avoirdupois. This is more than five times the worldwide production of silver in 1970 (*Encyclopedia Britannica*, 15th Edition, 1980, Vol. 16, p. 778).

eat many days. And the barrel of meal wasted not, neither did the cruse of oil fail. 1 Kings 17:12-13, 15-16.

Elijah brings fire from heaven, which consumes wet wood, and stones and dust.
And he put the wood in order, and cut the bullock in pieces, and laid him on the wood, and said, "Fill four barrels with water, and pour it on the burnt sacrifice, and on the wood." . . . Then the fire of the LORD fell, and consumed the burnt sacrifice, and the wood, and the stones, and the dust, and licked up the water that was in the trench. 1 Kings 18:33, 38.

A river divided by a magic mantle.
And Elijah took his mantle, and wrapped it together, and smote the waters, and they were divided hither and thither, so that they two went over on dry ground. 2 Kings 2:8.

Conditional inspiration: horses of fire: Elijah ascends to heaven in an element more suited to the other region; more magic mantle.
And it came to pass, when they were gone over, that Elijah said unto Elisha, "Ask what I shall do for thee, before I be taken away from thee." And Elisha said, "I pray thee, let a double portion of thy spirit be upon me." And he said, "Thou hast asked a hard thing: nevertheless, if thou see me when I am taken from thee, it shall be so unto thee; but if not, it shall not be so." And it came to pass, as they still went on, and talked, that, behold, there appeared a chariot of fire, and horses of fire, and parted them both asunder; and Elijah went up by a whirlwind into heaven. And Elisha saw it. . . . And he took the mantle of Elijah that fell from him . . . and when he also had smitten the waters, they parted hither and thither: and Elisha went over. 2 Kings 2:9-12, 14.

Leprosy transferred from one man to another.
The leprosy therefore of Naaman shall cleave unto thee, and unto thy seed for ever. And he went out from his presence a leper as white as snow. 2 Kings 5:27.

Iron floats.
But as one was felling a beam, the ax head fell into the water, and he cried, and said, "Alas, master!" for it was borrowed. And the man of God said, "Where fell it?" And he showed him the place. And he cut down a stick, and cast it in thither; and the iron did swim. 2 Kings 6:5, 6.

An army struck blind.

Therefore sent he thither horses, and chariots, and a great host: and they came by night, and compassed the city about. . . . And when they came down to him, Elisha prayed unto the LORD, and said, "Smite this people, I pray thee, with blindness." And he smote them with blindness according to the word of Elisha. And Elisha said unto them, "This is not the way, neither is this the city: follow me, and I will bring you to the man whom ye seek." But he led them to Samaria. And it came to pass, when they were come into Samaria, that Elisha said, "LORD, open the eyes of these men, that they may see." And the LORD opened their eyes, and they saw; and, behold, they were in the midst of Samaria. 2 Kings 6:14, 18-20.

A large army of 185,000 men suddenly discover that they are all dead corpses.

And it came to pass that night, that the angel of the LORD went out, and smote in the camp of the Assyrians an hundred fourscore and five thousand: and when they arose in the morning, behold, they were all dead corpses. 2 Kings 19:35.

Huge armies from small and barren districts.

And Abijah set the battle in array with an army of valiant men of war, even four hundred thousand chosen men: Jeroboam also set the battle in array against him with eight hundred thousand chosen men, being mighty men of valour. 2 Chron. 13:3.

Incredible slaughter.

And Abijah and his people slew them with a great slaughter: so there fell down slain of Israel five hundred thousand chosen men. 2 Chron. 13:17.

A wall crushes 27,000 warriors.

A wall fell upon twenty and seven thousand of the men that were left. 1 Kings 20:30.

The sun goes back to guarantee a fig poultice.

And Hezekiah wept sore. . . . And Isaiah said, "Take a lump of figs." And they took and laid it on the boil, and he recovered. And Hezekiah said unto Isaiah, "What shall be the sign that the LORD will heal me?" . . . And Isaiah the prophet cried unto the LORD: and he brought the shadow ten degrees backward, by which it had gone down in the dial of Ahaz. 2 Kings 20:3, 7-8, 11.

Juvenile depravity.

Jehoiachin was eight years old when he began to reign, and he reigned three months and ten days in Jerusalem: and he did that which was evil in the sight of the LORD. 2 Chron. 36:9.

Satan and God on friendly terms.

Now there was a day when the sons of God came to present themselves before the LORD, and Satan came also among them. And the LORD saith unto Satan, "Whence comest thou?" And Satan answered the LORD, and said, "From going to and fro in the earth, and from walking up and down in it." Job 1:6, 7.

Curious loveliness.

Thou art beautiful, O my love, as Tirzah, comely as Jerusalem ... thy hair is as a flock of goats that appear from Gilead. Thy teeth are as a flock of sheep which go up from the washing . . . thine eyes like the fishpools . . . thy nose is as the tower of Lebanon which looketh towards Damascus. Song of Sol. 6:4-6; 7:4.

Fabulous animals are treated as really existent.

(1) Unicorns.

Will the unicorn be willing to serve thee, or abide by thy crib? Canst thou bind the unicorn with his band in the furrow? or will he harrow the valleys after thee? Wilt thou trust him, because his strength is great? or wilt thou leave thy labour to him? Job 39:9-11.

Thou hast heard me from the horns of the unicorns. Ps. 22:21.

He hath as it were the strength of a unicorn. Num. 23:22; 24:8.

And his horns are like the horns of unicorns. Deut. 33:17.

He maketh them also to skip like a calf; Lebanon and Sirion like a young unicorn. Ps. 29:6.

But my horn shalt thou exalt like the horn of a unicorn. Ps. 92:10.

And the unicorns shall come down with them. Isa. 34:7.

(2) Cockatrices.

And the lion shall eat straw like the ox. And the sucking child shall play on the hole of the asp, and the weaned child shall put his hand on the cockatrice' den. Isa. 11:7, 8.

Out of the serpent's root shall come forth a cockatrice. Isa. 14:29.

They hatch cockatrice' eggs. Isa. 59:5.

"For, behold, I will send serpents, cockatrices, among you, which will not be charmed, and they shall bite you," saith the LORD. Jer. 8:17.

85

[A cockatrice was a serpent hatched from the egg of a cock. In the Revised Version "basilisk" is substituted for "cockatrice." The basilisk, or cockatrice, was supposed to drive all other serpents away by its hissing, and to kill with its mere glance.]

(3) Dragons.

It shall be an habitation of dragons, and a court for owls. Isa. 34:13.

The young lion and the dragon shalt thou trample under feet. Ps. 91:13.

Praise the Lord from the earth, ye dragons. Ps. 148:7.

The beast of the field shall honour me, the dragons and the owls: because I give waters in the wilderness, and rivers in the desert, to give drink to my people, my chosen. Isa. 43:20.

Thou breakest the heads of the dragons in the waters. Ps. 74:13.

The poison of dragons. Deut. 32:33.

And the wild asses did stand in the high places, they snuffed up the wind like dragons. Jer. 14:6.

Therefore I will wail and howl, I will go stripped and naked: I will make a wailing like the dragons, and mourning as the owls. Micah 1:8.

I am a brother to dragons, and a companion to owls. Job 30:29.

And the wild beasts of the islands shall cry in their desolate houses, and dragons in their pleasant palaces. Isa. 13:22.

In that day the LORD with his sore and great and strong sword shall punish leviathan the piercing serpent, even leviathan that crooked serpent; and he shall slay the dragon that is in the sea. Isa. 27:1.

And I will make Jerusalem heaps, and a den of dragons. Jer. 9:11.

Behold, the noise of the bruit is come, and a great commotion out of the north country, to make the cities of Judah desolate, and a den of dragons. Jer. 10:22.

(4) Satyrs.

The wild beasts of the deserts shall also meet with the wild beasts of the island, and the satyr shall cry to his fellow; the screech owl also shall rest there. Isa. 34:14.

Owls shall dwell there, and satyrs shall dance there. Isa. 13:21.

(5) Fiery serpents.

And the LORD sent fiery serpents among the people, and they bit the people; and much people of Israel died. Num. 21:6.

Terrible wilderness, wherein were fiery serpents, and scorpions. Deut. 8:15.

(6) Winged serpents.
The young and old lion, the viper and fiery flying serpent. Isa. 30:6.
Out of the serpent's root shall come forth a cockatrice, and his fruit shall be a fiery flying serpent. Isa. 14:29.

A roaring god.
The LORD shall go forth as a mighty man . . . he shall cry, yea, roar. Isa. 42:13.
The LORD shall roar from on high . . . he shall mightily roar upon his habitation. Jer. 25:30.
They shall walk after the LORD: he shall roar like a lion: when he shall roar, then the children shall tremble from the west. Hosea 11:10.
The LORD also shall roar out of Zion. Joel 3:16.

A hissing god.
And he will lift up an ensign to the nations from far, and will hiss unto them from the end of the earth. Isa. 5:26.
I will hiss for them. Zech. 10:8.
The LORD shall hiss for the fly that is in the uttermost part of the rivers of Egypt, and for the bee that is in the land of Assyria. And they shall come. Isa. 7:18, 19.

A barber god.
In the same day shall the Lord shave with a razor that is hired. Isa. 7:20.

Curious mercy.
To him that smote Egypt in their firstborn: for his mercy endureth for ever. . . . And slew famous kings: for his mercy endureth for ever. Ps. 136:10, 18.

Hallelujah dragons, pious mountains, and holy beasts.
Praise him, ye heavens of heavens, and ye waters that be above the heavens. . . . Praise the LORD from the earth, ye dragons, and all deeps: fire, and hail: snow and vapours; stormy wind fulfilling his word: mountains, and all hills: fruitful trees, and all cedars: beasts, and all cattle; creeping things, and flying fowl . . . let them praise the name of the LORD. Ps. 148:4, 7-10, 13.

A penitent god.
I am weary with repenting. Jer. 15:6.

And it repented the LORD that he had made man on the earth, and it grieved him at his heart. Gen. 6:6.

And the LORD repented of the evil which he thought to do unto his people. Exod. 32:14.

And the LORD repented that he had made Saul King over Israel. 1 Sam. 15:35.

And God repented of the evil, that he had said that he would do unto them; and he did it not. Jon. 3:10.

The LORD repented for this: "It shall not be," saith the LORD. Amos 7:3.

A furious god.

The LORD . . . is furious. Nahum 1:2.

A wild-beast god.

He was unto me as a bear lying in wait, and as a lion in secret places. Lam. 3:10.

For I will be unto Ephraim as a lion, and as a young lion to the house of Judah. Hos. 5:14.

A carnivorous god.

I will meet them as a bear that is bereaved of her whelps, and will rend the caul of their heart, and there will I devour them like a lion: the wild beast shall tear them. Hos. 13:8.

God deceives his own prophets.

O LORD, thou hast deceived me, and I was deceived: thou art stronger than I, and hast prevailed: I am in derision daily, every one mocketh me. Jer. 20:7.

The prophet wears a yoke.

Thus said the LORD to me: "Make thee bonds and yokes, and put them upon thy neck." . . . Then Hananiah the prophet took the yoke from off the prophet Jeremiah's neck, and brake it. Jer. 27:2; 28:10.

Inspired uncleanliness.

Thus saith the LORD unto me, "Go and get thee a linen girdle and put it upon thy loins, and put it not in water." Jer. 13:1.

Inspired follies.

And the word of the LORD came unto me the second time, saying,

"Take the girdle that thou hast got, which is upon thy loins, and arise, go to Euphrates, and hide there in a hole of the rock." So I went, and hid it by Euphrates, as the LORD commanded me. And it came to pass after many days, that the LORD said unto me, "Arise, go to Euphrates, and take the girdle from thence, which I commanded thee to hide there." Then I went to Euphrates, and digged, and took the girdle from the place where I had hid it: and, behold, the girdle was marred, it was profitable for nothing. Jer. 13:3-7.

[The Euphrates was hundreds of miles away across desert country.]

More inspired folly.

And thou, son of man, take thee a sharp knife, take thee a barber's razor, and cause it to pass upon thine head and upon thy beard: then take thee balances to weigh, and divide the hair. Thou shalt burn with fire a third part in the midst of the city, when the days of the siege are fulfilled: and thou shalt take a third part, and smite about it with a knife: and a third part thou shalt scatter in the wind; and I will draw out a sword after them. Thou shalt also take thereof a few in number, and bind them in thy skirts. Ezek. 5:1-3.

More inspiration.

The hand of the LORD God fell there upon me. Then I beheld, and lo a likeness as the appearance of fire. . . . And he put forth the form of an hand, and took me by a lock of mine head: and the spirit lifted me up between the earth and the heaven, and brought me in the visions of God to Jerusalem. Ezek. 8:1-3.

And I did so as I was commanded: I brought forth my stuff by day, as stuff for captivity, and in the even I digged through the wall with mine hand; I brought it forth in the twilight, and I bare it upon my shoulder in their sight. Ezek. 12:7.

Dry bones made alive.

The hand of the LORD was upon me, and carried me out in the spirit of the LORD, and set me down in the midst of the valley which was full of bones. . . . He said unto me, "Prophesy upon these bones, and say unto them, 'O ye dry bones, hear the word of the LORD.' " . . . And as I prophesied, there was a noise, and behold a shaking, and the bones came together, bone to his bone. . . . And the breath came unto them, and they lived, and stood up upon their feet, an exceeding great army. Ezek. 37:1, 4, 7, 10.

[This is usually explained as a vision, but the text speaks as if describing an actual occuurrence.]

Four-headed fowl.

The word of the LORD came expressly unto Ezekiel the priest. . . .
And I looked, and behold . . . four living creatures . . . they had the
likeness of a man. And every one had four faces, and every one had four
wings. And their feet were straight feet; and the sole of their feet was
like the sole of a calf's foot; and they sparkled like the colour of
burnished brass. And they had the hands of a man under their wings
on their four sides. . . . As for the likeness of their faces, they four had
the face of a man, and the face of a lion on the right side; and they four
had the face of an ox on the left side; they four also had the face of an
eagle. Ezek.1:3-8, 10. [Ezek. 10:14 substitutes cherub for ox.]

And their whole body, and their backs, and their hands, and their
wings . . . were full of eyes round about. Ezek. 10:12.

Ezekiel besieges a tile.

Thou also, son of man, take thee a tile, and lay it before thee, and
pourtray upon it the city, even Jerusalem; and lay siege against it, and
build a fort against it, and cast a mount against it; set the camp also
against it, and set battering rams against it round about. . . . Lie thou
also upon thy left side, and lay the iniquity of the house of Israel upon
it . . . so shalt thou bear the iniquity of the house of Israel. And when
thou hast accomplished them, lie again on thy right side, and thou shalt
bear the iniquity of the house of Judah forty days. . . . and thou shalt
not turn thee from one side to another, till thou hast ended the days of
thy siege. Ezek. 4:1-2, 4-6, 8.

A forgotten dream revealed and interpreted.

The king answered and said to the Chaldeans, "The thing is gone
from me; if ye will not make known unto me the dream, with the
interpretation thereof, ye shall be cut in pieces, and your houses shall
be made a dunghill." . . . And the decree went forth that the wise men
should be slain; and they sought Daniel and his fellows to be slain. . .
. Daniel answered. . . . "Thy dream, and the visions of thy head upon
thy bed, are these. . . . Thou, O king, sawest, and behold a great image.
. . . This image's head was of fine gold, his breast and his arms of silver,
his belly and his thighs of brass, his legs of iron, his feet part of iron and
part of clay." . . . Then the king Nebuchadnezzar fell upon his face, and
worshipped Daniel. Dan. 2:5, 13, 27, 28, 31-33, 46.

A disproportionate image.

Nebuchadnezzar, the king, made an image of gold, whose height was

threescore cubits, and the breadth thereof six cubits. Dan. 3:1.
[The height was ten times the width; fancy a statue ten feet high by one foot broad!]

Incombustible fire-kings.
And whoso falleth not down and worshippeth shall the same hour be cast into the midst of a burning fiery furnace. . . . Then was Nebuchadnezzar full of fury, and the form of his visage was changed against Shadrach, Meshach, and Abednego: therefore he spake and commanded that they should heat the furnace one seven times more than it was wont to be heated. And he commanded the most mighty men that were in his army to bind Shadrach, Meshach, and Abednego, and to cast them into the burning fiery furnace. Then these men were bound in their coats, their hosen, and their hats, and their other garments, and were cast into the midst of the burning fiery furnace. Therefore, because the king's commandment was urgent, and the furnace exceeding hot, the flame of the fire slew those men that took up Shadrach, Meshach, and Abednego. . . . Then Nebuchadnezzar the king was astonied, and rose up in haste, and spake, and said unto his counsellors, "Did not we cast three men bound into the midst of the fire?" They answered and said unto the king, "True, O king." He answered and said, "Lo, I see four men loose, walking in the midst of the fire, and they have no hurt; and the form of the fourth is like the Son of God." . . . Then Shadrach, Meshach, and Abednego, came forth of the midst of the fire. And the princes, governors, and captains, and the king's counsellors, being gathered together, saw these men, upon whose bodies the fire had no power, nor was an hair of their head singed, neither were their coats changed, nor the smell of fire had passed on them. Dan. 3:6, 19-22, 24-25, 26-27.

A hand out of a wall.
In the same hour came forth fingers of a man's hand, and wrote over against the candlestick upon the plaister of the wall of the king's palace: and the king saw the part of the hand that wrote. Dan. 5:5.

An inedible prophet.
Then the king commanded, and they brought Daniel, and cast him into the den of lions. . . . Then said Daniel unto the king, "O king, live for ever. My God hath sent his angel, and hath shut the lions' mouths, that they have not hurt me." . . . So Daniel was taken up out of the den, and no manner of hurt was found upon him, because he believed in his God. Dan. 6:16, 21-23.

Amos interviews God.

I saw the LORD standing upon the altar: and he said, "Smite the lintel of the door, that the posts may shake: and cut them in the head, all of them: and I will slay the last of them with the sword . . . and he that escapeth of them shall not be delivered. Though they dig into hell, thence shall mine hand take them; though they climb up to heaven, thence will I bring them down . . . and though they be hid from my sight in the bottom of the sea, thence will I command the serpent, and he shall bite them." Amos 9:1-3.

Fleeing from Omnipresence.

But Jonah rose up to flee unto Tarshish from the presence of the LORD, and went down to Joppa; and he found a ship going to Tarshish: so he paid the fare thereof, and went down into it, to go with them unto Tarshish from the presence of the LORD. Jon. 1:3.

Casting lots detects a culprit, and throwing him overboard pacifies a howling storm.

But the LORD sent out a great wind into the sea, and there was a mighty tempest in the sea, so that the ship was like to be broken. . . . And they said every one to his fellow, "Come, and let us cast lots, that we may know for whose cause this evil is upon us." So they cast lots, and the lot fell upon Jonah. . . . And he said unto them, "Take me up, and cast me forth into the sea; so shall the sea be calm unto you." . . . So they took up Jonah, and cast him forth into the sea: and the sea ceased from her raging. Jon. 1:4, 7, 12, 15.

Jonah resides in a whale.

Now the LORD had prepared a great fish to swallow up Jonah. And Jonah was in the belly of the fish three days and three nights. Jon. 1:17.

Jesus Christ guarantees the truth of the whale story.

For as Jonas was three days and three nights in the whale's belly; so shall the Son of man be three days and three nights in the heart of the earth. Matt. 12:40.

[A whale is not a fish, but Jesus had not been to a Council school.]

Prayer-meeting in a whale.

Then Jonah prayed unto the LORD his God out of the fish's belly, and said. . . ."The waters compassed me about, even to the soul: the depth closed me round about, the weeds were wrapped about my head. I went

92

down to the bottoms of the mountains: the earth with her bars was about me for ever." Jon. 2:1-6.

A whale vomits a man.

And the LORD spake unto the fish, and it vomited out Jonah upon the dry land. Jon. 2:10.

Penitent cattle.

Let man and beast be covered with sackcloth, and cry mightily unto God: yea, let them turn every one from his evil way, and from the violence that is in their hands. . . . And God saw their works, that they turned from their evil way; and God repented of the evil, that he had said he would do unto them; and he did it not. Jon. 3:8, 10.

Rapid growth of a gourd and rapid destruction by a curious worm.

God prepared a gourd, and made it to come up over Jonah, that it might be a shadow over his head. . . . But God prepared a worm when the morning rose the next day and it smote the gourd that it withered . . . which came up in a night, and perished in a night. Jon. 4:6-7, 10.

Habakkuk's God.

God came from Teman, and the Holy One from mount Paran . . . he had horns coming out of his hand. . . . Before him went the pestilence, and burning coals went forth at his feet. He stood, and measured the earth. Hab. 3:3-6.

More nonsense about God.

There went up a smoke out of his nostrils, and fire out of his mouth devoured: coals were kindled by it. . . . And he rode upon a cherub, and did fly: and he was seen upon the wings of the wind. 2 Sam. 22:9, 11.

A land which the LORD thy God careth for: the eyes of the LORD thy God are always upon it, from the beginning of the year even unto the end of the year. Deut. 11:12.

The Lord is a man of war. Exod. 15:3.

The eyes of the LORD run to and fro throughout the whole earth. 2 Chron. 16:9; Zech. 4:10.

Zechariah's vision.

In the first chariot were red horses; and in the second chariot black horses; and in the third chariot white horses; and in the fourth chariot grisled and bay horses. Then I answered and said unto the angel that talked with me, "What are these, my lord?" And the angel answered and said unto me, "These are the four spirits of the heavens, which go forth from standing before the LORD of all the earth." Zech. 6:2-5.

II. THE NEW TESTAMENT

Zacharias struck dumb for not believing an angel.
And they had no child, because that Elisabeth was barren, and they both were now well stricken in years. . . . But the angel said unto him, "Fear not, Zacharias: for thy prayer is heard; and thy wife Elisabeth shall bear thee a son, and thou shalt call his name John. . . . And behold, thou shalt be dumb, and not be able to speak, until the day that these things shall be performed, because thou believest not my words." Luke 1:7, 13, 20.

An inspired infant.
He shall be filled with the Holy Ghost, even from his mother's womb. Luke 1:15.

Joseph has two fathers.
Jacob begat Joseph. Matt. 1:16.
Joseph, which was the son of Heli. Luke 3:23.

A ghost is the father of a baby.
Now the birth of Jesus Christ was on this wise: When as his mother Mary was espoused to Joseph, before they came together, she was found with child of the Holy Ghost. Matt. 1:18.

A dream satisfies Joseph.
But while he thought on these things, behold, the angel of the Lord appeared unto him in a dream, saying, "Joseph, thou son of David, fear not to take unto thee Mary thy wife: for that which is conceived in her is of the Holy Ghost." Matt. 1:20.

A virgin mother.
Now all this was done, that it might be fulfilled which was spoken of the Lord by the prophet, saying, "Behold, a virgin shall be with child, and shall bring forth a son." Matt. 1:22, 23.

A baby God; or the "Incarnation."
And she brought forth her firstborn son, and wrapped him in swad-

dling clothes, and laid him in a manger; because there was no room for them in the inn. Luke 2:7.

God was manifest in the flesh. 1 Tim. 3:16.

In the beginning was the Word, and the Word was with God, and the Word was God. . . . And the Word was made flesh, and dwelt among us. John 1:1, 14.

But when the fulness of the time was come, God sent forth his Son, made of a woman. Gal. 4:4

Who, being in the form of God, thought it not robbery to be equal with God: but made himself of no reputation, and took upon him the form of a servant. Phil. 2:6, 7.

[Christ was thus supreme God and helpless infant in one — that is, he was infinite and finite, almighty and weak, omniscient and ignorant, omnipresent and not omnipresent, at one and the same time.]

Three persons are one.

For there are three that bear record in heaven, the Father, the Word, and the Holy Ghost: and these three are one. 1 John 5:7.

[This verse, being demonstrated a forgery, is omitted from the Revised Version. It is the only text distinctly asserting the doctrine of the Trinity, which is really a Christian invention or development of later date than the Bible.]

A son as old as his father, and identical with his father.

In the beginning was the Word . . . and the Word was God . . . and the Word was made flesh. . . . For God so loved the world, that he gave his only begotten Son. John 1:1, 14; 3:16.

A wonderful star.

There came wise men from the east to Jerusalem, saying, "Where is he that is born King of the Jews? for we have seen his star in the east . . . and, lo, the star, which they saw in the east, went before them, till it came and stood over where the young child was. Matt. 2:1, 2, 9.

[Try to ascertain what house or person any particular star stands over.]

Revelation misdirected; only obscure nobodies are enlightened.

And there were in the same country shepherds abiding in the field, keeping watch over their flock by night. And, lo, the angel of the Lord came upon them, and the glory of the Lord shone around about them: and they were sore afraid. And the angel said unto them, "Fear not: for, behold, I bring you good tidings of great joy, which shall be to all people. For unto you is born this day in the city of David, a Saviour, which is Christ the Lord." Luke 2:8-11.

[The Lord revealeth the birth of the saviour of the world to anonymous shepherds and apocryphal "wise men from the east," but not to known historians and learned men who could leave a trustworthy written record duly attested and confirmed.]

A mutilated, but perfect, baby God.

And when eight days were accomplished for the circumcising of the child, his name was called JESUS. Luke 2:21.

The immaculate virgin is purified.

And when the days of her purification according to the law of Moses were accomplished, they brought him to Jerusalem, to present him to the Lord. . . . And to offer a sacrifice according to that which is said in the law of the Lord, A pair of turtle-doves, or two young pigeons. Luke 2:22, 24.

Herod, a sensible and polite ruler, kills all the babies in Bethlehem on account of the silly superstition of the "wise men."

Then Herod, when he saw that he was mocked of the wise men, was exceeding wroth, and sent forth, and slew all the children that were in Bethlehem, and in all the coasts thereof, from two years old and under, according to the time which he had diligently inquired of the wise men. Matt. 2:16.

A family party: the Trinity in Unity meet in public.

And Jesus, when he was baptized, went up straightway out of the water: and, lo, the heavens were opened unto him, and he saw the Spirit of God descending like a dove, and lighting upon him: and lo a voice from heaven, saying, "This is my beloved Son, in whom I am well pleased." Matt. 3:16, 17.

And the Holy Ghost descended in a bodily shape like a dove upon him, and a voice came from heaven, which said, "Thou art my beloved Son; in thee I am well pleased." Luke 3:22.

[God is dipped; he likewise flies down from heaven as a pigeon and settles on his own head; and at the same time he shouts down from heaven his approbation of himself as his own Son. Baptism, too, signifying repentance and a new birth to righteousness, was particularly inappropriate to a perfect being like Jesus. John discreetly omits

97

Christ's baptism. John 1:32-34: And John bare record, saying. . . . "I knew him not: but he that sent me to baptize with water, the same said unto me, 'Upon whom thou shalt see the Spirit descending, and remaining on him, the same is he which baptizeth with the Holy Ghost.'" And I saw, and bare record that this is the Son of God.]

God is full of God.
Jesus being full of the Holy Ghost. Luke 4:1.
[Is the Holy Ghost ever full of Jesus?]

God is led by God and tempted by the devil.
Then was Jesus led up of the spirit into the wilderness to be tempted of the devil. Matt. 4:1.
And immediately the spirit *driveth* him into the wilderness. And he was there in the wilderness forty days, tempted of Satan; and was with the wild beasts; and the angels ministered unto him. Mark 1:12, 13.

Extraordinary fasting.
And when he had fasted forty days and forty nights, he was *afterward* an hungred. Matt. 4:2.

A meaningless temptation.
And when the tempter came to him, he said, "If thou be the Son of God, command that these stones be made bread." But he answered and said, "It is written, 'Man shall not live by bread alone, but by every word that proceedeth out of the mouth of God.'" Matt. 4:3, 4.

God trusts himself in the hands of the devil, who flies off with him and seats him on a pinnacle of his own temple.
Then the devil taketh him up into the holy city, and setteth him on a pinnacle of the temple, and saith unto him, "If thou be the Son of God, cast thyself down: for it is written, 'he shall give his angels charge concerning thee: and in their hands they shall bear thee up, lest at any time thou dash thy foot against a stone.'" Jesus said unto him, "It is written again, 'Thou shalt not tempt the Lord thy God.'" Matt. 4:5-7.
[The crass stupidity of the devil in playing such childish and senseless tricks on God is only equalled by the asinine folly of the inventors, writers, and supporters of such inspired rubbish.]

Seeing round a globe.
Again, the devil taketh him up into an exceeding high mountain, and

sheweth him all the kingdoms of the world, and the glory of them; and saith unto him, "All these things will I give thee, if thou wilt fall down and worship me." Matt. 4:8, 9.

[The devil offered Jesus what was already his — "the earth is the LORD's, and the fulness thereof." Ps. 24:1.]

An anti-teetotal miracle.

And there were set there six waterpots of stone . . . containing two or three firkins apiece. Jesus saith unto them, "Fill the waterpots with water." And they filled them up to the brim. And he saith unto them, "Draw out now, and bear unto the governor of the feast." And they bare . . . the water that was made wine. . . . This beginning of miracles did Jesus in Cana of Galilee, and manifested forth his glory; and his disciples believed on him. John 2:6-9, 11.

[One would expect Omnipotence to commence with a far worthier display of solemn power and wisdom than this imitation of a common conjurer's trick.]

Unclean spirits talk to Christ, and Christ evicts them.

And there was in their synagogue a man with an unclean spirit; and he cried out, saying, "Let us alone; what have we to do with thee, thou Jesus of Nazareth? art thou come to destroy us? I know thee who thou art, the Holy One of God." And Jesus rebuked him, saying, "Hold thy peace, and come out of him." And when the unclean spirit had torn him, and cried with a loud voice, he came out of him. And they were all amazed. Mark 1:23-27.

When he saw Jesus, he cried out, and fell down before him, and with a loud voice said, "What have I to do with thee, Jesus, thou son of God most high? I beseech thee, torment me not." Luke 8:28.

Devils really take possession of men.

And he healed many that were sick of divers diseases, and cast out many devils; and suffered not the devils to speak, because they knew him. Mark 1:34.

And he said unto them, "Go ye, and tell that fox, 'Behold, I cast out devils.' " Luke 13:32.

Mary called Magdalene, out of whom went seven devils. Luke 8:2.

A devil sent out of a man into two thousand pigs.

And when he was come out of the ship, immediately there met him out of the tombs a man with an unclean spirit, who had his dwelling among the tombs; and no man could bind him, no, not with chains. . . . But when he saw Jesus afar off, he ran and worshipped him, and cried with a loud voice, and said, "What have I to do with thee, Jesus, thou Son of the most high God? I adjure thee by God, that thou torment me not." For he said unto him, "Come out of the man, thou unclean spirit." And he asked him, "What is thy name?" And he answered, saying, "My name is Legion: for we are many." And he besought him much that he would not send them away out of the country. Now there was there nigh unto the mountains a great herd of swine feeding. And all the devils besought him saying, "Send us into the swine, that we may enter unto them." And forthwith Jesus gave them leave. And the unclean spirits went out, and entered into the swine: and the herd ran violently down a steep place into the sea (they were about two thousand); and were choked in the sea. Mark 5:2-3, 6-13.

And when he was come to the other side of the country of the Gergesenes, there met him two possessed with devils, coming out of the tombs, exceeding fierce. . . . They cried out, saying, "What have we to do with thee, Jesus, thou Son of God? . . ." So the devils besought him, saying, "If thou cast us out, suffer us to go away into the herd of swine." And he said unto them, "Go." And when they were come out, they went into the herd of swine: and, behold, the whole herd of swine ran violently down a steep place into the sea, and perished in the waters. Matt. 8:28-19, 31-33.

And they arrived at the country of the Gadarenes. . . . There met him out of the city a certain man, which had devils long time. . . . When he saw Jesus, he cried out . . . "I beseech thee, torment me not." (For he had commanded the unclean spirit to come out of the man. . . .) And Jesus asked him, saying, "What is thy name?" And he said, "Legion": because many devils were entered into him. . . . And there was an herd of many swine feeding on the mountain: and they besought him that he would suffer them to enter into them. And he suffered them. Then went the devils out of the man, and entered into the swine: and the herd ran violently down a steep place into the lake, and were choked. Luke 8:26-30, 32-33.

[One devil, it appears, is at the same time many devils, thus outdoing the Trinity in Unity by a still more wonderful multiplicity in unity.]

The disciples also cast out devils.

Then he called his twelve disciples together, and gave them power and authority over all devils, and to cure diseases. Luke 9:1.

And the seventy returned again with joy, saying, "Lord, even the devils are subject unto us through thy name." Luke 10:17.

All believers can expel devils.
And these signs shall follow them that believe; in my name shall they cast out devils. Mark 16:17.

Devils are the cause of dumbness, blindness, epilepsy, lunacy, etc.
As they went out, behold, they brought to him a dumb man possessed with a devil. And when the devil was cast out, the dumb spake. Matt. 9:32, 33.

Then was brought unto him one possessed with a devil, blind, and dumb: and he healed him, insomuch that the blind and dumb both spake and saw. Matt. 12:22.

And lo, a spirit taketh him, and he suddenly crieth out; and it teareth him that he foameth again, and bruising him hardly departeth from him. . . . And as he was yet a coming, the devil threw him down, and tare him. And Jesus rebuked the unclean spirit, and healed the child, and delivered him again to his father. Luke 9:39, 42.

There came to him a certain man, kneeling down to him, and saying, "Lord, have mercy on my son: for he is lunatick, and sore vexed. . . ." And Jesus rebuked the devil; and he departed out of him: and the child was cured from that very hour. Matt. 17:14-15, 18.

Orthodox devils.
The devils also believe, and tremble. James 2:19.

Foolish teachings.
Resist not evil: but whosoever shall smite thee on thy right cheek, turn to him the other also. And if any man will sue thee at the law, and take away thy coat, let him have thy cloke also. And whosoever shall compel thee to go a mile, go with him twain. Give to him that asketh thee, and from him that would borrow of thee turn not thou away. Matt. 5:39-42.

Blessed are the poor in spirit. Matt. 5:3.

Judge not, that ye be not judged. Matt. 7:1.

[Christ's absurd reversals of true morality would place the good at the mercy of the bad, and would make an end of civilized society.]

Self-mutilation a virtue.
But I say unto you, That whosoever looketh on a woman to lust after her hath committed adultery with her already in his heart. And if thy right eye offend thee, pluck it out, and cast it from thee: for it is

101

profitable for thee that one of thy members should perish, and not that thy whole body should be cast into hell. And if thy right hand offend thee, cut it off, and cast it from thee: for it is profitable for thee that one of thy members should perish, and not that thy whole body should be cast into hell. Matt. 5:28-30.

For there are some eunuchs, which were so born from their mother's womb: and there are some eunuchs, which were made eunuchs of men: and there are eunuchs, which have made themselves eunuchs for the kingdom of heaven's sake. He that is able to receive it, let him receive it. Matt. 19:12.

Universal improvidence a great Christian duty.

Lay not up for yourselves treasures upon earth.... Take no thought for your life, what ye shall eat, or what ye shall drink; nor yet for your body, what ye shall put on.... Behold the fowls of the air: for they sow not, neither do they reap, nor gather into barns; yet your heavenly Father feedeth them. Are ye not much better than they?... Consider the lilies of the field, how they grow; they toil not, neither do they spin.... If God so clothe the grass of the field, which today is, and to morrow is cast into the oven, shall he not much more clothe you, O ye of little faith? Therefore take no thought, saying, "What shall we eat?" or, "What shall we drink?" or, "Wherewithal shall we be clothed?" (For after all these things do the Gentiles seek): for your heavenly Father knoweth that ye have need of all these things. But seek ye first the kingdom of God, and his righteousness; and all these things shall be added unto you. Take therefore no thought for the morrow: for the morrow shall take thought for the things of itself. Matt. 6:19, 25-26, 28, 30-34.

The power of prayer.

Ask, and it shall be given you; seek, and ye shall find; knock, and it shall be opened unto you: for every one that asketh receiveth; and he that seeketh findeth; and to him that knocketh it shall be opened. Matt. 7:7, 8.

And all things, whatsoever ye shall ask in prayer, believing, ye shall receive. Matt. 21:22.

The omnipotence of faith.

Verily, I say unto you, If ye have faith as a grain of mustard seed, ye shall say unto this mountain, "Remove hence to yonder place"; and it shall remove; and nothing shall be impossible unto you. Matt. 17:20.

102

Verily, I say unto you, He that believeth on me, the works that I do shall he do also; and greater works than these shall he do. John 14:12.

Believers can work miracles.

And these signs shall follow them that believe; In my name shall they cast out devils; they shall speak with new tongues; they shall take up serpents; and if they drink any deadly thing, it shall not hurt them; they shall lay hands on the sick, and they shall recover. Mark 16:17, 18.

God prefers the ignorant and foolish to the wise and prudent.

Thou hast hid these things from the wise and prudent, and hast revealed them unto babes. Even so, Father: for so it seemed good in thy sight. Matt. 11:25, 26.

An exceedingly erroneous estimate.

Verily, I say unto you, Among them that are born of women there hath not risen a greater than John the Baptist: notwithstanding he that is least in the kingdom of heaven is greater than he. Matt. 11:11.

[Christ thus guarantees that John is greater than Confucius, and Socrates, and Aristotle, and *himself* even.]

Faith-healing.

The same heard Paul speak: who stedfastly beholding him, and perceiving that he had faith to be healed, said with a loud voice, "Stand upright on thy feet." And he leaped and walked. Acts 14:9, 10.

And a certain man lame from his mother's womb was carried . . . to ask alms of them that entered into the temple. . . . Then Peter said, "Silver and gold have I none; but such as I have give I thee: In the name of Jesus Christ of Nazareth rise up and walk." . . . And he leaping up stood, and walked. . . . Acts 3:2, 6, 8. He said unto her, "Daughter, thy faith hath made thee whole; go in peace, and be whole of thy plague." Mark 5:34.

Miraculous virtue in a garment.

And a certain woman . . . came in the press behind, and touched his garment. . . . And straightway the fountain of her blood was dried up. . . . And Jesus, immediately knowing in himself that virtue had gone out of him, turned him about in the press, and said, "Who touched my clothes?" Mark 5:25, 27, 29-30.

As many as touched him were made whole. Mark 6:56.

Handkerchiefs work miracles.

From his body were brought unto the sick handkerchiefs or aprons, and the diseases departed from them, and the evil spirits went out of them. Acts 19:12.

A splendid caterer.

He commanded the multitude to sit down on the grass, and took the five loaves, and the two fishes. . . . And they did all eat, and were filled: and they took up of the fragments that remained twelve baskets full. And they that had eaten were about five thousand men, beside women and children. Matt. 14:19-21.

The champion wave-walker.

But the ship was now in the midst of the sea, tossed with waves: for the wind was contrary. And in the fourth watch of the night Jesus went unto them, walking on the sea. Matt. 14:24, 25.

Peter also treads the billows.

And when Peter was come down out of the ship, he walked on the water, to go to Jesus. But when he saw the wind boisterous, he was afraid; and beginning to sink, he cried, saying, "Lord, save me." Matt. 14:29, 30.

An obedient storm.

And behold, there arose a great tempest in the sea, insomuch that the ship was covered with the waves: but he was asleep. And his disciples came to him, and awoke him. . . . Then he arose, and rebuked the winds and the sea; and there was a great calm. Matt. 8:24-26.

A corpse reviver.

And he that was dead came forth, bound hand and foot with grave-cloths. John 11:44.

A monied fish.

Go thou to the sea, and cast an hook, and take up the fish that first cometh up; and when thou hast opened his mouth thou shalt find a piece of money; that take, and give unto them for me and thee. Matt. 17:27.

A fig tree withered by the curse of its disappointed God.

He was hungry: and seeing a fig tree afar off having leaves, he came, if haply he might find any thing thereon: and when he came to it, he found nothing but leaves; for the time of figs was not yet. . . . And in the morning, as they passed by, they saw the fig tree dried up from the roots. And Peter calling to remembrance saith unto him, "Master, behold, the fig tree which thou cursedst is withered away." Mark 11:12-13, 20-21.

[The alleged miracles of the Lord of all power and might are as petty and insignificant as the narrators of the silly stories are obscure and credulous. Why didn't Christ discover printing, or the steam-engine, or confer some obvious universal benefit as a lasting testimony of his power and beneficence?]

Stupid teaching.

Unto them that are without, all these things are done in parables: that seeing they may see, and not perceive; and hearing they may hear, and not understand; lest at any time they should be converted, and their sins should be forgiven them. Mark 4:11, 12.

Christ rides on two donkeys.

And brought the ass, and the colt, and put on them their clothes, and they set him thereon. Matt. 21:7.

God deserts himself.

And about the ninth hour Jesus cried with a loud voice, saying, "*Eli, eli, lama sabachthani?*" That is to say, "My God, my God, why hast thou forsaken me?" Matt. 27:46.

A human body floats up into the sky.

"Behold my hands and my feet, that it is I myself: handle me, and see; for a spirit hath not flesh and bones, as ye see me have." . . . And it came to pass, while he blessed them, he was parted from them, and carried up into heaven. Luke 24:39, 51.

Christ descended into hell.

Being put to death in the flesh, but quickened by the Spirit: by which also he went and preached unto the spirits in prison. 1 Peter 3:18, 19.

I believe in God the Father Almighty, creator of heaven and earth; and in Jesus Christ, his only Son, our Lord; who was conceived by the Holy Spirit, born of the Virgin Mary, suffered under Pontius Pilate, was crucified, died, and buried; *descended to hell*; on the third day rose again from the dead; ascended to the heavens; sits at the right hand of

God the Father Almighty; thence will come to judge the quick and the dead. *Apostles' Creed.*

A son in his own father, and vice versa.
I and my Father are one. John 10:30.
Believe me that I am in the Father, and the Father in me: or else believe me for the very works' sake. John 14:11.

Wandering corpses.
And the graves were opened; and many bodies of the saints which slept arose, and came out of the graves after his resurrection, and went into the holy city, and appeared unto many. Matt. 27:52, 53.

Angels.
Know ye not that we shall judge angels? 1 Cor. 6:3.
For this cause ought the woman to have power on her head because of the angels. 1 Cor. 11:10.

Several heavens.
I knew a man in Christ above fourteen years ago . . . caught up to the third heaven. . . . He was caught up into paradise, and heard unspeakable words, which it is not lawful for a man to utter. 2 Cor. 12:2, 4.

The power of faith.
By faith they passed through the Red Sea as by dry land. . . . By faith the walls of Jericho fell down. Heb. 11:29, 30.

Sickness is to be cured by praying and anointing.
Is any among you afflicted? let him pray. Is any merry? let him sing psalms. Is any sick among you? let him call for the elders of the church; and let them pray over him, anointing him with oil in the name of the Lord: and the prayer of faith shall save the sick, and the Lord shall raise him up; and if he have committed sins, they shall be forgiven him. James 5:13-15.

Long chains or clever devils.
God spared not the angels that sinned, but cast them down to hell, and delivered them into chains of darkness, to be reserved unto judgment. 2 Peter 2:4.
Your adversary, the devil, as a roaring lion, walketh about, seeking whom he may devour. 1 Peter 5:8.

The Christian method of acquiring wisdom.
If any of you lack wisdom, let him ask of God, that giveth to all men liberally, and upbraideth not; and it shall be given him. But let him ask in faith, nothing wavering. James 1:5, 6.

A four-cornered globe.
I saw four angels standing on the four corners of the earth, holding the four winds of the earth. Rev. 7:1.

John's description of Christ.
I saw seven golden candlesticks; and in the midst of the seven candlesticks one like unto the Son of man, clothed with a garment down to the foot, and girt about the paps with a golden girdle. His head and his hairs were white like wool, as white as snow; and his eyes were as a flame of fire; and his feet like unto fine brass, as if they burned in a furnace; and his voice as the sound of many waters. And he had in his right hand seven stars: and out of his mouth went a sharp two-edged sword; and his countenance was as the sun shineth in his strength. Rev. 1:12-16.
The Son of God, who hath his eyes like unto a flame of fire, and his feet are like fine brass. Rev. 2:18.

God is like a sardine stone.
And I will shew thee things which must be hereafter . . . a throne was set in heaven, and one sat on the throne. And he that sat was to look upon like a jasper and a sardine stone: and there was a rainbow round about the throne, in sight like unto an emerald. Rev. 4:1-3.

A curious throne.
And out of the throne proceeded lightnings and thunderings and voices: and there were seven lamps of fire burning before the throne, which are the seven Spirits of God. Rev. 4:5.

Heavenly beasts.
And before the throne there was a sea of glass like unto crystal: and in the midst of the throne, and round about the throne, were four beasts full of eyes before and behind. And the first beast was like a lion, and the second beast like a calf, and the third beast had a face as a man, and the fourth beast was like a flying eagle. And the four beasts had each of them six wings about him; and they were full of eyes within: and they rest not day and night, saying, "Holy, holy, holy, Lord God Almighty,

which was, and is, and is to come." And when those beasts give glory and honour and thanks to him that sat on the throne, who liveth for ever and ever, the four and twenty elders fall down before him that sat on the throne, and worship him that liveth for ever and ever, and cast their crowns before the throne. Rev. 4:6-10.

And I heard a voice in the midst of the four beasts say, "A measure of wheat for a penny." Rev. 6:6.

The Lamb of God.

And I beheld, and, lo, in the midst of the throne and of the four beasts, and in the midst of the elders, stood a Lamb as it had been slain, having seven horns and seven eyes, which are the seven Spirits of God sent forth into all the earth. Rev. 5:6.

Pious animals.

And the four beasts said, "Amen." Rev. 5:14.

Queer locusts.

And the shapes of the locusts were like unto horses prepared unto battle; and on their heads were as it were crowns like gold, and their faces were as the faces of men. And they had hair as the hair of women, and their teeth were as the teeth of lions. And they had breastplates, as it were breastplates of iron; and the sound of their wings was as the sound of chariots of many horses running to battle. And they had tails like unto scorpions, and there were stings in their tails: and their power was to hurt men five months. Rev. 9:7-10.

A wonderful angel.

And I saw another mighty angel come down from heaven, clothed with a cloud: and a rainbow was upon his head, and his face was as it were the sun, and his feet as pillars of fire: and he had in his hand a little book open: and he set his right foot upon the sea, and his left foot on the earth, and cried with a loud voice, as when a lion roareth: and when he had cried, seven thunders uttered their voices. Rev. 10:1-3.

Swallowing the Bible?

And I took the little book out of the angel's hand, and ate it up; and it was in my mouth sweet as honey: and as soon as I had eaten it, my belly was bitter. Rev. 10:10.

Heavenly wonders.

And there appeared a great wonder in heaven; a woman clothed with

108

the sun, and the moon under her feet, and upon her head a crown of twelve stars. . . . And there appeared another wonder in heaven; and behold a great red dragon, having seven heads and ten horns, and seven crowns upon his heads. And his tail drew the third part of the stars of heaven, and did cast them to the earth: and the dragon stood before the woman . . . for to devour her child. Rev. 12:1, 3-4.

War in heaven.
And there was war in heaven: Michael and his angels fought against the dragon; and the dragon fought and his angels. . . . And the great dragon was cast out, that old serpent, called the Devil, and Satan. Rev. 12:7, 9.

A seven-headed leopard.
And I stood upon the sand of the sea, and saw a beast rise up out of the sea, having seven heads and ten horns, and upon his horns ten crowns . . . like unto a leopard. Rev. 13:1, 2.

A lamb's wedding.
The marriage of the Lamb is come, and his wife hath made herself ready. Rev. 19:7.

110

BIBLE ATROCITIES

God designs and creates carnivora, etc.

And God made the beast of the earth after his kind . . . and everything that creepeth upon the earth after his kind: and God saw that it was good.

And God created great whales, and every living creature that moveth . . . and every winged fowl after his kind: And God saw that it was good. . . . . And God made the beast of the earth after his kind . . . and God saw that it was good. . . . And God saw everything that he had made, and, behold, it was very good. Gen. 1:21, 25, 31.

And out of the ground the LORD God formed every beast of the field, and every fowl of the air. Gen. 2:19.

[Sharks, serpents, tigers, vermin, entozoa, cholera germs, etc., were purposely made or evolved by god, who designed animals to prey upon each other for food, and then pronounced his horrible system of almost universal carnage "very good" (Gen. 1:31). The divine idea of what is "very good" differs very widely from man's idea of goodness.]

God condemns all men for the offence of one.

By one man sin entered into the world, and death by sin; and so death passed upon all men, for that all have sinned. Rom. 5:12.

By one man's offence death reigned by one . . . by the offence of one judgment came upon all men to condemnation . . . by one man's disobedience many were made sinners. Rom. 5:17-19.

For since by man came death, by man came also the resurrection of the dead. For as in Adam all die, even so in Christ shall all be made alive. 1 Cor. 15:21, 22.

[Christianity teaches that death was unknown till Adam munched the apple, so that the whole animal creation were first made liable to suffer death through the fall of man. (Geology, however, proves that animals suffered death enormous ages before man appeared upon the scene, but at present we deal with the *cruelty* and not the *falsity* of biblical doctrines.] Many circumstances add to the atrocity of the divine vengeance for apple-eating.

(a) Men are condemned to eternal torments hereafter, a terrible punishment of which Adam was never warned.

111

(b) Adam and Eve had no knowledge of the distinction between good and evil, or right and wrong, till *after* the petty crime which entailed so fearful and universal a penalty.

(c) God's threat of immediate death was a falsehood, while the statement of the serpent was perfectly true.

(d) To pluck the fruit of the tree of knowledge is a virtuous act rather than a punishable one.

(e) God, foreknowing all that would happen, deliberately planned and set his "damnation trap," and watched its action without interfering. He made Adam imperfect and punished all living beings for the unsatisfactory nature of a specimen of his own handiwork.]

The Deluge: all created beings are drowned because God had made one species imperfect.

And God saw that the wickedness of man was great in the earth. . . . And the LORD said, "I will destroy man whom I have created from the face of the earth; both man, and beast, and the creeping thing, and the fowls of the air." Gen. 6:5, 7.

And, behold, I, even I, do bring a flood of waters upon the earth, to destroy all flesh, wherein is the breath of life, from under heaven; and every thing that is in the earth shall die. Gen. 6:17.

And every living substance was destroyed which was upon the face of the ground, both man, and cattle, and the creeping things, and the fowl of the heaven; and they were destroyed from the earth. Gen. 7:23.

The innocent cursed for the guilty.

And Noah began to be an husbandman, and he planted a vineyard: And he drank of the wine, and was drunken; and he was uncovered within his tent. And Ham, the father of Canaan, saw the nakedness of his father, and told his two brethren without. . . . And Noah . . . said, "Cursed be Canaan; a servant of servants shall he be unto his brethren." Gen. 9:20-22, 24-25.

[Ham saw and reported his father's folly, and his innocent son Canaan and his future descendants were cursed. Christians attribute the subsequent destruction of the Canaanites and the horrors of the African slave trade to the divine effect of this holy curse.]

Human sacrifice commanded by God.

Notwithstanding no devoted thing, that a man shall devote unto the LORD of all that he hath, both of man and beast, and of the field of his possession, shall be sold or redeemed: every devoted thing is most holy unto the Lord. None devoted, which shall be devoted of men, shall be redeemed; but shall surely be put to death. Lev. 27:28, 29.

[The inhabitants of Jericho were thus devoted or "accursed" to the Lord (And the city shall be accursed, even it, and all that are therein, to the LORD: only Rahab the harlot shall live, she and all that are with her in the house, because she hid the messengers that we sent. Josh. 6:17). Jer. 7:30, 31 ("For the children of Judah have done evil in my sight," saith the LORD: "they have set their abominations in the house which is called by my name, to pollute it. And they have built the high places of Tophet, which is in the valley of the son of Hinnom, to burn their sons and their daughters in the fire; which I commanded them not, neither came it into my heart.") makes it obvious that the Jews burned their sons and daughters to Jehovah in comparatively late times. See also Ezek. 20:25, 26 ("Wherefore I gave them also statutes that were not good, and judgments whereby they should not live; And I polluted them in their own gifts, in that they caused to pass through the fire all that openeth the womb, that I might make them desolate, to the end that they might know that I am the LORD.") and Mic. 6:7 (Will the LORD be pleased with thousands of rams, or with ten thousands of rivers of oil? shall I give my first-born for my transgression, the fruit of my body for the sin of my soul?).]

God commands Abraham to sacrifice Isaac.

And he said, "Take now thy son, thine only son Isaac, whom thou lovest, and get thee into the land of Moriah; and offer him there for a burnt offering upon one of the mountains which I will tell thee of." . . . And they came to the place which God had told him of; and Abraham built an altar there, and laid the wood in order, and bound Isaac his son, and laid him on the altar upon the wood. And Abraham stretched forth his hand, and took the knife to slay his son. Gen. 22:2, 9, 10.

Jephthah burns his daughter.

Then the spirit of the LORD came upon Jephthah. . . . And Jephthah vowed a vow unto the LORD, and said, "If thou shalt without fail deliver the children of Ammon into mine hands, then it shall be, that whatsoever [whosoever] cometh forth of the doors of my house to meet me, when I return in peace from the children of Ammon, shall surely be the

LORD's, and I will offer it up for a burnt offering." Judg. 11:29-31.

And Jephthah came to Mizpeh unto his house, and, behold, his daughter came out to meet him with timbrels and with dances: and she was his only child. . . . And it came to pass at the end of two months, that she returned unto her father, who did with her according to his vow which he had vowed. Judg. 11:34, 39.

[Jephthah must have reasonably expected so noble and loving an only daughter to be the first to meet him. He desired a great boon, and, inspired by the LORD, he offered a sacrifice proportionately precious. [Modern Christians, in imbecile defiance of the plain language of the text, say that Jephthah's daughter was only condemned to perpetual virginity. That this pious snatching at straws is purely modern is shown by the account of the Jewish historian Josephus, who says distinctly that the girl was burnt.]

The man after God's own heart sends seven innocent men to be offered to the Lord to stay a famine.

Then there was a famine in the days of David three years, year after year; and David enquired of the LORD. And the LORD answered, "It is for Saul, and for his bloody house, because he slew the Gibeonites." . . . Wherefore David said unto the Gibeonites, "What shall I do for you?" . . . And the Gibeonites said unto him, . . . "The man that consumed us, and that devised against us that we should be destroyed from remaining in any of the coasts of Israel, let seven of his sons be delivered unto us, and we will hang them up unto the LORD in Gibeah of Saul, *whom the LORD did choose. (!)*" And the king said, "I will give them." . . . And he delivered them into the hands of the Gibeonites, and they hanged them in the hill before the LORD. . . . And after that God was intreated for the land. 2 Sam. 21:1, 3-6, 9, 14. [Compare Num. 25:4. ("And the LORD said unto Moses, "Take all the heads of the people, and hang them up before the LORD against the sun, that the fierce anger of the LORD may be turned away from Israel.").]

Pious Lot offers his daughters for indiscriminate outrage by a riotous mob.

Behold, now, I have two daughters which have not known man; let me, I pray you, bring them out unto you, and do ye to them as is good in your eyes. Gen. 19:8.

Jacob's sons, selected by God as the fighting progenitors of his chosen race, treacherously slay the Shechemites and steal their wives.

114

And Hamor communed with them, saying, "The soul of my son Shechem longeth for your daughter: I pray you give her him to wife." . . . And the sons of Jacob answered Shechem and Hamor his father deceitfully, and said, because he had defiled Dinah their sister: and they said unto them, "We cannot do this thing, to give our sister to one that is uncircumcised; for that were a reproach unto us: but in this will we consent unto you: If ye will be as we be, that every male of you be circumcised; then will we give our daughters unto you." . . . And the young man deferred not to do the thing, because he had delight in Jacob's daughter: and he was more honourable than all the house of his father. . . . And every male was circumcised. . . . And it came to pass on the third day, when they were sore, that two of the sons of Jacob, Simeon and Levi, Dinah's brethren, took each man his sword, and came upon the city boldly, and slew all the males. And they slew Hamor and Shechem his son with the edge of the sword. . . . And all their wealth, and all their little ones, and their wives took they captive. Gen. 34:8, 13-16, 19, 24-26, 29.

God hardens Pharaoh's heart as an excuse for punishing the Egyptians with terrible plagues.

I will harden Pharaoh's heart, and multiply my signs and my wonders in the land of Egypt. But Pharaoh shall not hearken unto you, that I may lay my hand upon Egypt. Exod. 7:3, 4, 13.

I have hardened his heart, and the heart of his servants, that I might show these my signs before him. Exod. 10:1, 20, 27.

And I, behold, I will harden the heart of the Egyptians, and they shall follow them: and I will get me honour upon Pharaoh, and upon all his host, upon his chariots, and upon his horsemen. Exod. 14:17.

The waters are turned into blood.

All the waters that were in the river were turned to blood. And the fish that was in the river died; and the river stank, and the Egyptians could not drink of the water of the river; and there was blood throughout all the land of Egypt. Exod. 7:20, 21.

After sending plagues of frogs, lice and flies (Exod. 8), God kills all the cattle of Egypt with a murrain.

Behold, the hand of the LORD is upon the cattle which is in the field, upon the horses, upon the asses, upon the camels, upon the oxen, and upon the sheep: there shall be a very grievous murrain. . . . And all the cattle of Egypt died. Exod. 9:3, 6.

Hailstones kill man and beast.

The hail shall come down upon them, and they shall die. . . . And the LORD sent thunder and hail, and the fire ran along upon the ground. . . . And the hail smote throughout all the land of Egypt all that was in the field, both man and beast. Exod. 9:19, 23, 25.

God, acting as a midnight assassin on the largest scale, murders the firstborn of every Egyptian family.

And it came to pass, that at midnight the LORD smote all the firstborn in the land of Egypt, from the firstborn of Pharaoh that sat on his throne unto the firstborn of the captive that was in the dungeon; and all the firstborn of cattle. And Pharaoh rose up in the night, he, and all his servants, and all the Egyptians: and there was a great cry in Egypt; for there was not a house where there was not one dead. Exod. 12:29, 30.

And Moses said, "Thus saith the LORD, 'About midnight will I go out into the midst of Egypt: and all the firstborn in the land of Egypt shall die, from the firstborn of Pharaoh that sitteth upon his throne, even unto the firstborn of the maidservant . . . and all the firstborn of beasts. And there shall be a great cry throughout all the land of Egypt.' " Exod. 11:3-6.

God gains himself honour by drowning the Egyptians.

And I will harden Pharaoh's heart, that he shall follow after them; and I will be honoured upon Pharaoh, and upon all his host. Exod. 14:4.

And it came to pass, that in the morning watch the LORD looked unto the host of the Egyptians through the pillar of fire and of the cloud, and troubled the host of the Egyptians, and took off their chariot wheels, that they drave them heavily . . . and the LORD overthrew the Egyptians in the midst of the sea. And the waters returned, and covered the chariots, and the horsemen, and all the host of Pharaoh that came into the sea after them; there remained not so much as one of them. Exod. 14:24-25, 27-28.

I have gotten me honour upon Pharaoh, upon his chariots, and upon his horsemen. Exod. 14:18.

God sanctions slavery.

If thou buy an Hebrew servant. . . . If his master have given him a wife, and she have born him sons or daughters; the wife and her children shall be her master's, and he shall go out by himself. And if the servant shall plainly say, "I love my master, my wife, and my children; I will not go out free": then his master shall bring him unto the judges; he shall also bring him to the door, or unto the door post; and his master shall bore his ear

116

through with an awl; and he shall serve him for ever. Exod. 21:2, 4-6.

Both thy bondmen, and thy bondmaids, which thou shalt have, shall be of the heathen that are round about you; of them shall ye buy bondmen and bondmaids. Moreover, of the children of the strangers that do sojourn among you, of them shall ye buy, and of their families. . . . And ye shall take them as an inheritance for your children after you, to inherit them for a possession; they shall be your bondmen for ever. Lev. 25:44-46.

A man may sell his daughter.

And if a man sell his daughter to be a maidservant, she shall not go out as the menservants do. Exod. 21:7.

God orders slave-capturing expeditions.

When thou comest nigh unto a city to fight against it, then proclaim peace unto it. And it shall be, if it make thee answer of peace, and open unto thee, then it shall be, that all the people that is found therein shall be tributaries unto thee, and they shall serve thee. And if it will make no peace with thee, but will make war against thee, then thou shalt besiege it: and when the LORD thy God hath delivered it into thine hands, thou shalt smite every male thereof with the edge of the sword: but the women, and the little ones, and the cattle, and all that is in the city, even all the spoil thereof, shalt thou take unto thyself. . . . Thus shalt thou do unto all the cities which are very far from thee, which are not of the cities of these nations. Deut. 20:10-15.

Women may be captured, violated, and then turned out of doors, helpless, friendless, and in a foreign land.

When thou goest forth to war against thine enemies, and the LORD thy God hath delivered them into thine hands, and thou hast taken them captive, and seest among the captives a beautiful woman, and hast a desire unto her . . . thou shalt go in unto her, and be her husband, and she shall be thy wife. And it shall be, if thou have no delight in her, then thou shalt let her go whither she will. Deut. 21:10-11, 13-14.

See also Num. 31:18, 35 (But all the women children, that have not known a man by lying with him, keep alive for yourselves. . . . And thirty and two thousand persons in all, of women that had not known man by lying with him.) and Deut. 24:1-4 (When a man hath taken a wife, and married her, and it come to pass that she find no favour in his eyes, because he hath found some uncleanness in her: then let him write her a bill of divorcement, and give it in her hand, and send her out of his house. And when she is departed out of his house, she may go and be another man's wife. And if the latter husband hate her, and write her a bill of divorcement, and giveth it in her hand, and sendeth her out of his house; or if the latter husband die, which took her to be his wife; her former husband ... may not take her again to be his wife, after that she is defiled.)

[In these his revealed instructions, God says nothing about such a trifle as obtaining the woman's consent.]

A slave might be slowly beaten to death.

And if a man smite his servant, or his maid, with a rod, and he die under his hand ... if he continue a day or two, he shall not be punished: for he is his money. Exod. 21:20, 21.

Witches are to be killed.

Thou shalt not suffer a witch to live. Exod. 22:8.

A man also or woman that hath a familiar spirit, or that is a wizard, shall surely be put to death: they shall stone them with stones: their blood shall be upon them. Lev. 20:27.

See also Deut. 18:10, 11. (There shall not be found among you any one that maketh his son or his daughter to pass through the fire, or that useth divination, or an observer of times, or an enchanter, or a witch, or a charmer, or a consulter with familiar spirits, or a wizard, or a necromancer.) and Gal. 5:19, 20 (Now the works of the flesh are manifest, which are these; adultery, fornication, uncleanness, lasciviousness, idolatry, witchcraft, hatred, variance, emulations, wrath, strife, seditions, heresies.).

[Hundreds of thousands of innocent women have been put to death through the Bible teaching concerning the purely imaginary crime of witchcraft.]

Death for consulting wizards.

And the soul that turneth after such as have familiar spirits, and after wizards ... I will even set my face against that soul, and will cut him off from among his people. Lev. 20:6.

Death for idolatry or heresy.

He that sacrificeth unto any god, save unto the LORD only, he shall be utterly destroyed. Exod. 22:20.

If there rise among you a prophet, or a dreamer of dreams, and giveth thee a sign or a wonder, and the sign or the wonder come to pass, whereof he spake unto thee, saying, "Let us go after other gods, which thou hast not known, and let us serve them" . . . that prophet, or that dreamer of dreams, shall be put to death. Deut. 13:1, 2, 5.

If it be truth, and the thing certain, that such abomination [serving other gods] is wrought among you; thou shalt surely smite the inhabitants of that city with the edge of the sword, destroying it utterly, and all that is therein, and the cattle thereof, with the edge of the sword. Deut. 13:14, 15.

If there be found among you . . . man or woman, that hath wrought wickedness in the sight of the LORD thy God. . . . And hath gone and served other gods, and worshipped them. . . . And it be told thee . . . and, behold, it be true, and the thing certain, that such abomination is wrought in Israel: Then thou shalt bring forth that man or that woman . . . and shall stone them with stones, till they die. Deut. 17:2-5.

But the prophet, which shall presume to speak a word in my name, which I have not commanded him to speak, or that shall speak in the name of other gods, even that prophet shall die. Deut. 18:20.

A father is to slay his own daughter, or wife, or son, or friend, for a difference of religion.

If thy brother, the son of thy mother, or thy son, or thy daughter, or the wife of thy bosom, or thy friend which is as thine own soul, entice thee secretly, saying, "Let us go and serve other gods." . . . Thou shalt not consent unto him, nor hearken unto him; neither shalt thine eye pity him: neither shalt thou spare him: neither shalt thou conceal him: but thou shalt surely kill him; thine hand shall be first upon him to put him to death, and afterwards the hand of all the people. And thou shalt stone him with stones that he die. Deut. 13:6, 8-10.

Death to him who "doeth ought presumptuously."

But the soul that doeth ought presumptuously, whether he be born in the land, or a stranger, the same reproacheth the LORD; and that soul shall be cut off from among his people. Num. 15:30.

And the man that will do presumptuously, and will not hearken unto the priest that standeth to minister there before the LORD thy God, or unto the judge, even that man shall die. Deut. 17:12.

[As some Christians will ignorantly or fraudulently pretend that being "cut off" does not mean being "put to death," it will be well to refer to passages like Exod. 31:14, 15 (See below) or the above, where "cut off" is replaced indifferently by the words "shall surely be put to death." Where exclusion is meant other expressions are used, as in Num. 5:2, 4

119

(See also below), Num. 12:14, 15, and Deut. 23:1-3.

Ye shall keep the sabbath . . . whosever does any work therein, that soul shall be cut off from among his people. . . . the sabbath of rest, holy to the LORD: whosoever doeth any work in the sabbath day, he shall surely be put to death. Exod. 31:14, 15.

Whosoever shall commit any of these abominations, even the souls that commit them shall be cut off from among their people. Lev. 19:29.

Command the children of Israel, that they put out of the camp every leper, and every one that hath an issue, and whosoever is defiled by the dead. . . . And the children of Israel did so. Num. 5:2, 4.

And the LORD said unto Moses, "Let her be shut out from the camp seven days, and after that let her be received in again." . . . And Miriam was shut out from the camp seven days. Num. 12:14-15.

He that is wounded in the stones, or hath his privy member cut off, shall not enter into the congregation of the LORD. A bastard shall not enter into the congregation of the LORD. . . . An Ammonite or Moabite shall not enter into the congregation of the LORD. . . . Deut. 23:1-3.]

Death to all sabbath-breakers.

Ye shall keep the sabbath therefore; for it is holy unto you: everyone that defileth it shall surely be put to death: for whosoever doeth any work therein, that soul shall be cut off from among his people. Six days may work be done; but in the seventh is the sabbath of rest, holy to the LORD: whosoever doeth any work in the sabbath day, he shall surely be put to death. Exod. 31:14, 15.

Death for kindling a fire on the seventh day.

Whosoever doeth work therein shall be put to death. Ye shall kindle no fire throughout your habitations upon the sabbath day. Exod. 35:2, 3.

Every one that defileth it shall surely be put to death. Exod. 31:14.

Death for picking up sticks on the Saturday.

And while the children of Israel were in the wilderness, they found a man that gathered sticks upon the sabbath day. . . . And the LORD saith unto Moses, "The man shall be surely put to death: all the congregation shall stone him with stones without the camp." And all the congregation brought him without the camp, and stoned him with stones, and he died; as the LORD commanded Moses. Num. 15:32, 35-36.

[Christian congregations forget that they are continually breaking God's law by not stoning to death those who work or kindle a fire on the

120

sacred seventh day, which is Saturday. They ignore the (biblical) fact that God the creator worked on Sunday and rested on Saturday, wherefore the LORD blessed the Saturday and hallowed it.]

Death for not keeping the feast of the passover.

The man that is clean, and is not in a journey, and forbeareth to keep the passover, even the same soul shall be cut off from among his people: because he brought not the offering of the LORD in his appointed season, that man shall bear his sin. Num. 9:13.

Death for eating leavened bread during the passover.

Whosoever eateth leavened bread from the first day until the seventh, that soul shall be cut off from Israel. Exod. 12:15.

Seven days shall there be no leaven found in your houses: for whosoever eateth that which is leavened, even that soul shall be cut off from the congregation of Israel, whether he be a stranger, or born in the land. Exod. 12:19.

Death for eating fat.

And the LORD spake unto Moses, saying, "Speak unto the children of Israel, saying, 'Ye shall eat no manner of fat, of ox, or of sheep, or of goat. . . . For whosoever eatest the fat of the beast, of which men offer an offering made by fire unto the LORD, even the soul that eateth it shall be cut off from his people.' " Lev. 7:22, 25.

Death for eating blood.

All the fat is the LORD's. It shall be a perpetual statute for your generations throughout all your dwellings, that ye eat neither fat nor blood. Lev. 3:16, 17.

Ye shall eat no manner of blood, whether it be of fowl or of beast, in any of your dwellings. Whatsoever soul it be that eateth any manner of blood, even that soul shall be cut off from his people. Lev. 7:26, 27.

And whatsoever man there be of the house of Israel, or of the strangers that sojourn among you, that eateth any manner of blood; I will even set my face against that soul that eateth blood, and will cut him off from among his people. For the life of the flesh is in the blood: and I have given it to you upon the altar to make an atonement for your souls: for it is the blood that maketh an atonement for the soul. Therefore I said unto the children of Israel, "No soul of you shall eat blood, neither shall any stranger that sojourneth among you eat blood." And whatsoever man there be of the children of Israel, or of the strangers that sojourn among you, which hunteth and catcheth any beast or fowl that may be eaten; he shall even pour out the blood thereof, and cover it with dust. For it is the life of all flesh; the blood of it is for the life thereof: therefore I said unto the children of Israel, "Ye shall eat the blood of no manner of flesh": for the life of all flesh is the blood thereof: whosoever eateth it shall be cut off. And every soul that eateth that which died of itself, or that which was torn with beasts, whether it be one of your own country, or a stranger, he shall both wash his clothes, and bathe himself in water, and be unclean until the even: then shall he be clean. But if he wash them not, nor bathe his flesh; then he shall bear his iniquity. Lev. 17:10-16.

[A stranger who should eat a blood-pudding would have to suffer capital punishment for his atrocious crime.]

Death to children for not being circumcised.

And the uncircumcised man child whose flesh of his foreskin is not circumcised, that soul shall be cut off from his people; he hath broken my covenant. Gen. 17:14.

Death for imitating holy ointment, or putting any of it upon a stranger.

Moreover the LORD spake unto Moses, saying, "Take thou also unto thee principal spices.... And thou shalt make it an oil of holy ointment, an ointment compound after the art of the apothecary; it shall be an holy anointing oil.... Whosoever compoundeth any like it, or whosoever putteth any of it upon a stranger, shall even be cut off from his people." Exod. 30:22, 25, 33.

Death for making perfume.

And the LORD said unto Moses, "Take unto thee sweet spices, stacte, and onycha, and galbanum; these sweet spices with pure frankincense: of each shall there be a like weight: and thou shalt make it a perfume, a confection after the art of the apothecary, tempered together, pure and holy.... Whosoever shall make like unto that, to smell thereto, shall even be cut off from his people." Exod. 30:34-35, 38.

Death for eating a day too late.

And if ye offer a sacrifice of peace offerings ... it shall be eaten the same day ye offer it, and on the morrow... And if it be eaten at all on the third day, it is abominable.... Everyone that eateth it shall bear his iniquity, because he hath profaned the hallowed thing of the LORD: and that soul shall be cut off from among his people. Lev. 19:5-8.

And if any of the flesh of the sacrifice of his peace offerings be eaten at all on the third day, it shall not be accepted, neither shall it be imputed unto him that offereth it: it shall be an abomination, and the soul that eateth of it shall bear his iniquity. Lev. 7:18.

Death for sacrificing without the priests' aid.

Whatsoever man there be of the house of Israel, or of the strangers which sojourn among you, that offereth a burnt offering or sacrifice, and bringeth it not unto the door of the tabernacle of the congregation, to offer it unto the LORD; even that man shall be cut off from among his people. Lev. 17:8, 9.

Death for killing cattle without bringing an offering to the priests.

This is the thing which the LORD had commanded, saying, "What man soever there be of the house of Israel, that killeth an ox, or lamb, or goat, in the camp, or that killeth it out of the camp, and bringeth it not unto the door of the tabernacle of the congregation, to offer an offering unto the LORD before the tabernacle of the LORD; blood shall be imputed unto that man; he hath shed blood; and that man shall be cut off from among his people: to the end that the children of Israel may bring their sacrifices . . . unto the priest." Lev. 17:2-5.

Death for purely ceremonial offences.

But the soul that eateth of the flesh of the sacrifice of peace offerings, that pertain unto the LORD, having his uncleanness upon him, even that soul shall be cut off from his people. Moreover the soul that shall touch any unclean thing, as the uncleanness of man, or any unclean beast, or any abominable unclean thing, and eat of the flesh of sacrifice of peace offerings, which pertain unto the LORD, even that soul shall be cut off from his people. Lev. 7:20, 21.

Say unto them, "Whosoever he be of all your seed among your generations, that goeth unto the holy things, which the children of Israel hallow unto the LORD, having his uncleanness upon him, that soul shall be cut off from my presence: I am the LORD. . . . They shall therefore keep mine ordinance, lest they bear sin for it, and die therefore, if they profane it: I the LORD do sanctify them." Lev. 22:3, 9.

[Eating a peace offering after touching a pig or entering the house of the dying thus entailed the penalty of death.]

Death for touching a holy thing.

The sons of Kohath shall come to bear it [the ark]: but they shall not touch any holy thing, lest they die. Num. 4:15.

And when they came to Nachon's threshingfloor, Uzzah put forth his hand to the ark of God, and took hold of it; for the oxen shook it. And the anger of the LORD was kindled against Uzzah; and God smote him there for his error; and there he died by the ark of God. 2 Sam. 6:6-7.

Death for approaching the holy candlestick.

And they shall keep thy charge, and the charge of all the tabernacle: only they shall not come nigh the vessels of the sanctuary and the altar, that neither they, nor ye also, die. Num. 18:3.

Death for entering the holy place.

But they shall not go in to see when the holy things are covered, lest they die. Num. 4:20.

Death for entering the holy place without giving notice to God by the sound of tinkling bells hung on the dress.

A golden bell and a pomegranate, a golden bell and a pomegranate, upon the hem of the robe round about. And it shall be upon Aaron to minister: and his sound shall be heard when he goeth in unto the holy place before the LORD, and when he cometh out, that he die not. Exod. 28:34, 35.

Death for entering the holy place without linen breeches.

And thou shalt make them linen breeches to cover their nakedness; from the loins even unto the thighs they shall reach: and they shall be upon Aaron, and upon his sons, when they come in unto the tabernacle of the congregation, or when they come near unto the altar to minister to the holy place: that they bear not iniquity, and die: it shall be a statute for ever unto him and his seed after him. Exod. 28:42, 43.

Death for not being purified.

Or if a soul touch any unclean thing, whether it be a carcase of an unclean beast, or a carcase of unclean cattle, or the carcase of unclean creeping things, and if it be hidden from him, he also shall be unclean, and guilty. Lev. 5:2.

The man that shall be unclean, and shall not purify himself, that soul shall be cut off from among the congregation. Num. 19:20.

Whosoever . . . that goeth unto the holy things, which the children of Israel hallow unto the LORD, having his uncleanness upon him, that soul shall be cut off. . . . They shall therefore keep mine ordinance, lest they bear sin for it, and die therefore, if they profane it: I the LORD do sanctify them. Lev. 22:3, 9.

Whosoever toucheth the dead body of any man that is dead, and purifieth not himself, defileth the tabernacle of the LORD; and that soul shall be cut off from Israel; because the water of separation was not sprinkled upon him. Num. 19:13.

[The uncleanliness was mostly of an imaginary character. It was incurred by touching persons already ceremonially unclean (See below) or unclean things such as pork or oysters or an owl or swan or by touching any dead animal or in innumerable other ways. Being unclean in the modern sense of the word, that is being actually dirty or filthy, does not seem to have been mentioned by God as an offence needing purification or penalty.

Or whosoever toucheth any creeping thing, whereby he may be made unclean, or a man of whom he may take uncleanness, whatsoever uncleanness he hath; The soul which hath touched any such shall be unclean until even, and shall not eat of the holy things, unless he wash his flesh with water. Lev. 22:5-6.

Nevertheless these shall ye not eat of them that chew the cud, or of them that divide the hoof: as the camel, because he cheweth the cud, but divideth not the hoof; he is unclean unto you. . . . And the swine, though he divide the hoof, and be clovenfooted, yet he cheweth not the cud; he is unclean to you. . . . And all that have not fins and scales in the seas, and in the rivers of all that move in the waters, and of any living thing which is in the waters, they shall be an abomination unto you. . . . Whatsoever hath no fins nor scales in the waters, that shall be an abomination unto you. And these are they which ye shall have in abomination among the fowls; they shall not be eaten, they are an abomination: the eagle, and the ossifrage, and the ospray, And the vulture, and the kite after his kind; Every raven after his kind; And the owl, and the night hawk, and the cuckow, and the hawk after his kind, And the little owl, and the cormorant, and the great owl, And the swan, and the pelican, and the gier eagle, And the stork, the heron after her kind, and the lapwing, and the bat. All fowls that creep, going upon all four, shall be an abomination unto you. . . . And for these ye shall be unclean: whosoever toucheth the carcase of them shall be unclean until the even. . . . And whatsoever goeth upon his paws, among all manner of beasts that go on all four, those are unclean unto you: whoso toucheth their carcase shall be unclean until the even. Lev. 11:4, 7, 10, 12-20, 24, 27.

And if any beast, of which ye may eat, die; he that toucheth the carcase thereof shall be unclean until the even. Lev. 11:39.]

Death for eating animals that have died a natural death or been killed or wounded by hunting dogs, ferrets, falcons, or wild beasts.

That which dieth of itself, or is torn with beasts, he shall not eat to defile himself therewith: I am the LORD. They shall therefore keep mine ordinance, lest they bear sin for it, and die therefore, if they profane it. Lev. 22:8, 9.

And whatsoever man there be of the children of Israel, or of the strangers that sojourn among you, which hunteth and catcheth any beast or fowl that may be eaten; he shall even pour out the blood thereof, and cover it with dust. For it is the life of all flesh; the blood of it is for the life thereof: therefore I said unto the children of Israel, "Ye shall eat the blood of no manner of flesh": for the life of all flesh is the blood thereof: whosoever eateth it shall be cut off. And every soul that eateth that which died of itself, or that which was torn with beasts, whether it be one of your own country, or a stranger, he shall both wash his clothes, and bathe himself in water, and be unclean until the even: then shall he be clean. But if he wash them not, nor bathe his flesh; then he shall bear his iniquity. Lev. 17:13-16.

[Animals that died of disease might, however, freely be sold for food to the stranger, because the Israelites were a holy people unto the Lord and strangers were not (Deut. 14:21: Ye shall not eat of any thing that dieth of itself: thou shalt give it unto the stranger that is in thy gates, that he may eat it; or thou mayest sell it unto an alien: for thou art an holy people unto the LORD thy God. Thou shalt not seethe a kid in his mother's milk.).]

Death for working on the day of atonement, or for not afflicting one's soul.

For whatever soul it be that shall not be afflicted in that same day, he shall be cut off from among his people. And whatsoever soul it be that doeth any work in that same day, the same soul will I destroy from among his people. Lev. 23:29, 30.

Death for straying near the tabernacle.

When the tabernacle is to be pitched, the Levites shall set it up, and the stranger that cometh nigh shall be put to death. Num. 1:51.

Neither must the children of Israel henceforth come nigh the tabernacle of the congregation, lest they bear sin, and die. Num. 18:22.

Whosoever cometh any thing near unto the tabernacle of the LORD shall die: shall we be consumed with dying? Num. 17:13.

Death for approaching too near the clergy during divine service.
Thou shalt appoint Aaron and his sons, and they shall wait on their priest's office: and the stranger that cometh nigh shall be put to death. Num. 3:10.

Therefore thou and thy sons with thee shall keep your priest's office for every thing of the altar, and within the vail; and ye shall serve: I have given your priest's office unto you as a service of gift: and the stranger that cometh nigh shall be put to death. Num. 18:7.

But those that encamp before the tabernacle toward the east, even before the tabernacle of the congregation eastward, shall be Moses, and Aaron and his sons, keeping the charge of the sanctuary for the charge of the children of Israel; and the stranger that cometh nigh shall be put to death. Num. 3:38.

Death for blasphemy.
And he that blasphemeth the name of the LORD, he shall surely be put to death, and all the congregation shall surely stone him: as well as the stranger, as he that is born in the land, when he blasphemeth the name of the LORD, shall be put to death. Lev. 24:16.

The son of the Israelitish woman and a man of Israel strove together in the camp; and the Israelitish woman's son blasphemed the name of the LORD, and cursed. . . . And the LORD spake unto Moses, saying, "Bring forth him that hath cursed without the camp; and let all that heard him lay their hands upon his head, and let all the congregation stone him." . . . And the children of Israel did as the LORD commanded Moses. Lev. 24:10-11, 13-14, 23.

Death for unchastity, or for natural or accidental imperfection of structure.
But if this thing be true, and the tokens of virginity be not found for the damsel: then they shall bring out the damsel to the door of her father's house, and the men of her city shall stone her with stones that she die: because she hath wrought folly in Israel. Deut. 22:20, 21.

[God assigns no punishment for similar unchastity on the part of man. Medical men now know that under God's law many perfectly innocent women would be disgraced and judicially murdered. The man who brought a false charge of this kind against his bride was only fined a penalty of silver. Priests' daughters were burnt alive for unchastity (And the daughter of any priest, if she profane herself by playing the whore, she profaneth her father: she shall be burnt with fire. Lev. 21:9.]

Death for sexual intercourse during menstruation.

And if a man shall lie with a woman having her sickness, and shall uncover her nakedness; he hath discovered her fountain, and she hath uncovered the fountain of her blood: and both of them shall be cut off from among their people. Lev. 20:18.

Worshippers of the golden calf are slain by friends and brothers.

And he said unto them, "Thus saith the LORD God of Israel, 'Put every man his sword by his side, and go in and out from gate to gate throughout the camp, and slay every man his brother, and every man his companion, and every man his neighbour.'" And the children of Levi did according to the word of Moses: and there fell of the people that day about three thousand men. For Moses had said, "Consecrate yourselves today to the LORD, even every man upon his son, and upon his brother; that he may bestow upon you a blessing this day." . . . And the LORD plagued the people, because they made the calf, which Aaron made. Exod. 32:27-29, 35.

People burnt to death for complaining.

And when the people complained, it displeased the LORD; and the LORD heard it; and his anger was kindled, and the fire of the LORD burnt among them, and consumed them that were in the uttermost parts of the camp. Num. 11:1.

People killed for wanting a change of diet.

And the mixt multitude that was among them fell a lusting: and the children of Israel also wept again, and said, "Who shall give us flesh to eat? We remember the fish, which we did eat in Egypt freely; the cucumbers, and the melons, and the leeks, and onions, and the garlick: but now our soul is dried away: there is nothing at all, besides this manna, before our eyes." . . . And there went forth a wind from the LORD, and brought quails from the sea, and let them fall by the camp. . . . And while the flesh was yet between their teeth, ere it was chewed, the wrath of the LORD was kindled against the people, and the LORD smote the people with a very great plague. And he called the name of that place Kibrothhattaavah: because there they buried the people that lusted. Num. 11:4-6, 31, 33-34.

Priests burnt alive for using the wrong sort of fire.

And Nadab and Abihu, the sons of Aaron, took either of them his censer, and put fire therein, and put incense thereon, and offered strange fire before the LORD, which he commanded them not. And there went out fire from the LORD, and devoured them, and they died before the LORD. Lev. 10:1, 2.

Opposition crushed by fire, earthquake, and pestilence.

And they gathered themselves together against Moses and against Aaron, and saith unto them, "Ye take too much upon you, seeing all the congregation are holy, every one of them, and the LORD is among them: wherefore then lift ye up yourselves above the congregation of the LORD?" . . . and the LORD spake unto Moses and unto Aaron saying, "Separate yourselves from among this congregation, that I may consume them in a moment." And they fell upon their faces, and said, "O God, the God of the spirits of all flesh, shall one man sin, and wilt thou be wroth with all the congregation?" . . . And Datham and Abiram came out, and stood in the door of their tents, and their wives, and their sons, and their little children. . . . The ground clave asunder that was under them: and the earth opened her mouth, and swallowed them up, and their houses, and all the men that appertained unto Korah, and all their goods. They, and all that appertained to them, went down alive into the pit, and the earth closed upon them: and they perished from among the congregation. . . . And there came out a fire from the LORD, and consumed the two hundred and fifty men that offered incense. Num. 16:3, 20-22, 27, 31-33, 35.

Now they that died in the plague were fourteen thousand and seven hundred, beside them that died about the matter of Korah. Num. 16:49.

God answers complaints by sending fiery serpents.

And the people spake against God, and against Moses. "Wherefore have ye brought us up out of Egypt to die in the wilderness? for there is no bread, neither is there any water; and our soul loatheth this light bread." And the LORD sent fiery serpents among the people, and they bit the people; and much people of Israel died. Num. 21:5, 6.

Holy massacre; capture of 32,000 girls as booty; wholesale murder of helpless women and children.

And the LORD spake unto Moses, saying, "Avenge the children of Israel of the Midianites." . . . And the children of Israel took all the women of Midian captives, and their little ones, and took the spoil of all their cattle, and all their flocks, and all their goods. And they burnt all their cities wherein they dwelt, and all their goodly castles, with fire. And they took all the spoil, and all the prey, both of men and of beasts. . . .

129

and Moses was wroth. . . . And Moses said unto them, "Have ye saved all the women alive? . . . Now therefore kill every male among the little ones, and kill every woman that hath known man by lying with him. But all the women children, that have not known a man by lying with him, keep alive for yourselves." Num. 31:1-2, 9-11, 14-18.

[The Midianites had sheltered Moses for forty years when he fled for life from Egypt (See below.). Moses repays their hospitality in this horribly pious way. The Midianites were the descendants of Midian, son of Abraham, and were thus closely related to the Israelites. The Moabites and Ammonites, the offspring of Lot's incest, were specially protected by the Lord.]

Now when Pharaoh heard this thing, he sought to slay Moses. But Moses fled from the face of Pharaoh, and dwelt in the land of Midian: and he sat down by a well. Exod. 2:15.

Then again Abraham took a wife, and her name was Keturah. And she bare him Zimran, and Jokshan, and Medan, and Midian, and Ishbak, and Shuah. Gen. 25:1-2.

And when we passed by from our brethren the children of Esau, which dwelt in Seir, through the way of the plain from Elath, and from Eziongaber, we turned and passed by the way of the wilderness of Moab. . . . And the Lord said unto me, "Distress not the Moabites, neither contend with them in battle: for I will not give thee of their land for a possession; because I have given Ar unto the children of Lot for a possession. . . . And when thou comest nigh over against the children of Ammon, distress them not, nor meddle with them: for I will not give thee of the land of the children of Ammon any possession; because I have given it unto the children of Lot for a possession."Deut. 2:8-9, 19.

The Lord divides the human "prey" between the warriors and the congregation, and takes a share of the girls for himself.

And the LORD spake unto Moses, saying, "Take the sum of the prey that was taken, both of man and of beast . . . and divide the prey into two parts; between them that took the war upon them, who went out to battle, and between all the congregation: and levy a tribute unto the LORD of the men of war which went out to battle: one soul of five hundred, both of the persons, and of the beeves, and of the asses, and of the sheep: take it of their half, and give it unto Eleazar the priest, for an heave offering of the LORD. And of the children of Israel's half thou shalt take one portion of fifty, of the persons, of the beeves, of the asses, and of the flocks, of all manner of beasts, and give them unto the Levites, which keep the charge of the tabernacle of the LORD." Num. 31:25-30.

And the booty, being the rest of the prey which the men of war had caught, was six hundred thousand and seventy thousand and five thousand sheep. . . . and thirty and two thousand persons in all, of women that had not known man by lying with him. . . . And the asses were thirty thousand and five hundred; of which the LORD's tribute was threescore and one. And the persons were sixteen thousand; of which the LORD's tribute was thirty and two persons. Num. 31:32, 35, 39-40.

[The priests of the tabernacle thus received thirty-two young girls, as their share of the "booty."]

God's pleasant love for ungrateful enemies and negligent friends.

I will also send wild beasts among you, which shall rob you of your children. Lev. 26:22.

Then I will walk contrary unto you also in fury; and I, even I, will chastise you seven times for your sins. And ye shall eat the flesh of your sons, and the flesh of your daughters shall ye eat. Lev. 26:28, 29.

Infinite love corrects imperfect man for working on Saturdays, making images or pictures, sparing witches' lives, not killing a heretic wife, and so forth.

The LORD shall smite thee with a consumption, and with a fever, and with an inflammation, and with an extreme burning, and with the sword, and with blasting, and with mildew; and they shall pursue thee until thou perish. And thy heaven that is over thy head shall be brass, and the earth that is under thee shall be iron. The LORD shall make the rain of thy land powder and dust: from heaven shall it come down upon thee, until thou be destroyed. . . . And thy carcase shall be meat unto all fowls of the air, and unto the beasts of the earth, and no man shall fray them away. The LORD will smite thee with the botch of Egypt, and with the emerods, and with the scab, and with the itch, whereof thou canst not be healed. The LORD shall smite thee with madness, and blindness, and astonishment of heart. Deut. 28:22-24, 26-28.

And thou shalt eat the fruit of thine own body, the flesh of thy sons and of thy daughters, which the LORD thy God hath given thee, in the siege, and in the straitness, wherewith thine enemies shall distress thee. Deut. 28:53.

For a fire is kindled in mine anger, and shall burn unto the lowest hell, and shall consume the earth with her increase, and set on fire the foundations of the mountains. I will heap mischiefs upon them; I will spend mine arrows upon them. They shall be burnt with hunger, and devoured with burning heat, and with bitter destruction: I will also send the teeth of the beasts upon them, with the poison of serpents of the dust. The sword without, and terror within, shall destroy both the young man and the virgin, the suckling also with the man of grey hairs. . . . I will make mine arrows drunk with blood, and my sword shall devour flesh; and that with the blood of the slain and of the captives. Deut. 32:22-25, 42.

Massacre of a whole nation.

But Sihon king of Heshbon would not let us pass by him: for the LORD thy God hardened his spirit, and made his heart obstinate, that he might deliver him into thy hand. . . . And we took all his cities at that time, and utterly destroyed the men, and the women, and the little ones, of every city, we left none to remain. Deut. 2:30, 34.

All Bashan massacred.

And we utterly destroyed them, as we did unto Sihon, king of Heshbon, utterly destroying the men, women, and children, of every city. Deut. 3:6.

Seven nations of Canaan to be utterly destroyed and expropriated.

Seven nations greater and mightier than thou; and when the LORD thy God shall deliver them before thee; thou shalt smite them, and utterly destroy them; thou shalt make no covenant with them, nor shew mercy unto them. . . . For thou art an holy people unto the LORD thy God: the LORD thy God hath chosen thee to be a special people unto himself, above all people that are upon the face of the earth. Deut. 7:1-2, 6.

But of all the cities of these people, which the LORD thy God doth give thee for an inheritance, thou shalt save alive nothing that breatheth: but thou shalt utterly destroy them; namely the Hittites, and the Amorites, the Canaanites, and the Perizzites, the Hivites, and the Jebusites; as the LORD thy God hath commanded thee. Deut. 20:6, 17.

Murderous hornets.

Moreover the LORD thy God will send the hornet among them, until they that are left, and hide themselves from thee, be destroyed. Thou shalt not be affrighted at them: for the LORD thy God is among you, a mighty God and terrible. Deut. 7:20, 21.

God's children faithfully obey their loving Father's command to mas-sacre innocent babes, women, and men indiscriminately.

So Joshua smote all the country of the hills, and of the south, and of the vale, and of the springs, and all their kings: he left none remaining, but utterly destroyed all that breathed, as the LORD God of Israel commanded. Josh. 10:40.

And that day Joshua took Makkedah, and smote it with the edge of the sword, and the king thereof he utterly destroyed, them, and all the souls that were therein; he let none remain. . . . Then Joshua passed from Makkedah, and all Israel with him, unto Libnah, and fought against Libnah: And the LORD delivered it also, and the king thereof, into the hand of Israel; and he smote it with the edge of the sword, and all the souls that were therein; he let none remain in it; but did unto the king thereof as he did unto the king of Jericho. And Joshua passed from Libnah, and all Israel with him, unto Lachish, and encamped against it, and fought against it: And the LORD delivered Lachish into the hand of Israel, which took it on the second day, and smote it with the edge of the sword, and all the souls that were therein, according to all that he had done to Libnah. Then Horam king of Gezer came up to help Lachish; and Joshua smote him and his people, until he had left him none remaining. And from Lachish Joshua passed unto Eglon, and all Israel with him; and they encamped against it, and fought against it: And they took it on that day, and smote it with the edge of the sword, and all the souls that were therein he utterly destroyed that day, according to all that he had done to Lachish. And Joshua went up from Eglon, and all Israel with him, unto Hebron; and they fought against it: And they took it, and smote it with the edge of the sword, and the king thereof, and all the cities thereof, and all the souls that were therein; he left none remaining. . . . And Joshua returned, and all Israel with him, to Debir; and fought against it: And he took it, and the king thereof, and all the cities thereof; and they smote them with the edge of the sword, and utterly destroyed all the souls that were therein; he left none remaining. . . . So Joshua smote all the country of the hills, and of the south, and of the vale, and of the springs, and all their kings: he left none remaining, but utterly destroyed all that breathed, as the LORD God of Israel commanded. Josh. 10:28-40.

And Joshua at that time turned back, and took Hazor, and smote the king thereof with the sword: for Hazor beforetime was the head of all those kingdoms. And they smote all the souls that were therein with the edge of the sword, utterly destroying them: there was not any left to breathe: and he burnt Hazor with fire. And all the cities of those kings, and all the kings of them, did Joshua take, and smote them with the edge of the sword, and he utterly destroyed them, as Moses the servant of the LORD commanded. . . . And all the spoil of these cities, and the cattle, the children of Israel took for a prey unto themselves; but every man they smote with the edge of the sword, until they had destroyed them, neither left they any to breathe. As the LORD commanded Moses his servant, so did Moses command Joshua, and so did Joshua; he left nothing undone of all that the LORD commanded Moses. . . . For it was of the LORD to harden their hearts, that they should come against Israel in battle, that he might destroy them utterly, and that they might have no favour, but that he might destroy them, as the LORD commanded Moses. And at that time came Joshua, and cut off the Anakim, from the mountains, from Hebron, from Debir, from Anab, and from all the mountains of Judah, and from all the mountains of Israel: Joshua destroyed them utterly with their cities. Josh. 11:10-12, 14, 15, 20, 21.

For Joshua drew not his hand back, wherewith he stretched out the spear, until he had utterly destroyed all the inhabitants of Ai. Josh. 8:26.

The holy massacre at Jericho.

And the city shall be accursed, even it, and all that are therein, to the LORD: only Rahab the harlot shall live, she and all that are with her in the house, because she hid the messengers [spies] that we sent. . . . And they utterly destroyed all that was in the city, both man and woman, young and old, ox and sheep, and ass, with the edge of the sword. Josh.6:17, 21.

Achan's family stoned and burnt to satisfy God.

And the LORD said unto Joshua . . . he that is taken with the accursed thing shall be burnt with fire, he and all that he hath. . . . And Joshua, and all Israel with him, took Achan . . . and his sons, and his daughters, and his oxen, and his asses, and his sheep, and his tent, and all that he had. . . . And all Israel stoned him with stones, and burned them with fire, after they had stoned them with stones. . . . So the LORD turned from the fierceness of his anger. Josh. 7:10, 15, 24-26.

[Achan had taken some gold from the city, and had kept it back from the priests. This was in God's eyes a most odious crime, for which the thief's children must be burnt. But the murder of the whole population of the city was a most virtuous and pious act of obedience to the Infinite Benevolence that makes hell and orders murder on the hugest scale.]

134

Holy assassination.

But when the children of Israel cried unto the LORD, the LORD raised them up a deliverer, Ehud the son of Gera, a Benjamite, a man left-handed: and by him the children of Israel sent a present unto Eglon the king of Moab. But Ehud made him a dagger which had two edges, of a cubit length; and he did girt it under his raiment upon his right thigh. . . . and said, "I have a secret errand unto thee, O king": who said, "Keep silence." And all that stood by him went out from him. And Ehud came unto him; and he was sitting in a summer parlour, which he had for himself alone. And Ehud said, "I have a message from God unto thee." And he arose out of his seat. And Ehud put forth his left hand, and took the dagger from his right thigh, and thrust it into his belly: and the haft also went in after the blade; and the fat closed upon the blade, so that he could not draw the dagger out of his belly; and the dirt came out. Judg. 3:15-16, 19-22.

Treachery and assassination belauded.

For the LORD shall sell Sisera into the hand of a woman. . . . Howbeit Sisera flew away on his feet to the tent of Jael the wife of Heber the Kenite: for there was peace between Jabin the king of Hazor and the house of Heber the Kenite. And Jael went out to meet Sisera, and said unto him, "Turn in, my lord, turn in to me; fear not." And when he had turned in unto her into the tent, she covered him with a mantle. . . . Then Jael Heber's wife took a nail of the tent, and took an hammer in her hand, and went softly unto him, and smote the nail into his temples, and fastened it into the ground: for he was fast asleep and weary. So he died. . . . Behold, Sisera lay dead, and the nail was in his temples. So God subdued on that day Jabin the king of Canaan before the children of Israel. Judges 4:9, 17-18, 21, 23.

Blessed above women shall Jael the wife of Heber the Kenite be, blessed shall she be above women in the tent. . . . She put her hand to the nail, and her right hand to the workmen's hammer; and with the hammer she smote Sisera, she smote off his head, when she had pierced and stricken through his temples. . . . So let all thine enemies perish, O LORD. Judg. 5:24, 26, 31.

Samson, being inspired, kills thirty men in order to pay a Christmas forfeit with their garments.

And the spirit of the LORD came upon him, and he went down to Ashkelon, and slew thirty men of them, and took their spoil, and gave change of garments unto them which expounded the riddle. Judg. 14:19.

Cruelty to animals, and incendiarism.

And Samson went and caught three hundred foxes, and took fire-brands, and turned tail to tail, and put a firebrand in the midst between two tails. And when he had set the brands on fire, he let them go into the standing corn of the Philistines, and burnt up both the shocks, and also the standing corn, with the vineyards and olives. Judg. 15:4, 5.

Samson's destructiveness.

And the Spirit of the LORD came mightily upon him. . . . And he found a new jawbone of an ass, and put forth his hand, and took it, and slew a thousand men therewith. Judg. 15:14, 15.

And Samson took hold of the two middle pillars upon which the house stood. . . . And he bowed himself with all his might; and the house fell upon the lords, and upon all the people that were therein. So the dead which he slew at his death were more than they which he slew in his life. Judg. 16:29, 30.

Pious slaughter of peaceful citizens.

And the priest said unto them, "Go in peace: before the LORD is your way wherein ye go." Then the five men departed, and came to Laish, and saw the people that were therein, how they dwelt careless, after the manner of the Zidonians, quiet and secure. . . . And they smote them with the edge of the sword, and burnt the city with fire. Judg. 18:6—7, 27.

A pious method of obtaining wives.

How shall we do for wives. . . . And the congregation sent thither twelve thousand men of the valiantest, and commanded them, saying, "Go and smite the inhabitants of Jabeshgilead with the edge of the sword, with the women and the children. And this is the thing that ye shall do, Ye shall utterly destroy every male, and every woman that hath lain by man." And they found among the inhabitants of Jabeshgilead four hundred young virgins, that had known no man by lying with any male. . . . And Benjamin came again at that time; and they gave them wives which they had saved alive of the women of Jabeshgilead. Judg. 21:7, 10-12, 14.

God's pleasant method of vindicating his superiority to fish-god Dagon.

When the Philistines took the ark of God, they brought it into the house of Dagon, and set it by Dagon. . . . But the hand of the LORD was heavy upon them of Ashdod, and he destroyed them, and smote them

136

with emerods [hemorrhoids], even Ashdod and the coasts thereof. . . . They sent therefore and gathered all the lords of the Philistines unto them, and said, "What shall we do with the ark of the God of Israel?" And they answered, "Let the ark of the God of Israel be carried about unto Gath." And they carried the ark of the God of Israel about thither. And it was so, that, after they had carried it about, the hand of the LORD was against the city with a very great destruction: and he smote the men of the city, both small and great, and they had emerods in their secret parts. Therefore they sent the ark of God to Ekron. And it came to pass, as the ark of God came to Ekron, that the Ekronites cried out, saying, "They have brought about the ark of the God of Israel to us, to slay us and our people." 1 Sam. 4:2, 6, 8-10.

God murders 50,070 men for looking inside a box.

And he smote the men of Bethshemesh, because they had looked into the ark of the LORD, even he smote of the people fifty thousand and threescore and ten men: and the people lamented, because the LORD had smitten many of the people with a great slaughter. 1 Sam. 6:19.

God has the Amalekites massacred for an offence 400 years old.

Samuel also said unto Saul. . . . "Thus saith the LORD of hosts, 'I remember that which Amalek did to Israel, how he laid wait for him in the way, when he came up from Egypt. Now go and smite Amalek, and utterly destroy all that they have, and spare them not; but slay both man and woman, infant and suckling, ox and sheep, camel and ass.' " . . . And he took Agag the king of the Amalekites alive, and utterly destroyed all the people with the edge of the sword. 1 Sam. 15:1-3, 8.

[God was so angry with Saul for sparing Agag's life that he transferred the crown to David. (Then came the word of the LORD unto Samuel, saying, "It repenteth me that I have set up Saul to be king: for he is turned back from following me, and hath not performed my commandments." And it grieved Samuel; and he cried unto the LORD all night. . . . And Saul said unto Samuel, "Yea, I have obeyed the voice of the LORD, and have gone the way which the LORD sent me, and have brought Agag the king of Amalek, and have utterly destroyed the Amalekites. But the people took of the spoil, sheep and oxen, the chief of the things which should have been utterly destroyed, to sacrifice unto the LORD thy God in Gilgal." And Samuel said, "Hath the LORD as great delight in burnt offerings and sacrifices, as in obeying the voice of the LORD? Behold, to obey is better than sacrifice, and to hearken than the fat of rams. For rebellion is as the sin of witchcraft, and stubbornness is as iniquity and idolatry. Because thou hast rejected the word of the LORD, he hath also rejected thee from being king." 1 Sam. 15:10, 11, 20-23.)]

Agag hewn to pieces.
And Samuel hewed Agag in pieces before the LORD in Gilgal. 1 Sam. 15:33.

David slays and mutilates two hundred Philistines.
Wherefore David arose and went, he and his men, and slew of the Philistines two hundred men; and David brought their foreskins, and they gave them in full tale to the king, that he might be the king's son in law. 1 Sam. 18:27.

[Scalping by Indians is quite a respectable piece of savagery beside this feat of the man after God's own heart.]

David lives by massacre and robbery and blackmail.
And David and his men went up, and invaded the Geshurites, and the Gezrites, and the Amalekites. . . . And David smote the land, and left neither man nor woman alive, and took away the sheep, and the oxen, and the asses, and the camels, and the apparel. 1 Sam. 27:8, 9.

And David sent out ten young men, and David said unto the young men, "Get you up to Carmel, and go to Nabal, and greet him in my name: and thus shall ye say to him that liveth in prosperity, . . . 'Wherefore let the young men find favor in thine eyes: for we come in a good day: give, I pray thee, whatsoever cometh to thine hand unto thy servants, and to thy son David.' " . . . And Nabal answered David's servants, and said "Who is David? . . . there be many servants now a days that break away every man from his master." . . . And David said unto his men, "Gird ye on every man his sword." And they girded on every man his sword; and David also girded on his sword: and there went up after David about four hundred men; and two hundred abode by the stuff. 1 Sam. 25:5, 6, 8, 10, 13.

The Amalekites retaliating by theft without bloodshed, David shows them that extermination is the true policy.
They [the Amalekites] slew not any, either great or small, but carried them away, and went on their way. . . . But David pursued . . . and David smote them from the twilight even unto the evening of the next day: and there escaped not a man of them, save four hundred young men, which rode upon camels, and fled. And David recovered all that the Amale-

kites had carried away: and David rescued his two wives. 1 Sam. 30:2, 10, 17, 18.

God strikes Uzzah dead for saving the ark from falling.
And when they came to Nachon's threshingfloor, Uzzah put forth his hand to the ark of God, and took hold of it; for the oxen shook it. And the anger of the LORD was kindled against Uzzah; and God smote him there for his error; and there he died by the ark of God. 2 Sam. 6:6, 7.

David kills two-thirds of his Moabitish prisoners, and maims the captured horses.
And he smote Moab, and measured them with a line, casting them down to the ground; even with two lines measured he to put to death, and with one full line to keep alive. 2 Sam. 8:2.
And David took from him a thousand chariots . . . and David houghed all the chariot horses. 2 Sam. 8:4.

The man after God's own heart commits adultery with Uriah's wife and has Uriah slain.
And it came to pass in an eveningtide, that David arose from off his bed, and walked upon the roof of the king's house: and from the roof he saw a woman washing herself; and the woman was very beautiful to look upon. . . . And David sent messengers, and took her; and she came in unto him, and he lay with her; for she was purified from her uncleanness: and she returned unto her house. . . . And it came to pass in the morning, that David wrote a letter to Joab, and sent it by the hand of Uriah. And he wrote in the letter, saying, "Set ye Uriah in the forefront of the hottest battle, and retire ye from him, that he may be smitten, and die." 2 Sam. 11:2, 4, 14, 15

The man after God's own heart tortures the Ammonites.
And he brought out the people that were in it and cut them with saws, and with harrows of iron, and with axes. Even so dealt David with all the cities of the children of Ammon. 1 Chron. 20:3.
And [he] put them under saws, and under harrows of iron, and under axes of iron, and made them pass through the brickkiln. 2 Sam. 12:31.

God sends his angel to kill 70,000 men for having been enumerated in a census.
And Satan stood up against Israel, and provoked David to number Israel. . . . So Gad came to David, and said unto him, "Thus saith the

LORD, 'Choose thee either three years' famine; or three months to be destroyed before thy foes, while that the sword of thine enemies overtaketh thee; or else three days the sword of the LORD, even the pestilence, in the land, and the angel of the LORD, destroying throughout all the coasts of Israel.' " . . . So the LORD sent pestilence upon Israel: and there fell of Israel seventy thousand men. And God sent an angel unto Jerusalem to destroy it. 1 Chron. 21:1, 11, 14-15.

So the LORD sent a pestilence upon Israel from the morning even to the time appointed: and there died of the people from Dan even to Beersheba seventy thousand men. 2 Sam. 24:15.

[If the pestilence destroyed women and children as well as men, nearly a quarter of a million human beings must have been slain by God for the terrible crime of having been counted. David, the real culprit, was allowed to choose a punishment that fell on his people instead of himself.]

Secret orders of the man after God's own heart on his deathbed.
Let not his [Joab's] hoar head go down to the grave in peace. . . . And, behold, thou hast with thee Shimei . . . cursed me . . . and I sware to him by the LORD, saying, "I will not put thee to death with the sword" . . . his hoar head bring thou down to the grave with blood. 1 Kings 2:6, 8-9.

[Joab was David's commander-in-chief. David's orders were duly carried out by Solomon. See 1 Kings 2:29, 34, 46: And it was told king Solomon that Joab was fled unto the tabernacle of the LORD. . . . Then Solomon sent Benaiah the son of Jehoida, saying, "Go, fall upon him." . . . So Benaiah the son of Jehoida went up, and fell upon him, and slew him. . . . So the king commanded Benaiah the son of Jehoida. . . . And the kingdom was established in the hand of Solomon.]

The Lord's prophet has four hundred and fifty rival priests slain in cold blood.
And Elijah said unto them, "Take the prophets of Baal; let not one of them escape." And they took them: and Elijah brought them down to the brook Kishon, and slew them there. 1 Kings 18:40.

Elijah consumes a hundred men with fire from heaven.
And Elijah answered and said to the captain of fifty, "If I be a man of God, then let fire come down from heaven, and consume thee and thy fifty." And there came down fire from heaven, and consumed him and his fifty. Again also he sent unto him another captain of fifty with his fifty . . . . And the fire of God came down from heaven, and consumed him and his fifty. 2 Kings 1:10-12.

Forty-two children killed by bears for annoying Elisha.

And he went up from thence into Bethel: and as he was going up by the way, there came forth little children out of the city, and mocked him, and said unto him, "Go up, thou bald head; go up, thou bald head." And he turned back, and looked on them and cursed them in the name of the LORD. And there came forth two she bears out of the wood, and tare forty and two children of them. 2 Kings 2:23, 24.

God entices Ahab to his death by a lying spirit.

And the LORD said, "Who shall entice Ahab king of Israel, that he may go up and fall at Ramothgi lead?" . . . A spirit . . . said, "I will go out, and be a lying spirit in the mouth of all his prophets." And the LORD said. "Thou shalt entice him, and thou shalt also prevail: go out, and do even so." Now, therefore, behold, the LORD hath put a lying spirit in the mouth of these thy prophets. 2 Chron. 18:19-22.

God's prophets cause political and religious massacres.

And Ahab said to Elijah, "Hast thou found me, O mine enemy?" And he answered, "I have found thee: because thou hast sold thyself to work evil in the sight of the LORD. Behold, I will bring evil upon thee, and will take away thy posterity, and will cut off from Ahab him that pisseth against the wall, and him that is shut up and left in Israel, and will make thine house like the house of Jeroboam the son of Nebat, and like the house of Baasha the son of Ahijah, for the provocation wherewith thou hast provoked me to anger, and made Israel to sin." And of Jezebel also spake the LORD, saying, "The dogs shall eat Jezebel by the wall of Jezreel. Him that dieth of Ahab in the city the dogs shall eat; and him that dieth in the field shall the fowls of the air eat." 1 Kings 21:20-24.

And he arose, and went into the house; and he poured the oil on his head, and said unto him, "Thus saith the LORD God of Israel, 'I have anointed thee king over the people of the LORD, even over Israel. And thou shalt smite the house of Ahab thy master, that I may avenge the blood of all the servants of the LORD, at the hand of Jezebel. For the whole house of Ahab shall perish: and I will cut off from Ahab him that pisseth against the wall, and him that is shut up and left in Israel: and I will make the house of Ahab like the house of Jeroboam the son of Nebat, and like the house of Baasha the son of Ahijah: And the dogs shall eat Jezebel in the portion of Jezreel, and there shall be none to bury her.' " 2 Kings 9:6-10.

Know now that there shall fall unto the earth nothing of the word of the LORD, which the LORD spake concerning the house of Ahab: for the LORD hath done that which he spake by his servant Elijah. So Jehu slew all that remained of the house of Ahab in Jezreel, and all his great men, and his kinsfolks, and his priests, until he left him none remaining. 2 Kings 10:10, 11.

And he said, "Come with me, and see my zeal for the LORD." So they made him ride in his chariot. And when he came to Samaria, he slew all that remained unto Ahab in Samaria, till he had destroyed them, according to the saying of the LORD, which he spake to Elijah. And Jehu gathered all the people together, and said unto them, "Ahab served Baal a little; but Jehu shall serve him much. Now therefore call unto me all the prophets of Baal, all his servants, and all his priests; let none be wanting: for I have a great sacrifice to do to Baal; whosoever shall be wanting, he shall not live." But Jehu did it in subtilty, to the intent that he might destroy the worshippers of Baal. . . . And it came to pass, as soon as he had made an end of offering the burnt offering, that Jehu said to the guard and to the captains, "Go in, and slay them; let none come forth." And they smote them with the edge of the sword; and the guard and the captains cast them out, and went to the city of the house of Baal. . . . Thus Jehu destroyed Baal out of Israel. . . . And the LORD said unto Jehu, "Because thou has done well in executing that which is right in mine eyes . . . thy children of the fourth generation shall sit on the throne of Israel." 2 Kings 10:16-19, 25, 28, 30.

God's angel slays 185,000 men in one night.

And it came to pass that night, that the angel of the LORD went out, and smote in the camp of the Assyrians an hundred fourscore and five thousand: and when they arose early in the morning, behold, they were all dead corpses. 2 Kings 19:35.

Children punished for their fathers' sins.

Prepare slaughter for his children for the iniquity of their fathers. Isa. 14:21.

Visiting the iniquity of the fathers upon the children, and upon the children's children, unto the third and to the fourth generation. Exod. 34:7; Num. 14:18.

Foreign wives and their children abandoned by pious husbands and fathers.

We have trespassed against our God, and have taken strange wives of the people of the land: yet now there is hope in Israel concerning this thing. Now therefore let us make a covenant with our God to put away

142

all the wives, and such as are born of them, according to the counsel of my lord, and of those that tremble at the commandment of our God. Ezra 10:2, 3.

God allows Satan to kill Job's servants and children merely to test Job's piety.

And the LORD said unto Satan, "Behold, all that he hath is in thy power; only upon himself put not forth thine hand." So Satan went forth from the presence of the LORD. . . . And there came a messenger unto Job, and said, "The oxen were plowing, and the asses feeding beside them: and the Sabeans fell upon them, and took them away; yea, they have slain the servants with the edge of the sword; and I only am escaped alone to tell thee." While he was yet speaking, there came also another, and said, "Thy sons and thy daughters were eating and drinking wine in their eldest brother's house: and, behold, there came forth a great wind from the wilderness, and smote the four corners of the house, and it fell upon the young men, and they are dead; and I only am escaped alone to tell thee." Job 1:12, 14, 18-19.

God deceives prophets as an excuse for slaying them.

And if the prophet be deceived when he hath spoken a thing, I the LORD have deceived that prophet, and I will stretch out my hand upon him, and will destroy him from the midst of my people Israel. Ezek. 14:19.

Inspired cursings.

When he shall be judged, let him be condemned: and let his prayer become sin. Let his days be few; and let another take his office. Let his children be fatherless, and his wife a widow. Let his children be continually vagabonds, and beg: let them seek their bread also out of their desolate places. . . . Let there be none to extend mercy unto him: neither let there be any to favour his fatherless children. . . . Let this be the reward of mine adversaries from the LORD, and of them that speak evil against my soul. Ps. 109:7-10, 12, 20.

Happy shall he be, that taketh and dasheth thy little ones against the stones. Ps. 137:9.

Curious mercies.

O give thanks unto the God of gods. . . . To him that smote Egypt in their firstborn: for his mercy endureth for ever. . . . But overthrew Pharaoh and his host in the Red sea: for his mercy endureth for ever. . . .

To him which smote great kings: for his mercy endureth for ever: and slew famous kings: for his mercy endureth for ever: Sihon king of the Amorites: for his mercy endureth for ever: and Og the king of Bashan: for his mercy endureth for ever: and gave their land for an heritage: for his mercy endureth for ever. Ps. 136:2, 10, 15, 17-21.

Pretty prophecies.

For the indignation of the Lord is upon all nations, and his fury upon all their armies: he hath utterly destroyed them, he hath delivered them to the slaughter. Their slain also shall be cast out, and their stink shall come up out of their carcases, and the mountains shall be melted with their blood. And all the host of heaven shall be dissolved, and the heavens shall be rolled together as a scroll. . . . The sword of the LORD is filled with blood, it is made fat with fatness. Isa. 34:2-6.

Therefore deliver up their children to the famine and pour out their blood by the force of the sword; and let their wives be bereaved of their children, and be widows; and let their men be put to death. Jer. 18:21.

No city shall escape: the valley also shall perish, and the plain shall be destroyed, as the LORD hath spoken. . . . Cursed be he that doeth the work of the LORD deceitfully, and cursed be he that keepeth back his sword from blood. Jer. 48:8, 10.

A pleasant deity.

The young and the old lie on the ground in the streets: my virgins and my young men are fallen by the sword; thou hast slain them in the day of thine anger; thou hast killed, and not pitied. Lam. 2:21.

He was unto me as a bear lying in wait, and as a lion in secret places. He hath turned aside my ways, and pulled me in pieces: he hath made me desolate. Lam. 3:10, 11.

Therefore I will be unto them as a lion: as a leopard by the way will I observe them: I will meet them as a bear that is bereaved of her whelps, and will rend the caul of their heart, and there will I devour them like a lion: the wild beast shall tear them. Hos. 13:7, 8.

He that is far off shall die of the pestilence; and he that is near shall fall by the sword; and he that remaineth and is besieged shall die by the famine: thus will I accomplish my fury upon them. Then shall ye know that I am the LORD. Ezek. 6:12, 13.

And, lo, they put the branch to their nose. Therefore will I also deal in fury: mine eye shall not spare, neither will I have pity. Ezek. 8:17, 18.

Howl ye; for the day of the LORD is at hand; it shall come as a destruction from the Almighty. . . . Behold, the day of the LORD

cometh, cruel both with wrath and fierce anger, to lay the land desolate
.... Their children also shall be dashed to pieces before their eyes; their
houses shall be spoiled, and their wives ravished. Behold, I will stir up
the Medes. . . . And they shall have no pity on the fruit of the womb;
their eye shall not spare children. Isa. 13:6, 9, 16-18.

God is jealous . . . the LORD revengeth, and is furious; the LORD will
take vengeance on his adversaries, and he reserveth wrath for his
enemies. . . . The LORD hath his way in the whirlwind and in the storm
.... The mountains quake at him, and the hills melt, and the earth is
burned at his presence, yea, the world, and all that dwell therein. Who
can stand before his indignation? and who can abide in the fierceness
of his anger? his fury is poured out like fire, and the rocks are thrown
down by him. Nah. 1:2-3, 5-6.

Before him went the pestilence, and burning coals went forth at his
feet. Hab. 3:5.

"I will utterly consume all things from off the land, "saith the LORD."
I will consume man and beast; I will consume the fowls of the heaven,
and the fishes of the sea . . . and I will cut off man from off the land,"
saith the LORD. Zeph. 1:2, 3.

*The New Testament sanctifies and upholds innumerable atrocities of the
Old Testament.*

If they hear not Moses and the prophets, neither will they be
persuaded, though one rose from the dead. Luke 16:31.

Think not that I am come to destroy the law,* or the prophets: I am
come not to destroy, but to fulfil. For verily I say unto you, Till heaven
and earth pass, one jot or one tittle shall in no wise pass from the law
till all be fulfilled. Whosoever, therefore, shall break one of these least
commandments, and shall teach men so, he shall be called the least in
the kingdom of heaven: but whosoever shall do and teach them, the
same shall be called great in the kingdom of heaven. Matt. 5:17-19.

It is easier for heaven and earth to pass, than one tittle of the law to
fail. Luke 16:17.

From a child thou hast known the holy scriptures, which are able to
make thee wise unto salvation through faith which is in Christ Jesus. All
scripture is given by inspiration of God, and is profitable for doctrine for

---

*Among the Jews "the law" meant the Pentateuch (John 1:17 and 8:5: For the
law was given by Moses, but grace and truth came by Jesus Christ. . . . "Now
Moses in the law commanded us, that such should be stoned: but what sayest
thou?"). The law thus sanctioned by Jesus allowed slavery, etc., and mercilessly
put to death heretics, sabbath-breakers, witches, etc.

reproof, for correction, for instruction in righteousness. 2 Tim. 3:15, 16.

Search the scriptures; for in them ye think ye have eternal life: and they are they which testify of me. . . . For had ye believed Moses, you would have believed me: for he wrote of me. But if ye believe not his writings, how shall ye believe my words: John 5:39, 46, 47.

Then he said unto them, "O fools, and slow of heart to believe all that the prophets have spoken." . . . And beginning at Moses and all the prophets, he expounded unto them in all the scriptures the things concerning himself. Luke 24:25, 27.

By faith Abraham, when he was tried, offered up Isaac. . . . By faith the walls of Jericho fell down, after they were compassed about seven days. By faith the harlot Rahab perished not with them that believed not, when she had received the spies with peace. Heb. 11:17, 30-31.

Was not Abraham our father justified by works, when he had offered Isaac his son upon the altar? Seest thou how faith wrought with his works, and by works was faith made perfect? James 2:21, 22.

The New Testament adds worse terrors and atrocities of its own in the shape of ETERNAL TORMENTS.

It is better for thee to enter into life halt or maimed, rather than having two hands or two feet to be cast into everlasting fire. Matt. 18:8.

Then shall he say also unto them on the left hand, "Depart from me, ye cursed, into everlasting fire, prepared for the devil and his angels." . . . And these shall go away into everlasting punishment: but the righteous into life eternal. Matt. 25:41, 46.

And if thy hand offend thee, cut if off: it is better for thee to enter into life maimed, than having two hands to go into hell, into the fire that never shall be quenched: where their worm dieth not, and the fire is not quenched. And if thy foot offend thee, cut it off: it is better for thee to enter halt into life, than having two feet to be cast into hell, into the fire that shall never be quenched: where their worm dieth not, and the fire is not quenched. And if thine eye offend thee, pluck it out: it is better for thee to enter into the kingdom of God with one eye, than having two eyes to be cast into hell fire: where their worm dieth not and the fire is not quenched. Mark 9:43-48.

But I will forewarn you whom ye shall fear: Fear him, which after he had killed hath power to cast into hell; yea, I say unto you, Fear him. Luke 12:5.

But rather fear him which is able to destroy both soul and body in hell. Matt. 10:28.

Ye serpents, ye generation of vipers, how can ye escape the damnation of hell? Matt. 23:33.

A more particular description of hell as given by Christ to the multitude.
And in hell he lift up his eyes, being in torments, and seeth Abraham afar off, and Lazarus in his bosom. And he cried and said, "Father Abraham, have mercy upon me, and send Lazarus, that he may dip the tip of his finger in water, and cool my tongue; for I am tormented in this flame." Luke 16:23, 24.

[Some modern Christians protest that this kind of thing is only figurative. But what is it figurative of, except of agony of either mind or body? Surely the "eternal punishment" of Matt. 25:46 (See above.) must mean eternal punishment. If such expressions are allegorised into nothing, then Christ has been guilty of successfully terrorizing Christendom for nearly two thousand years by vulgar lies and atrocious threats.]

John the Divine's description of hell and the rejoicing of the saints over the sufferings of the tormented.
If any man worship the beast and his image, and receive his mark in his forehead, or in his hand, The same shall drink of the wine of the wrath of God which is poured out without mixture into the cup of his indignation; and he shall be tormented with fire and brimstone in the presence of the holy angels, and in the presence of the Lamb; And the smoke of their torment ascendeth up for ever and ever: and they have no rest day nor night, who worship the beast and his image, and whosoever receiveth the mark of his name. Rev. 14: 9-11.

And after these things I heard a great voice of much people in heaven saying, "Alleluia. . . ." And again they said "Alleluia." And her smoke rose up for ever and ever. And the four and twenty elders and the four beasts fell down and worshipped God that sat on the throne, saying, "Amen; Alleluia." Rev. 19:1, 3-4.

These both were cast alive into a lake of fire burning with brimstone. Rev. 19:20.

And I saw an angel come down from heaven, having the key of the bottomless pit and a great chain in his hand. And he laid hold on the dragon, that old serpent, which is the Devil, and Satan, and bound him a thousand years, and cast him into the bottomless pit, and shut him up. Rev. 20:1-3.

And the devil that deceived them was cast into the lake of fire and brimstone, where the beast and the false prophet are, and shall be tormented day and night for ever and ever. Rev. 20:10.

The New Testament first proclaims that condemnation to these eternal torments is the heritage of all because Adam sinned.

Wherefore, as by one man sin entered into the world, and death by sin; and so death passed upon all men, for that all have sinned: . . . By the offence of one judgment came upon all men to condemnation. Rom. 5:12, 18.

For since by man came death, by man came also the resurrection of the dead. For as in Adam all die even so in Christ shall all be made alive. 1 Cor. 15:21, 22.

But the scripture hath concluded all under sin. Gal. 3:22.

The great majority of mankind will go to hell.

Strait is the gate and narrow is the way, which leadeth into life, and few there be that find it. Matt. 7:14.

There shall be weeping and gnashing of teeth. For many are called but few are chosen. Matt. 22:13, 14.

Then said one unto him, "Lord, are there few that be saved?" And he said unto them, "Strive to enter in at the strait gate: for many, I say unto you, will seek to enter in, and shall not be able." Luke 13:23, 24.

Idolaters to go to hell.

Idolators . . . shall have their part in the lake which burneth with fire and brimstone. Rev. 21:8.

Know ye not that the unrighteous shall not inherit the kingdom of God? Be not deceived: neither fornicators, nor idolaters, nor adulterers, nor effeminate, nor abusers of themselves with mankind. 1 Cor. 6:9.

[Hindoos, Africans, etc., are thus doomed in the most wholesale manner to a hell of which they have never even heard.]

Damnation for not knowing God.

The Lord Jesus shall be revealed from heaven with his mighty angels, in flaming fire, taking vengeance on them that know not God, and that obey not the gospel of our Lord Jesus Christ: who shall be punished with everlasting destruction from the presence of the Lord. 2 Thess. 1:7, 9.

Neither is there salvation in any other: for there is none other name under heaven given among men whereby we must be saved. Acts 4:12.

The wicked shall be turned into hell, and all the nations that forget God. Ps. 9:17.

148

Hell-fire for describing a fool correctly.
Whosoever shall say, "Thou fool," shall be in danger of hell-fire. Matt. 5:22.

[Carlyle, who described the population of England as "mostly fools," must be in considerable danger of hell-fire. Christ also is in danger of hell-fire himself, for he often called people fools and also vipers, children of hell and so forth:
(Ye fools and blind: for whether is greater, the gold, or the temple that sanctifieth the gold? Matt. 23:17.

Ye fools, did not he that made that which is without make that which is within also? Luke 11:40.

O fools, and slow of heart to believe all that the prophets have spoken. . . . Luke 24:25.

But when he saw many of the Pharisees and Sadducees come to his baptism, he said unto them, "O generation of vipers, who hath warned you to flee from the wrath to come?" Matt. 3:7.

O generation of vipers, how can ye, being evil, speak good things? for out of the abundance of the heart the mouth speaketh. Matt. 12:34.

Ye serpents, ye generation of vipers, how can ye escape the damnation of hell? Matt. 23:33.).]

Damnation for unbelief.
But the fearful, and unbelieving, and the abominable, and murderers and whoremongers, and sorcerers and idolaters, and all liars, shall have their part in the lake which burneth with fire and brimstone. Rev. 21:8.

He that believeth not the Son shall not see life; but the wrath of God abideth on him. John 3:36.

The lord of that servant . . . will appoint him his portion with the unbelievers. Luke 12:46.

He that believeth not shall be damned. Mark 16:16.

Damnation for being rich.
It is easier for a camel to go through the eye of a needle, than for a rich man to enter into the kingdom of God. Matt 19:24.

But woe unto you that are rich! for ye have received your consolation. Luke 6:24.

There was a certain rich man, which was clothed in purple and fine linen, and fared sumptuously every day: And there was a certain beggar named Lazarus, which was laid at his gate, full of sores. And desiring to be fed with the crumbs which fell from the rich man's table: moreover the dogs came and licked his sores. And it came to pass, that the beggar died, and was carried by the angels into Abraham's bosom: the rich man

149

also died, and was buried; And in hell he lift up his eyes, being in torments, and seeth Abraham afar off, and Lazarus in his bosom. And he cried and said, "Father Abraham, have mercy on me, and send Lazarus that he may dip the tip of his finger in water, and cool my tongue; for I am tormented in this flame." But Abraham said, "Son, remember that thou in thy lifetime receivedst thy good things, and likewise Lazarus evil things: but now he is comforted, and thou art tormented. And beside all this, between us and you there is a great gulf fixed: so that they which would pass from hence to you cannot; neither can they pass to us, that would come from thence." Then he said, "I pray thee therefore, father, that thou wouldest send him to my father's house: For I have five brethren; that he may testify unto them, lest they also come into this place of torment." Abraham saith unto him, "They have Moses and the prophets; let them hear them." And he said, "Nay, father Abraham: but if one went unto them from the dead, they will repent." And he said unto him, "If they hear not Moses and the prophets, neither will they be persuaded, though one rose from the dead." Luke 16:19-31.

A licensed devil.

Your adversary, the devil, as a roaring lion, walketh about, seeking whom he may devour. 1 Pet. 5:8.

The working of Satan with all power and signs and lying wonders. . . . 2 Thess. 2:9.

Devils are allowed to take possession of men and children.

And behold, a man of the company cried out, saying, "Master, I beseech thee, look upon my son; for he is mine only child, And, lo, a spirit taketh him, and he suddenly crieth out; and it teareth him that he foameth again, and bruising him hardly departeth from him. And I besought thy disciples to cast him out: and they could not." . . . And as he was yet a coming, the devil threw him down, and tare him. Luke 9:38-40, 42.

When the even was come, they brought unto him many that were possessed with devils. Matt. 8:16.

Mary called Magdalene, out of whom went seven devils. . . . Luke 8:2.

Sacrifice of an innocent person appeases God's anger against the guilty.

Christ our passover is sacrificed for us. 1 Cor. 5:7.

Who did no sin, neither was guile found in his mouth. 1 Pet. 2:22.

150

But now once in the end of the world hath he appeared to put away sin by the sacrifice by himself. Heb. 9:26.

For he hath made him to be sin for us, who knew no sin. 2 Cor. 5:21.

If any man sin, we have an advocate with the Father, Jesus Christ the righteous; And he is the propitiation for our sins: and not for ours only, but also for the sins of the whole world. 1 John 2:1, 2.

Who his own self bare our sins in his own body on the tree, that we, being dead to sins, should live unto righteousness: by whose stripes ye were healed. 1 Pet. 2:24.

Blood is the remedy and atonement for sin.

The blood of Jesus Christ his Son cleanseth us from all sin. 1 John 1:7.

And almost all things are by the law purged with blood; and without shedding of blood is no remission. . . . So Christ was once offered to bear the sins of many. Heb. 9: 22, 28.

This is my blood of the new testament, which is shed for many for the remission of sins. Matt. 26:28.

The church of God, which he hath purchased with his own blood. Acts. 20:28.

In whom we have redemption through his blood, the forgiveness of sins. . . . Eph. 1:7; 7 Col. 1:14.

Jesus Christ . . . washed us from our sins in his own blood. . . . Rev. 1:5.

Thou wast slain, and hast redeemed us to God by thy blood. . . . Rev. 5:9.

Neither by the blood of goats and calves, but by his own blood he entered in once into the holy place, having obtained eternal redemption for us. For if the blood of bulls and of goats, and the ashes of an heifer sprinkling the unclean, sanctifieth to the purifying of the flesh: How much more shall the blood of Christ, who through the eternal Spirit offered himself without spot to God, purge your conscience from dead works to serve the living God? Heb. 9:12-14.

Of how much sorer punishment, suppose ye, shall he be thought worthy, who hath trodden under foot the Son of God, and hath counted the blood of the covenant, wherewith he was sanctified, an unholy thing, and hath done despite unto the Spirit of grace? Heb. 10:29.

Elect according to the foreknowledge of God the Father, through sanctification of the Spirit, unto obedience and sprinkling of the blood of Jesus Christ. 1 Pet. 1:2.

And he said to me, "These are they which came out of great

tribulation, and have washed their robes, and made them white in the blood of the Lamb." Rev. 7:14.

A father requires the agonising death of an only son as a victim before he can relinquish his vengeance on sinners whom he made imperfect.

For God so loved the world, that he gave his only begotten Son, that whosoever believe in him should not perish, but have everlasting life. John 3:16.

He humbled himself, and became obedient unto death, even the death of the cross. Phil. 2:8.

For it pleased the Father that . . . having made peace through the blood of the cross. . . . Col. 1:19, 20.

God . . . sent his Son to be the propitiation for our sins. 1 John 4:10.

Christ hath redeemed us from the curse of the law, being made a curse for us. Gal. 3:13.

For there is one God, and one mediator between God and men, the man Christ Jesus; Who gave himself a ransom for all. . . . 1 Tim. 2:5-6.

But now in Christ Jesus ye who sometimes were far off are made nigh by the blood of Christ. . . . And that he might reconcile both unto God in one body by the cross, having slain the enmity thereby. Eph. 2:13, 16.

Being justified freely by his grace through the redemption that is in Christ Jesus: Whom God hath set forth to be a propitiation through faith in his blood, to declare his righteousness for the remission of sins that are past through the forbearance of God. Rom. 3:24, 15.

Who was delivered for our offences, and was raised again for our justification. Rom. 4:25.

Therefore being justified by faith, we have peace with God through our Lord Jesus Christ. . . . Christ died for the ungodly. . . . While we were yet sinners, Christ died for us. Much more then, being now justified by his blood, we shall be saved from wrath through him. . . . We were reconciled to God by the death of his Son . . . by whom we have now received the atonement. Rom. 5:1, 6, 8-11.

God sends a delusion to entrap people into damnation.

God shall send them strong delusion, that they should believe a lie: That they all might be damned who believed not the truth. . . . 2 Thess. 2:11, 12.

Christ speaks in unintelligible parables, so that people may not understand and be saved.

Unto them that are without, all these things are done in parables:

That seeing they may see, and not perceive; and hearing they may hear, and not understand; lest at any time they should be converted, and their sins should be forgiven them. Mark 4:11, 12.

God hardens people's hearts, so that they shall not be saved from hell.
Therefore they could not believe, because that Esaias said again, "He hath blinded their eyes, and hardened their heart; that they should not see with their eyes, nor understand with their heart, and be converted, and I should heal them." John 12:39, 40.

Man is helpless to save himself from hell.
And not only this; but when Rebecca also had conceived by one, even by our father Isaac; (For the children being not yet born, neither having done any good or evil, that the purpose of God according to election might stand, not of works, but of him that calleth;) It was said unto her, "The elder shall serve the younger. As it is written, 'Jacob have I loved, but Esau have I hated.' " . . . So then it is not of him that willeth, nor of him that runneth, but of God that sheweth mercy. . . . Therefore hath he mercy on whom he will have mercy, and whom he will he hardeneth. . . . Hath not the potter power over the clay, of the same lump to make one vessel unto honour, and another unto dishonour? What if God, willing to shew his wrath, and to make his power known, endured with much long suffering the vessels of wrath fitted to destruction? Rom. 9:9-13, 16, 18, 21-22.

Predestination.
For whom he did foreknow, he also did predestinate to be conformed to the image of his Son, that he might be the firstborn among his brethren. Moreover whom he did predestinate, them he also called; and whom he called, them he also justified: and whom he justified, them he also glorified. Rom. 8:29, 30.

The election hath obtained it, and the rest were blinded (according as it is written, God hath given them the spirit of slumber, eyes that they should not see, and ears that they should not hear); unto this day. And David saith, "Let their table be made a snare, and a trap, and a stumbling block, and a recompense unto them: let their eyes be darkened, that they may not see, and bow down their back alway." Rom. 11:7-10.

He hath chosen us in him before the foundation of the world. . . . having predestinated us unto the adoption of children by Jesus Christ. Eph. 1:4, 5.

Whose names were not written in the book of life from the foundation of the world. Rev. 17:8.

And whosoever was not found written in the book of life was cast into the lake of fire. Rev. 20:15.

Antinomianism*: murder no crime, vice no sin, natural morality a snare.

Who shall lay anything to the charge of God's elect? It is God that justifieth. Rom. 8:33.

By him all that believe are justified from all things. Acts 13:39.

All things are lawful unto me, but all things are not expedient: all things are lawful for me, but I will not be brought under the power of any. 1 Cor. 6:12.

Whosoever is born of God doth not commit sin; for his seed remaineth in him: and he cannot sin, because he is born of God. 1 John 3:9.

Whosoever believeth that Jesus is the Christ is born of God. 1 John 5:1.

Justified by faith. Rom. 5:1.

But to him that worketh not, but believeth on him that justifieth the ungodly, his faith is counted for righteousness.... Blessed is the man to whom the Lord will not impute sin. Rom. 4:5, 8.

Being then made free from sin. Rom. 6:18, 22.

If any man come to me, and hate not his father, and mother, and wife, and children, and brethren, and sisters, yea, and his own life also, he cannot be my disciple. Luke 14:26.

[Antinomianism is a logical result of Christianity, and in all times, especially during seasons of active belief, it has had to be fought and crushed by the more practical members of society or the Church. Seeing that Christians are taught that the Holy Spirit will dwell within them and inspire their thoughts and actions, it necessarily follows that these are of God and above human law. Hence the excesses of fanatics like those of Munster (where Anabaptists proclaimed a "kingdom of heaven" in 1534) are really indulged in as inspirational privileges of the saints who cannot sin, and who, being of the elect or predestinate, cannot be lost. Besides, Christ's blood has paid the ransom for all sin in those who believe. Hence pleasant vice and convenient crime are felt to

---

*Antinomianism — the doctrine that under the gospel dispensation of grace the moral law is of no use or obligation because faith alone is necessary to salvation.

be no longer of the nature of sin. Acts like the extermination of the Canaanites and Albigenses — and Christian atrocities generally — are really examples of public religious antinomianism. The private mischief caused by superseding "cold morality" by faith and personal inspiration is probably infinitely greater than Christians would care to acknowledge.]

Idealised cannibalism.

Then Jesus said unto them, "Verily, verily, I say unto you, Except ye eat the flesh of the Son of man, and drink his blood, ye have no life in you. Whoso eateth my flesh, and drinketh my blood, hath eternal life; and I will raise him up at the last day. For my flesh is meat indeed, and my blood is drink indeed. He that eateth my flesh, and drinketh my blood, dwelleth in me, and I in him." John 6:53-56.

A man and his wife killed for keeping part of their own property.

As many as were possessors of lands or houses sold them, and brought the prices of the things that were sold, and laid them down at the apostles' feet: and distribution was made. . . . But a certain man named Ananias, with Sapphira his wife, sold a possession, and kept back part of the price, his wife also being privy to it, and brought a certain part, and laid it at the apostles' feet. But Peter said, "Ananias, why hath Satan filled thine heart to lie to the Holy Ghost, and to keep back part of the price of the land?" . . . And Ananias hearing these words fell down, and gave up the ghost: and great fear came on all them that heard these things. And the young men arose, wound him up, and carried him out, and buried him. And it was about the space of three hours after, when his wife, not knowing what was done, came in. And Peter answered unto her, "Tell me whether ye sold the land for so much?" And she said, "Yea, for so much." Then Peter said unto her, "How is it that ye have agreed together to tempt the Spirit of the Lord? Behold, the feet of them which have buried thy husband are at the door, and shall carry thee out." Then she fell down straightway at his feet, and yielded up the ghost: and the young men came in, and found her dead, and, carrying her forth, buried her by her husband. And great fear came upon all the church, and upon as many as heard these things. Acts 4:34, 35; 5:1-3, 5-11.

A man struck blind for opposing Christianity.

But Elymas the sorcerer (for so is his name by interpretation) withstood them, seeking to turn away the deputy from the faith. Then

Saul (who also is called Paul), filled with the Holy Ghost, set his eyes on him, and said, "O full of all subtilty and all mischief, thou child of the devil, thou enemy of all righteousness, wilt thou not cease to pervert the right ways of the Lord? And now, behold, the hand of the Lord is upon thee, and thou shalt be blind, not seeing the sun for a season." And immediately there fell on him a mist and a darkness; and he went about seeking some to lead him by the hand. Acts 13:8-11.

The Judgment Day.

But the end of all things is at hand: be ye therefore sober, and watch unto prayer. 1 Peter 4:7.

But the same day that Lot went out of Sodom it rained fire and brimstone from heaven, and destroyed them all. Even thus shall it be in the day when the Son of man is revealed. Luke 17:29, 30.

But the heavens and the earth, which are now, by the same word are kept in store, reserved unto fire against the day of judgment and perdition of ungodly men. . . . But the day of the Lord will come as a thief in the night; in the which the heavens shall pass away with a great noise, and the elements shall melt with fervent heat, the earth also, and the works that are therein shall be burned up. 2 Peter 3:7, 10.

The day of wrath and revelation of the righteous judgment of God. Rom. 2:5.

There was a great earthquake; and the sun became black as sackcloth of hair, and the moon became as blood; and the stars of heaven fell upon the earth, even as a fig tree casteth her untimely figs, when she is shaken of a mighty wind. And the heaven departed as a scroll when it is rolled together; and every mountain and island were moved out of their places. And the kings of the earth, and great men, and the rich men, and the chief captains, and, mighty men, and every bondman, and every free man, hid themselves in the dens and in the rocks of the mountains; and said to the mountains and rocks, "Fall on us, and hide us from the face of him that sitteth on the throne, and from the wrath of the Lamb: for the great day of his wrath is come; and who shall be able to stand?" Rev. 6:12-17.

Then shall he say also unto them on the left hand, "Depart from me, ye cursed, into everlasting fire, prepared for the devil and his angels: For I was an hungred, and ye gave me no meat: I was thirsty, and ye gave me no drink: I was a stranger, and ye took me not in: naked, and ye clothed me not: sick, and in prison, and ye visited me not." Then shall they also answer him, saying, "Lord, when saw we thee an hungred, or athirst, or a stranger, or naked, or sick, or in prison, and did not minister unto thee?" Then shall he answer them, saying, "Verily, I say unto you, Inasmuch as ye did it not to one of the least of these, ye did it not to me. And these shall go away into everlasting punishment: but the righteous into life eternal." Matt. 25:41-46.

UNFULFILLED PROPHECIES
AND BROKEN PROMISES
I. OLD TESTAMENT

Adam to die on the day he ate the apple.

And the LORD God commanded the man, saying, "Of every tree of the garden thou mayest freely eat: but of the tree of knowledge of good and evil, thou shalt not eat of it: for in the day that thou eatest thereof thou shalt surely die." Gen. 2:16, 17.

[Adam and Eve did not die in the day on which they ate the forbidden fruit. Eve lived to bear several children, and Adam lived to the ripe old age of nine hundred and thirty years. (Gen. 5:5 — "And all the days that Adam lived were nine hundred and thirty years: and he died.")]

Dust to be the serpent's food.

And the LORD God said unto the serpent, "Because thou hast done this . . . dust shall thou eat all the days of thy life." Gen. 3:14.

[Serpents do not eat dust, except in the sense in which we all eat our peck of dust before we die. Isaiah also prophesies that "dust shall be the serpent's meat" (Isa. 65:25). This is a common oriental fancy.]

Cain to be a wanderer.

And the LORD said unto Cain. . . . "A fugitive and a vagabond shalt thou be in the earth." Gen. 4:9,12.

[Verses 16 and 17 show that Cain lived a settled life and was far from being a vagabond or wanderer upon the face of the earth. He "dwelt" in the land of Nod, and "builded a city, and called the name of the city after the name of his son, Enoch."]

Harvest never to cease.

While the earth remaineth, seed time and harvest, and cold and heat, and summer and winter, and day and night shall not cease. Gen. 8:22.

[Gen. 41:56 states that for several years harvest ceased all over the face of the earth. ("And the famine was all over the face of the earth: and Joseph opened all the storehouses, and sold unto the Egyptians; and the famine waxed sore in the land of Egypt.")]

Abraham to receive the land of Canaan, and his descendants, the Jews, to retain it for ever.

And Abram fell on his face: and God talked with him, saying.... "I will give unto thee, and to thy seed after thee, the land wherein thou art a stranger, all the land of Canaan, for an everlasting possession." Gen. 17:3, 8.

For all the land which thou seest, to thee will I give it, and to thy seed for ever. Gen. 13:15.

Remember Abraham, Isaac, and Israel, thy servants, to whom thou swearest by thine own self, and saidst unto them, "I will multiply your seed as the stars of heaven, and all this land that I have spoken of will I give unto your seed, and they shall inherit it for ever." Exod. 32:13.

[That Abraham never received the land that God promised to him is evident from the biblical narrative, and from Acts 7:5, where it is acknowledged that God gave Abraham "none inheritance in it, no, not so much as to set his foot on." That the Jews have not received "all the land of Canaan for an everlasting possession" is evident from the facts of history. The Jews were conquered by the Romans, and have never recovered complete possession of their country.]

The Israelites to be afflicted as slaves in Egypt for 400 years.

And he said unto Abram, "Know of a surety that thy seed shall be a stranger in a land that is not theirs, and shall serve them; and they shall afflict them four hundred years." Gen. 15:13.

[According to the orthodox biblical chronology, the Israelites were only in Egypt for 215 years in all. Jacob entered Egypt in B.C. 1706, and the exodus under Moses took place in B.C. 1491. Of the 215 years the first portion under Joseph was a time of great prosperity for the Israelites. Dr. Pinnock makes the period of affliction only eighty-two years. Exod. 12:40 ("Now the sojourning of the children of Israel, who dwelt in Egypt, was four hundred and thirty years.") makes the "sojourning" 430 years, but Gal. 3:16, 17 ("Now to Abraham and his seed were the promises made.... And this I say, that the covenant, that was confirmed before of God in Christ, the law, which was four hundred and thirty years after, cannot disannul, that it should make the promise of none effect.") makes it evident that this period commences from the call of Abraham, and was *not* the period of bondage and affliction in Egypt foretold by God. Acts 7:6 ("And God spake on this wise, That his seed should sojourn in a strange land; and that they should bring them into bondage, and entreat them evil four hundred years."), however, accepts and repeats the erroneous view which Paul and the orthodox chronology have to correct. Moses was only the great grandson of Levi (Exod. 6:16, 18, 20: And these are the names of the sons of Levi according to their generations; Gershon, and Kohath, and Merari: and the years of the life of Levi were an hundred thirty and seven years. . . . And the sons of Kohath; Amram, and Izhar, and Hebron, and Uzziel: and the years of the life of Kohath were an hundred thirty and three years. . . . And Amram took him Jochebed his father's sister to wife; and she bare him Aaron and Moses: and the years of the life of Amram were an hundred and thirty and seven years.), and to make four generations cover 430 years would be absurd. Josephus (*Antiquities, book 2, chapter 15*) says the Jews were in Egypt 215 years, and this agrees with the Samaritan and the Septuagint.]

The Jews to return from Egypt in the fourth generation from Abraham.

And thou [Abram*] shalt go to thy fathers in peace; thou shalt be buried in a good old age. But in the fourth generation they shall come hither again. Gen. 15:15,16.

[The Jews did not return from their Egyptian slavery in the fourth generation from Abraham, nor till long afterwards. Joseph and his brethren were the fourth generation from Abraham.]

Jewish territory to extend from the Nile to the Euphrates.

In the same day the LORD made a covenant with Abram, saying, "Unto thy seed have I given this land, from the river of Egypt unto the great river, the river Euphrates." Gen. 15:18.

Turn you, and take your journey, and go to the mount of the Amorites, and unto all the places nigh thereunto, in the plain, in the hills, and in the vale, and in the south, and by the sea side, to the land of the Canaanites, and unto Lebanon, unto the great river, the river Euphrates. Behold, I have set the land before you: go in and possess the land which the LORD sware unto your fathers, Abraham, Isaac, and Jacob, to give unto them and to their seed after them. Deut. 1:7, 8.

[The Israelitish territory never extended to the river of Egypt, and it is questionable whether it ever extended to the Euphrates.]

Sarah to be a mother of nations.

And God said unto Abraham, "As for Sarai thy wife . . . I will bless her,

---

*The name of Abram was changed to Abraham by God's order. (Gen. 17:5: Neither shall thy name any more be called Abram, but thy name shall be Abraham; for a father of many nations have I made thee.) In this text, all citations prior to Gen. 17:5 give Abram and all those after use Abraham.

and she shall be a mother of nations." Gen. 17:15, 16.

[The only nation descended from Sarah were the Jews. God also promised Abraham that he should be the father of many nations, but only four nations appear to have descended from him, namely the Jews, the Ishmaelites, the Midianites, and the Edomites.]

Canaan promised to Jacob.

And, behold, the LORD stood above it, and said, "I am the LORD God of Abraham thy father, and the God of Isaac: the land whereon thou liest, to thee will I give it, and to thy seed." Gen. 28:13.

[Jacob never received the promised land, and it is questionable whether the spot on which he then lay ever came into the possession of his descendants.]

Abraham, Jacob, and the Jews to be a blessing to all mankind.

In thee [Abram] shall all families of the earth be blessed. Gen. 12:3.

And in thy seed shall all the nations of the earth be blessed. Gen. 22:18; 26:4.

And in thee [Jacob] and in thy seed shall all the families of the earth be blessed. Gen. 28:14.

[All the nations of the earth have not been particularly blessed in Abraham, or in Jacob, or in their descendants, the Jews. The Christians claim that Christ fulfilled this prophecy by giving Christianity to the world (Acts 3:25, 26: Ye are the children of the prophets, and of the covenant which God made with our fathers, saying unto Abraham, "And in thy seed shall all the kindred, of the earth be blessed." Unto you first God, having raised up his Son Jesus, sent him to bless you, in turning away every one of you from his iniquities"; Gal. 3:8, 9: And the scripture, foreseeing that God would justify the heathen through faith, preached before the gospel unto Abraham, saying, "In thee shall all nations be blessed." So then they which be of faith are blessed with faithful Abraham.). But this assumes that Christianity has been a blessing, whereas history shows that it has been a curse. Even supposing, for argument's sake, that Christianity is a blessing, the prophecy remains unfulfilled. The Chinese, the Hindus, the Jews themselves, and, in fact, the larger part of the population of the globe, are still unbelievers in Christ. Christ said he came not to bring peace, but a sword. The household strife which he promised, and the national and religious strife of which it was the type can hardly be described as blessing all families of all nations. And as the majority of people are to go to hell, the absurdity of describing Christianity as a blessing to *all* families and nations on earth is obvious.]

Jacob to return from Egypt.

And he said, "I am God. . . . I will go down with thee into Egypt; and I will also surely bring thee up again." Gen. 46:3,4.

[God did not bring Jacob back again from Egypt, as he promised. And Jacob lived in the land of Egypt seventeen years: so the whole age of Jacob was an hundred forty and seven years. And the time drew nigh that Israel must die: and he called his son Joseph, and said unto him, "If now I have found grace in thy sight, put, I pray thee, thy hand under my thigh, and deal kindly and truly with me; bury me not, I pray thee, in Egypt." Gen. 47:28, 29.]

Judah to remain an independent state till Christ (?) came.

The sceptre shall not depart from Judah, nor a lawgiver from between his feet, until Shiloh come; and unto him shall the gathering of the people be. Gen. 49:10.

[Shiloh was a place where the national gatherings took place before Jerusalem was taken by David. The true reading is "until he come to Shiloh" (see marginal note in Revised Version). The Christians pretend that Shiloh means Christ; but, if so, the prophecy was falsified, for the King of Judah was carried away captive by Nebuchadnezzar, Jerusalem and the temple were burnt, and all the leading Jews were taken away to Babylon. All this took place 588 years before the alleged birth of Christ, the alleged Shiloh of the prophecy.]

The promised land to be fertile and extensive.

And the LORD said, "I have surely seen the affliction of my people which are in Egypt. . . . And I am come down . . . to bring them up out of that land unto a good land and a large, unto a land flowing with milk and honey." Exod. 3:7, 8.

[Palestine was neither a good land nor a large. Far from being a land which might poetically be described as flowing with milk and honey, it is, and always must have been within historic times, a barren and desolate land in the main. In size it was little larger than Wales. Of course, the Jews were infatuated with their own land, but this is no reason why other people should accept their patriotic illusions as facts.]

Christ (?) to smite the corners of Moab.

There shall come a Star out of Jacob, and a Sceptre shall rise out of Israel, and shall smite the corners of Moab, and destroy all the children of Sheth. Num. 24:17.

[Christians, stupidly enough, say this is a remarkable prophecy of

Christ, but Christ had no sceptre except a mock one; and he did not smite the corners of Moab or destroy the children of Sheth. Some say it refers to Christ, through David, who was a type and ancestor of Jesus Christ.]

Phinehas and his sons to retain the priesthood for ever.

And the LORD spake unto Moses, saying, "Phinehas, the son of Eleazar, the son of Aaron the priest, hath turned my wrath away from the children of Israel. . . . Wherefore say, 'Behold, I give unto him my covenant of peace: and he shall have it, and his seed after him, even the covenant of an everlasting priesthood.' "Num. 25:10-13.

[The "everlasting" priesthood was subsequently transferred to the descendants of another son of Aaron. It was restored, however, by Solomon to Zadok, who was descended from Phineas (1 Chron. 6:4-8: And Phinehas begat Abishua, and Abishua begat Bukki, and Bukki begat Uzzi, and Uzzi begat Zerahiah, and Zerahiah begat Meraioth, Meraioth begat Amariah, and Amariah begat Ahitub. And Ahitub begat Zadok.), with whose family the eternal priesthood continued as long as it lasted.]

The earth to be destroyed and to remain for ever.

The earth, which the LORD thy God giveth thee, for ever. Deut. 4:40.

The earth abideth for ever. Eccles. 1:4.

Who laid the foundations of the earth, that it should not be removed for ever. Ps. 104:5.

The earth also and the works that are therein shall be burned up . . . all these things shall be dissolved. 2 Peter 3:10, 11.

[One of these two conflicting outcomes will evidently be falsified.]

The Jews to be borrowers, and not lenders.

He shall lend to thee, and thou shalt not lend to him . . . all these curses shall come upon thee . . . and they shall be upon thee for a sign and for a wonder, and upon thy seed for ever. Deut. 28:44-46.

[If the Jews were always in debt instead of being great money lenders, Christians would claim this as a most remarkable prophecy.]

Naphtali's possessions wrongly assigned.

And of Naphtali he said, "O Naphtali . . . possess thou the west and the south." Deut. 33:23.

[Naphtali received a district in the north of Palestine, but none in the south or west.]

164

God falsifies his promise to Eli, and makes another almost equally futile concerning Samuel.

And there came a man of God unto Eli, and said unto him. . . . "The LORD God of Israel saith, 'I said indeed that thy house, and the house of thy father, should walk before me for ever:' but now the LORD saith, 'Be it far from me. . . . And I will raise me up a faithful priest, that shall do according to that which is in mine heart and in my mind: and I will build him a sure house; and he shall walk before mine anointed for ever.' " 1 Sam. 2:27, 30, 35.

[God's idea of revoking his "sure" prophecies, and making them conditional when it suits him, is rich. Samuel is clearly the faithful priest who was to replace Eli; but he had no sure house built up, and his sons were almost as bad as Eli's (1 Sam. 8:3: And his sons walked not in his ways, but turned aside after lucre, and took bribes, and perverted judgment.). Neither he nor descendants of his walked before God's anointed for ever, unless "for ever" means an exceedingly limited period.]

David's kingdom to be eternal, and his descendants to rule for ever.

I have made a covenant with my chosen, I have sworn unto David my servant, "Thy seed will I establish for ever, and build up thy throne to all generations." Ps. 89:3, 4.

Once have I sworn by my holiness that I will not lie unto David. His seed shall endure for ever, and his throne as the sun before me. It shall be established for ever as the moon, and as a faithful witness in heaven. Ps. 89:35-37.

And thine house and thy kingdom shall be established for ever before thee: thy throne shall be established for ever. 2 Sam. 7:16.

For thus saith the LORD: David shall never want a man to sit upon the throne of the house of Israel. Jer. 33:17.

[These flattering promises have certainly not been kept. Christians pretend that a spiritual kingdom is meant, of which Christ is king. This interpretation does violence to the whole spirit and language of the divine promises made to King David.]

Solomon's throne to be everlasting.

I will stablish his throne [Solomon's] for ever. . . . I will settle him in mine house and in my kingdom for ever: and his throne shall be established for evermore. 1 Chron. 17:12, 14.

I will stablish the throne of his kingdom for ever. 2 Sam. 7:13.

["Evermore" meant about four hundred years, at the end of which period the kingdom ceased and was never restored. The greater part of the kingdom, moreover, revolted from the sway of Solomon's own son, and it was never brought into subjection again; so firmly was the kingdom "stablished" for evermore.]

Israel to be established in their own land for ever.

Because thy God loved Israel, to establish them for ever. 2 Chron. 9:8.

Moreover, I will appoint a place for my people Israel, and will plant them, that they may dwell in a place of their own, and move no more; neither shall the children of wickedness afflict them any more, as beforetime. 2 Sam. 7:10.

[This is still unfulfilled, for the Jews are scattered over the world.]

Josiah's end to be peaceful.

Thou [Josiah] shalt be gathered into thy grave in peace. 2 Kings 22:20.

[Notwithstanding this prophecy, Josiah was slain in battle. (In his days Pharaoh nechoh king of Egypt went up against the king of Assyria to the river Euphrates: and king Josiah went against him; and he slew him at Megiddo, when he had seen him. And his servants carried him in a chariot dead from Megiddo, and brought him to Jerusalem, and buried him in his own sepulchre. And the people of the land took Jehoahaz the son of Josiah, and anointed him, and made him king in his father's stead. 2 Kings 23:29, 30.]

Ahaz is assured that the Syrian league against him shall fail.

Then said the LORD unto Isaiah, "Go forth now to meet Ahaz. . . . And say unto him, 'Take heed, and be quiet; fear not, neither be fainthearted for the two tails of these smoking firebrands, for the fierce anger of Rezin with Syria, and of the son of Remaliah. Because Syria, Ephraim, and the son of Remaliah, have taken evil counsel against thee, saying, "Let us go up against Judah, and vex it, and let us make a breach therein for us, and set a king in the midst of it, even the son of Tabeal"'": Thus said the LORD God, "It shall not stand, neither shall it come to pass." Isa. 7:3-7.

[If King Ahaz trusted in the divine assurances put forward by Isaiah, he must have been woefully deceived, for we read in 2 Chron. 28:5, 6 that "The LORD his God delivered him into the hand of the king of Syria; and they smote him, and carried away a great multitude of them captives, and brought them to Damascus. And he was also delivered into the hand of the king of Israel, who smote him with a great slaughter. For Pekah the son of Remaliah slew in Judah an hundred and twenty thousand in one day, which were all valiant men." Ahaz sought assistance from the king of Assyria, but he only "distressed him" and "helped him not." 2 Chron. 28:20, 21.]

Universal peace.

Out of Zion shall go forth the law, and the word of the LORD from Jerusalem. And he shall judge among the nations, and shall rebuke many people: and they shall beat their swords into plowshares, and their spears into pruninghooks: nation shall not lift up sword against nation, neither shall they learn war any more. Isa. 2:3, 4.

[Neither figuratively nor literally have these optimistic anticipations come to pass. Christians pretend that their talk about peace and love fulfills these prophecies in the spirit. But the same Christians also point out how strikingly Christ's declaration, that he came not to send peace, but a sword, has been fulfilled in the religious and political wars that have desolated the earth.]

Pretended prophecy of a virgin mother.

Therefore the Lord himself shall give you a sign; Behold, a virgin shall conceive, and bear a son, and shall call his name Immanuel. Butter and honey shall he eat, that he may know to refuse the evil, and choose the good. For before the child shall know to refuse the evil, and choose the good, the land that thou abhorrest shall be forsaken of both her kings. Isa. 7:14-16.

[Christians persist in claiming this as one of the most striking prophecies of Christ, although the context clearly shows that it is nothing of the kind. But Christ was *not* born of a virgin. The Christians assert that he was, and then take their utterly unfounded and unproven assertion of an impossible occurrence as proof of the fulfillment of a prophecy which they have distorted from its plain original meaning and purpose. Christ was not called Immanuel except by those who do so in order to fulfill the alleged prophecy. He was called Jesus. The word translated virgin only means a young woman, and the context (Isa. 8:1-4: Moreover the LORD said unto me, "Take thee a great roll, and write in it with a man's pen concerning Mahershalalhashbaz." And I took unto me faithful witnesses to record, Uriah the priest, and Zechariah the son of Jeberechiah. And I went unto the prophetess; and she conceived, and bare a son. Then said the LORD to me, "Call his name Mahershalalhashbaz. For before the child shall have knowledge to cry, 'My father,' and 'My mother,' the riches of Damascus and the spoil of Samaria shall be taken away before the king of Assyria.") describing how the prophet set about fulfilling his prophecy, shows that the conception of the child was to be in a purely natural way. There is nothing remarkable in the expectation that a person who is a virgin *now*, shall become a mother at some future date.]

Christ's governorship and titles.

For unto us a child is born, unto us a son is given: and the government shall be upon his shoulder: and his name shall be called Wonderful, Counsellor, The mighty God, The everlasting Father, The Prince of Peace. Isa. 9:6.

[Christians claim this as a prophecy of Jesus Christ. But the government was never upon his shoulder. Nobody calls Jesus by the name "Wonderful," or "Counsellor." Jesus is scarcely called, or thought of as, the mighty God, but as the redeeming or atoning God. He is never termed the everlasting Father. He is the everlasting *Son*, and Christians can hardly suppose that the Holy Ghost inspired Isaiah to commit the damnable heresy of confounding the persons. Christ has indeed been flatteringly *called* the "Prince of Peace," but his own emphatic declaration was that he came "not to send peace, but a sword" (Matt. 10:34). This latter prediction has certainly been fulfilled. A Prince of Peace who brings not peace but a sword is very convenient for fulfilling conflicting prophecies.]

Christ to destroy the wicked and establish peace.

And there shall come forth a rod out of the stem of Jesse, and a Branch shall grow out of his roots. . . . And he shall smite the earth with the rod of his mouth, and with the breath of his lips shall he slay the wicked. . . . The wolf also shall dwell with the lamb, and the leopard shall lie down with the kid; and the calf and the young lion and the fatling together; and a little child shall lead them. And the cow and the bear shall feed; their young ones shall lie down together: and the lion shall eat straw like the ox. Isa. 11:1, 4, 6, 7.

[Christians say this prophecy refers to Christ. But the meek victim who went as a lamb to the slaughter can hardly be described as slaying the wicked with the breath of his mouth. Certainly he never brought the era of universal peace with him. Beasts and nations still fight and slay as of yore.]

Circumstances connected with Christ's coming.

And in that day there shall be a root of Jesse, which shall stand for an ensign of the people; to it shall the Gentiles seek.... And he shall set up an ensign for the nations, and shall assemble the outcasts of Israel, and gather together the dispersed of Judah from the four corners of the earth. The envy also of Ephraim shall depart, and the adversaries of Judah shall be cut off.... They shall spoil them of the east together: they shall lay their hand upon Edom and Moab; and the children of Ammon shall obey them. And the LORD shall utterly destroy the tongue of the Egyptian sea; and with his mighty wind shall he shake his hand over the river, and shall smite it in the seven streams, and make men go over dryshod. Isa. 11:12-15.

[There is a continuation of the prophecy already given. Christians say the root of Jesus is Jesse, to whom Gentiles seek even more than do the Jews. But the lost tribes are irrevocably lost, except in the imagination of certain fanatics. They have not been restored together with the people of Judah from the four corners of the earth, and it is difficult to see how they ever can be. Another difficulty is how the universal peace, etc., prophesied in verses 5 to 9 (See above.) is to be accompanied by the cutting off of adversaries (verse 13) and the spoiling of them of the east, etc. (verse 14). The destruction of the Sinatic gulf and the drying up of the Nile are as yet unmentioned in history.]

Damascus to be destroyed.

The burden of Damascus. Behold, Damascus is taken away from being a city, and it shall be a ruinous heap. Isa. 17:10.

[Damascus has been fortunate rather than otherwise. It is still in a fairly prosperous condition.]

Egypt's troubles; the Nile to be dried up, etc.

The burden of Egypt.... The waters shall fail from the sea, and the river shall be wasted and dried up.... Neither shall there be any work for Egypt, which the head or tail, branch or rush, may do.... And the land of Judah shall be a terror unto Egypt, every one that maketh mention thereof shall be afraid in himself. Isa. 19:1, 5, 15, 17.

[History fails to record the fulfillment of these inspired predictions launched against Egypt.]

Fabulous animals to exist.

The weaned child shall put his hand on the cockatrice' den. Isa. 11:8. And the unicorns shall come down with them, and the bullocks with the bulls. Isa. 34:7.

Babylon . . . satyrs shall dance there . . . and dragons. Isa. 13:19-22.

[Seeing that cockatrices (serpents hatched from cock's eggs), unicorns, satyrs, and dragons are purely imaginary creatures, it is difficult to see how these prophecies can be fulfilled. Those who think that Isaiah spoke figuratively in *all* these cases should read the context.]

Jerusalem to enjoy perpetual safety.

Thine eyes shall see Jerusalem a quiet habitation, a tabernacle that shall not be taken down; not one of the stakes thereof ever be removed, neither shall any of the cords thereof be broken. Isa. 33:20.

[If Jerusalem had suffered no calamities after the return from captivity, this would be pointed to as a highly significant prophecy. As it is unfulfilled, its realization is postponed to a distant future.]

Every high place or person to be brought low, and vice versa. The whole of mankind to behold God's glory revealed.

Every valley shall be exalted, and every mountain and hill shall be made low. . . . And the glory of the LORD shall be revealed, and all flesh shall see it together: for the mouth of the LORD hath spoken it. Isa. 40:4, 5.

[Christians refer this prophecy to Christ; but "all flesh" have not seen the glorious revelation, or even heard of it, although nearly two thousand years have elapsed since the boasted fulfillment in Christ.]

Christ not to lift up his voice in the street, or to be violent or be discouraged.

He shall not cry, nor lift up, nor cause his voice to be heard in the street. A bruised reed shall he not break, and the smoking flax shall he not quench. . . . He shall not fail nor be discouraged, till he have set judgment in the earth. Isa. 42:2-4.

[Christians consider that these prophecies were wonderfully fulfilled in Jesus Christ. But Christ often cried aloud and lifted up his voice in public thoroughfares and open spaces. Scourging tradesmen and upsetting their tables does not display great tenderness or gentleness of disposition. Christ failed and was discouraged long before he set judgment in the earth, unless the latter phrase be twisted into meaning anything the Christian chooses. Christ's exclamation, "My God, my God, why hast thou forsaken me?" (Matt. 27:46; Mark 15:34) shows that Christ *was* discouraged.]

170

No uncircumcised or unclean persons to enter Jerusalem.
Awake, awake; put on thy strength, O Zion; put on thy beautiful garments, O Jerusalem, the holy city; for henceforth there shall no more come into thee the uncircumcised and the unclean. Isa. 52:1.
[As this has obviously not been fulfilled so far as the real Jerusalem is concerned, Christians have to refer it to a spiritual Jerusalem, or ideal state of good. To prophesy that ideal good shall not admit the morally bad is like prophesying a kind of whiteness which shall not be black.]

The Lord's salvation to be seen by all the world.
The LORD had made bare his holy arm in the eyes of all the nations; and all the ends of the earth shall see the salvation of our God. Isa. 52:10.
[The bulk of mankind has never heard of the Christian scheme of salvation even yet; so that this prophecy is still unfulfilled, however much Christian fanatics may boast to the contrary.]

Christ (?) to be extolled, but his form and visage to be dreadfully marred.
Behold, my servant shall deal prudently, he shall be exalted and extolled, and be very high. As many were astonied at thee; his visage was so marred more than any man, and his form more than the sons of men. Isa. 52:13, 14.
[Christians refer this to Christ, and have to explain it all away as fulfilled in some roundabout spiritual way, by which means anything can be made to mean anything required.]

Christ (?) to be withered and ugly.
For he shall grow up before him as a tender plant, and as a root out of a dry ground; he hath no form nor comeliness; and when we shall see him, there is no beauty that we should desire him. Isa. 53:2.
[According to Luke 2:40 the child Jesus "grew and waxed strong in spirit, filled with wisdom: and the grace of God was upon him." He "increased in wisdom and stature, and in favour with God and man" (Luke 2:52). There are no indications that Christ was a tender plant, or a withered root, or that he was frightfully ugly. As the "common people heard him gladly" (Mark 12:37), and he was "glorified of all" (Luke 4:15), the deformity prophesied of Christ can hardly be explained as repulsiveness of manners or morals.]

Christ (?) to bear our sickness, sorrows, and sins for us.
Surely he hath borne our griefs and carried our sorrows. . . . with his

stripes we are healed . . . and the LORD hath laid on him the iniquity of us all. Isa. 53:4, 5, 6.

[Christians assert that all this is fulfilled by the atoning death of Jesus, whose sacrifice on the cross was the propitiation for the sins of the whole world. But they are totally unable to produce any proofs of their assertion. We suffer our sorrows and the natural punishments of our "sins" just the same as ever. The empty pretence that Christ bore all the sins of the whole world is a worthless and mischievous falsehood. A similar criticism applies to many other prophecies which Christians regard as fulfilled by virtue of their mere assertion to that effect. The word translated "griefs" is sicknesses in the original; see Revised Version, marginal note.]

Christ (?) to be silent before his judges.

As a sheep before her shearers is dumb, so he openeth not his mouth. Isa. 53:7.

[Although apparently supported by Matt. 27:14 (See below.) this prophecy was falsified according to John 18:20-23, 33-37 (See below.), which shows that Christ answered Pilate and the chief priest at some little length.]

And he answered him to never a word; insomuch that the governor marvelled greatly. Matt. 27:14.

Jesus answered him, "I spake openly to the world; I ever taught in the synagogue, and in the temple, whither the Jews always resort; and in secret have I said nothing. Why askest thou me? ask them which heard me, what I have said unto them: behold, they know what I said." And when he had thus spoken, one of the officers which stood by struck Jesus with the palm of his hand, saying, "Answerest thou the high priest so?" Jesus answered him, "If I have spoken evil, bear witness of the evil: but if well, why smitest thou me?" . . . Then Pilate entered into the judgment hall again, and called Jesus, and said unto him, "Art thou the King of the Jews?" Jesus answered him, "Sayest thou this thing of thyself, or did others tell it thee of me?" Pilate answered, "Am I a Jew? Thine own nation and the chief priest have delivered thee unto me: what hast thou done?" Jesus answered, "My kingdom is not of this world: if my kingdom were of this world, then would my servants fight, that I should not be delivered to the Jews: but now is my kingdom not from hence." Pilate therefore said unto him, "Art thou a king then?" Jesus answered, "Thou sayest that I am a king. To this end was I born, and for this cause came I into the world, that I should bear witness unto the truth. Every one that is of the truth heareth my voice." John 18:20-23, 33-37.

172

Christ (?) to be buried with criminals and to be executed in company with rich men.

And he made his grave with the wicked, and with the rich in his death. Isa. 53:9.

[According to the Gospel narrative, this prophecy was falsified by being reversed. Christ made his *grave* with the *rich* by being buried in the sepulchre of the rich Joseph of Arimathea: and he was with the *wicked* (the crucified thieves, not rich people) in his *death*.]

Christ (?) never to employ any violence or deceit.

Because he had done no violence, neither was any deceit in his mouth. Isa. 53:9

[Christ *had* committed acts of violence, if the New Testament is true. Scourge in hand, he had raised a disgraceful riot in the sacred precincts of the Temple. He had driven forth the dealers in sacred articles headlong, and had overturned the tables of the money-changers (John 2:15: And when he had made a scourge of small cords, he drove them all out of the temple, and the sheep, and the oxen; and poured out the changer's money, and overthrew the tables; Mark 11:15: And Jesus went into the temple, and began to cast out them that sold and bought in the temple, and overthrew the tables of the moneychangers, and the seats of them that sold doves.). The Christian pretence that Christ fulfilled the prophecy by never employing deceit is also stupidly untrue. We can only spare space to mention a few of his many equivocations and falsehoods. When he told the Jews he would raise the Temple in three days (Matt. 26:61; 27:40; Mark 14:58; 15:29; John 2:19-21), while secretly he referred only to the "temple" of his body, he used deceit. When he quickened the zeal of his disciples by telling them that the end of the world and his own triumphant return to judge all men should occur before the generation then living had passed away, he used deceit. And if the modern Christians who reduce hell-fire to a mere figure of speech are correct, Christ used diabolical deceit in terrifying the masses with such a horrible and debasing doctrine. The broken promises given later on in this work will afford further instances of the deceit which Christ employed for the purpose of alluring or terrifying the credulous.]

Christ's soul to be sacrificed; yet he is to prolong his days and see his descendants.

When thou shalt make his soul an offering for sin, he shall see his seed, he shall prolong his days. Isa. 53:10.

[Christ's *soul* was not sacrificed, but only his body. Christ had no children. He did not prolong his days by his crucifixion. Spiritual interpretations, of course, have to be resorted to here. "Seed" is made to mean "converts." Prolonging the days of the already eternal Jesus must mean making his life longer than eternity.]

Nations that do not submit to the Jewish sway are to perish.
For the nation and kingdom that will not serve thee shall perish; yea, those nations shall be utterly wasted. Isa. 60:12.

[Nations that remain unsubjugated by the Jews manage to flourish as yet, notwithstanding this inspired prophecy. If this poetical expression of a Jew's national hopes is perverted into a reference to Christ or his Church, then it may be pointed out that China and many other nations have flourished without Christ. As predictions like the above are unfulfilled, they will be postponed to a remote future, when "unto me every knee shall bow, every tongue shall swear" (Isa. 45:23; Phil. 2:10). But the majority, who are in hell, would falsify this prophecy, unless hell, as well as heaven, is to be peopled with worshippers.]

The sun's light to be sevenfold; violence to cease, etc.
The light of the moon shall be as the light of the sun, and the light of the sun shall be sevenfold, as the light of seven days. Isa. 30:26.

Violence shall no more be heard in thy land, wasting nor destruction within thy borders; but thou shalt call thy walls Salvation, and thy gates Praise. The sun shall be no more thy light by day; neither for brightness shall the moon give light unto thee; but the LORD shall be unto thee an everlasting light, and thy God thy glory. . . . Thy people also shall be all righteous: they shall inherit the land for ever. Isa. 60:18, 19, 21.

A new heaven and earth peopled with centenarians and peaceful carnivora.
For, behold, I create new heavens and a new earth: and the former shall not be remembered, nor come into mind. . . . There shall be no more thence an infant of days, nor an old man that hath not filled his days: for the child shall die an hundred years old. . . . The wolf and the lamb shall feed together, and the lion shall eat straw like the bullock: and dust shall be the serpent's meat. Isa. 65:17, 20, 25.

[Being partly figurative, perhaps, most partly literal, these extravagant predictions of longevity, peace, light, etc., will be made to mean whatever best suits Christian requirements.]

The Lord will and will not keep anger for ever.

"I am merciful," saith the Lord "and I will not keep anger for ever." Jer. 3:12.

Ye have kindled a fire in mine anger, which shall burn for ever. Jer. 17:4.

[One of these contradictory announcements will have to be falsified.]

Jerusalem to be supreme, and the lost tribes to be restored.

At that time they shall call Jerusalem the throne of the LORD; and all the nations shall be gathered unto it, to the name of the LORD, to Jerusalem: neither shall they walk any more after the imagination of their evil heart. In those days the house of Judah shall walk with the house of Israel, and they shall come together out of the land of the north to the land that I have given for an inheritance unto your fathers. Jer. 3:17, 18.

[As the ten "lost tribes" of Israel have disappeared, it is not easy to see how they can walk with the tribe of Judah.]

Christ (?) to be our Righteousness; to gather the dispersed Jews; and to reign over them as a prosperous king.

(3) "And I will gather the remnant of my flock out of all countries whither I have driven them, and will bring them again to their folds; and they shall be fruitful and increase.

(4) "And I will set up shepherds over them which shall feed them: and they shall fear no more, nor be dismayed, neither shall they be lacking," saith the LORD.

(5) "Behold, the days come," saith the LORD, "that I will raise unto David a righteous Branch, and a King shall reign and prosper, and shall execute judgment and justice in the earth.

(6) "In his days Judah shall be saved, and Israel shall dwell safely: and this is his name whereby he shall be called, THE LORD OUR RIGHTEOUSNESS.

(7) "Therefore, behold, the days come," saith the LORD, "that they shall no more say, 'The LORD liveth, which brought up the children of Israel out of the land of Egypt'; But, the LORD liveth, which brought up and which led the seed of the house of Israel out of the north country, and from all countries whither I had driven them; and they shall dwell in their own land." Jer. 23:3-8.

[The context as here given shows that the famous Christian prophecy of verses 5 and 6 is not fulfilled. No such restoration of the

175

Jews has taken place. Christ is not shown to be descended from David except by a clumsy piece of Christian sophistry, since Joseph was not his father. He was never a king, he did not reign, he did not prosper, and he did not execute judgment and still less justice in the earth. In his days Judah remained ignominiously subjugated by Gentiles, and Israel had apparently disappeared amidst captivities and misfortunes. The name whereby he was called was the very common one of Jesus, or Joshua, and there are no indications of his being called "the Lord of our righteousness," except occasionally by a few people who do so in order to fulfill the prophecy. The title really should be, as Matthew Arnold points out, "The Lord *is* our righteousness." But a dishonest translation, literally correct but morally a fraud, suited the Christian theory best. Our Revised Version, however, has to adopt the correct translation. The Douay Version translates the names as "The Lord our just one," thus depriving the prophecy of its apparently remarkable reference to the all-important Christian doctrine of imputed righteousness by faith in Christ.]

Christ (?) to reign and Judah to be our righteousness.
At that time, will I cause the Branch of righteousness to grow up unto David; and he shall execute justice and righteousness in the land. In those days shall Judah be saved, and Jerusalem shall dwell safely: and this is the name wherewith she shall be called, The LORD our righteousness. Jer. 33:15, 16.
[This is substantially a repetition of verses 5 and 6 in the preceding prophecy. But it differs in one important respect. It is *she* this time, and not *he*, that is to be called "The Lord our righteousness." Which is the correct version? As the special compound name is only applied in this latter case to Jerusalem or Judah, the translators have not attempted to bias the reader's mind by printing it in large capitals, as they did when it might plausibly be pointed to as a wonderful anticipation of an atoning redeemer, whose righteousness would be transferred to us. Neither Jerusalem nor Judah was actually called by the name prophesied.]

Egypt and all other nations to fall with wide and terrible slaughter, and to rise no more.
Then took I the cup at the LORD's hand, and made all the nations to drink, unto whom the LORD had sent me: to wit, Jerusalem, and the cities of Judah, and the kings thereof, and the princes thereof, to make them a desolation, an astonishment, an hissing, and a curse; as it is this day; Pharaoh king of Egypt, and his servants, and his princes, and all his

people. . . . and all the kingdoms of the world, which are upon the face of the earth. . . . Therefore thou shalt say unto them, "Thus said the LORD of hosts, the God of Israel: 'Drink ye, and be drunken, and spue, and fall, and rise no more. . . . The LORD shall roar from on high, and utter his voice from his holy habitation. . . . A great whirlwind shall be raised up from the coasts of the earth. And the slain of the LORD shall be at that day from one end of the earth even unto the other end of the earth: they shall not be lamented, neither gathered, nor buried; they shall be dung upon the ground.' " Jer. 25:17-19, 26, 27, 30, 32, 33.

[Egypt and "all the kingdoms of the world" have not fallen so as to "rise no more." The LORD's roaring from his holy habitation and the day of worldwide slaughter are as yet unrecorded in history.]

The ten tribes to be restored at the same time with Judah.

And I will cause the captivity of Judah and the captivity of Israel to return, and will build them, as at the first. Jer. 33.7

[There was no restoration of the "lost tribes" of Israel, only of Judah; and even Judah was not by any means re-established in its ancient power and freedom.]

Zedekiah to die in peace.

Yet hear the word of the LORD, O Zedekiah king of Judah. . . . that shalt die in peace. Jer. 34:4,5.

[Jeremiah's assurance was not worth much, for the prophet himself subsequently records that "the king of Babylon slew the sons of Zedekiah before his eyes. . . . Then he put out the eyes of Zedekiah; and the king of Babylon bound him in chains, and carried him to Babylon, and put him in prison till the day of his death." (Jer. 52:10, 11). This is hardly what an uninspired writer would describe as dying in peace.]

Jehoiakim to leave no offspring to sit on the throne of David.

Therefore thus saith the LORD of Jehoiakim king of Judah; "He shall have none to sit on the throne of David." Jer. 36:30.

[Jehoiakim was succeeded on the throne by his son Jehoiachin (2 Kings 24:6: So Jehoiakim slept with his fathers: and Jehoiachin his son reigned in his stead.), called also Jeconiah (1 Chron. 3:15, 16: And the sons of Josiah were, the firstborn Johanan, the second Jehoiakim, and third Zedekiah, the fourth Shallum. And the sons of Jehoiakim: Jeconiah his son, Zedekiah his son.), from whom Matthew traces the descent of Jesus (See below.).]

[Matt 1:11: And Josias begat Jechonias and his brethren, about the time they were carried away to Babylon."; note the discrepancy in Matthew of the missing Jehoiakim, and compare Matt. 1:12: (And after they were brought into Babylon, Jechonias begat Salathiel; and *Salathiel* begat *Zorobabel.*) with 1 Chron. 3:17-19 (And the sons of Jeconiah; Assir, Salathiel his son, Malchiram also, and Pedaiah, and Shenazar, Jecamiah, Hoshama, and Nedabiah. And the sons of *Pedaiah* were, *Zerubbabel,* and Shimei."). Christ was thus included in this prophecy, and if Christians say (truly enough) that he did not sit on the throne of David, then many prophecies which they say describe their Christ as sitting on the throne of David must have been falsified. Christians will probably reconcile these conflicting prophecies by pretending that Christ *did* and *did not* sit on the throne of David; he *was* king of Israel and he *was not.*]

Jehoiakim's body to be shamefully treated.
Therefore thus saith the LORD concerning Jehoiakim the son of Josiah king of Judah.... "He shall be buried with the burial of an ass, drawn and cast beyond the gates of Jerusalem." Jer. 22:18, 19.

His dead body shall be cast out in the day to the heat, and in the night to the frost. Jer. 36:30.

[2 Kings 24:6 shows that "Jehoiakim slept with his fathers." If the prophecy had been fulfilled, it is hardly likely that Jeremiah or the compilers of Kings and Chronicles would have misled readers by their subsequent silence, and by language implying the direct contrary of the prophecy.]

Nebuchadnezzar to capture Tyre and destroy it for ever.
Therefore thus saith the LORD God; "Behold, I am against thee, O Tyrus, and will cause many nations to come up against thee, as the sea causeth his waves to come up. And they shall destroy the walls of Tyrus, and break down her towers. . . . It shall be a place for the spreading of nets in the midst of the sea: for I have spoken it," saith the LORD God: and it shall become a spoil to the nations. . . . For thus saith the LORD God; "Behold, I will bring upon Tyrus Nebuchadnezzar king of Babylon . . . thy walls shall shake at the noise of the horsemen, and of the wheels, and of the chariots, when he shall enter into thy gates, as men enter into a city wherein is made a breach. With the hoofs of his horses shall he tread down all thy streets. . . . The sound of thy harps shall be no more heard. And I will make thee like the top of a rock: thou shalt be a place to spread nets upon; thou shalt be built no more: for I

the LORD have spoken it," saith the LORD God. Ezek. 26:3-5, 7, 10. 13-14.

Thou shalt be a terror, and never shalt be any more. Ezek. 27:36.

[Notwithstanding these prophecies, Nebuchadrezzar, or Nebuchadnezzar as the name is more usually spelled, failed to capture or destroy Tyre — a feat which was reserved for Alexander the Great, 240 years afterwards. Subsequently in spite of the prophecy, Tyre *was* built again, and is mentioned in the New Testament (See below.) The siege by Nebuchadnezzar lasted thirteen years. He took the outworks, but the town itself, being on an island, remained impregnable. Tyre is now inhabited by over 10,000 people.]

Acts 12:20: And Herod was highly displeased with them of Tyre and Sidon."

Luke 10:13: Woe unto thee, Chorazin! woe unto thee, Bethsaida! for if the mighty works had been done in Tyre and Sidon, which have been done in you, they had a great while ago repented, sitting in sackcloth and ashes.)

Nebuchadnezzar to seize the riches of Tyre.

And they shall make a spoil of thy riches, and make a prey of thy merchandise. Ezek. 26:12.

[This prophecy was falsified by the event, for Ezekiel himself (29:18) subsequently says: "Nebuchadrezzar king of Babylon caused his army to serve a great service against Tyrus: every head was made bald, and every shoulder was peeled: yet had he no wages, nor his army, for Tyrus, for the service that he had served against it." The inhabitants and their riches were on the island.]

Egypt to be utterly desolate for forty years..

Set thy face against Pharaoh king of Egypt, and prophesy against him, and against all Egypt. . . . And the land of Egypt shall be desolate and waste. . . . I will make the land of Egypt utterly waste and desolate, from the tower of Syrene even unto the border of Ethiopia. No foot of man shall pass through it, nor foot of beast shall pass through it, neither shall it be inhabited forty years. And I will make the land of Egypt desolate in the midst of the countries that are desolate, and her cities among the cities that are laid waste shall be desolate forty years: and I will scatter the Egyptians among the nations, and will disperse them through the countries. Yet thus saith the LORD God; At the end of forty years will I gather the Egyptians from the people whither they were scattered: and I will bring again the captivity of Egypt, and will cause them to return. Ezek. 29:2, 9, 10-14.

[There never has been a time since this rash prophecy when Egypt has been uninhabited for forty years, or indeed for a single day.]

Judah and the lost tribes to be reunited under one king.

And say unto them, "Thus said the LORD God: 'Behold, I will take the children of Israel from among the heathen, whither they be gone, and will gather them on every side, and bring them into their own land: and I will make them one nation in the land upon the mountains of Israel; and one king shall be king to them all; and they shall be no more two nations, neither shall they be divided into two kingdoms any more at all. . . . And they shall dwell in the land that I have given unto Jacob my servant, wherein your fathers have dwelt; and they shall dwell therein, even they, and their children, and their children's children for ever: and my servant David shall be their prince for ever.' " Ezek. 37:21, 22, 25.

[Unfulfilled prophecies of the restoration and union of the two kingdoms of Judah and Israel under a king are either deferred to a distant future or are interpreted spiritually as referring to Christ.]

Dates in Daniel.

(24) Seventy weeks are determined upon thy people and upon thy holy city, to finish the transgression, and to make an end of sins, and to make reconciliation for iniquity, and to bring in everlasting righteousness, and to seal up the vision and prophecy, and to anoint the most Holy.

(25) Know therefore and understand, that from the going forth of the commandment to restore and to build Jerusalem unto the Messiah the Prince shall be seven weeks, and threescore and two weeks: the street shall be built again, and the wall, even in troublous times.

(26) And after threescore and two weeks shall Messiah be cut off, but not for himself. Dan. 9:24-26.

[Christians pretend that this is a strikingly accurate prediction of the time of Christ's appearance and death. The "seventy weeks" they say mean prophetical weeks of years, though really they referred to the seventy years' captivity, which was a past event to the forger of the Book of Daniel. But seventy weeks of years, that is seventy sevens, equals 490 years; and as the orthodox chronology makes Daniel die B.C. 534, the prophecy must be at least 44 years out if it refers to the birth of Christ. Really it would be at least 77 years out, for the crucifixion or atonement must be looked to as the fulfillment of the prophecy. Verse 25 makes the period 483 years from the edict to restore Jerusalem,

180

which was issued by Cyrus in B.C. 536. So that this is wrong by at least 53 years. The prophecy in verse 25, that Messiah shall be cut off 434 years after his appearance is absurd; Jesus only lived 33 years. To date the period from the edict of restoration is inadmissible, because this would extinguish Messiah some fifty years before his appearance. (For fuller examination of this prophecy see the *Freethinker* for May 31 and June 7, 1885). The important alterations made in the Revised Version show the obscure nature of the original words and the bias which led our translators to colour their translation with Christian ideas. Thus the decisive word "Messiah" disappears altogether in the newer and more honest version, and the general phrase, "the anointed one," takes its place. The period between the edict and Christ's coming in verse 25 is also reduced from 69 weeks to seven weeks. And yet prophecies which have been thus misinterpreted or falsified in our Bible are held up as convincing proofs of the truth of Christianity! The prophecy that Messiah's death shall be "not for himself" becomes "he shall have nothing" in the Revised Version, while in the Douay Version it reads "the people that shall deny him shall not be his." Of what value are prophecies of so uncertain or flexible a nature that Christians can interpret them so variously?]

Universal inspiration.
And my people shall never be ashamed. And it shall come to pass afterward, that I will pour out my spirit upon all flesh; and your sons and your daughters shall prophesy, your old men shall dream dreams, your young men shall see visions. Joel 2:27, 28.
[Christians say this was fulfilled on the day of Pentecost and subsequently. But God did not by any means pour out his spirit on "all flesh." Nor are the Jews so hardened as never to have been ashamed amidst their poverty and afflictions.]

At the return from captivity all nations were to assemble near Jerusalem, and no strangers were henceforth to pass through that city; Egypt was to be desolate, and the restoration of Judah was to be everlasting.
For, behold, in those days, and in that time, when I shall bring again the captivity of Judah and Jerusalem, I will also gather all nations, and will bring them down into the valley of Jehoshaphat, and will plead with them there for my people and for my heritage Israel. . . . The LORD also shall roar out of Zion. . . . then shall Jerusalem be holy, and there shall no strangers pass through her any more. . . . Egypt shall be a desolation

181

. . . but Judah shall dwell for ever, and Jerusalem from generation to generation. Joel 3:1, 2, 16, 17, 19, 20.

[God did "bring again" the captivity — that is, he restored the Jews to their native land; but many of the events which were to accompany that restoration have altogether failed to happen.]

Israel to rise and not to rise.

The virgin of Israel is fallen; she shall no more rise. Amos 5:2.

Again I will build thee, and thou shalt be built, O virgin of Israel: thou shalt again be adorned with thy tabrets, and shalt go forth in the dances of them that make merry. Jer. 31:4.

[As these prophecies contradict each other, one of them must be fulfilled.]

Curses on Amaziah.

Then answered Amos and said to Amaziah . . . "Thus saith the LORD; 'Thy wife shall be an harlot in the city, and thy sons and thy daughters shall fall by the sword, and thy land shall be divided by line: and thou shalt die in a polluted land.' " Amos 7:14,17.

[The Bible in recording the events of Amaziah's reign (2 Kings 14; 2 Chron. 25) gives no hint of his wife's unfaithfulness or of his children's slaughter. His son Uzziah succeeded him on the throne and died a leper (See below.), so that he at least was not slain by the sword. Amaziah himself . . . was killed at Lachish (See below.) in Judah, a territory which at least was less "polluted" than any other in the ages of the prophets.]

Then all the people of Judah took Uzziah, who was sixteen years old, and made him king in the room of his father Amaziah. . . . And Uzziah the king was a leper unto the day of his death, and dwelt in a several house, being a leper. 2 Chron. 26:1, 21.

And the rest of the acts of Amaziah, are they not written in the book of the chronicles of the kings of Judah? Now they made a conspiracy against him in Jerusalem: and he fled to Lachish; but they sent after him to Lachish, and slew him there. 2 Kings 14:18, 19.

This is the inheritance of the tribe of the children of Judah according to their families. . . . Lachish, and Bozkath, and Eglon. Josh. 15:20, 39.

The restoration to be eternal.

"And I will bring again the captivity of my people of Israel, and they shall build the waste cities, and inhabit them. . . . and they shall no more be pulled up out of their land which I have given them," saith the LORD thy God. Amos 9:14, 15.

182

[The prophecy of the return from captivity was fulfilled; but the flattering prediction of a continued possession of the land has been falsified.]

The alleged prophecy of Christ's birth at Bethlehem.

But thou, Bethlehem Ephratah, though thou be little among the thousands of Judah, yet out of thee shall he come forth unto me that is to be ruler in Israel; whose goings forth have been from of old, from everlasting. . . . And this man shall be the peace, when the Assyrian shall come into our land: and when he shall tread in our palaces, then shall we raise against him seven shepherds, and eight principal men. And they shall waste the land of Assyria with the sword, and the land of Nimrod in the entrances thereof; thus shall he deliver us from the Assyrian, when he cometh into our land, and when he treadeth within our borders. Mic. 5:2, 5, 6.

[Christians say this refers to Christ, who came from Nazareth in Galilee, but who is represented as having been born at Bethlehem in Judea. Bethlehem, the son of Ephratah, is mentioned among the descendants of Judah (1 Chron. 4:4: These are the sons of Hur, the firstborn of Ephratah, the father of Bethlehem.) Matthew, while grasping at the prophecy which he endeavours to fulfill by making Christ born at Bethlehem, yet in his translation of the prophecy describes this Bethlehem as not the least among the *princes* of Judah. David himself was of this race or locality (See below.) So that the remarkable part of the prophecy was evidently no prophecy at all, but merely a reference to the genealogy or birthplace of the great David, who in the person of a descendant was expected to restore the kingdom to Israel. Probably such prophecies as this and the lamentation in Psalm 22:1, 16-18 (See below.), gave birth to the traditions which are supposed to record their fulfillment. The reference to the "goings forth" of this expected ruler as having "been from of old, from everlasting," looks like a wonderful anticipation of the Christian doctrine that Jesus was also the eternal God himself. But, as Matthew Arnold points out, such language could only have been applied to Jehovah, and the true rendering undoubtedly could be "out of thee shall he that is to be ruler of Israel come forth unto me (Jehovah) whose goings forth have been from of old, from everlasting." The eternity ascribed to Jehovah by the prophet is transferred by the Christian translators to the expected king of the line of David. Thus prophecies are manufactured. Christ did not fulfill the prophecy, for he never was ruler in Israel, and did not deliver Israel from the Assyrian when he came into the land.]

183

Now David was the son of that Ephrathite of Bethlehemjudah, whose name was Jesse.... And David answered, "I am the son of thy servant Jesse the Bethlehemite." 1 Sam. 17:12, 58.

And Joseph also went up from Galilee ... into Judea, unto the city of David, which is called Bethlehem. Luke 2:4.

My God, my God, why hast thou forsaken me? why art thou so far from helping me, and from the words of my roaring? ... For dogs have compassed me: the assembly of the wicked have inclosed me; they pierced my hands and my feet. I may tell all my bones: they look and stare upon me. They part my garments among them, and cast lots upon my vesture. Ps. 22:1, 16-18.

The Jews to destroy all their enemies as a lion among sheep.

And the remnant of Jacob shall be among the Gentiles in the midst of many people as a lion among the beasts of the forest, as a young lion among the flocks of sheep: who, if he go through, both treadeth down, and teareth in pieces, and none can deliver. Thine hand shall be lifted up upon thine adversaries, and all thine enemies shall be cut off. Mic. 5:8, 9.

[This is a continuation of the prophecy just given. Christ's birth at Bethlehem was never accompanied or followed by the circumstances prophesied. The remnant of Jacob did not exterminate all their enemies, or rage as successfully among them as a lion among sheep.]

The Jews to be a guileless race.

The remnant of Israel shall not do iniquity, nor speak lies; neither shall a deceitful tongue be found in their mouth. Zeph. 3:13.

[Jews are not very specially conspicuous as absolutely truthful and just.]

Christ to come after a universal earthquake; and the second temple to be more glorious than the first.

For thus saith the LORD of hosts: "Yet once, it is a little while, and I will shake the heavens, and the earth, and the sea, and the dry land; and I will shake all nations, and the desire of all nations shall come: and I will fill this house with glory," saith the LORD of hosts.... "The glory of this latter house shall be greater than of the former," saith the LORD of hosts: "and in this place will I give peace," saith the LORD of hosts. Hag. 2:6-7, 9.

[The universal earthquake which was to precede Christ's coming appears to have passed unnoticed. Christ was not "the desire of all nations," as Christians pretend. The Revised Version alters this into

184

"the desirable things of the nations shall come." The glory of the second temple never exceeded that of the first, although Christians boast that it did because Christ entered it. So far from Christ coming in "a little while," he did not come till 500 years after the prophecy. Verses 21-23 (Speak to Zerubbabel, governor of Judah, saying, "I will shake the heavens and the earth; And I will overthrow the throne of kingdoms, and I will destroy the strength of the kingdoms of the heathen; and I will overthrow the chariots, and those that ride in them; and the horses and their riders shall come down, every one by the sword of his brother. In that day," saith the LORD of hosts, "I will take thee, O Zerubbabel, my servant, the son of Shealtiel," saith the LORD, "and will make thee as a signet: for I have chosen thee," saith the LORD of hosts.) show that Zerubbabel, the then governor of Jerusalem, was to be taken by the LORD "in that day" and made as a signet, showing clearly that Haggai's prophecy referred to the immediate future, and not to Jesus.]

No rain for nations that do not keep an annual feast at Jerusalem.
And it shall be, that whoso will not come up of all the families of the earth into Jerusalem to worship the King, the LORD of hosts, even upon them shall be no rain. And if the family of Egypt go not up, and come not, that have no rain; there shall be the plague, wherewith the LORD will smite the heathen that come not up to keep the feast of tabernacles. This shall be the punishment of Egypt, and the punishment of all nations that come not up to keep the feast of tabernacles. In that day shall there be upon the bells of the horses, "HOLINESS UNTO THE LORD." Zech. 14:17-20.
[There is no sign of the fulfillment of this prophecy as yet, nor is there likely to be.]

Elijah to return to earth to prepare the world for Christ's coming.
Behold, I will send you Elijah the prophet before the coming of the great and dreadful day of the LORD: and he shall turn the heart of the fathers to the children, and the heart of the children to their fathers, lest I come and smite the earth with a curse. Mal. 4:5, 6.
[As Elijah did not come, Jesus fulfills the prophecy in a very easy fashion by declaring that John the Baptist was this "Elias, which was for to come" (Matt. 11:14). The "great and dreadful day" which Elijah was to herald does not seem to have arrived yet. John and Jesus did not cause union among the Jews, but only further division and strife. Jesus says that Elias or John came before him and "restoreth all things" (See

below.) — a prophecy or announcement which is absurdly wide of the mark.]

And they asked him, saying, "Why say the scribes that Elias must first come?" And he answered and told them, "Elias verily cometh first, and restoreth all things; and how it is written of the Son of man, that he must suffer many things, and be set at naught. But I say unto you, that Elias is indeed come, and they have done unto him whatsoever they listed, as it is written of him." Mark 9:11-13.

II. NEW TESTAMENT

Jesus to be enthroned as the king of the Jews.

The LORD God shall give unto him the throne of his father David: And he shall reign over the house of Jacob for ever. . . . Luke 1:32, 33.

[As Jesus never received the throne of David, nor reigned over the house of Jacob, who indeed rejected him, this prophecy is interpreted in a spiritual or figurative sense. Even then it is still unfulfilled, for the Jews still reject the Gospel, so that Jesus does not reign over them except in a sense which makes him reign over everything as God.]

Jesus to deliver the Jews from their foes.

That we should be saved from our enemies, and from the hand of all that hate us; to perform the mercy promised to our fathers, and to remember his holy covenant; the oath which he swore to our father Abraham, that he would grant unto us, that we being delivered out of the hand of our enemies might serve him without fear, in holiness and righteousness before him, all the days of our life. Luke 1:71-75.

[Neither John the Baptist nor Jesus Christ brought about the fulfillment of this inspired prophecy, or the fulfillment of God's covenant with Abraham. The Jews were *not* delivered from the hands of their enemies, but remained in subjection under the Romans until the horrors of the siege of Jerusalem, excited by fanatical hopes of Messianic deliverance, ended in national destruction and the hardships of dispersion and exile.]

Meekness will bring proprietorship of land.

Blessed are the meek: for they shall inherit the earth. Matt. 5:5.

[This divine promise is not particularly well kept at present. The strong and enterprising nations still conquer the weak, and the meek lag behind in the race of life. Half the soil of England is owned by the House of Lords, and they are a particularly "meek" body! The meek *may* inherit the earth, but they have not made a beginning yet.]

Christ not to abolish the law, which is eternal and unalterable.

Think not that I am come to destroy the law, or the prophets: I am not come to destroy, but to fulfil. For verily I say unto you, Till heaven and earth pass, one jot or one tittle shall in no wise pass from the law, till all be fulfilled. Whosoever therefore shall break one of these least commandments, and shall teach men so, he shall be called the least in the kingdom of heaven: but whosoever shall do and teach them, the same shall be called great in the kingdom of heaven. Matt. 5:17-19.

And it is easier for heaven and earth to pass, than one tittle of the law to fail. Luke 16:17.

[Paul, on the contrary, declares that Christ "abolished" the law (Eph. 2:15: Having abolished in his flesh the enmity, even the law of commandments contained in ordinances. . .), that he "delivered" us from the law (Rom. 7:6: But now we are delivered from the law, that being dead wherein we were held; that we should serve in newness of spirit, and not in the oldness of the letter.), that Christians "are not under the law" (Rom. 6:14: For sin shall not have dominion over you: for ye are not under the law, but under grace; Rom. 3:28: Therefore we conclude that a man is justified by faith without the deeds of the law.), and that "Christ hath redeemed us from the curse of the law" (Gal. 3:13: Christ hath redeemed us from the curse of the law, being made a curse for us: for it is written, "Cursed is every one that hangeth on a tree."). Jesus said that all who came before him —including, of course, Moses and the prophets — are thieves and robbers. (John 10:8: All that ever came before me are thieves and robbers: but the sheep did not hear them.) Christians contend that the expression "till all be fulfilled" limited the supremacy of the law to Christ's crucifixion, which they pretend fulfilled all the law, and ended it or abolished it without destroying it. If Jesus meant this, he was guilty of paltry equivocation. He tried to make himself popular with the Jews by a most emphatic but most delusive promise, which he privately understood in a non-natural sense. Why did he use the emphatic words "till heaven and earth pass" if he only meant a period of three years at most? If he secretly meant that Christianity would only carry out the Mosaic law in some spiritual sense, he cheated the Jews by not explaining this important mental reservation to them.]

Pious improvidence will secure all things needful.

Take therefore no thought for the morrow: for the morrow shall take thought for the things of itself. Matt. 6:34.

If then God so clothe the grass, which is to day in the field, and to morrow is cast into the oven; how much more will he clothe you, O ye of little faith? And seek not ye what ye shall eat, or what ye shall drink, neither be ye of doubtful mind. . . . But rather seek ye the kingdom of God; and all these things shall be added unto you. Luke 12:28, 29, 31.

[If mankind were to trust to this most fallacious and pernicious promise, the result would be universal misery and starvation.]

Requests to be granted.

Ask, and it shall be given you; seek, and ye shall find; knock, and it shall be opened unto you: for every one that asketh receiveth; and he that seeketh findest; and to him that knocketh it shall be opened. Matt. 7:7, 8.

[Millions have sought and have not found. It is simply a monstrous falsehood to say that everyone who asketh receiveth.]

The omnipotence of belief.

Verily, verily, I say unto you, He that believeth on me, the works that I do shall he do also; and greater works than these shall he do. John 14:12.

Jesus said unto him, "If thou canst believe, all things are possible to him that believeth." Mark 9:23.

Verily I say unto you, If ye have faith as a grain of mustard seed, ye shall say unto this mountain, "Remove hence to yonder place;" and it shall remove; and nothing shall be impossible unto you. Matt 17:20.

Jesus answered and said unto them, "Verily I say unto you, If ye have faith, and doubt not, ye shall not only do this which is done to the fig tree, but also if ye shall say unto this mountain, 'Be thou removed, and be thou cast into the sea'; it shall be done." Matt. 21:21.

For verily I say unto you, That whosoever shall say unto this mountain, "Be thou removed, and be thou cast into the sea"; and shall not doubt in his heart, but shall believe that those things which he saith shall come to pass; he shall have whatsoever he saith. Mark 11:23.

And the Lord said, "If ye had faith as a grain of mustard seed, ye might say unto this sycamine tree, "Be thou plucked up by the root, and be thou planted in the sea"; and it should obey you." Luke 17:6.

[Christ's promises of the omnipotence of human faith have been miserably broken. Some of the failures are recorded in Scripture. The apostles, for example, failed to cast out a certain devil, and Jesus had to confess that "this kind can come forth by nothing, but by prayer and fasting" (Mark 9:29). Even of Jesus it is said "he could there do no mighty work. . . " (Mark 6:5). If a modern preacher promised the trees and mountains should obey human commands, he would be treated as insane or as a contemptible impostor.]

Prayer and faith conjoined to be omnipotent.

And all things, whatsoever ye shall ask in prayer, believing, ye shall receive. Matt. 21:22.

Therefore I say unto you, What things soever ye desire, when ye pray, believe that ye receive them, and ye shall have them. Mark 11:24.

And whatsoever ye shall ask in my name, that will I do, that the father may be glorified in the Son. If ye shall ask any thing in my name, I will do it. John 14:13, 14.

If ye abide in me, and my words abide in you, ye shall ask what ye will, and it shall be done unto you. . . . but I have chosen you, and ordained you, that ye should go and bring forth fruit, and that your fruit should remain: that whatsoever ye shall ask of the Father in my name, he may give it you. John 15:7, 16.

[Christ's promise of the universal efficacy of prayer has proved as miserable a sham as his promise of the omnipotence of faith.]

Prayer to heal the sick.

Is any sick among you? let him call for the elders of the church; and let them pray over him, anointing him with oil in the name of the Lord: And the prayer of faith shall save the sick, and the Lord shall raise him up. . . James 5:14, 15.

[The apostle's promise is just as fallacious as his master's.]

Judas and the other apostles to sit on twelve thrones judging the twelve tribes of Israel.

When the Son of man shall sit in the throne of his glory, ye also shall sit upon twelve thrones, judging the twelve tribes of Israel. Matt. 19:28.

And I appoint unto you a kingdom, as my Father hath appointed unto me; That ye may eat and drink at my table in my kingdom, and sit on thrones judging the twelve tribes of Israel. Luke 22:29, 30.

[This promise to the twelve apostles is still unfulfilled, and in the case of the apostle Judas, the "son of perdition," it is difficult to see how it can ever be fulfilled. (Matt. 26:24: But woe unto that man by whom the Son of man is betrayed! it had been good for that man if he had not been born.)]

The believer in Jesus will never hunger or thirst.

And Jesus said unto them, "I am the bread of life: he that cometh to me shall never hunger; and he that believeth on me shall never thirst." John 6:35.

[Taken literally or figuratively, this promise is often broken. Believers are liable to mental miseries just as they are to physical hunger and thirst. Those who pretend to the contrary are simply brazen-faced quacks or fanatics, on whom the most obvious facts produce no impression whatsoever.]

Cannibalism to secure eternal life.
Then Jesus said unto them, "Verily, verily, I say unto you, Except ye eat the flesh of the Son of man, and drink his blood, ye have no life in you. Whoso eateth my flesh, and drinketh my blood, hath eternal life; and I will raise him up at the last day." John 6:53, 54.
[This must be falsified in many instances, for many saints fall from grace. Judas himself partook of the mystic flesh and blood. Paul says that it is impossible for fallen saints to renew their repentance. (Heb. 6:4-6: For it is impossible for those who were once enlightened, and have tasted of the heavenly gift, and were made partakers of the Holy Ghost, And have tasted the good word of God, and the powers of the world to come, If they shall fall away, to renew them again unto repentance; seeing they crucify to themselves the Son of God afresh, and put him to an open shame.)]

Saints will never die.
Verily, verily, I say unto you, If a man keep my saying, he shall never see death. John 8:51.
[Christians have to say that "never see death" means "never see the *second* death," or "never *fear* death."]

Christ's followers to be mentally and morally enlightened.
Then spake Jesus again unto them saying, "I am the light of the world: he that followeth me shall not walk in darkness, but shall have the light of life." John 8:12.
[The world became Christian, and walked from the light of Roman civilization into the universal ignorance, superstition, and depravity of the Dark Ages.]

Christian unity.
And there shall be one fold, and one shepherd. John 10:16.
[The warring sects of Christendom have never been in one fold with Jesus as their shepherd, and are never likely to be.]

Jesus to be glorified, to judge the world, to cast out the Devil, and to draw all men to him.
And Jesus answered them saying, "The hour is come, that the Son of man should be glorified. . . . Now is the judgment of this world: now shall

the prince of this world be cast out. And I, if I be lifted up from the earth, will draw all men unto me." John 12:23, 31, 32.

[Christ was lifted up, but he is far from having drawn all men unto him. The great majority have not even heard his name. The judgment of the world and the casting out of the Devil, although announced in the present tense, are still in the distant future.]

The Holy Ghost to teach all knowledge and all truth, scientific, historical, and otherwise.

But the Comforter, which is the Holy Ghost, whom the Father will send in my name, he shall teach you all things. . . . John 14:26.

When he, the Spirit of truth, is come, he will guide you into all truth. John 16:13.

[Although the Holy Ghost was to teach the disciples "all things" and "all truth," it is evident that the "ignorant and unlearned" apostles knew but little more after they were inspired than before. When Paul withstood Peter to the face because he was to be blamed (Gal. 2:11: But when Peter was come to Antioch, I withstood him to the face, because he was to be blamed.), it is evident that the Holy Ghost did not teach both of them the truth.]

Peter to deny Christ thrice before the cock crew.

Jesus said unto him, "Verily I say unto thee, That this night, before the cock crow, thou shalt deny me thrice." Matt. 26:34.

I tell thee, Peter, the cock shall not crow this day, before that thou shalt thrice deny that thou knowest me. Luke 22:34.

[Mark 14:58-72: (But he denied, saying, "I know not, neither understand I what thou sayest." And he went out into the porch; and the cock crew. And a maid saw him again, and began to say to them that stood by, "This is one of them." And he denied it again. And a little after, they that stood by said again to Peter, "Surely thou art one of them: for thou art a Galilaean, and thy speech agreeth thereto." But he began to curse and to swear, saying, "I know not this man of whom ye speak." And the second time the cock crew.) shows that the cock crew at each successive denial, and did not wait till the conclusion ·of the three denials.]

Jesus, as a second Jonah, to be three days and three nights in the grave.

But he answered and said unto them, "An evil and adulterous generation seeketh after a sign; and there shall no sign be given to it, but

192

the sign of the prophet Jonas: For as Jonas was three days and three nights in the whale's belly; so shall the Son of man be three days and three nights in the heart of the earth." Matt. 12:39, 40.

For as Jonas was a sign unto the Ninevites, so shall also the Son of man be to this generation. Luke 11:30.

And he began to teach them, that the Son of man must suffer many things . . . and be killed, and after three days rise again. Mark 8:31.

[Christ has not risen again, nor made his resurrection a sign to the world. Christians pretend he has, but their evidence of so wonderful and all-important an event is not sufficient to hang a cat on. If the Christian legend of his resurrection is true, Jesus did not fulfill the prophecy so far as the element of time is concerned, for he was not three days and three nights "in the heart of the earth," if we may so call a grave. Buried on Friday evening, and risen before the early dawn on Sunday morning, he was only in the sepulchre for one day and part of two nights.]

No sign whatever to be given to the generation then living.

And he sighed deeply in his spirit, and saith, "Why doth this generation seek after a sign? verily I say unto you, There shall no sign be given unto this generation." And he left them. . . . Mark 8:12, 13.

[This must have been falsified if the prophecies of a sign to be given were fulfilled. Christ, moreover, is alleged to have worked many "miracles and wonders and *signs*" during his lifetime. (Acts 2:22: Ye men of Israel, hear these words; Jesus of Nazareth, a man approved of God among you by miracles and wonders and signs, which God did by him in the midst of you, as ye yourselves also know.)]

Christ's solemn predictions of his speedy return in glory.

And as he sat upon the mount of Olives, the disciples came unto him privately, saying, "Tell us, when shall these things be? and what shall be the sign of thy coming, and of the end of the world?" And Jesus answered and said unto them. . . . "As the lightning cometh out of the east, and shineth even unto the west; so shall also the coming of the Son of man be. . . . Immediately after the tribulation of those days shall the sun be darkened, and the moon shall not give her light, and the stars shall fall from heaven, and the powers of the heavens shall be shaken: And then shall appear the sign of the Son of man in heaven: and then shall all the tribes of the earth mourn, and they shall see the Son of man coming in the clouds of heaven with power and great glory. And he shall send his angels with a great sound of a trumpet, and they shall gather together his elect from the four winds, from one end of heaven to the other.... Verily I say unto you, THIS GENERATION SHALL NOT PASS, TILL ALL THESE THINGS BE FULFILLED. Heaven and earth shall pass away, but my words shall not pass away." Matt. 24:3, 4, 27, 29-31, 34, 35.

And the stars of heaven shall fall, and the powers that are in heaven shall be shaken. And then shall they see the Son of man coming in the clouds with great power and glory. And then shall he send his angels, and shall gather together his elect from the four winds, from the uttermost part of the earth to the uttermost part of heaven.... Verily I say unto you, THAT THIS GENERATION SHALL NOT PASS, TILL ALL THESE THINGS BE DONE. Mark 8:25, 30.

And when ye shall see Jerusalem compassed with armies, then know that the desolation thereof is nigh. Then let them which are in Judaea flee to the mountains; and let them which are in the midst of it depart out; and let not them that are in the countries enter thereinto. For these be the days of vengeance, that all things which are written may be fulfilled. But woe unto them that are with child, and to them that give suck, in those days! for there shall be great distress in the land, and wrath upon the people. And they shall fall by the edge of the sword, and shall be led away captive into all nations: and Jerusalem shall be trodden down of the Gentiles, until the times of the Gentiles be fulfilled. And there shall be signs in the sun, and in the moon, and in the stars; and upon the earth distress of nations, with perplexity; the sea and the waves roaring; Men's hearts failing them for fear, and for looking after those things which are coming on the earth: for the powers of heaven shall be shaken, And then shall they see the Son of man coming in a cloud with power and great glory. And when these things begin to come to pass, then look up, and lift up your heads; for your redemption draweth nigh.... Verily I say unto you, THIS GENERATION SHALL NOT PASS AWAY, TILL ALL BE FULFILLED. Luke 21:20-28, 32.

[This prophecy by the Son of God is more specific in point of time than prophecies usually are, and so forms a good test of the reality of Christ's pretensions. Nearly 2,000 years have elapsed, and it is still unfulfilled, although Christ himself most emphatically declared that it should be completely fulfilled within the lifetime of the generation then living. Generation after generation has passed away, and the prophet of Nazareth stands a convicted impostor. The prophecy was exceedingly useful in its day, because it terrified people into the arms of the Church; now it remains on record as a gigantic falsehood. The Son of man has *not* come like the lightning shining from the east to the west, and all the tribes of the earth have *not* seen him coming in the clouds of heaven

194

with power and great glory. Nor has he sent his angels with sound of trumpet gathering the elect from all parts of the world. Nor have the stars of heaven fallen; they are still there, and the constellations appear much the same as in the time of Job.]

Christ announces the Day of Judgment as close at hand.

The hour is coming, in which all that are in the graves shall hear his voice, And shall come forth; they that have done good, unto the resurrection of life; and they that have done evil, unto the resurrection of damnation. John 5:28, 29.

For the Son of man shall come in the glory of his Father with his angels; and then he shall reward every man according to his works. Verily I say unto you, There be some standing here, which shall not taste of death, till they see the Son of man coming in his kingdom. Matt. 16:27, 28.

And he said unto them, "Verily I say unto you, That there be some of them that stand here, which shall not taste of death, till they have seen the kingdom of God come with power." Mark 9:1.

But I tell you of a truth, there be some standing here, which shall not taste of death, till they see the kingdom of God. Luke 9:27.

Jesus saith unto him, "If I will that he tarry till I come, what is that to thee?" John 21:22.

[These passages, like the prophecies previously given, show clearly that Christ's coming in power and glory to judge the quick and the dead was to take place during the lifetime of then-existing persons. Either these prophecies were spoken by Christ, or they were not. If he uttered them, he stands ignominiously condemned as a false prophet. If he did not, the Evangelists have put them into his mouth without warrant, and the Gospels are "unreliable fabrications." In either case Christianity is based on falsehood.]

Living Christians of the apostolic age to be caught up into the clouds.

For this we say unto you by the word of the Lord, that we which are alive and remain unto the coming of the Lord shall not prevent them which are asleep. For the Lord himself shall descend from heaven with a shout, with the voice of the archangel, and with the trump of God: and the dead in Christ shall rise first: Then we which are alive and remain shall be caught up together with them in the clouds, to meet the Lord in the air: and so shall we ever be with the Lord. Wherefore comfort one another with these words. 1 Thess. 4:15-18.

[Paul shared the delusion taught by Christ; he expected to be snatched up bodily into heaven with other saints then living, who would thus never taste death.]

Some more of Paul's references to the approaching end of the world.
In these last days. Heb. 1:2.
The time is short. 1. Cor. 7:29.
But now once in the end of the world hath he appeared to put away sin by the sacrifice of himself. Heb. 9:26.
For yet a little while, and he that shall come will come, and will not tarry. Heb. 10:37.
I give thee charge in the sight of God . . . that thou keep this commandment without spot, unrebukeable, until the appearing of our Lord Jesus Christ. 1 Tim. 6:13, 14.
[Texts like the above show clearly that Paul taught his converts that Christ's coming and the end of the world were close at hand.]

Peter's prediction of the speedy destruction of the world by fire.
But the end of all things is at hand. 1 Pet. 4:7.
Who shall give account to him that is ready to judge the quick and the dead. 1 Pet. 4:5.
The heavens and the earth, which are now, by the same word are kept in store, reserved unto fire against the day of judgment and perdition of ungodly men. . . . The day of the Lord will come as a thief in the night; in the which the heavens shall pass away with a great noise, and the elements shall melt with fervent heat. . . . Looking for and hasting unto the coming of the day of God, wherein the heavens being on fire shall be dissolved, and the elements shall melt with fervent heat. Nevertheless we, according to his promise, look for new heavens and a new earth, wherein dwelleth righteousness. Wherefore, beloved, seeing that ye look for such things, be diligent that ye may be found of him in peace, without spot, and blameless. 2 Pet. 3:7, 10, 12-14.
Others mocking said, "These men are full of new wine." But Peter, standing up with the eleven, lifted up his voice, and said unto them, ". . . For these [men] are not drunken, as ye suppose, seeing it is but the third hour of the day. But this is that which was spoken by the prophet Joel; 'And it shall come to pass in the last days,' saith God, 'I will pour out of my Spirit upon all flesh: and your sons and your daughters shall prophesy, and your young men shall see visions, and your old men shall dream dreams: And on my servants and on my handmaidens I will pour out in those days of my Spirit; and they shall prophesy: And I will shew wonders in heaven above, and signs in the earth beneath; blood, and

fire, and vapour of smoke: The sun shall be turned into darkness, and the moon ihto blood, before that great and notable day of the Lord come: And it shall come to pass that whosoever shall call upon the name of the Lord shall be saved.' " Acts 2:13-21.

In these last times. 1 Pet. 1:20.

[Peter agreed with Paul in announcing the approaching end of the world, however much he may have quarrelled with him over other matters where there was room for difference of opinion.]

James also predicts Christ's coming as close at hand.

Be patient, therefore, brethren, unto the coming of the Lord. . . . For the coming of the Lord draweth nigh. . . . Behold, the judge standeth before the door. James 5:7-9.

[This shows that the apostle James also deluded the early Christians with the promise of the speedy return of the Lord Jesus, and with the threat of the swift approach of the great Day of Judgment.]

Christ's broken promise to the crucified thief.

And Jesus said unto him, "Verily, I say unto thee, To day shalt thou be with me in paradise." Luke 23:43.

[This promise could not have been kept, unless Christ went to heaven that day, which is contrary to the Christian doctrine that when he was dead he spent the succeeding three days and nights in the heart of the earth or (according to the *Apostle's Creed*) in hell.]

Signs of belief.

And these signs shall follow them that believe; In my name shall they cast out devils; they shall speak with new tongues; They shall take up serpents; and if they drink any deadly thing, it shall not hurt them; they shall lay hands on the sick, and they shall recover. Mark 16:17, 18.

[These signs do not follow belief. Christ's precious promises break down when put to a practical test. What living believer is there who can cast out devils and take poison unharmed? Are we to conclude that belief is now extinct?]

The predictions in the Book of Revelation were shortly to come to pass.

The Revelation of Jesus Christ, which God gave unto him, to shew unto his servants things which must shortly come to pass. Rev. 1:1.

Christ to come quickly and be seen by everybody, including those who pierced him.

Behold, he cometh with clouds; and every eye shall see him, and they

197

also which pierced him: and all kindreds of the earth shall wail because of him. Even so, Amen. Rev. 1:7.

Behold, I come quickly. Rev. 3:11.

["Quickly" means at least nineteen hundred years; how much more it means only fanatics and charlatans can inform us. Christian imbecility pleads that with the Lord a thousand years are as a day and a day is as a thousand years. But the Lord was addressing — and grossly *deceiving* — human beings with whom a day is no more a thousand years than a penny is a thousand pounds. A man who promised some money in one day's time and then postponed payment for a thousand years would be regarded as a liar; but the Christian God is above the rules of human morality.]

Satan bound during the Millennium.

And he laid hold of the dragon, that old serpent, which is the Devil, and Satan, and bound him a thousand years, And cast him into the bottomless pit and shut him up, and set a seal upon him, that he should deceive the nations no more, till the thousand years should be fulfilled. Rev. 20:2, 3.

And they [the saints] lived and reigned with Christ a thousand years. But the rest of the dead lived not again until a thousand years were finished. This is the first resurrection. Rev. 20:4, 5.

[If a thousand years are as a day with the Lord, perhaps this "thousand years" means only four-and-twenty hours. Who is to tell?]

Satan's campaign; and his punishment.

And when the thousand years are expired, Satan shall be loosed out of his prison, And shall go out to deceive the nations which are in the four quarters of the earth, Gog and Magog, to gather them together to battle: the number of whom is as the sand of the sea. And they went up on the breadth of the earth, and compassed the camp of the saints about, and the beloved city: and the fire came down from God out of heaven, and devoured them. And the devil that deceived them was cast into the lake of fire and brimstone, where the beast and the false prophet are, and shall be tormented day and night for ever and ever. Rev. 20:7-10.

The end of the world; the resurrection of the dead; the damnation of the lost; a new heaven and earth without any sea.

And I saw a great white throne, and him that sat on it, from whose face the earth and the heaven fled away; and there was found no place for them . . . . And the sea gave up the dead which were in it; and death and hell delivered up the dead which were in them: and they were judged every man according to their works. And death and hell were cast into the lake of fire. This is the second death. And whatsoever was not found written in the book of life was cast into the lake of fire. Rev. 20:11, 12-15.

And I saw a new heaven and a new earth: for the first heaven and the first earth were passed away; and there was no more sea. Rev. 21:1.

The Day of Judgment close at hand.

And he said unto me, "These sayings are faithful and true": and the Lord God of the holy prophets sent his angel to shew unto his servants the things which must shortly be done. . . . And he saith unto me, "Seal not the sayings of the prophecy of this book: for the time is at hand. . . . And, behold, I come quickly; and my reward is with me, to give every man according as his work shall be." . . . He which testifieth these things saith, "Surely I come quickly." Amen. Even so, come, Lord Jesus. Rev. 22:6, 10, 12, 20.

[These inspired predictions of "things which must *shortly come to pass*" (Rev. 1:1) are still unfulfilled after a lapse of over nineteen centuries. The Evil One has *not* been chained up, the Millennium has *not* come, neither the first nor second resurrection has happened, the nations have not besieged the camp of the saints nor been devoured by fire from heaven, the earth and the heaven have not passed away, the judgment day is still postponed, the sea has not given up its dead, death and hell are not cast into the lake of fire, a similar fate has not befallen all those whose names are not written in the book of life, and a new earth has not been created without any sea. And yet all these things and many more were "shortly to come to pass"! Christ was to "come quickly"! What better evidence could anyone require to convince him that Christian prophecies are a mass of impudent quackery or fanatical delusion?]

BIBLE IMMORALITIES, INDECENCIES AND OBSCENITIES

The world peopled by incest.

And Cain knew his wife; and she conceived, and bare Enoch: and he builded a city, and called the name of the city, after the name of his son, Enoch. . . . And to Seth, to him also there was born a son; and he called his name Enos: then began men to call upon the name of the LORD. Gen. 4:17, 26.

[It is obvious that the sons and daughters of Adam and Eve must have committed incest. God might easily have prevented this by creating *two* separate pairs of human beings with which to start.]

Noah exposes himself.

And Noah began to be an husbandman, and he planted a vineyard: And he drank of the wine, and was drunken; and he was uncovered within his tent. And Ham, the father of Canaan, saw the nakedness of his father, and told his two brethren without. And Shem and Japheth took a garment, and laid it upon both their shoulders, and went backward, and covered the nakedness of their father; and their faces were backward, and they saw not their father's nakedness. And Noah awoke from his wine, and knew what his younger son had done unto him. And he said, "Cursed be Canaan; a servant of servants shall he be unto his brethren." Gen. 9:20-25.

[This "perfect" man (Gen. 6:9: Noah was a just man and perfect in his generations, and Noah walked with God.), having been just saved from water, fell under the influence of wine, and in his drunkenness failed to observe the laws of decency. The just and perfect patriarch subsequently cursed, not himself, but the son who had observed his nakedness, and this son's posterity after him.]

Abraham marries his father's daughter.

And yet indeed she is my sister; she is the daughter of my father, but not the daughter of my mother, and she became my wife. Gen. 20:12.

Abraham traffics in his wife's honour.

And it came to pass, when he was come near to enter into Egypt, that he said unto Sarai his wife, "Behold now, I know that thou art a fair woman to look upon: Therefore it shall come to pass, when the Egyptians shall see thee, that they shall say, 'This is his wife:' and they will kill me, but they will save thee alive. Say, I pray thee, thou art my sister: that it may be well with me for thy sake; and my soul shall live because of thee." And it came to pass, that, when Abram was come into Egypt, the Egyptians beheld the woman that she was very fair. The princes also of Pharaoh saw her, and commended her before Pharaoh: and the woman was taken into Pharaoh's house. And he entreated Abram well for her sake: and he had sheep, and oxen, and he asses, and menservants, and maidservants, and she asses, and camels. And the LORD plagued Pharaoh and his house with great plagues because of Sarai Abram's wife. And Pharaoh called Abram, and said, "What is this that thou hast done unto me? why didst thou not tell me that she was thy wife? Why saidst thou, 'She is my sister?' so I might have taken her to me to wife: now therefore behold thy wife, take her, and go thy way." Gen. 12:11-19.

And Abraham said of Sarah his wife, "She is my sister:" and Abimelech king of Gerar sent, and took Sarah. But God came to Abimelech in a dream by night, and said to him, "Behold, thou art but a dead man, for the woman which thou hast taken; for she is a man's wife." But Abimelech had not come near her: and he said, "LORD, wilt thou slay also a righteous nation? Said he not unto me, 'She is my sister?' and she, even she herself said, 'He is my brother:' in the integrity of my heart and innocency of my hands have I done this." And God said unto him in a dream, "Yea, I know that thou didst this in the integrity of thy heart; for I also withheld thee from sinning against me: therefore suffered I thee not to touch her. Now therefore restore the man his wife; for he is a prophet, and he shall pray for thee, and thou shalt live: and if thou restore her not, know thou that thou shalt surely die, thou, and all that are thine." . . . Then Abimelech called Abraham, and said unto him, "What hast thou done unto us? and what have I offended thee, that thou hast brought on me and on my kingdom a great sin? thou hast done deeds unto me that ought not to be done." And Abimelech said unto Abraham, "What sawest thou, that thou hast done this thing?" And Abraham said, "Because I thought, 'Surely the fear of God is not in this place; and they will slay me for my wife's sake.' And yet indeed she is my sister; she is the daughter of my father, but not the daughter of my mother; and she became my wife." . . . And Abimelech took sheep, and oxen, and menservants, and womenservants, and gave them unto Abraham, and restored him Sarah his wife. And Abimelech said, 'Behold, my land is before thee: dwell where it pleaseth thee." And unto Sarah he said, "Behold, I have given thy brother a thousand pieces of silver: behold, he is to thee a covering of the eyes, unto all that are with thee," and with all other: thus she was reproved. So Abraham prayed unto God: and God healed Abimelech, and his wife, and his maidservants; and they bare children. For the LORD had fast closed up all the wombs of the house of Abimelech, because of Sarah Abraham's wife. Gen. 20:2-18.

[Abraham passed his beautiful wife off as his sister and allowed Pharaoh to take her to his royal palace, receiving in return "sheep, and oxen, and he asses, and menservants, and maidservants, and she asses, and camels." After the LORD had plagued Pharaoh and his house with great plagues, Pharaoh sent her back to her husband, who, however, does not appear to have returned the valuable consideration which he had received of the king. Abraham also played the same trick on good King Abimelech, and received a thousand pieces of silver. (Gen. 20:16: And unto Sarah [Abimelech] said. "Behold, I have given thy brother a thousand pieces of silver. . . .")]

Abraham takes a concubine.

And he went in unto Hagar, and she conceived: and when she saw that she had conceived, her mistress was despised in her eyes. Gen. 16:4.

God institutes the obscene rite of circumcision.

This is my covenant, which ye shall keep, between me and you and thy seed after thee; Every man child among you shall be circumcised. And ye shall circumcise the flesh of your foreskin; and it shall be a token of the covenant betwixt me and you. And he that is eight days old shall be circumcised among you, every man child in your generations, he that is born in the house, or bought with money of any stranger, which is not of thy seed. He that is born in thy house, and he that is bought with thy money, must needs be circumcised: and my covenant shall be in your flesh for an everlasting covenant. And the uncircumcised man child whose flesh of his foreskin is not circumcised, that soul shall be cut off from his people; he hath broken my covenant. . . . And Abraham took Ishmael his son, and all that were born in his house, and all that were bought with his money, every male among the men of Abraham's house; and circumcised the flesh of their foreskin in the selfsame day, as

God had said unto him. And Abraham was ninety years old and nine, when he was circumcised in the flesh of his foreskin. And Ishmael his son was thirteen years old, when he was circumcised in the flesh of his foreskin. In the selfsame day was Abraham circumcised, and Ishmael his son. And all the men of his house, born in the house, and bought with money of the stranger, were circumcised with him. Gen. 17:10-14, 23-27.

And in the eighth day the flesh of his foreskin shall be circumcised. Lev. 12:3.

[What could have put this wicked idea into God's mind? Did he wish to show that religion and obscenity are intimately connected?]

Lot offers his daughters to a mob of Sodomites.

And there came two angels to Sodom at even; and Lot sat in the gate of Sodom: . . . But before they lay down, the men of the city, even the men of Sodom, compassed the house round, both old and young, all the people from every quarter: And they called unto Lot, and said unto him, "Where are the men which came in to thee this night? bring them out unto us, that we may know them." And Lot went out at the door unto them, and shut the door after him. And said, "I pray you, brethren, do not so wickedly. Behold now, I have two daughters which have not known man; let me, I pray you, bring them out unto you, and do ye to them as is good in your eyes: only unto these men do nothing; for therefore came they under the shadow of my roof." Gen. 19:1-8.

[Lot, the nephew of Abraham, was one of the saints whom God saved from the cities of the plain (Gen. 19:15: And when the morning arose, then the angels hastened unto Lot, saying, "Arise, take thy wife, and thy two daughters, which are here; lest thou be consumed in the iniquity of the city."). His offer of his two young daughters to be indiscriminately violated by a lustful mob reaches the lowest depth of cowardly infamy. But the Bible seems to regard the offer as an honourable one because he sought thereby to save two angels from filthy outrage.]

Two sisters seduce their drunken father.

And Lot went up out of Zoar, and dwelt in the mountain, and his two daughters with him; for he feared to dwell in Zoar: and he dwelt in a cave, he and his two daughters. And the firstborn said unto the younger, "Our father is old, and there is not a man in the earth to come in unto us after the manner of all the earth: Come, let us make our father drink wine, and we will lie with him, that we may preserve seed of our father." And they made their father drink wine that night: and the firstborn went in, and lay with her father; and he perceived not when she lay down, nor when she arose. And it came to pass on the morrow, that the firstborn said unto the younger, "Behold, I lay yesternight with my father: let us make him drink wine this night also; and go thou in, and lie with him, that we may preserve seed of our father." And they made their father drink wine that night also: and the younger arose, and lay with him; and he perceived not when she lay down, nor when she arose. Thus were both the daughters of Lot with child by their father. And the firstborn bare a son, and called his name Moab: the same is the father of the Moabites unto this day. And the younger, she also bare a son, and called his name Benammi: the same is the father of the children of Ammon unto this day. Gen. 19:30-38.

[Lot's wife was struck dead (converted into a pillar of salt — Gen. 19:26: But his wife looked back from behind him, and she became a pillar of salt.) for the trivial offence of looking back at a city on fire, but God's Bible never records the slightest disapproval or punishment of this incest. (2 Pet. 2:7, 8: And delivered just Lot, vexed with the filthy conversation of the wicked: [For that righteous man dwelling among them, in seeing and hearing, vexed his righteous soul from day to day with their unlawful deeds;].) God made the children the progenitors of great nations, and Jesus was descended from one of them through Ruth. (Ruth 4:9, 10, 21, 22: And Boaz said unto the elders, and unto all the people . . . "Ruth the Moabitess, the wife of Mahlon, have I purchased to be my wife, to raise up the name of the dead upon his inheritance, that the name of the dead be not cut off from among his brethren, and from the gate of his place." . . . And Salmon begat Boaz, and Boaz begat Obed, and Obed begat Jesse, and Jesse begat David.)]

The birth of twins described.
And Rebekah his wife conceived. And the children struggled together within her; . . . And when her days to be delivered were fulfilled, behold, there were twins in her womb. And the first came out red, all over like an hairy garment; and they called his name Esau. And after that came his brother out, and his hand took hold on Esau's heel; and his name was called Jacob: and Isaac was threescore years old when she bare them. Gen. 25:21, 22, 24-26.

Isaac repeats Abraham's trick and passes his wife off as his sister.
And Isaac dwelt in Gerar: And the men of the place asked him of his wife; and he said, "She is my sister;" for he feared to say, "She is my

wife"; lest said he, the men of the place should kill me for Rebekah; because she was fair to look upon. And it came to pass, when he had been there a long time, that Abimelech king of the Philistines looked out at a window, and saw, and, behold, Isaac was sporting with Rebekah his wife. And Abimelech called Isaac, and said, "Behold, of a surety she is thy wife: and how saidst thou, 'She is my sister?' " And Isaac said unto him, "Because I said, Lest I die for her." And Abimelech said, "What is this thou hast done unto us? one of the people might lightly have lien with thy wife, and thou shouldest have brought guiltiness upon us." And Abimelech charged all his people, saying, "He that toucheth this man or his wife shall surely be put to death." Then Isaac sowed in that land, and received in the same year an hundredfold: And the LORD blessed him. Gen. 26:6-12.

Jacob marries two sisters and takes concubines as well.

And it came to pass in the evening, that he took Leah his daughter, and brought her to him; and he went in unto her. And Laban gave unto his daughter Leah Zilpah his maid for an handmaid. And it came to pass, that in the morning, behold, it was Leah: and he said to Laban, "What is this thou hast done unto me? did not I serve with thee for Rachel? wherefore then hast thou beguiled me?" And Laban said, "It must not be so done in our country, to give the younger before the firstborn. Fulfill her week, and we will give thee this also for the service which thou shalt serve with me yet seven other years." And Jacob did so, and fulfilled her week: and he gave him Rachel his daughter to wife also. And Laban gave to Rachel his daughter Bilhah his handmaid to be her maid. And he went in also unto Rachel, and he loved also Rachel more than Leah, and served with him yet seven other years. Gen. 29:23-30.

And she [Rachel] said, "Behold my maid Bilhah, go in unto her; and she shall bear upon my knees, that I may also have children by her." And she gave him Bilhah her handmaid to wife: and Jacob went in unto her. And Bilhah conceived, and bare Jacob a son. And Rachel said, "God hath judged me, and hath also heard my voice, and hath given me a son:" therefore called she his name Dan. And Bilhah Rachel's maid conceived again, and bare Jacob a second son. And Rachel said, "With great wrestlings have I wrestled with my sister, and I have prevailed": and she called his name Naphtali. When Leah saw that she had left bearing, she took Zilpah her maid, and gave her to Jacob to wife. And Zilpah Leah's maid bare Jacob a son. And Leah said, "A troop cometh": and she called his name Gad. And Zilpah Leah's maid bare Jacob a second son. Gen. 30:3-10.

Dinah being ravished, the Shechemites on circumcising themselves are treacherously slain by Jacob's sons.

And Dinah the daughter of Leah, which she bare unto Jacob, went out to see the daughters of the land. And when Shechem the son of Hamor the Hivite, prince of the country, saw her, he took her, and lay with her, and defiled her. And his soul clave unto Dinah the daughter of Jacob, and he loved the damsel, and spake kindly unto the damsel. And Shechem spake unto his father Hamor, saying "Get me this damsel to wife." . . . And Hamor . . . went out unto Jacob to commune with him. And the sons of Jacob came out of the field when they heard it: and the men were grieved, and they were very wroth, because he had wrought folly in Israel in lying with Jacob's daughter; which thing ought not to be done. And Hamor communed with them, saying, "The soul of my son Shechem longeth for your daughter: I pray you give her him to wife. And make ye marriages with us, and give your daughters unto us, and take our daughters unto you. And ye shall dwell with us: and the land shall be before you; dwell and trade ye therein, and get you possessions therein." And Shechem said unto her father and unto her brethren, "Let me find grace in your eyes, and what ye shall say unto me I will give. Ask me never so much dowry and gift, and I will give according as ye shall say unto me: but give me the damsel to wife." And the sons of Jacob answered Shechem and Hamor his father deceitfully, and said, because he had defiled Dinah their sister: . . . "We cannot do this thing, to give our sister to one that is uncircumcised; for that were a reproach unto us: But in this will we consent unto you: if ye will be as we be, that every male of you be circumcised; Then will we give our daughters unto you, and we will take your daughters to us, and we will dwell with you, and we will become one people. But if ye will not hearken unto us, to be circumcised; then will we take our daughter, and we will be gone." . . . And the young man deferred not to do the thing, because he had delight in Jacob's daughter: and he was more honourable than all the house of his father. And Hamor and Shechem his son came unto the gate of their city, and communed with the men of their city, saying, "These men are peaceable with us; therefore let them dwell in the land, and trade therein; for the land, behold, it is large enough for them; let us take their daughters to us for wives, and let us give them our daughters. Only herein will the men consent unto us for to dwell with us, to be one people, if every male among us be circumcised, as they are circumcised. Shall not their cattle and their substance and every beast of theirs be ours? only let us consent unto them, and they will dwell with us." . . . and every male was circumcised, all that went out of the gate of his city. And

207

it came to pass on the third day, when they were sore, that two of the sons of Jacob, Simeon and Levi, Dinah's brethren, took each man his sword, and came upon the city boldly, and slew all the males. And they slew Hamor and Shechem his son with the edge of the sword, and took Dinah out of Shechem's house, and went out. The sons of Jacob came upon the slain, and spoiled the city, because they had defiled their sister. They took their sheep, and their oxen, and their asses, and that which was in the city, and that which was in the field. And all their wealth, and all their little ones, and their wives took they captive, and spoiled even all that was in the house. Gen. 34:1-29.

Reuben commits incest with his father's concubine.

And it came to pass, when Israel dwelt in that land, that Reuben went and lay with Bilhah his father's concubine: and Israel heard it. Gen. 35:22.

Reuben, thou art my firstborn, my might, and the beginning of my strength, the excellency of dignity, and the excellency of power: Unstable as water, thou shalt not excel; because thou wentest up to thy father's bed; then defiledst thou it: he went up to my couch. Gen. 49:3, 4.

Onanism.

And Er, Judah's firstborn, was wicked in the sight of the LORD; and the LORD slew him. And Judah said unto Onan, "Go in unto thy brother's wife, and marry her, and raise up seed to thy brother." And Onan knew that the seed should not be his; and it came to pass, when he went in unto his brother's wife, that he spilled it on the ground, lest that he should give seed to his brother. Gen. 38:7-9.

Judah has sons by his daughter-in-law Tamar.

And it was told Tamar, saying, "Behold thy father in law goeth up to Timnath to shear his sheep." And she put her widow's garments off from her, and covered her with a vail, and wrapped herself, and sat in an open place, which is by the way to Timnath; for she saw that Shelah was grown, and she was not given unto him to wife. When Judah saw her, he thought her to be an harlot; because she had covered her face. And he turned unto her by the way, and said, "Go to, I pray thee, let me come in unto thee:" (for he knew not that she was his daughter in law.) And she said, "What wilt thou give me, that thou mayest come in unto me?" And he said, "I will send thee a kid from the flock." And she said, "Wilt thou give me a pledge, till thou send it?" And he said, "What pledge shall I give thee?" And she said, "Thy signet, and thy bracelets, and thy staff that is in thine hand." And he gave it her, and came in unto her, and she conceived by him. And she arose, and went away, and laid by her vail from her, and put on the garments of her widowhood. And Judah sent the kid by the hand of his friend the Adullamite, to receive his pledge from the woman's hand: but he found her not. Then he asked the men of that place, saying, "Where is the harlot, that was openly by the way side?" And they said, "There was no harlot in this place." And he returned to Judah, and said, "I cannot find her; and also the men of the place said, that there was no harlot in this place." And Judah said, "Let her take it to her, lest we be shamed: behold, I sent this kid, and thou hast not found her." And it came to pass about three months after, that it was told Judah, saying, "Tamar thy daughter in law hath played the harlot; and also, behold, she is with child by whoredom." And Judah said, "Bring her forth, and let her be burnt." When she was brought forth, she sent to her father in law, saying, "By the man, whose these are, am I with child:" and she said, "Discern, I pray thee, whose are these, the signet, and bracelets, and staff." And Judah acknowledged them, and said, "She hath been more righteous than I; because that I gave her not to Shelah my son." And he knew her again no more. And it came to pass in the time of her travail, that, behold, twins were in her womb. Gen. 38:13-27.

Another birth of twins described.

And it came to pass in the time of her travail, that, behold, twins were in her womb. And it came to pass, when she travailed, that the one put out his hand: and the midwife took and bound upon his hand a scarlet thread, saying, "This came out first." And it came to pass, as he drew back his hand, that, behold, his brother came out: and she said, "How hast thou broken forth? this breach be upon thee:" therefore his name was called Pharez. And afterward came out his brother, that had the scarlet thread upon his hand: and his name was called Zarah. Gen. 38:27-30.

[This beastly 38th chapter of Genesis, like other Bible filth, was appointed to be read in the churches. See table of Lessons in the Prayer Book.]

The story of Potiphar's wife and the chaste Joseph.

And it came to pass after these things, that his master's wife cast her eyes upon Joseph; and she said, "Lie with me." But he refused, and said unto his master's wife, "Behold, my master wotteth not what is with me in the house, and he hath committed all that he hath to my hand; There is none greater in this house than I; neither hath he kept back any thing from me but thee, because thou art his wife: how then can I do this great wickedness, and sin against God?" And it came to pass, as she spake to Joseph day by day, that he hearkened not unto her, to lie by her, or to be with her. And it came to pass about this time, that Joseph went into the house to do his business; and there was none of the men of the house there within. And she caught him by his garment, saying, "Lie with me": and he left his garment in her hand, and fled, and got him out. And it came to pass, when she saw that he had left his garment in her hand, and was fled forth, That she called unto the men of her house, and spake unto them, saying, "See, he hath brought in an Hebrew unto us to mock us; he came in unto me to lie with me, and I cried with a loud voice: And it came to pass, when he heard that I lifted up my voice and cried, that he left his garment with me, and fled, and got him out." And she laid up his garment by her, until his lord came home. And she spake unto him according to these words, saying, "The Hebrew servant, which thou hast brought unto us, came in unto me to mock me: And it came to pass, as I lifted up my voice and cried, that he left his garment with me, and fled out." And it came to pass, when his master heard the words of his wife, which she spake unto him, saying, "After this manner did thy servant to me"; that his wrath was kindled. And Joseph's master took him, and put him into the prison, a place where the king's prisoners were bound: and he was there in the prison. Gen. 39:7-20.

Zipporah has to circumcise her son in order to restrain the Lord from killing Moses.

And it came to pass by the way in the inn, that the LORD met him, and sought to kill him. Then Zipporah took a sharp stone, and cut off the foreskin of her son, and cast it at his feet, and said, "Surely a bloody husband art thou to me." So he let him go. Exod. 4:24-26.

God displays his rear end; he moons Moses.

And I will take away mine hand, and thou shalt see my back parts: but my face shall not be seen. Exod. 33:23.

Laws describing bestiality, sodomy, and incest.
  Bestiality.
Whosoever lieth with a beast shall surely be put to death. Exod. 22:19.
Neither shalt thou lie with any beast to defile thyself therewith:

210

neither shall any woman stand before a beast to lie down thereto: it is confusion. Lev. 18:23.

And if a man lie with a beast, he shall surely be put to death: and ye shall slay the beast. And if a woman approach unto any beast, and lie down thereto, thou shalt kill the woman, and the beast: they shall surely be put to death; their blood shall be upon them. Lev. 20:15, 16.

Sodomy.

Thou shalt not lie with mankind, as with womankind: it is abomination. Lev. 18:22.

If a man also lie with mankind, as he lieth with a woman, both of them have committed an abomination: they shall surely be put to death; their blood shall be upon them. Lev. 20:13.

For this cause God gave them up unto vile affections: for even their women did change the natural use into that which is against nature: And likewise also the men, leaving the natural *use* of the woman, burned in their lust one toward another; men with men working that which is unseemly, and receiving in themselves that recompence of their error which was meet. Rom. 1:26, 27.

Various kinds of incest.

The nakedness of thy father's wife shalt thou not uncover: it is thy father's nakedness. The nakedness of thy sister, the daughter of thy father, or daughter of thy mother, whether she be born at home, or born abroad, even their nakedness thou shalt not uncover. The nakedness of thy son's daughter, or of thy daughter's daughter, even their nakedness thou shalt not uncover: for theirs is thine own nakedness. The nakedness of thy father's wife's daughter, begotten of thy father, she is thy sister, thou shalt not uncover her nakedness. Thou shalt not uncover the nakedness of thy father's sister: she is thy father's near kinswoman. Thou shalt not uncover the nakedness of thy mother's sister: for she is thy mother's near kinswoman. Thou shalt not uncover the nakedness of thy father's brother, thou shalt not approach to his wife: she is thine aunt. Thou shalt not uncover the nakedness of thy daughter in law: she is thy son's wife; thou shalt not uncover her nakedness. Thou shalt not uncover the nakedness of thy brother's wife: it is thy brother's nakedness. Thou shalt not uncover the nakedness of a woman and her daughter, neither shalt thou take her son's daughter, or her daughter's daughter, to uncover her nakedness; for they are her near kinswomen: it is wickedness. Neither shalt thou take a wife to her sister, to vex her, to uncover her nakedness, beside the other in her life time. Lev. 18:8-18.

And the man that lieth with his father's wife hath uncovered his father's nakedness: both of them shall surely be put to death; their blood shall be upon them. And if a man lie with his daughter in law, both of them shall surely be put to death: they have wrought confusion; their blood shall be upon them.... And if a man take a wife and her mother, it is wickedness: they shall be burnt with fire, both he and they; that there be no wickedness among you.... And if a man shall take his sister, his father's daughter, or his mother's daughter, and see her nakedness, and she see his nakedness; it is a wicked thing; and they shall be cut off in the sight of their people: he hath uncovered his sister's nakedness; he shall bear his iniquity. And if a man shall lie with a woman having her sickness, and shall uncover her nakedness; he hath discovered her fountain, and she hath uncovered the fountain of her blood: and both of them shall be cut off from among their people. And thou shalt not uncover the nakedness of thy mother's sister, nor of thy father's sister: for he uncovereth his near kin: they shall bear their iniquity. And if a man shall lie with his uncle's wife, he hath uncovered his uncle's nakedness: they shall bear their sin; they shall die childless. And if a man shall take his brother's wife, it is an unclean thing: he hath uncovered his brother's nakedness; they shall be childless. Lev. 20:11-14, 17-21.

[Surely such laws and *such suggestions* should not be included in a book intended for universal reading by young and old. What would be thought of any Council School book, except the Bible, if it introduced laws concerning rape, incest, and unnatural crime, to the notice of children? Surely such regulations could be issued in a separate volume. The patriarchs were not noted for observing the laws against incest. Abraham ought to have been put to death for marrying his father's daughter (Lev. 20:17); Jacob for marrying his wife's sister during his first wife's lifetime (Neither shalt thou take a wife to her sister, to vex her, to uncover her nakedness, beside the other in her life time. ... For whosoever shall commit any of these abominations, even the souls that commit them shall be cut off from among their people. Lev. 18:18, 29); Judah and his daughter-in-law for their joint sin (Lev. 20:12); Reuben for incestuous intercourse with his father's concubine (Lev. 20:11); and Amram, the father of Moses, for marrying his aunt (And Amram took him Jochebed his father's sister to wife; and she bare him Aaron and Moses: and the years of the life of Amram were an hundred and thirty and seven years. Exod. 6:20; Lev. 20:19).]

212

Other laws describing various sexual offences, etc.

Rape.

But if a man find a betrothed damsel in the field, and the man force her, and lie with her: then the man only that lay with her shall die: But unto the damsel thou shalt do nothing; there is in the damsel no sin worthy of death: for as when a man riseth against his neighbour, and slayeth him, even so is this matter: For he found her in the field, and the betrothed damsel cried, and there was none to save her. If a man find a damsel that is a virgin, which is not betrothed, and lay hold on her, and lie with her, and they be found; Then the man that lay with her shall give unto the damsel's father fifty shekels of silver, and she shall be his wife; because he hath humbled her, he may not put her away all his days. Deut. 22:25-29.

Miscellaneous filth.

And if any man's seed of copulation go out from him, then he shall wash all his flesh in water, and be unclean until the even. . . . The woman also with whom man shall lie with seed of copulation, they shall both bathe themselves in water, and be unclean until the even. . . . And if any man lie with her at all, and her flowers be upon him, he shall be unclean seven days; and all the bed whereon he lieth shall be unclean. . . . This is the law of him that hath an issue, and of him whose seed goeth from him, and is defiled therewith; And of her that is sick of her flowers, and of him that hath an issue, of the man, and of the woman, and of him that lieth with her that is unclean. Lev. 15:16, 18, 24, 32, 33.

And if a man shall lie with a woman having her sickness, and shall uncover her nakedness; he hath discovered her fountain, and she hath uncovered the fountain of her blood: and both of them shall be cut off from among their people. Lev. 20:18.

Indecency.

When men strive together one with another, and the wife of the one draweth near for to deliver her husband out of the hand of him that smiteth him, and putteth forth her hand, and taketh him by the secrets: Then thou shalt cut off her hand, thine eye shall not pity her. Deut. 25:11, 12

Fornication.

And whosoever lieth carnally with a woman, that is a bondmaid, betrothed to an husband, and not at all redeemed, nor freedom given her; she shall be scourged; they shall not be put to death, because she was not free. Lev. 19:20.

And the daughter of any priest, if she profane herself by playing the whore, she profaneth her father: she shall be burnt with fire. Lev. 21:9.

Adultery.

If a man be found lying with a woman married to an husband, then they shall both of them die, both the man that lay with the woman, and the woman: so shalt thou put away evil from Israel. Deut. 22:22.

Unchastity.

But if this thing be true, and the tokens of virginity be not found for the damsel: Then they shall bring out the damsel to the door of her father's house, and the men of her city shall stone her with stones that she die: because she hath wrought folly in Israel, to play the whore in her father's house: so shalt thou put evil away from among you. Deut. 22:20, 21.

Castration.

He that is wounded in the stones, or hath his privy member cut off, shall not enter into the congregation of the LORD. Deut. 23:1.

For there are some eunuchs, which were so born from their mother's womb: and there are some eunuchs, which were made eunuchs of men: and there be eunuchs, which have made themselves eunuchs for the kingdom of heaven's sake. He that is able to receive it, let him receive it. Matt. 19:12.

Women reputed "unclean" after childbirth.

And the LORD spake unto Moses, saying, "Speak unto the children of Israel, saying, 'If a woman have conceived seed, and born a man child: then she shall be unclean seven days; according to the days of the separation for her infirmity shall she be unclean. And in the eighth day the flesh of his foreskin shall be circumcised. And she shall then continue in the blood of her purifying three and thirty days; she shall touch no hallowed thing, nor come into the sanctuary, until the days of her purifying be fulfilled. But if she bear a maid child, then she shall be unclean two weeks, as in her separation; and she shall continue in the blood of her purifying threescore and six days. And when the days of her purifying are fulfilled, for a son, or for a daughter, she shall bring a lamb of the first year for a burnt offering, and a young pigeon, or a turtledove, for a sin offering, unto the door of the tabernacle of the congregation, unto the priest: Who shall offer it before the LORD, and make an atonement for her; and she shall be cleansed from the issue of her blood. This is the law for her that hath born a male or a female. And if she be not able to bring a lamb, then she shall bring two turtles, or two young pigeons; the one for the burnt offering, and the other for a sin offering: and the priest shall make an atonement for her, and she shall be clean.' " Lev. 12:1-8.

[Why should motherhood be insulted as impure before God and man? Surely it should be held as honourable and as pure as any event can be.]

Motherhood pruriently stigmatized as sinful.
Behold, I was shapen in iniquity; and in sin did my mother conceive me. Ps. 51:5.

Effects of holy water on unfaithful wives.
Then the priest shall charge the woman with an oath of cursing, and the priest shall say unto the woman, "The LORD make thee a curse and an oath among thy people, when the LORD doth make thy thigh to rot: and thy belly to swell; And this water that causeth the curse shall go into thy bowels to make thy belly to swell, and thy thigh to rot:" And the woman shall say, "Amen, amen." . . . And when he hath made her to drink the water, then it shall come to pass, that, if she be defiled, and have done trespass against her husband, that the water that causeth the curse shall enter into her, and become bitter, and her belly shall swell, and her thigh shall rot: and the woman shall be a curse among her people. Num. 5:21, 22, 27.

[God did not trouble to institute any similar test for unfaithful husbands.]

Another religious cure for immorality or for marrying a foreigner.
And, behold, one of the children of Israel came and brought unto his brethren a Midianitish woman in the sight of Moses, and in the sight of all the congregation of the children of Israel, who were weeping before the door of the tabernacle of the congregation. And when Phinehas, the son of Eleazar, the son of Aaron the priest, saw it, he rose up from among the congregation, and took a javelin in his hand; And he went after the man of Israel into the tent, and thrust both of them through, the man of Israel, and the woman through her belly. So the plague was stayed from the children of Israel. . . . For they vex you with their wiles, wherewith they have beguiled you in the matter of Peor, and in the matter of Cozbi, the daughter of a prince of Midian, their sister, which was slain in the day of the plague for Peor's sake. Num. 25:6-8, 18.

Virgins and female children made "prey" and divided among God's warriors and priests.
"Now therefore kill every male among the little ones, and kill every woman that hath known man by lying with him. But all the women

children, that have not known a man by lying with him, keep alive for yourselves." ... And the booty, being the rest of the prey which the men of war had caught, was ... thirty and two thousand persons in all, of women that had not known man by lying with him. . . . of which the LORD's tribute was thirty and two persons. Num. 31:17, 18, 32, 35, 40.

[Thirty-two thousand women and children are thus alleged to have been captured as booty and divided between the congregation and the Lord.]

Filthy language used unnecessarily.

Then I will set my face against that man, and against his family, and will cut him off, and all that go a whoring after him, to commit whoredom with Molech, from among their people. And the soul that turneth after such as have familiar spirits, and after wizards, to go a whoring after them, I will even set my face against that soul, and will cut him off from among his people. Lev. 20:5, 6.

And they shall no more offer their sacrifices unto devils, after whom they have gone a whoring. This shall be a statute for ever unto them throughout their generations. Lev. 17:7.

Thou hast played the whore also with the Assyrians, because thou wast unsatiable; yea, thou hast played the harlot with them, and yet couldest not be satisfied. Ezek. 16:28.

The word of the LORD came again unto me, saying, "Son of man, there were two women, the daughters of one mother: And they committed whoredoms in Egypt; they committed whoredoms in their youth: there were their breasts pressed, and there they bruised the teats of their virginity. And the names of them were Aholah the elder, and Aholibah her sister: and they were mine, and they bare sons and daughters. Thus were their names; Samaria is Aholah, and Jerusalem Aholibah. And Aholah played the harlot when she was mine; and she doted on her lovers, on the Assyrians her neighbours, which were clothed with blue, captains and rulers, all of them desirable young men, horsemen riding upon horses. Thus she committed her whoredoms with them, with all them that were the chosen men of Assyria, and with all on whom she doted: with all their idols she defiled herself. Neither left she her whoredoms brought from Egypt: for in her youth they lay with her, and they bruised the breasts of her virginity, and poured their whoredom upon her. Wherefore I have delivered her into the hand of her lovers, into the hand of the Assyrians, upon whom she doted. These discovered her nakedness: they took her sons and her daughters, and slew her with the sword: and she became famous among women; for

216

they had executed judgment upon her. And when her sister Aholibah saw this, she was more corrupt in her inordinate love than she, and in her whoredoms more than her sister in her whoredoms. She doted upon the Assyrians her neighbours, captains and rulers clothed most gorgeously, horsemen riding upon horses, all of them desirable young men. Then I saw that she was defiled, that they took both one way. And that she increased her whoredoms: for when she saw men pourtrayed upon the wall, the images of the Chaldeans pourtrayed with vermilion, Girded with girdles upon their loins, exceeding in dyed attire upon their heads, all of them princes to look to, after the manner of the Babylonians of Chaldea, the land of their nativity: And as soon as she saw them with her eyes, she doted upon them, and sent messengers unto them into Chaldea. And the Babylonians came to her into the bed of love, and they defiled her with their whoredom, and she was polluted with them, and her mind was alienated from them. So she discovered her whoredoms, and discovered her nakedness: then my mind was alienated from her, like as my mind was alienated from her sister. Yet she multiplied her whoredoms, in calling to remembrance the days of her youth, wherein she had played the harlot in the land of Egypt. For she doted upon their paramours, whose flesh is as the flesh of asses, and whose issue is like the issue of horses. Thus thou calledst to remembrance the lewdness of thy youth, in bruising thy teats by the Egyptians for the paps of thy youth.

Therefore, O Aholibah, thus saith the Lord GOD; 'Behold, I will raise up thy lovers against thee, from whom thy mind is alienated, and I will bring them against thee on every side; The Babylonians, and all the Chaldeans, Pekod, and Shoa, and Koa, and all the Assyrians with them: all of them desirable young men, captains and rulers, great lords and renowned, all of them riding upon horses. And they shall come against thee with chariots, wagons, and wheels, and with an assembly of people, which shall set against thee buckler and shield and helmet round about: and I will set judgment before them, and they shall judge thee according to their judgments. And I will set my jealousy against thee, and they shall deal furiously with thee: they shall take away thy nose and thine ears; and thy remnant shall fall by the sword: they shall take thy sons and thy daughters; and thy residue shall be devoured by the fire. They shall also strip thee out of thy clothes, and take away thy fair jewels. Thus will I make thy lewdness to cease from thee, and thy whoredom brought from the land of Egypt: so that thou shalt not lift up thine eyes unto them, nor remember Egypt any more.' For thus saith the Lord GOD; 'Behold, I will deliver thee into the hand of them whom thou hatest, into the hand of them from whom thy mind is alienated: And they shall deal with thee hatefully, and shall take away all thy labour, and shall leave thee naked and bare: and the nakedness of thy whoredoms shall be discovered, both thy lewdness and thy whoredoms. I will do these things unto thee, because thou hast gone a whoring after the heathen, and because thou art polluted with their idols. Thou hast walked in the way of thy sister; therefore will I give her cup into thine hand.' Thus saith the Lord GOD; 'Thou shalt drink of thy sister's cup deep and large: thou shalt be laughed to scorn and had in derision; it containeth much. Thou shalt be filled with drunkenness and sorrow, with the cup of astonishment and desolation, with the cup of thy sister Samaria. Thou shalt even drink it and suck it out, and thou shalt break the sherds thereof, and pluck off thine own breasts: for I have spoken it,' saith the Lord GOD. Therefore thus saith the Lord GOD; 'Because thou hast forgotten me, and cast me behind thy back, therefore bear thou also thy lewdness and thy whoredoms.' "

The LORD said moreover unto me; "Son of man, wilt thou judge Aholah and Aholibah? yea, declare unto them their abominations; That they have committed adultery, and blood is in their hands, and with their idols have they committed adultery, and have also caused their sons, whom they bare unto me, to pass for them through the fire, to devour them. Moreover this they have done unto me: they have defiled my sanctuary in the same day, and have profaned my sabbaths. For when they had slain their children to their idols, then they came the same day into my sanctuary to profane it; and, lo, thus have they done in the midst of mine house. And furthermore, that ye have sent for men to come from far, unto whom a messenger was sent; and, lo, they came: for whom thou didst wash thyself, paintedst thy eyes, and deckedst thyself with ornaments, And satest upon a stately bed, and a table prepared before it, whereupon thou hast set mine incense and mine oil. And a voice of a multitude being at ease was with her: and with the men of the common sort were brought Sabeans from the wilderness, which put bracelets upon their hands, and beautiful crowns upon their heads. Then I said unto her that was old in adulteries, 'Will they now commit whoredoms with her, and she with them?' Yet they went in unto her, as they go in unto a woman that playeth the harlot: so went they in unto Aholah and unto Aholibah, the lewd women.

And the righteous men, they shall judge them after the manner of adulteresses, and after the manner of women that shed blood; because they are adulteresses, and blood is in their hands. For thus saith the Lord GOD; 'I will bring up a company upon them, and will give them to

218

be removed and spoiled. And the company shall stone them with stones, and dispatch them with their swords; they shall slay their sons and their daughters, and burn up their houses with fire. Thus will I cause lewdness to cease out of the land, that all women may be taught not to do after your lewdness. And they shall recompense your lewdness upon you, and ye shall bear the sins of your idols: and ye shall know that I am the Lord GOD.' " Ezek. 23:1-49.

And they that escape of you shall remember me among the nations whither they shall be carried captives, because I am broken with their whorish heart, which hath departed from me, and with their eyes, which go a whoring after their idols: and they shall loathe themselves for the evils which they have committed in all their abominations. Ezek. 6:9.

And it came to pass through the lightness of her whoredom, that she defiled the land, and committed adultery with stones and with stocks. Jer. 3:9.

And there came one of the seven angels which had the seven vials, and talked with me, saying unto me, "Come hither; I will shew unto thee the judgment of the great whore that sitteth upon many waters: With whom the kings of the earth have committed fornication, and the inhabitants of the earth have been made drunk with the wine of her fornication." So he carried me away in the spirit into the wilderness: and I saw a woman sit upon a scarlet coloured beast, full of names of blasphemy, having seven heads and ten horns. And the woman was arrayed in purple and scarlet colour, and decked with gold and precious stones and pearls, having a golden cup in her hand full of abominations and filthiness of her fornication: And upon her forehead was a name written, MYSTERY, BABYLON THE GREAT, THE MOTHER OF HARLOTS AND ABOMINATIONS OF THE EARTH. . . . And he saith unto me, "The waters which thou sawest, where the whore sitteth, are peoples, and multitudes, and nations, and tongues. And the ten horns which thou sawest upon the beast, these shall hate the whore, and shall make her desolate and naked, and shall eat her flesh, and burn her with fire." Rev. 17:1-5, 15, 16.

My people ask counsel at their stocks, and their staff declareth unto them: for the spirit of whoredoms hath caused them to err, and they have gone a whoring from under their God. Hos. 4:12.

I have seen an horrible thing in the house of Israel: there is the whoredom of Ephraim, Israel is defiled. Hos. 6:10.

Rejoice not, O Israel, for joy, as other people: for thou hast gone a whoring from thy God, thou hast loved a reward upon every cornfloor. Hos. 9:1.

Because of the multitude of the whoredoms of the wellfavoured harlot, the mistress of witchcrafts, that selleth nations through her whoredoms, and families through her witchcrafts. Nah. 3:4.

Lest thou make a covenant with the inhabitants of the land, and they go a whoring after their gods, and do sacrifice unto their gods, and one call thee, and thou eat of his sacrifice; And thou take of their daughters unto thy sons, and their daughters go a whoring after their gods, and make thy sons go a whoring after their gods. Exod. 34:15, 16.

And it shall be unto you for a fringe, that ye may look upon it, and remember all the commandments of the LORD, and do them; and that ye seek not after your own heart and your own eyes, after which ye use to go a whoring. Num. 15:39.

For, lo, they that are far from thee shall perish: thou hast destroyed all them that go a whoring from thee. Ps. 73:27.

Thus were they defiled with their own works, and went a whoring with their own inventions. Ps. 106:39.

And yet they would not hearken unto their judges, but they went a whoring after other gods, and bowed themselves unto them: they turned quickly out of the way which their fathers walked in, obeying the commandments of the LORD; but they did not so. Judges 2:17.

And it came to pass, as soon as Gideon was dead, that the children of Israel turned again, and went a whoring after Baalim, and made Baalberith their god. Judges 8:33.

So and more also do God unto the enemies of David, if I leave of all that pertain to him by the morning light any that pisseth against the wall .... For in very deed, as the LORD God of Israel liveth, which hath kept me back from hurting thee, except thou hadst hasted and come to meet me, surely there had not been left unto Nabal by the morning light any that pisseth against the wall. 1 Sam. 25:22, 34. [Conversation addressed by David to a lady.]

Therefore, behold, I will bring evil upon the house of Jeroboam, and will cut off from Jeroboam him that pisseth against the wall, and him that is shut up and left in Israel, and will take away the remnant of the house of Jeroboam, as a man taketh away dung, till it be all gone. 1 Kings 14:10.

And it came to pass, when he began to reign, as soon as he sat on his throne, that he slew all the house of Baasha: he left him not one that pisseth against a wall, neither of his kinsfolks, nor of his friends. 1 Kings 16:11.

Behold, I will bring evil upon thee, and will take away thy posterity, and will cut off from Ahab him that pisseth against the wall, and him that is shut up and left in Israel. 1 Kings 21:21.

For the whole house of Ahab shall perish: and I will cut off from Ahab him that pisseth against the wall, and him that is shut up and left in Israel. 2 Kings 9:8.

But Rabshakeh said unto them, "Hath my master sent me to thy master, and to thee, to speak these words? hath he not sent me to the men which sit on the wall, that they may eat their own dung, and drink their own piss with you?" 2 Kings 18:27.

But Rabshakeh said, "Hath my master sent me to thy master and to thee to speak these words? hath he not sent me to the men that sit upon the wall, that they may eat their own dung, and drink their own piss with you?" Isa. 36:12.

Circumcise therefore the foreskin of your heart, and be no more stiffnecked. Deut. 10:16.

And the LORD thy God will circumcise thine heart, and the heart of thy seed, to love the LORD thy God with all thine heart, and with all thy soul, that thou mayest live. Deut. 30:6.

Circumcise yourselves to the LORD, and take away the foreskins of your heart, ye men of Judah and inhabitants of Jerusalem: lest my fury come forth like fire, and burn that none can quench it, because of the evil of your doings. Jer. 4:4.

Filthy ideas on the part of God.

Behold, I will corrupt your seed, and spread dung upon your faces.... Mal. 2:3.

And thou shalt eat it as barley cakes, and thou shalt bake it with dung that cometh out of man, in their sight. Ezek. 4:12.

Unnecessary references to parturition, menstruation, conception, begetting, harlotry, fornication, belly, womb, etc.

And toward her young one that cometh out from between her feet, and toward her children which she shall bear: for she shall eat them for want of all things secretly in the siege and straitness, wherewith thine enemy shall distress thee in thy gates. Deut. 28:57.

Woe unto him that saith unto his father, "What begettest thou?" or to the woman, "What hast thou brought forth?" Isa. 45:10.

And if a woman have an issue, and her issue in her flesh be blood, she shall be put apart seven days: and whosoever toucheth her shall be unclean until the even. And every thing that she lieth upon in her separation shall be unclean: every thing also that she sitteth upon shall be unclean. And whosoever toucheth her bed shall wash his clothes, and bathe himself in water, and be unclean until the even. And whosoever toucheth any thing that she sat upon shall wash his clothes, and bathe himself in water, and be unclean until the even. And if it be on her bed, or on any thing whereon she sitteth, when he toucheth it, he shall be unclean until the even. . . . And of her that is sick of her flowers, and of him that hath an issue, of the man, and of the woman, and of him that lieth with her that is unclean. Lev. 15:19-23, 33.

And it came to pass, that, when Elisabeth heard the salutation of Mary, the babe leaped in her womb; and Elisabeth was filled with the Holy Ghost. And she spake out with a loud voice, and said, "Blessed art thou among women, and blessed is the fruit of thy womb. . . . For, lo, as soon as the voice of thy salutation sounded in mine ears, the babe leaped in my womb for joy." Luke 1:41, 42, 44.

And when the LORD saw that Leah was hated, he opened her womb: but Rachel was barren. Gen. 29:31.

And David comforted Bathsheba his wife, and went in unto her, and lay with her: and she bare a son, and he called his name Solomon: and the LORD loved him. 2 Sam. 12:24.

Hearken unto me, O house of Jacob, and all the remnant of the house of Israel, which are borne by me from the belly, which are carried from the womb. Isa. 46:3.

And it shall come to pass after the end of seventy years, that the LORD will visit Tyre, and she shall turn to her hire, and shall commit fornication with all the kingdoms of the world upon the face of the earth. Isa. 23:17.

Because of the multitude of the whoredoms of the wellfavoured harlot, the mistress of witchcrafts, that selleth nations through her whoredoms, and families through her witchcrafts. Nahum 3:4.

With whom the kings of the earth have committed fornication, and the inhabitants of the earth have been made drunk with the wine of her fornication. Rev. 17:2.

[It is needless to give any more of the innumerable instances of language of this kind. The free use of such words and ideas is not in good taste, and is extremely objectionable in a book intended for general use.]

God will cause wives to be ravished.

Their children also shall be dashed to pieces before their eyes; their houses shall be spoiled, and their wives ravished. Isa. 13:16.

For I will gather all nations against Jerusalem to battle; and the city shall be taken, and the houses rifled, and the women ravished; and half of the city shall go forth into captivity, and the residue of the people shall not be cut off from the city. Zech. 14:2.

Thus saith the LORD, "Behold, I will raise up evil against thee out of thine own house, and I will take thy wives before thine eyes, and give them unto thy neighbour, and he shall lie with thy wives in the sight of this sun." 2 Sam. 12:11.

Therefore will I give their wives unto others, and their fields to them that shall inherit them: for every one from the least even unto the greatest is given to covetousness, from the prophet even unto the priest every one dealeth falsely. Jer. 8:10.

And their houses shall be turned unto others, with their fields and wives together: for I will stretch out my hand upon the inhabitants of the land, saith the LORD. Jer. 6:12.

Thou shalt betroth a wife, and another man shall lie with her: thou shalt build an house, and thou shalt not dwell therein: thou shalt plant a vineyard, and shalt not gather the grapes thereof. Deut. 28:30.

Women may be captured and married, and then dismissed at will.

When thou goest forth to war against thine enemies, and the LORD thy God hath delivered them into thine hands, and thou hast taken them captive, And seest among the captives a beautiful woman, and hast a desire unto her, that thou wouldest have her to thy wife; Then thou shalt bring her home to thine house; and she shall shave her head, and pare her nails; And she shall put the raiment of her captivity from off her, and shall remain in thine house, and bewail her father and her mother a full month: and after that thou shalt go in unto her, and be her husband, and she shall be thy wife. And it shall be, if thou have no delight in her, then thou shalt let her go whither she will; but thou shalt not sell her at all for money, thou shalt not make merchandise of her, because thou hast humbled her. Deut. 21:10-14.

Polygamy sanctioned.

If a man have two wives, one beloved, and another hated, and they have born him children, both the beloved and the hated; and if the firstborn son be hers that was hated: Deut. 21:15.

[The habitual polygamy of David, Solomon, and the patriarchs, shows conclusively that the Bible had not prohibited such customs.]

Divorce at will.

When a man hath taken a wife, and married her, and it come to pass that she find no favour in his eyes, because he hath found some uncleanness in her: then let him write her a bill of divorcement, and give it in her hand, and send her out of his house. Deut. 24:1-3.

They say unto him, "Why did Moses then command to give a writing of divorcement, and to put her away?" He saith unto them, "Moses because of the hardness of your hearts suffered you to put away your wives: but from the beginning it was not so." Matt. 19:7, 8.

And they said, "Moses suffered to write a bill of divorcement, and to put her away." Mark 10:4.

And it shall be, if thou have no delight in her, then thou shalt let her go whither she will; but thou shalt not sell her at all for money, thou shalt not make merchandise of her, because thou hast humbled her. Deut. 21:14.

And Abraham rose up early in the morning, and took bread, and a bottle of water, and gave it unto Hagar, putting it on her shoulder, and the child, and sent her away: and she departed, and wandered in the wilderness of Beersheba. Gen. 21:14.

Men are to have children by their brother's widow.

If brethren dwell together, and one of them die, and have no child, the wife of the dead shall not marry without unto a stranger: her husband's brother shall go in unto her, and take her to him to wife, and perform the duty of an husband's brother unto her. And it shall be, that the firstborn which she beareth shall succeed in the name of his brother which is dead, that his name be not put out of Israel. And if the man like not to take his brother's wife, then let his brother's wife go up to the gate unto the elders, and say, "My husband's brother refuseth to raise up unto his brother a name in Israel, he will not perform the duty of my husband's brother." Then the elders of his city shall call him, and speak unto him: and if he stand to it, and say, "I like not to take her;" Then shall his brother's wife come unto him in the presence of the elders, and loose his shoe from off his foot, and spit in his face, and shall answer and say, "So shall it be done unto that man that will not build up his brother's house." And his name shall be called in Israel, "The house of him that hath his shoe loosed." Deut. 25:5-10.

Master, Moses wrote unto us, "If a man's brother die, and leave his wife behind him, and leave no children, that his brother should take his wife, and raise up seed unto his brother." Now there were seven brethren: and the first took a wife, and dying left no seed. And the second took her, and died, neither left he any seed: and the third likewise. And the seven had her, and left no seed: last of all the woman died also. In the resurrection therefore, when they shall rise, whose wife shall she be of them? for the seven had her to wife. Mark 12:19-23.

[In the case put before Jesus in Mark 12:19-23 seven brothers successively are supposed to have taken the same woman. This wife was evidently in addition to any others a man might have.]

Rahab the harlot.

And Joshua the son of Nun sent out of Shittim two men to spy secretly, saying, "Go view the land, even Jericho." And they went, and came into an harlot's house, named Rahab, and lodged there. Josh. 2:1.

And the city shall be accursed, even it, and all that are therein, to the LORD: only Rahab the harlot shall live, she and all that are with her in the house, because she hid the messengers that we sent. . . . And Joshua saved Rahab the harlot alive, and her father's household, and all that she had; and she dwelleth in Israel even unto this day; because she hid the messengers, which Joshua sent to spy out Jericho. Josh. 6:17, 25.

[This harlot is commended for her treachery in Heb. 11:31: (By faith the harlot Rahab perished not with them that believed not, when she had received the spies with peace.) and James 2:25: (Likewise also was not Rahab the harlot justified by works, when she had received the messengers, and had sent them out another way?).]

Joshua circumcises all the males of Israel.

At that time the LORD said unto Joshua, "Make thee sharp knives, and circumcise again the children of Israel the second time." And Joshua made him sharp knives, and circumcised the children of Israel at the hill of the foreskins. And this is the cause why Joshua did circumcise: All the people that came out of Egypt, that were males, even all the men of war, died in the wilderness by the way, after they came out of Egypt. Now all the people that came out were circumcised: but all the people that were born in the wilderness by the way as they came forth out of Egypt, them they had not circumcised. For the children of Israel walked forty years in the wilderness, till all the people that were men of war, which came out of Egypt, were consumed, because they obeyed not the voice of the LORD: unto whom the LORD sware that he would not shew them the land, which the LORD sware unto their fathers that he would give us, a land that floweth with milk and honey. And their children, whom he raised up in their stead, them Joshua circumcised: for they were uncircumcised, because they had not circumcised them by the way. And it came to pass, when they had done circumcising all the people, that they abode in their places in the camp, till they were whole. Josh. 5:2-8.

Gideon has many wives and a concubine.
And Gideon had threescore and ten sons of his body begotten: for he had many wives. And his concubine that was in Shechem, she also bare him a son, whose name he called Abimelech. Judg. 8:30, 31.

Women conceive after interviews with men of God.
And the angel of the LORD appeared unto the woman, and said unto her, "Behold now, thou art barren, and bearest not: but thou shalt conceive, and bear a son." . . . Then the woman came and told her husband, saying, "A man of God came unto me, and his countenance was like the countenance of an angel of God, very terrible: but I asked him not whence he was, neither told he me his name." . . . And God hearkened to the voice of Manoah; and the angel of God came again unto the woman as she sat in the field: but Manoah her husband was not with her. . . . And the woman bare a son, and called his name Samson: and the child grew, and the LORD blessed him. Judg. 13:3, 6, 9, 24.

Now there was a certain man of Ramathaimzophim, of mount Ephraim, and his name was Elkanah, the son of Jeroham, the son of Elihu, the son of Tohu, the son of Zuph, an Ephrathite: And he had two wives; the name of the one was Hannah, and the name of the other Peninnah: and Peninnah had children, but Hannah had no children. . . . Now Hannah, she spake in her heart; only her lips moved, but her voice was not heard: therefore Eli thought she had been drunken. And Eli said unto her, "How long wilt thou be drunken? put away thy wine from thee." And Hannah answered and said, "No, my Lord, I am a woman of a sorrowful spirit: I have drunk neither wine nor strong drink, but have poured out my soul before the LORD." . . . Then Eli answered and said, "Go in peace: and the God of Israel grant thee thy petition that thou hast asked of him." . . . Wherefore it came to pass, when the time was come about after Hannah had conceived, that she bare a son, and called his name Samuel, saying, "Because I have asked him of the LORD." 1 Sam. 1:1, 2, 13-15, 17, 20.

And it fell on a day, that he came thither, and he turned into the chamber and lay there. And he said to Gehazi his servant, "Call this Shunammite. And when he had called her, she stood before him. . . . And he said, "About this season, according to the time of life, thou shalt embrace a son." And she said, "Nay, my lord, thou man of God, do not lie unto thine handmaid." And the woman conceived, and bare a son at

226

that season that Elisha had said unto her, according to the time of life. 2 Kings 4:11-12, 16-17.

[God might easily have taken away all suspicion of impropriety by employing lady messengers or lady angels in these delicate cases.]

Samson and the harlot.

Then went Samson to Gaza, and saw there an harlot, and went in unto her. And it was told the Gazites, saying, "Samson is come hither." And they compassed him in, and laid wait for him all night in the gate of the city, and were quiet all the night, saying, "In the morning, when it is day, we shall kill him." And Samson lay till midnight, and arose at midnight, and took the doors of the gate of the city, and the two posts, and went away with them, bar and all, and put them upon his shoulders, and carried them up to the top of an hill that is before Hebron. Judg. 16:1-3.

[Samson was inspired by the "spirit of the LORD" ("And the Spirit of the LORD began to move him at times in the camp of Dan between Zorah and Eshtaol." — Judg. 13:25; "And the Spirit of the LORD came upon him, and he went down to Ashkelon, and slew thirty men of them, and took their spoil, and gave change of garments unto them which expounded the riddle. And his anger was kindled, and he went up to his father's house." Judg. 14:19). Did the "divine spirit" inspire him during his numerous amours?]

Samson and Delilah.

And it came to pass afterward, that he loved a woman in the valley of Sorek, whose name was Delilah. And the lords of the Philistines came up unto her, and said unto her, "Entice him, and see wherein his great strength lieth, and by what means we may prevail against him, that we may bind him to afflict him: and we will give thee every one of us eleven hundred pieces of silver." And Delilah said to Samson, "Tell me, I pray thee, wherein thy great strength lieth, and wherewith thou mightest be bound to afflict thee." . . . And it came to pass, when she pressed him daily with her words, and urged him, so that his soul was vexed unto death; That he told her all his heart, and said unto her, "There hath not come a razor upon mine head; for I have been a Nazarite unto God from my mother's womb: if I be shaven, then my strength will go from me, and I shall become weak, and be like any other man." And when Delilah saw that he had told her all his heart, she sent and called for the lords of the Philistines, saying, "Come up this once, for he hath shewed me all his heart." Then the lords of the Philistines came up unto her, and brought money in their hand. And she made him sleep upon her knees; and she called for a man, and she caused him to shave off the seven locks of his head; and she began to afflict him, and his strength went from him. And she said, "The Philistines be upon thee, Samson." And he awoke out of his sleep, and said, "I will go out as at other times before, and shake myself." And he wist not that the LORD was departed from him. But the Philistines took him, and put out his eyes, and brought him down to Gaza, and bound him with fetters of brass; and he did grind in the prison house. Judg. 16:4-6, 16-21.

A cowardly priest thrusts forth his concubine to a lustful mob.

Now as they were making their hearts merry, behold, the men of the city, certain sons of Belial, beset the house round about, and beat at the door, and spake to the master of the house, the old man, saying, "Bring forth the man that came into thine house, that we may know him." And the man, the master of the house, went out unto them, and said unto them, "Nay, my brethren, nay, I pray you, do not so wickedly; seeing that this man is come into mine house, do not this folly. Behold, here is my daughter a maiden, and his concubine; them I will bring out now, and humble ye them, and do with them what seemeth good unto you: but unto this man do not so vile a thing." But the men would not hearken to him: so the man took his concubine, and brought her forth unto them; and they knew her, and abused her all the night until the morning: and when the day began to spring, they let her go. Then came the woman in the dawning of the day, and fell down at the door of the man's house where her lord was, till it was light. And her lord rose up in the morning, and opened the doors of the house, and went out to go his way: and, behold, the woman his concubine was fallen down at the door of the house, and her hands were upon the threshold. And he said unto her, "Up, and let us be going." But none answered. Then the man took her up upon an ass, and the man rose up, and gat him unto his place. And when he was come into his house, he took a knife, and laid hold on his concubine, and divided her, together with her bones, into twelve pieces, and sent her into all the coasts of Israel. And it was so, that all that saw it said, "There was no such deed done nor seen from the day that the children of Israel came up out of the land of Egypt unto this day: consider of it, take advice, and speak your minds." Judg. 19:22-30.

[In this filthy story the lusts of a beastly crowd are satiated upon the concubine until she falls dead in the morning light. The priestly dastard who has thus sacrificed his property, then cuts up her body and sends pieces to the tribes.]

228

Four hundred wives seized.

"And this is the thing that ye shall do, Ye shall utterly destroy every male, and every woman that hath lain by man." And they found among the inhabitants of Jabeshgilead four hundred young virgins, that had known no man by lying with any male: and they brought them unto the camp to Shiloh, which is in the land of Canaan. And the whole congregation sent some to speak to the children of Benjamin that were in the rock Rimmon, and to call peaceably unto them. And Benjamin came again at that time; and they gave them wives which they had saved alive of the women of Jabeshgilead: and yet so they sufficed them not. Judg. 21:11-14.

More wives seized at a friendly feast.

Then they said, "Behold, there is a feast of the LORD in Shiloh yearly in a place which is on the north side of Bethel, on the east side of the highway that goeth up from Bethel to Shechem, and on the south of Lebonah." Therefore they commanded the children of Benjamin, saying, "Go and lie in wait in the vineyards; And see, and, behold, if the daughters of Shiloh come out to dance in dances, then come ye out of the vineyards, and catch you every man his wife of the daughters of Shiloh, and go to the land of Benjamin. And it shall be, when their fathers or their brethren come unto us to complain, that we will say unto them, 'Be favorable unto them for our sakes: because we reserved not to each man his wife in the war: for ye did not give unto them at this time, that ye should be guilty.' " And the children of Benjamin did so, and took them wives, according to their number, of them that danced, whom they caught: and they went and returned unto their inheritance, and repaired the cities, and dwelt in them. Judg. 21:19-23.

Ruth's adventures in the barn with Boaz.

"And it shall be, when he lieth down, that thou shalt mark the place where he shall lie, and thou shalt go in, and uncover his feet, and lay thee down; and he will tell thee what thou shalt do." And she said unto her, "All that thou sayest unto me I will do." And she went down unto the floor, and did according to all that her mother in law bade her. And when Boaz had eaten and drunk, and his heart was merry, he went to lie down at the end of the heap of corn: and she came softly, and uncovered his feet, and laid her down. And it came to pass at midnight, that the man was afraid, and turned himself: and, behold, a woman lay at his feet. And he said, "Who art thou?" And she answered, "I am Ruth thine handmaid: spread therefore thy skirt over thine handmaid; for thou art a near kinsman." And he said, "Blessed be thou of the LORD, my daughter: for thou hast shewed more kindness in the latter end than at the beginning, inasmuch as thou followedst not young men, whether poor or rich. And now, my daughter, fear not; I will do to thee all that thou requirest: for all the city of my people doth know that thou art a virtuous woman. And now it is true that I am thy near kinsman: howbeit there is a kinsman nearer than I. Tarry this night, and it shall be in the morning, that if he will perform unto thee the part of a kinsman, well; let him do the kinsman's part: but if he will not do the part of a kinsman to thee, then will I do the part of a kinsman to thee, as the LORD liveth: lie down until the morning." And she lay at his feet until the morning: and she rose up before one could know another. And he said, "Let it not be known that a woman came into the floor." Also he said, "Bring the vail that thou hast upon thee, and hold it." And when she held it, he measured six measures of barley, and laid it on her: and she went into the city. Ruth 3:4-15.

[Whatever may have been the ancient custom, this is hardly an edifying story for modern maidens. A girl who lay down by a man in the dark, and asked him to spread his skirt over her, and who departed secretly next morning with a present, would hardly meet with modern approval.]

Eli's lecherous sons.

Now Eli was very old, and heard all that his sons did unto all Israel; and how they lay with the women that assembled at the door of the tabernacle of the congregation. 1 Sam. 2:22.

God's filthy revenge on those who captured the ark.

But the hand of the LORD was heavy upon them of Ashdod, and he destroyed them, and smote them with emerods, even Ashdod and the coasts thereof. . . . And it was so, that, after they had carried it about, the hand of the LORD was against the city with a very great destruction: and he smote the men of the city, both small and great, and they had emerods in their secret parts. . . . And the men that died not were smitten with the emerods: and the cry of the city went up to heaven. 1 Sam. 5:6, 9, 12.

[Emerods (hemorrhoids) are "livid, painful, bleeding tubercles about the anus." Golden emerods were subsequently sent to the LORD as a trespass-offering. ("Wherefore ye shall make images of your emerods, and images of your mice that mar the land; and ye shall give glory unto the God of Israel: peradventure he will lighten his hand from off you, and from off your gods, and from off your land.". . . And they laid the ark of the LORD upon the cart, and the coffer with the mice of gold and the images of their emerods. 1 Sam. 6:5, 11). Voltaire refers to them as golden anuses.]

A dowry of a hundred foreskins.

And Saul said, "Thus shall ye say to David, 'The king desireth not any dowry, but an hundred foreskins of the Philistines, to be avenged of the king's enemies.'" But Saul thought to make David fall by the hand of the Philistines. . . . Wherefore David arose and went, he and his men, and slew of the Philistines two hundred men; and David brought their foreskins, and they gave them in full tale to the king, that he might be the king's son in law. And Saul gave him Michal his daughter to wife. 1 Sam. 18:25, 27.

[King Saul asked only a hundred foreskins of Philistines in return for the hand of his daughter Michal. David cut off two hundred. Voltaire supposes they were sent as a necklace to the bride won by this remarkable present, of which David and Saul were evidently more proud than Indians of their captured scalps.]

King Saul's prophecies and nakedness.

And he went thither to Naioth in Ramah: and the Spirit of God was upon him [Saul] also, and he went on, and prophesied, until he came to Naioth in Ramah. And he stripped off his clothes also, and prophesied before Samuel in like manner, and lay down naked all that day and all that night. Wherefore they say, "Is Saul also among the prophets?" 1 Sam. 19:23, 24.

The man after God's own heart practices polygamy and concubinage.

And David took him more concubines and wives out of Jerusalem, after he was come from Hebron: and there were yet sons and daughters born to David. 2 Sam. 5:13.

And Nathan said to David, "Thou art the man. Thus saith the LORD God of Israel, 'I anointed thee king over Israel, and I delivered thee out of the hand of Saul; And I gave thee thy master's house, and thy master's wives into thy bosom, and gave thee the house of Israel and of Judah; and if that had been too little, I would moreover have given unto thee such and such things.'" 2 Sam. 12:7, 8.

And David came to his house at Jerusalem; and the king took the ten women his concubines, whom he had left to keep the house, and put them in ward, and fed them, but went not in unto them. So they were shut up unto the day of their death, living in widowhood. 2 Sam. 20:3.

231

David's indecent dancing before the ark.
And David danced before the LORD with all his might; and David was girded with a linen ephod. So David and all the house of Israel brought up the ark of the LORD with shouting, and with the sound of the trumpet. And as the ark of the LORD came into the city of David, Michal Saul's daughter looked through a window, and saw king David leaping and dancing before the LORD; and she despised him in her heart. . . . Then David returned to bless his household. And Michal the daughter of Saul came out to meet David, and said, "How glorious was the king of Israel to day, who uncovered himself to day in the eyes of the handmaids of his servants, as one of the vain fellows shamelessly uncovereth himself!" And David said unto Michal, "It was before the LORD, which chose me before thy father, and before all his house, to appoint me ruler over the people of the LORD, over Israel: therefore will I play before the LORD. And I will yet be more vile than thus, and will be base in mine own sight: and of the maidservants which thou hast spoken of, of them shall I be had in honour." Therefore Michal the daughter of Saul had no child unto the day of her death. 2 Sam. 6:14-16, 20-23.

David commits adultery.
And it came to pass in an eveningtide, that David arose from off his bed, and walked upon the roof of the king's house: and from the roof he saw a woman washing herself; and the woman was very beautiful to look upon. And David sent and enquired after the woman. And one said, "Is not this Bathsheba, the daughter of Eliam, the wife of Uriah the Hittite?" And David sent messengers, and took her; and she came in unto him, and he lay with her; for she was purified from her uncleanness: and she returned unto her house. And the woman conceived, and sent and told David, and said, "I am with child." And David sent to Joab, saying, "Send me Uriah the Hittite." And Joab sent Uriah to David. And when Uriah was come unto him, David demanded of him how Joab did, and how the people did, and how the war prospered. And David said to Uriah, "Go down to thy house, and wash thy feet." And Uriah departed out of the king's house, and there followed him a mess of meat from the king. But Uriah slept at the door of the king's house with all the servants of his lord, and went not down to his house. And when they had told David, saying, "Uriah went not down unto his house," David said unto Uriah, "Camest thou not from thy journey? why then didst thou not go down unto thine house?" And Uriah said unto David, "The ark, and Israel, and Judah, abide in tents;

and my lord Joab, and the servants of my lord, are encamped in the open fields; shall I then go into mine house, to eat and to drink, and to lie with my wife? as thou livest, and as thy soul liveth, I will not do this thing." And David said to Uriah, "Tarry here to day also, and to morrow I will let thee depart." So Uriah abode in Jerusalem that day, and the morrow. And when David had called him, he did eat and drink before him; and he made him drunk: and at even he went out to lie on his bed with the servants of his lord, but went not down to his house. And it came to pass in the morning, that David wrote a letter to Joab, and sent it by the hand of Uriah. And he wrote in the letter, saying, "Set ye Uriah in the forefront of the hottest battle, and retire ye from him, that he may be smitten, and die." And it came to pass, when Joab observed the city, that he assigned Uriah unto a place where he knew that valiant men were. And the men of the city went out, and fought with Joab: and there fell some of the people of the servants of David; and Uriah the Hittite died also. Then Joab sent and told David all the things concerning the war; and charged the messenger, saying, "When thou hast made an end of telling the matters of the war unto the king, and if so be that the king's wrath arise, and he say unto thee, 'Wherefore approached ye so nigh unto the city when ye did fight? knew ye not that they would shoot from the wall? Who smote Abimelech the son of Jerubbesheth? did not a woman cast a piece of millstone upon him from the wall, that he died in Thebez? why went ye nigh the wall?' then say thou, 'Thy servant Uriah the Hittite is dead also.' So the messenger went, and came and shewed David all that Joab had sent him for. And the messenger said unto David, "Surely the men prevailed against us, and came out unto us into the field, and we were upon them even unto the entering of the gate. And the shooters shot from off the wall upon thy servants; and some of the king's servants be dead, and thy servant Uriah the Hittite is dead also." Then said David unto the messenger, "Thus shalt thou say unto Joab, 'Let not this thing displease thee, for the sword devoureth one as well as another: make thy battle more strong against the city, and overthrow it:' and encourage thou him." And when the wife of Uriah heard that Uriah her husband was dead, she mourned for her husband. And when the mourning was past, David sent and fetched her to his house, and she became his wife, and bare him a son. But the thing that David had done displeased the LORD. 2 Sam. 11:2-27.

[David, however, was pious, if immoral. The Bible carefully informs us that Bathsheba was "purified" from her ceremonial "uncleanness" before the act of adultery took place. (2 Sam. 11:4.)]

God punishes adultery with open incest "before all Israel and before the sun."

Thus saith the LORD, "Behold, I will raise up evil against thee out of thine own house, and I will take thy wives before thine eyes, and give them unto thy neighbour, and he shall lie with thy wives in the sight of this sun. For thou didst it secretly: but I will do this thing before all Israel, and before the sun." 2 Sam. 12:11, 12.

And Ahithophel said unto Absalom, "Go in unto thy father's concubines, which he hath left to keep the house; and all Israel shall hear that thou art abhorred of thy father: then shall the hands of all that are with thee be strong." So they spread Absalom a tent upon the top of the house; and Absalom went in unto his father's concubines in the sight of all Israel. And the counsel of Ahithophel, which he counselled in those days, was as if a man had enquired at the oracle of God: so was all the counsel of Ahithophel both with David and with Absalom. 2 Sam. 16:21-23.

Ammon ravishes his sister Tamar.

And it came to pass after this, that Absalom the son of David had a fair sister, whose name was Tamar; and Amnon the son of David loved her. And Amnon was so vexed, that he fell sick for his sister Tamar; for she was a virgin; and Amnon thought it hard for him to do any thing to her. But Amnon had a friend, whose name was Jonadab, the son of Shimeah David's brother: and Jonadab was a very subtil man. And he said unto him, "Why art thou, being the king's son, lean from day to day? wilt thou not tell me?" And Amnon said unto him, "I love Tamar, my brother Absalom's sister." And Jonadab said unto him, "Lay thee down on thy bed, and make thyself sick: and when thy father cometh to see thee, say unto him, 'I pray thee, let my sister Tamar come, and give me meat, and dress the meat in my sight, that I may see it, and eat it at her hand.'" So Amnon lay down, and made himself sick: and when the king was come to see him, Amnon said unto the king, "I pray thee, let Tamar my sister come, and make me a couple of cakes in my sight, that I may eat at her hand." Then David sent home to Tamar, saying, "Go now to thy brother Amnon's house, and dress him meat." So Tamar went to her brother Amnon's house; and he was laid down. And she took flour, and kneaded it, and made cakes in his sight, and did bake the cakes. And she took a pan, and poured them out before him; but he refused to eat. And Amnon said, "Have out all men from me." And they went out every man from him. And Amnon said unto Tamar, "Bring the meat into the chamber, that I may eat of thine hand." And Tamar took

234

the cakes which she had made, and brought them into the chamber to Amnon her brother. And when she had brought them unto him to eat, he took hold of her, and said unto her, "Come lie with me, my sister." And she answered him, "Nay, my brother, do not force me; for no such thing ought to be done in Israel: do not thou this folly. And I, whither shall I cause my shame to go? and as for thee, thou shalt be as one of the fools in Israel. Now therefore, I pray thee, speak unto the king; for he will not withhold me from thee." Howbeit he would not hearken unto her voice: but, being stronger than she, forced her, and lay with her. Then Amnon hated her exceedingly; so that the hatred wherewith he hated her was greater than the love wherewith he had loved her. And Amnon said unto her, "Arise, be gone." And she said unto him, "There is no cause: this evil in sending me away is greater than the other that thou didst unto me." But he would not hearken unto her. Then he called his servant that ministered unto him, and said, "Put now this woman out from me, and bolt the door after her." And she had a garment of divers colours upon her: for with such robes were the king's daughters that were virgins apparelled. Then his servant brought her out, and bolted the door after her. And Tamar put ashes on her head, and rent her garment of divers colours that was on her, and laid her hand on her head, and went on crying. And Absalom her brother said unto her, "Hath Amnon thy brother been with thee? but hold now thy peace, my sister: he is thy brother; regard not this thing." So Tamar remained desolate in her brother Absalom's house. But when king David heard of all these things, he was very wroth. And Absalom spake unto his brother Amnon neither good nor bad: for Absalom hated Amnon, because he had forced his sister Tamar. 2 Sam. 13:1-22.

Reviving a bedridden old saint with a young virgin.
Wherefore his servants said unto him, "Let there be sought for my lord the king a young virgin: and let her stand before the king, and let her cherish him, and let her lie in thy bosom, that my lord the king may get heat." 1 Kings 1:2.

Solomon's great harem.
But King Solomon loved many strange women. . . . And he had seven hundred wives, princesses, and three hundred concubines: and his wives turned away his heart. 1 Kings 11:1, 3.

Foreign wives dismissed wholesale as an act of piety.
And Shechaniah the son of Jehiel, one of the sons of Elam, answered

and said unto Ezra, "We have trespassed against our God, and have taken strange wives of the people of the land: yet now there is hope in Israel concerning this thing. Now therefore let us make a covenant with our God to put away all the wives, and such as are born of them, according to the counsel of my lord, and of those that tremble at the commandment of our God; and let it be done according to the law." ... And Ezra the priest stood up, and said unto them, "Ye have transgressed, and have taken strange wives, to increase the trespass of Israel. Now therefore make confession unto the LORD God of your fathers, and do his pleasure: and separate yourselves from the people of the land, and from the strange wives." ... And they made an end with all the men that had taken strange wives by the first day of the first month. Ezra 10:2-3, 10-11, 17.

In those days also saw I Jews that had married wives of Ashdod, of Ammon, and of Moab: And their children spake half in the speech of Ashdod, and could not speak in the Jews' language, but according to the language of each people. And I contended with them, and cursed them, and smote certain of them, and plucked off their hair, and made them swear by God, saying, "Ye shall not give your daughters unto their sons, nor take their daughters unto your sons, or for yourselves. Did not Solomon king of Israel sin by these things? yet among many nations was there no king like him, who was beloved of his God, and God made him king over all Israel: nevertheless even him did outlandish women cause to sin. Shall we then hearken unto you to do all this great evil, to transgress against our God in marrying strange wives?" And one of the sons of Joiada, the son of Eliashib the high priest, was son in law to Sanballat the Horonite: therefore I chased him from me. Remember them, O my God, because they have defiled the priesthood, and the covenant of the priesthood, and of the Levites. Thus cleansed I them from all strangers, and appointed the wards of the priests and the Levites, every one in his business. Neh. 13:23-30.

Polygamy and concubinage illustrated in the story of Esther.
Then said the king's servants that ministered unto him, "Let there be fair young virgins sought for the king." ... Now when every maid's turn was come to go in to king Ahasuerus, after that she had been twelve months, according to the manner of the women (for so were the days of their purifications accomplished, to wit, six months with oil of myrrh, and six months with sweet odours, and with other things for the purifying of the women;) Then thus came every maiden unto the king; whatsoever she desired was given her to go with her out of the house of

the women unto the king's house. In the evening she went, and on the morrow she returned into the second house of the women, to the custody of Shaashgaz, the king's chamberlain, which kept the concubines: she came in unto the king no more, except the king delighted in her, and that she were called by name. . . . And the king loved Esther above all the women, and she obtained grace and favour in his sight more than all the virgins; so that he set the royal crown upon her head, and made her queen instead of Vashti. Esther 2:2, 12-14, 17.

Then the king returned out of the palace garden into the place of the banquet of wine; and Haman was fallen upon the bed whereon Esther was. Then said the king, "Will he force the queen also before me in the house?" As the word went out of the king's mouth, they covered Haman's face. Esther 7:8.

Lascivious descriptions in the song of Solomon.

A bundle of myrrh is my well-beloved unto me; he shall lie all night betwixt my breasts. . . . Behold, thou art fair, my beloved, yea, pleasant: also our bed is green. Song of Sol. 1:13, 16.

He brought me to the banqueting house, and his banner over me was love. Stay me with flagons, comfort me with apples: for I am sick of love. His left hand is under my head, and his right hand doth embrace me. I charge you, O ye daughters of Jerusalem, by the roes, and by the hinds of the field, that ye stir not up, nor awake my love, till he please. Song of Sol. 2:4-7.

By night on my bed I sought him whom my soul loveth: I sought him, but I found him not. I will rise now, and go about the city in the streets, and in the broad ways will I seek him whom my soul loveth: I sought him, but I found him not. The watchmen that go about the city found me: to whom I said, "Saw ye him whom my soul loveth?" It was but a little that I passed from them, but I found him whom my soul loveth: I held him, and would not let him go, until I had brought him into my mother's house, and into the chamber of her that conceived me. I charge you, O ye daughters of Jerusalem, by the roes, and by the hinds of the field, that ye stir not up, nor awake my love, till he please. Song of Sol. 3:1-5.

Thy two breasts are like two young roes that are twins, which feed among the lilies. Song of Sol. 4:5.

I sleep, but my heart waketh: it is the voice of my beloved that knocketh, saying, "Open to me, my sister, my love, my dove, my undefiled: for my head is filled with dew, and my locks with the drops of the night. I have put off my coat; how shall I put it on? I have washed my feet; how shall I defile them?" My beloved put in his hand by the hole of the door, and my bowels were moved for him. I rose up to open to my beloved; and my hands dropped with myrrh, and my fingers with sweet smelling myrrh, upon the handles of the lock. . . . His hands are as gold rings set with the beryl: his belly is as bright ivory overlaid with sapphires. His legs are as pillars of marble, set upon sockets of fine gold: his countenance is as Lebanon, excellent as the cedars. Song of Sol. 5:2-5, 14-15.

How beautiful are thy feet with shoes, O prince's daughter! the joints of thy thighs are like jewels, the work of the hands of a cunning workman. Thy navel is like a round goblet, which wanteth not liquor: thy belly is like an heap of wheat set about with lilies. Thy two breasts are like two young roes that are twins. . . . How fair and how pleasant art thou, O love, for delights! This thy stature is like to a palm tree, and thy breasts to clusters of grapes. I said, "I will go up to the palm tree, I will take hold of the boughs thereof: now also thy breasts shall be as clusters of the vine, and the smell of thy nose like apples." Song of Sol. 7:1-3, 6-8.

[The headings of the chapters treat the Song of Solomon as a description of the mutual love between Christ and his Church. The piety that can spiritualize an erotic song in this fashion is absolutely asinine in its fatuous imbecility. If it were not included in the Bible, the Song of Solomon would be prohibited to young ladies as dangerously immoral reading. Luscious as our English translation is, scholars know very well that the original is in some parts absolutely untranslatable, being not simply *blue*, but *purple*.]

God causes his prophet to walk about stark naked for three years.

At the same time spake the LORD by Isaiah the son of Amoz, saying, "Go and loose the sackcloth from off thy loins, and put off thy shoe from thy foot." And he did so, walking naked and barefoot. And the LORD said, "Like as my servant Isaiah hath walked naked and barefoot three years for a sign and wonder upon Egypt and upon Ethiopia; So shall the king of Assyria lead away the Egyptians prisoners, and the Ethiopians captives, young and old, naked and barefoot, even with their buttocks uncovered, to the shame of Egypt." Isa. 20:2-4.

[Micah also says he will wail and howl and "go stripped and naked." ("Therefore I will wail and howl, I will go stripped and naked: I will make a wailing like the dragons, and mourning as the owls." Mic. 1:8.)]

A curious question.

Woe unto him that saith unto his father, "What begettest thou?" or to the woman, "What hast thou brought forth?" Isa. 45:10.

Jeremiah's elegant figures of speech.

They say, If a man put away his wife, and she go from him, and become another man's, shall he return unto her again? shall not that land be greatly polluted? but thou hast played the harlot with many lovers; yet return again to me," saith the LORD. "Lift up thine eyes unto the high places, and see where thou hast not been lien with. In the ways hast thou sat for them, as the Arabian in the wilderness; and thou hast polluted the land with thy whoredoms and with thy wickedness. Therefore the showers have been withholden, and there hath been no latter rain; and thou hadst a whore's forehead, thou refusedst to be ashamed." . . . The LORD said also unto me in the days of Josiah the king, "Hast thou seen that which backsliding Israel hath done? she is gone up upon every high mountain and under every green tree, and there hath played the harlot. And I said after she had done all these things, 'Turn thou unto me.' But she returned not. And her treacherous sister Judah saw it. And I saw, when for all the causes whereby backsliding Israel committed adultery I had put her away, and given her a bill of divorce; yet her treacherous sister Judah feared not, but went and played the harlot also. And it came to pass through the lightness of her whoredom, that she defiled the land, and committed adultery with stones and with stocks." Jer. 3:1-3, 6-9.

Ezekiel's filthy cookery.

"And thou shalt eat as barley cakes, and thou shalt bake it with dung that cometh out of man, in their sight." And the LORD said, "Even thus shall the children of Israel eat their defiled bread among the Gentiles, whither I will drive them." Then said I, "Ah Lord GOD! behold, my soul hath not been polluted: for from my youth up even till now have I not eaten of that which dieth of itself, or is torn in pieces; neither came there abominable flesh into my mouth." Then he said unto me, "Lo, I have given thee cow's dung for man's dung, and thou shalt prepare thy bread therewith." Ezek. 4:12-15.

[God commanded Ezekiel to cook publicly his bread with "dung which cometh out of man." Ezekiel revolted against this, on ceremonial grounds apparently, and cow's dung was graciously substituted.]

Ezekiel's elegant figures of speech.

"Now when I passed by thee, and looked upon thee, behold, thy time was the time of love; and I spread my skirt over thee, and covered thy nakedness: yea, I sware unto thee, and entered into a covenant with thee," saith the Lord GOD, "and thou becamest mine. . . . But thou didst trust in thine own beauty, and playedst the harlot because of thy renown, and pouredst out thy fornications in every one that passed by; his it was. And of thy garments thou didst take, and deckedst thy high places with divers colours, and playedst the harlot thereupon: the like things shall not come, neither shall it be so. Thou hast also taken thy fair jewels of my gold and of my silver, which I had given thee, and madest to thyself images of men, and didst commit whoredom with them. . . . Moreover thou hast taken thy sons and thy daughters, whom thou hast borne unto me, and these hast thou sacrificed unto them to be devoured. Is this of thy whoredoms a small matter. . . . And in all thine abominations and thy whoredoms thou hast not remembered the days of thy youth, when thou wast naked and bare, and wast polluted in thy blood. . . . Thou hast also committed fornication with the Egyptians thy neighbours, great of flesh; and hast increased thy whoredoms, to provoke me to anger. . . . Thou hast played the whore also with the Assyrians, because thou wast unsatiable; yea, thou hast played the harlot with them, and yet couldest not be satisfied. Thou hast moreover multiplied thy fornication in the land of Canaan unto Chaldea; and yet thou wast not satisfied herewith. How weak is thine heart," saith the Lord GOD, "seeing thou doest all these things, the work of an imperious whorish woman; In that thou buildest thine eminent place in the head of every way, and makest thine high place in every street; and hast not been as an harlot, in that thou scornest hire; But as a wife that committeth adultery, which taketh strangers instead of her husband! They give gifts to all whores: but thou givest thy gifts to all thy lovers, and hirest them, that they may come unto thee on every side for thy whoredom. And the contrary is in thee from other women in thy whoredoms, whereas none followeth thee to commit whoredoms: and in that thou givest a reward, and no reward is given unto thee, therefore thou art contrary. Wherefore, O harlot, hear the word of the LORD:" Thus saith the Lord GOD; "Because thy filthiness was poured out, and thy nakedness discovered through thy whoredoms with thy lovers, and with all the idols of thy abominations, and by the blood of thy children, which thou didst give unto them; Behold, therefore I will gather all thy lovers, with whom thou hast taken pleasure, and all them that thou hast loved, with all them that thou hast hated; I will even gather them round about against thee, and will discover thy nakedness unto them, that they may see all thy nakedness." Ezek. 16: 8, 15-17, 20, 22, 26, 28-37.

Ezekiel's inspired story of two harlots and their doings.
See pages 216-219. Ezek. 23:1-49.

[Some parts of this story are inexpressibly beastly in the Hebrew. Were these translated literally fathers would have to keep the Bible under lock and key.]

Hosea's inspired immoralities.

The beginning of the word of the LORD by Hosea. And the LORD said to Hosea, "Go, take unto thee a wife of whoredoms and children of whoredoms: for the land hath committed great whoredom, departing from the LORD." So he went and took Gomer the daughter of Diblaim; which conceived and bare him a son. . . . And she conceived again, and bare a daughter. And God said unto him, "Call her name Loruhamah: for I will no more have mercy upon the house of Israel; but I will utterly take them away. . . . Now when she had weaned Loruhamah, she conceived, and bare a son. Hos. 1:2, 3, 6, 8.

Say ye unto your brethren, Ammi; and to your sisters, Ruhamah. Plead with your mother, plead: for she is not my wife, neither am I her husband: let her therefore put away her whoredoms out of her sight, and her adulteries from between her breasts; Lest I strip her naked, and set her as in the day that she was born, and make her as a wilderness, and set her like a dry land, and slay her with thirst. Hos. 2:1-3.

Hosea's threats.

For they shall eat, and not have enough: they shall commit whoredom, and shall not increase: because they have left off to take heed to the LORD. Whoredom and wine and new wine take away the heart. My people ask counsel at their stocks, and their staff declareth unto them: for the spirit of whoredoms hath caused them to err, and they have gone a whoring from under their God. They sacrifice upon the tops of the mountains, and burn incense upon the hills, under oaks and poplars and elms, because the shadow thereof is good: therefore your daughters shall commit whoredom, and your spouses shall commit adultery. I will not punish your daughters when they commit whoredom, nor your spouses when they commit adultery: for themselves are separated with whores, and they sacrifice with harlots: therefore the people that doth not understand shall fall. Hos. 4:10-14.

Samaria shall become desolate; for she hath rebelled against her God: they shall fall by the sword: their infants shall be dashed in pieces, and their women with child shall be ripped up. Hos. 13:16.

Christ begotten.

I will declare the decree: the LORD hath said unto me, "Thou art my

241

Son; this day have I begotten thee." Ps. 2:7.

God hath fulfilled the same unto us their children, in that he hath raised up Jesus again; as it is also written in the second psalm, "Thou art my Son, this day have I begotten thee." Acts 13:33.

For unto which of the angels said he at any time, "Thou art my Son, this day have I begotten thee?" And again, "I will be to him a Father, and he shall be to me a Son?" And again, when he bringeth in the firstbegotten into the world, he saith, "And let all the angels of God worship him." Heb. 1:5, 6.

No man hath seen God at any time; the only begotten Son, which is in the bosom of the father, he hath declared him. John 1:18.

For God so loved the world that he gave his only begotten son, that whosoever believeth in him should not perish, but have everlasting life. John 3:16.

[Do Christians ever attempt to realize the meaning of the word begotten? Misappropriated from the Old Testament, where it was used figuratively, they adopt the word in some actual sense which they do not stop to define. Christians who resent Ingersoll's phrase, the "Presbyterian God," as "grossly offensive," yet preach a "begotten" God, as if the idea of God's begetting a son were not infinitely more shocking to believers in a deity utterly above such human methods of propagation. No wonder the Mohammedans so indignantly repudiate the prurient blasphemy on which Christianity is founded. As God, the only begotten son of the Father, existed from all eternity, being co-eternal with his Father, he was begotten a second time when he was born of the Virgin Mary. This time he was begotten of the Holy Ghost, instead of the Father. Why the duty of male parentage was thus delegated to the third person of the Trinity is not explained.]

Conception through intercourse with a ghost.

Now the birth of Jesus Christ was on this wise: When as his mother Mary was espoused to Joseph, before they came together, she was found with child of the Holy Ghost. . . . But while he [Joseph] thought on these things, behold, the angel of the LORD appeared unto him in a dream, saying, "Joseph, thou son of David, fear not to take unto thee Mary thy wife: for that which is conceived in her is of the Holy Ghost." . . . Now all this was done, that it might be fulfilled which was spoken of the LORD by the prophet, saying, "Behold, a virgin shall be with child, and shall bring forth a son, and they shall call his name Emmanuel, which being interpreted is, 'God with us.' " Matt. 1:18, 20, 22, 23.

Then said Mary unto the angel, "How shall this be, seeing I know not a man?" And the angel answered and said unto her, "The Holy Ghost shall come upon thee, and the power of the Highest shall overshadow thee: therefore also that holy thing which shall be born of thee shall be called the Son of God." Luke 1:34, 35.

[This lying dogma of birth by a Virgin Mother is filthily prurient and insulting in its very basis. What is there more degrading in male parentage than in female? If God could be the child of a human mother, why not of a human father also? If a miracle was to be worked why was the visit of a beautiful *male* angel Gabriel necessary? And why should the Holy Ghost come upon a virgin bride like Jupiter upon Danae in a golden cloud? To a truly reverent believer in an all-perfect Supreme Spirit, the Christian doctrines of celestial impregnation and divine begetting must be inexpressibly revolting and most hideously blasphemous.]

Elizabeth's conception after an angel's visit.

And they had no child, because that Elizabeth was barren, and they both were now well stricken in years. . . . But the angel said unto him, "Fear not, Zacharias: for thy prayer is heard; and thy wife Elizabeth shall bear thee a son, and thou shalt call his name John." Luke 1:7, 13.

John the Baptist's pre-natal performance.

And it came to pass, that, when Elizabeth heard the salutation of Mary, the babe leaped in her womb; and Elizabeth was filled with the Holy Ghost. And she spake out with a loud voice, and said, . . . "For, lo, as soon as the voice of thy salutation sounded in mine ears, the babe leaped in my womb for joy." Luke 1:41, 42, 44.

John and Jesus are piously mutilated in their private parts.

And it came to pass, that on the eighth day they came to circumcise the child; and they called him Zacharias, after the name of his father. And his mother answered and said, "Not so; but he shall be called John." Luke 1:59, 60.

And when eight days were accomplished for the circumcising of the child, his name was called JESUS, which was so named of the angel before he was conceived in the womb. Luke 2:21.

Jesus has nothing to say against the Jewish custom of raising up seed to a brother.

Then came to him certain of the Sadducees, which deny that there is any resurrection; and they asked him, Saying, "Master, Moses wrote unto us, 'If any man's brother die, having a wife, and he die without children, that his brother should take his wife, and raise up seed unto his brother.' There were therefore seven brethren: and the first took a wife, and died without children. And the second took her to wife, and he died childless. And the third took her; and in like manner the seven also: and they left no children, and died. Last of all the woman died also. Therefore in the resurrection whose wife of them is she? for seven had her to wife." And Jesus answering said unto them, "The children of this world marry, and are given in marriage." Luke 20:27-34.

Jesus refuses to condemn an adulteress caught in the act.

And the scribes and Pharisees brought unto him a woman taken in adultery; and when they had set her in the midst, They say unto him, "Master, this woman was taken in adultery, in the very act. Now Moses in the law commanded us, that such should be stoned: but what sayest thou?" This they said, tempting him, that they might have to accuse him. But Jesus stooped down, and with his finger wrote on the ground, as though he heard them not. So when they continued asking him, he lifted up himself, and said unto them, "He that is without sin among you, let him first cast a stone at her." And again he stooped down, and wrote on the ground. And they which heard it, being convicted by their own conscience, went out one by one, beginning at the eldest, even unto the last: and Jesus was left alone, and the woman standing in the midst. When Jesus had lifted up himself, and saw none but the woman, he said unto her, "Woman, where are those thine accusers? hath no man condemned thee?" She said, "No man, LORD" And Jesus said unto her, "Neither do I condemn thee: go, and sin no more." John 8:3-11.

[Christ seems to have favored harlots generally. "Whether of them twain did the will of his father?" They say unto him, "The first." Jesus saith unto them, "Verily I say unto you, That the publicans and the harlots go into the kingdom of God before you. For John came unto you in the way of righteousness, and ye believed him not: but the publicans and the harlots believed him: and ye, when ye had seen it, repented not afterward, that ye might believe him." Matt: 21:31, 32.

And it came to pass, that, as Jesus sat at meat in his house, many publicans and sinners sat also together with Jesus and his disciples: for there were many, and they followed him. And when the scribes and Pharisees saw him eat with publicans and sinners, they said unto his disciples, "How is it that he eateth and drinketh with publicans and sinners?" Mark 2:15, 16.

And, behold, a woman in the city, which was a sinner, when she knew

244

that Jesus sat at meat in the Pharisee's house, brought an alabaster box of ointment, And stood at his feet behind him weeping, and began to wash his feet with tears, and did wipe them with the hairs of her head, and kissed his feet, and anointed them with the ointment. Now when the Pharisee which had bidden him saw it, he spake within himself, saying, "This man, if he were a prophet, would have known who and what manner of woman this is that toucheth him: for she is a sinner." Luke 7:37-39.

Jesus saith unto her, "Go, call thy husband, and come hither." The woman answered and said, "I have no husband." Jesus saith unto her, "Thou hast well said, 'I have no husband:' For thou hast had five husbands; and he whom thou now hast is not thy husband: in that saidst thou truly." John 4:16-18.

Castration recommended by Jesus.

For there are some eunuchs, which were so born from their mother's womb: and there are some eunuchs, which were made eunuchs of men: and there be eunuchs, which have made themselves eunuchs for the kingdom of heaven's sake. He that is able to receive it, let him receive it. Matt. 19:12.

Wherefore if thy hand or thy foot offend thee, cut them off, and cast them from thee: it is better for thee to enter into life halt or maimed, rather than having two hands or two feet to be cast into everlasting fire. And if thine eye offend thee, pluck it out, and cast it from thee: it is better for thee to enter into life with one eye, rather than having two eyes to be cast into hell fire. Matt. 18:8, 9.

But I say unto you, That whosoever looketh on a woman to lust after her hath committed adultery with her already in his heart. And if thy right eye offend thee, pluck it out, and cast it from thee: for it is profitable for thee that one of thy members should perish, and not that thy whole body should be cast into hell. And if thy right hand offend thee, cut it off, and cast it from thee: for it is profitable for thee that one of thy members should perish, and not that thy whole body should be cast into hell. Matt. 5:28-30.

[Origen and other early Christians faithfully carried out the divine injunction. A Christian sect in Russia long practiced castration as an act of obedience to Christ's command.]

Celibacy recommended by Jesus.

His disciples say unto him, "If the case of the man be so with his wife, it is not good to marry." But he said unto them, "All men cannot receive this saying, save they to whom it is given. For there are some eunuchs, which were so born from their mother's womb: and there are some eunuchs, which were made eunuchs of men: and there be eunuchs, which have made themselves eunuchs for the kingdom of heaven's sake. He that is able to receive it, let him receive it." Matt. 19:10-12.

Hatred of parents and of wife and family recommended by Jesus.

If any man come to me, and hate not his father, and mother, and wife, and children, and brethren, and sisters, yea, and his own life also, he cannot be my disciple. Luke 14:26.

Desertion of wife and children recommended by Jesus.

So likewise, whosoever he be of you that forsaketh not all that he hath, he cannot be my disciple. Luke 14:33.

And when they had brought their ships to land, they forsook all, and followed him. Luke 5:11.

And every one that hath forsaken houses, or brethren, or sisters, or father, or mother, or wife, or children, or lands, for my name's sake, shall receive an hundredfold, and shall inherit everlasting life. Matt. 19:29.

And another of his disciples said unto him, "Lord, suffer me first to go and bury my father." But Jesus said unto him, "Follow me; and let the dead bury their dead." Matt. 8:21, 22.

Second birth.

Jesus answered and said unto him, "Verily, verily, I say unto thee, Except a man be born again, he cannot see the kingdom of God." Nicodemus saith unto him, "How can a man be born when he is old? can he enter the second time into his mother's womb, and be born?" John 3:3, 4

Paul recommends celibacy and deprecates marriage.

Now concerning the things whereof ye wrote unto me: It is good for a man not to touch a woman. . . . For I would that all men were even as I myself. But every man hath his proper gift of God, one after this manner, and another after that. I say therefore to the unmarried and widows, It is good for them if they abide even as I. But if they cannot contain, let them marry: for it is better to marry than to burn. . . . Art thou bound unto a wife? seek not to be loosed. Art thou loosed from a wife? seek not a wife. . . . But I would have you without carefulness. He that is unmarried careth for the things that belong to the Lord, how he may please the Lord: But he that is married careth for the things that are of the world, how he may please his wife. There is a difference also between a wife and a virgin. The unmarried woman careth for the things of the Lord, that she may be holy both in body and in spirit: but she that is married careth for the things of the world, how she may please her husband. And this I speak for your own profit; not that I may cast a snare upon you, but for that which is comely, and that ye may attend upon the Lord without distraction. . . . Nevertheless he that standeth stedfast in his heart, having no necessity, but hath power over his own will, and hath so decreed in his heart that he will keep his virgin, doeth well. So then he that giveth her in marriage doeth well; but he that giveth her not in marriage doeth better. The wife is bound by the law as long as her husband liveth; but if her husband be dead, she is at liberty to be married to whom she will; only in the Lord. But she is happier if she so abide, after my judgment: and I think also that I have the spirit of God. 1 Cor. 7:1, 7-9, 27, 32-35, 37-40.

Immoralities prevalent among early Christians.

It is reported commonly that there is fornication among you, and such fornication as is not so much as named among the Gentiles, that one should have his father's wife. And ye are puffed up, and have not rather mourned, that he that hath done this deed might be taken away from among you. . . . Your glorying is not good. Know ye not that a little leaven leaveneth the whole lump? 1 Cor. 5:1, 2, 6.

Know ye not that the unrighteous shall not inherit the kingdom of God? Be not deceived: neither fornicators, nor idolaters, nor adulterers, nor effeminate, nor abusers of themselves with mankind, . . . All things are lawful unto me, but all things are not expedient: all things are lawful for me, but I will not be brought under the power of any. Meats for the belly, and the belly for meats: but God shall destroy both it and them. Now the body is not for fornication, but for the Lord; and the Lord for the body. And God hath both raised up the Lord, and will also raise up us by his own power. Know ye not that your bodies are the members of Christ? shall I then take the members of Christ, and make them the members of an harlot? God forbid. What? Know ye not that he which is joined to an harlot is one body? for two, saith he, shall be one flesh. But he that is joined unto the Lord is one spirit. Flee fornication. Every sin that a man doeth is without the body; but he that committeth fornication sinneth against his own body. What? know ye not that your body is the temple of the Holy Ghost which is in you, which ye have of God, and ye are not your own? 1 Cor. 6:9, 12-19.

[The Christians gloried in the offence. They gloried in being set free from the law. They accepted Paul's saying, "All things are lawful unto me." Antinomianism has always been a great danger among believers, because it is a logical outcome of a Christian belief in inspiration and the "Atonement."]

Unseemly and disgusting expressions employed by St. John the Divine.

Notwithstanding I have a few things against thee, because thou sufferest that woman Jezebel, which calleth herself a prophetess, to teach and to seduce my servants to commit fornication, and to eat things sacrificed unto idols. And I gave her space to repent of her fornications; and she repent not. Rev. 2:20, 21.

Neither repented they of their murders, nor of their sorceries, nor of their fornication, nor of their thefts. Rev. 9:21.

And there followed another angel, saying, "Babylon is fallen, is fallen, that great city, because she made all nations drink of the wine of the wrath of her fornication." Rev. 14:8.

And there came one of the seven angels which had the seven vails, and talked with me, saying unto me, "Come hither; I will shew unto thee the judgment of the great whore that sitteth upon many waters: With whom the kings of the earth have committed fornication, and the inhabitants of the earth have been made drunk with the wine of her fornication." So he carried me away in the spirit into the wilderness: and I saw a woman sit upon a scarlet coloured beast, full of names and blasphemy, having seven heads and ten horns. And the woman was arrayed in purple and scarlet colour, and decked with gold and precious stones and pearls, having a golden cup in her hand full of abominations and filthiness of her fornication: And upon her forehead was a name written, "MYSTERY, BABYLON THE GREAT, THE MOTHER OF HARLOTS AND ABOMINATIONS OF THE EARTH." . . . And he saith unto me, "The waters which thou sawest, where the whore sitteth, are peoples, and multitudes, and nations, and tongues. And the ten horns which thou sawest upon the beast, these shall hate the whore, and shall make her desolate and naked, and shall eat her flesh, and burn her with fire." Rev. 17:1-5, 15, 16.

For all nations have drunk of the wine of the wrath of her fornication, and the kings of the earth have committed fornication with her, and the merchants of the earth are waxed rich through the abundance of her delicacies. Rev. 18:3.

For true and righteous are his judgments: for he hath judged the great whore, which did corrupt the earth with her fornication, and hath

248

avenged the blood of his servants at her hand. Rev. 19:2.

[These favored terms of theological insult are referred by Protestants to the elder (Roman) branch of the Church. If the house of Christianity is thus divided against itself, how shall it stand? Where is the sweet concord and brotherhood and unity which Christianity professes to establish?]

MORE CONTRADICTIONS
AND ABSURDITIES

Excerpted from:

Self-Contradictions of the Bible
144 Propositions
(Author unknown)

Bible Contradicts Itself
John Bowden

SELF-CONTRADICTIONS OF THE BIBLE
144 PROPOSITIONS

Author Unknown

(Presented here are only those contradictions which are not already covered in the Foote & Ball section of this book — a total of twenty-three.)

THEOLOGICAL DOCTRINES

God is satisfied with his works.
And God saw every thing that he had made, and, behold, it was very good. Gen. 1:31.

God is dissatisfied with his works.
And it repented the LORD that he had made man on the earth, and it grieved him at his heart. Gen. 6:6.

God dwells in chosen temples.
And the LORD appeared to Solomon by night, and said unto him, "I have heard thy prayer, and have chosen this place to myself for an house of sacrifice. . . . For now have I chosen and sanctified this house that my name may be there forever: and mine eyes and mine heart shall be there perpetually." 2 Chron. 7:12, 16.

God dwells not in temples.
Howbeit the most High dwelleth not in temples made with hands. Acts 7:48.

God dwells in light.
Dwelling in the light which no man can approach unto. . . . 1 Tim. 6:16.

God dwells in darkness.
Clouds and darkness are round about him. Ps. 97:2.

God is seen and heard.
And the LORD God called unto Adam, and said unto him, "Where art thou?" And he said, "I heard thy voice in the garden, and I was afraid." Gen. 3:9, 10.
In the year that King Uzziah died I saw also the LORD sitting upon a throne, high and lifted up. Isa. 6:1.

God is invisible and cannot be heard.
Ye have neither heard his voice at any time, nor seen his shape. John 5:37.

God is tired and rests.

For in six days the LORD made heaven and earth, and on the seventh day he rested, and was refreshed. Exod. 31:17

I am weary with repenting. Jer. 15:6.

Thou hast wearied me with thine iniquities. Isa. 43:24.

God is omnipresent, sees and knows all things.

Whither shall I flee from thy presence? If I ascend up into heaven, thou art there: if I make my bed in hell, behold, thou art there. If I take the wings of the morning, and dwell in the uttermost parts of the sea; Even there shall thy hand lead me, and thy right hand shall hold me. Ps. 139:7-10.

For his eyes are upon the ways of man, and he seeth all his goings. There is no darkness, nor shadow of death, where the workers of iniquity may hide themselves. Job 34:21, 22.

God knows the hearts of men.

Thou, Lord, which knowest the hearts of all men. . . . Acts 1:24.

Thou knowest my downsitting and mine uprising; thou understandest my thought afar off. Thou compassest my path and my lying down, and art acquainted with all my ways. Ps. 139:2, 3.

For he knoweth the secrets of the heart. Ps. 44:21.

God is never tired and never rests.

Hast thou not heard, that the everlasting God, the LORD, the Creator of the ends of the earth, fainteth not, neither is weary? Isa. 40:28.

God is not omnipresent, neither sees nor knows all things.

And Adam and his wife hid themselves from the presence of the LORD God amongst the trees of the garden. Gen. 3:8.

God tries men to find out what is in their hearts.

The LORD, your God proveth you, to know whether ye love the LORD your God with all your heart and with all your soul. Deut. 13:3.

The LORD thy God led thee these forty years in the wilderness, to humble thee, and to prove thee, to know what was in thy heart. . . . Deut. 8:2.

For now I know that thou fearest God, seeing thou hast not withheld thy son, thine only son from me. Gen. 22:12.

God is all-powerful.
There is nothing too hard for thee. . . . Behold, I am the LORD, the God of all flesh: is there any thing too hard for me? Jer. 32:17, 27.

God is not all-powerful.
And the LORD was with Judah; and he drave out the inhabitants of the mountain; but could not drive out the inhabitants of the valley, because they had chariots of iron. Judg. 1:19.

God is unchangeable.
I the LORD have spoken it: it shall come to pass, and I will do it; I will not go back, neither will I spare, neither will I repent. Ezek. 24:14.

God is changeable.
Wherefore the LORD God of Israel saith, "I said indeed that thy house, and the house of thy father, should walk before me forever:" but now the LORD saith, "Be it far from me. . . . Behold, the days come, that I will cut off thine arm, and the arm of thy father's house . . . ." 1 Sam. 2:30, 31.

In those days was Hezekiah sick unto death. And the prophet Isaiah the son of Amoz came to him, and said unto him, "Thus saith the LORD, 'Set thy house in order; for thou shalt die, and not live.' " . . . And it came to pass, afore Isaiah was gone out into the middle court, that the word of the LORD came unto him, saying, "Turn again, and tell Hezekiah the captain of my people, 'Thus saith the LORD, . . . "I have heard thy prayer, . . . and I will add unto thy days, fifteen years. . . ." ' " 2 Kings 20:1, 4-6.

And the LORD said unto Moses, "Depart, and go up hence, thou and the people. . . . For I will not go up in the midst of thee." . . . And the LORD said unto Moses, "I will do this thing also that thou hast spoken. . . . My presence shall go with thee, and I will give thee rest." Exod. 33:1, 3, 17, 14.

God is just and impartial.
The LORD is upright: . . . and there is no unrighteousness in him. Ps. 92:15.
Shall not the Judge of all the earth do right? Gen. 18:25.
Ye say, The way of the LORD is not equal. Hear now, O house of Israel; Is not my way equal? Ezek. 18:25.
He doth execute the judgment of the fatherless and widow, and loveth the stranger, in giving him food and raiment. Love ye, therefore the stranger. Deut. 10:18, 19.

God is unjust and partial.
Cursed be Canaan; a servant of servants shall he be unto his brethren. Gen. 9:25.
For I, the LORD thy God, am a jealous God, visiting the iniquity of the fathers upon the children unto the third and fourth generation. . . . Exod. 20:5.
For whosoever hath, to him shall be given, and he shall have more abundance; but whosoever hath not, from him shall be taken away even that he hath. Matt. 13:12.
Ye shall not eat of any thing that dieth of itself: thou shalt give it unto the stranger that is in thy gates, that he may eat it; or thou mayest sell it unto an alien. Deut. 14:21.
And David spake unto the LORD when he saw the angel that smote the people, and said, "Lo, I have sinned, and I have done wickedly: but these sheep, what have they done?" 2 Sam. 24:17.

God is not the author of evil.
The law of the LORD is perfect. . . . The statutes of the LORD are right. . . . The commandment of the LORD is pure. Ps. 19:7, 8.

God is the author of evil.
Out of the mouth of the most High proceedeth not evil and good? Lam. 3:38.
Thus saith the LORD, "Behold, I frame evil against you, and devise a device against you." Jer. 18:11.

258

God gives freely to those who ask.
If any of you lack wisdom, let him ask of God, that giveth to all men liberally and upbraideth not; and it shall be given him. James 1:5.
For every one that asketh receiveth; and he that seeketh findeth. Luke 11:10.

God is to be found by those who seek him.
Those that seek me early shall find me. Prov. 8:17.

God is peaceful.
God is not the author of confusion, but of peace. . . . 1 Cor. 14:33.

God is kind, merciful, and good.
The LORD is very pitiful, and of tender mercy. James 5:11.
For his mercy endureth forever. 1 Chron. 16:34.
I have no pleasure in the death

God withholds his blessings and prevents their reception.
For it was of the LORD to harden their hearts, that they should come against Israel in battle, that he might destroy them utterly, and that they might have no favor. . . . Josh. 11:20.
O LORD, why hast thou made us to err from thy ways, and hardened our heart. . .? Isa. 63:17.

God is not to be found by those who seek him.
Then shall they call upon me, but I will not answer; they shall seek me early, but they shall not find me. Prov. 1:28.
And when ye spread forth your hands, I will hide mine eyes from you; yea, when ye make many prayers, I will not hear. Isa. 1:15.
They cried, but there was none to save them; even unto the LORD, but he answered them not. Ps. 18:41.

God is warlike.
The LORD of hosts is his name. Isa. 51:15.
Blessed be the LORD, my strength, which teacheth my hands to war, and my fingers to fight. Ps. 144:1.

God is cruel, unmerciful, destructive, and ferocious.
I will not pity, nor spare, nor have mercy, but destroy them. Jer. 13:14.
The LORD cast down great

of him that dieth, saith the Lord GOD. Ezek. 18:32.

Good and upright is the LORD. Ps 25:8.

God's anger is slow, and endures but for a moment.

The LORD is merciful and gracious, slow to anger, and plenteous in mercy. Ps. 103:8.

His anger endureth but a moment. Ps. 30:5.

God commands, approves of, and delights in burnt offerings, sacrifices, and holy days.

Thou shalt offer every day a bullock for a sin offering for atonement. Exod. 29:36.

On the tenth day of this seventh month there shall be a day of atonement: it shall be an holy convocation unto you; and ye shall afflict your souls, and offer an offering made by fire unto the LORD. Lev. 23:27.

And thou shalt burn the whole ram upon the altar: ... it is a sweet savour; an offering made by fire unto the LORD. Exod. 29:18.

And the priest shall burn all on

stones from heaven upon them ... and they died. Josh. 10:11.

God's anger is fierce, frequent, and endures long.

And the LORD said unto Moses, "Take all the heads of the people, and hang them up before the LORD against the sun, that the fierce anger of the LORD may be turned away from Israel." Num. 25:4.

For ye have kindled a fire in mine anger which shall burn for ever. Jer. 17:4.

God is angry ["*with the wicked*," interpolated by the translators] every day. Ps. 7:11.

And ... the LORD met him, and sought to kill him. Exod. 4:24.

God disapproves of, and has no pleasure in, burnt offerings, sacrifices, and holy days.

For I spake not unto your fathers, nor commanded them in the day that I brought them out of the land of Egypt, concerning burnt offerings or sacrifices. Jer. 7:22.

Your burnt offerings are not acceptable, nor your sacrifices sweet unto me. Jer. 6:20.

I will not reprove thee for thy sacrifices or thy burnt offerings, to have been continually before me. I will take no bullock out of thy house, nor he goats out of thy folds. ... Will I eat of the flesh of

the altar, to be a burnt sacrifice, an offering made by fire, of a sweet savour unto the LORD. Lev. 1:9.

bulls, or drink the blood of goats? Offer unto God thanksgiving; and pay thy vows unto the most High. Ps. 1:8, 9, 13, 14.

Bring no more vain oblations; incense is an abomination unto me; the new moons and sabbaths, the calling of assemblies, I cannot away with; it is iniquity, even the solemn meeting. . . . To what purpose is the multitude of your sacrifices unto me? . . . I am full of the burnt offerings of rams, and the fat of fed beasts; and I delight not in the blood of bullocks, or of lambs, or of he goats. When ye come to appear before me, who hath required this at your hand . . . ? Isa. 1:13, 11, 12.

God forbids human sacrifice.

Take heed to thyself that thou be not snared by following them [the Gentile nations]; . . . for every abomination to the LORD which he hateth, have they done unto their gods; for even their sons and their daughters have they burnt in the fire to their gods. Deut. 12:30, 31.

God commands and accepts human sacrifice.

No devoted thing, that a man shall devote unto the LORD of all that he hath, both of *man* and of beast, and of the field of his possession, shall be sold or redeemed: every devoted thing is most holy unto the LORD. None devoted, which shall be devoted of men, shall be redeemed, but shall surely be put to death. Lev. 27:28, 29.

The king [David] took the two sons of Rizpah . . . and the five sons of Michael . . . and he delivered them into the hands of the Gibeonites, and they hanged them in the hill before the LORD. . . . And after that God was entreated for the land. 2 Sam. 21:8, 9, 14.

And he [God] said, "Take now

thy son, thine only son Isaac, whom thou lovest, and get thee into the land of Moriah; and offer him there for a burnt offering. . . ." Gen. 22:2.

And Jephthah vowed a vow unto the LORD, and said, "If thou shalt without fail deliver the children of Ammon into mine hands, Then it shall be, that whatsoever cometh forth of the doors of my house to meet me, when I return in peace from the children of Ammon, shall surely be the LORD's, and I will offer it up for a burnt offering." So Jephthah passed over unto the children of Ammon to fight against them; and the LORD delivered them into his hands. . . . And Jephthah came to Mizpeh unto his house, and, behold, his daughter came out to meet him. . . . And he sent her away for two months: and she went with her companions, and bewailed her virginity upon the mountains. And it came to pass at the end of two months, that she returned unto her father, who did with her according to his vow which he had vowed. Judg. 11:30, 31, 32, 34, 38, 39.

God tempts no man.

Let no man say when he is tempted, "I am tempted of God:" for God cannot be tempted with evil, neither tempteth he any man. James 1:13.

God does tempt men.

And the LORD said unto Satan, "Hast thou considered my servant Job, that there is none like him in the earth, a perfect and an upright man, one that feareth God and escheweth evil? and still he holdeth fast his integrity, although thou movedst me against him, to destroy him without cause." Job 2:3.

O LORD, thou hast deceived me, and I was deceived, [marginal reading, enticed]. Jer. 20:7.

God cannot lie.
It was impossible for God to lie . . . . Heb. 6:18.

God lies and deceives.
Ah, Lord GOD! surely thou hast greatly deceived this people. . . . Jer 4:10.

Wilt thou be altogether unto me as a liar . . .? Jer. 15:18.

For this cause God shall send them strong delusion, that they should believe a lie. 2 Thess. 2:11.

And if the prophet be deceived when he hath spoken a thing, I the LORD have deceived that prophet. . . . Ezek. 14:9.

Because of man's wickedness God destroys him.
And God saw that the wickedness of man was great in the earth, and that every imagination of the thoughts of his heart was only evil continually. . . . And the LORD said, "I will destroy man whom I have created." Gen. 6:5, 7.

Because of man's wickedness God will not destroy him.
And the LORD said in his heart, "I will not again curse the ground any more for man's sake; for the imagination of man's heart is evil from his youth; neither will I again smite any more every thing living . . . ." Gen. 8:21.

God's attributes revealed in his works.
For the invisible things of him from the creation of the world are clearly seen, being understood by the things that are made, even his eternal power and Godhead. Rom. 1:20.

God's attributes cannot be discovered.
Canst thou, by searching find out God? Job 11:7.

There is no searching of his understanding. Isa. 40:28.

There is but one God.
The LORD our God is one

There is a plurality of Gods.
And God said, "Let us make

263

LORD. Deut. 6:4.

There is none other God but one. 1 Cor. 8:4.

man in our image. . . ." Gen. 1:26.

And the LORD God said, "Behold, the man is become as one of us." Gen. 3:22.

And the LORD appeared unto him [Abraham] in the plains of Mamre. . . . And he lift up his eyes and looked, and, lo, three men stood by him: and when he saw them, he ran to meet them from the tent door, and bowed himself toward the ground, And said, "My Lord, if now I have found favour in thy sight, pass not away, I pray thee, from thy servant." Gen. 18:1, 2, 3.

MORAL PRECEPTS

Robbery commanded.

When ye go, ye shall not go empty: But every woman shall borrow of her neighbour, and of her that sojourneth in her house, jewels of silver, and jewels of gold, and raiment: and ye shall put them upon your sons, and upon your daughters; and ye shall spoil the Egyptians. Exod. 3:21, 22.

And they borrowed of the Egyptians jewels of silver, and jewels of gold, and raiment. . . . And they spoiled the Egyptians. Exod. 12:35, 36.

Robbery forbidden.

Thou shalt not defraud thy neighbour, neither rob him. Lev. 19:13.

Thou shalt not steal. Exod. 20:15.

Lying commanded, approved, and sanctioned.

And the LORD said unto Samuel, . . . "I will send thee to Jesse the Bethlehemite for I have provided me a king among his sons." And Samuel said, "How can I go? if Saul hear it he will kill me." And the LORD said, "Take an heifer with thee, and say, 'I am come to sacrifice to the LORD.'"
1 Sam. 16:1, 2.

And the woman [Rahab] took the two men, and hid them and said thus, "There came men unto me, but I wist not whence they were: and it came to pass about the time of shutting of the gate, when it was dark, that the men went out: whither the men went I

Lying forbidden.

Thou shalt not bear false witness. . . . Exod. 20:16.

All liars, shall have their part in the lake which burneth with fire and brimstone. Rev. 21:8.

wot not: pursue after them quickly; for ye shall overtake them." But she had brought them up to the roof of the house, and hid them with the stalks of flax. . . . Josh. 2:4-6.

Was not Rahab the harlot *justified* by works, when she had received the messengers, and had sent them out another way? James 2:25.

And the king of Egypt called for the midwives, and said unto them, "Why have ye done this thing, and have saved the men children alive?" And the midwives said unto Pharaoh, "Because the Hebrew women are not as the Egyptian women; for they are lively, and are delivered ere the midwives come in unto them." *Therefore God dealt well* with the midwives. Exod. 1:18-20.

Ye shall know my breach of promise. Num. 14:34.

For if the truth of God hath more abounded through my lie unto his glory; why yet am I also judged as a sinner? Rom. 3:7.

Being crafty, I caught you with guile. 2 Cor. 12:16.

Killing commanded and sanctioned.

So Jehu slew all that remained of the house of Ahab. . . . And the LORD said unto Jehu, "Because thou has done well in executing that which is right in mine eyes, and hast done unto the house of Ahab according to all that was in

Killing forbidden.

No murderer hath eternal life abiding in him. 1 John 3:15.

mine heart, thy children of the fourth generation shall sit on the throne of Israel." 2 Kings 10:11, 30.

The blood-shedder must die.

At the hand of every man's brother will I require the life of man. Who so sheddeth man's blood, by man shall his blood be shed. Gen. 9:5, 6.

The blood-shedder must not die.

And the LORD set a mark upon Cain, lest any finding him should kill him. Gen. 4:15.

Slavery and oppression ordained.

Cursed be Canaan; a servant of servants shall he be unto his brethren. Gen. 9:25.

Of the children of the strangers that do sojourn among you, of them shall ye buy. . . . They shall be your bondmen for ever: but over your brethren the children of Israel, ye shall not rule one over another with rigour. Lev. 25:45, 46.

I will sell your sons and daughters into the hands of the children of Judah, and they shall sell them to the Sabeans, to a people far off: for the LORD hath spoken it. Joel 3:8.

Slavery and oppression forbidden.

Undo the heavy burdens and . . . let the oppressed go free, and . . . break every yoke. Isa. 58:6.

Thou shalt neither vex a stranger, nor oppress him. Exod. 22:21.

He that stealeth a man, and selleth him, or if he be found in his hand, he shall surely be put to death. Exod. 21:16.

Neither be ye called masters. Matt. 23:10.

Improvidence enjoined.

Give to every man that asketh of thee; and of him that taketh away thy goods, ask them not again. . . . And lend, hoping for nothing again; and your reward shall be great. . . . Luke 6:30, 35.

Sell that ye have, and give alms. Luke 12:33.

Improvidence condemned.

A good man leaveth an inheritance to his children's children. Prov. 13:22.

Anger approved.

Be ye angry, and sin not. Eph. 4:26.

There came forth little children out of the city, and mocked him [Elisha], and said unto him, "Go up, thou bald head; go up, thou bald head." And he turned back and looked on them, and cursed them in the name of the LORD. And there came forth two she bears out of the wood, and tare forty and two children of them. 2 Kings 2:23, 24.

And when he had looked round about on them with anger . . . he saith unto the man, "Stretch forth thy hand." Mark 3:5.

Good works to be seen of men.

Let your light so shine before men, that they may see your good works. . . . Matt. 5:16.

Judging of others forbidden.

Judge not, that ye be not judged. For with what judgment ye judge, ye shall be judged. Matt. 7:1, 2.

Anger disapproved.

Be not hasty in thy spirit to be angry: for anger resteth in the bosom of fools. Eccles. 7:9.

Make no friendship with an angry man. Prov. 22:24.

The wrath of man worketh not the righteousness of God. James 1:20.

Good works not to be seen of men.

Take heed that ye do not your alms before men, to be seen of them. Matt. 6:1.

Judging of others approved.

Do ye not know that the saints shall judge the world? and if the world shall be judged by you, are ye unworthy to judge the smallest matters? Know ye not that we shall judge angels? how much more things that pertain to this life? If then ye have judgments of things pertaining to this life, set them to judge who are least esteemed in the church. 1 Cor. 6:2-4.

Do not ye judge them that are within? 1 Cor. 5:12.

Jesus taught non resistance.

Resist not evil: but whosoever shall smite thee on thy right cheek, turn to him the other also. Matt. 5:39.

All they that take the sword shall perish with the sword. Matt. 26:52.

Jesus warned his followers not to fear being killed.

Be not afraid of them that kill the body. . . .Luke 12:4.

Public prayer sanctioned.

And Solomon stood before the altar of the LORD in the presence of all the congregation of Israel, and spread forth his hands toward heaven. [Then follows the prayer.] And it was so, that when Solomon had made an end of praying all this prayer and supplication unto the LORD, he arose from before the altar of the LORD, from kneeling on his knees with his hands spread up to heaven. . . . And the LORD said unto him, "I have heard thy prayer and thy supplication, that thou hast made before me." 1 Kings 8:22, 54, and 9:3.

Importunity in prayer commended.

Because this widow troubleth me, I will avenge her, lest by her continual coming she weary me. . . . And shall not God avenge his own elect, which cry day and night

Jesus taught and practiced physical violence.

He that hath no sword, let him sell his garment, and buy one. Luke 22:36.

And when he had made a scourge of small cords, he drove them all out of the temple. . . . John 2:15.

Jesus himself avoided the Jews for fear of being killed.

After these things Jesus walked in Galilee: for he would not walk in Jewry, because the Jews sought to kill him. John 7:1.

Public prayer disapproved.

When thou prayest, thou shalt not be as the hypocrites are: for they love to pray standing in the synagogues and in the corners of the streets, that they may be seen of men. . . . But thou, when thou prayest, enter into thy closet, and when thou hast shut thy door, pray to thy Father which is in secret. Matt. 6:5, 6.

Importunity in prayer condemned.

But when ye pray, use not vain repetitions, as the heathen do: for they think that they shall be heard for their much speaking. Be not ye

unto him . . .? Luke 18:5, 7.

Because of his importunity he will rise and give him as many as he needeth. Luke 11:8.

The wearing of long hair by men sanctioned.

And no razor shall come on his head: for the child shall be a Nazarite unto God from the womb. Judg. 13:5.

All the days of the vow of his separation there shall no razor come upon his head: until the days be fulfilled, in the which he separateth himself unto the LORD, he shall be holy, and shall let the locks of the hair of his head grow. Num. 6:5.

Circumcision instituted.

This is my covenant, which ye shall keep between me and you and thy seed after thee; Every man child among you shall be circumcised. Gen. 17:10.

The sabbath instituted.

And God blessed the seventh day, and sanctified it. Gen. 2:3.

Remember the sabbath day, to keep it holy. Exod. 20:8.

therefore like unto them: for your Father knoweth what things ye have need of, before ye ask him. Matt. 6:7, 8.

The wearing of long hair by men condemned.

Doth not even nature itself teach you, that, if a man have long hair, it is a shame unto him? 1 Cor. 11:14.

Circumcision condemned.

Behold, I Paul say unto you, that if ye be circumcised, Christ shall profit you nothing. Gal. 5:2.

The sabbath repudiated.

The new moons and sabbaths, the calling of assemblies, I cannot away with; it is iniquity. . . . Isa. 1:13.

One man esteemeth one day above another: another man esteemeth every day alike. Let every man be fully persuaded in his own mind. Rom. 14:5.

Let no man therefore judge you in meat, or in drink, or in respect of an holyday, or of the new moon: or of the sabbath days. Col. 2:16.

No work to be done on the sabbath under penalty of death.

Whosoever doeth any work in the sabbath day, he shall surely be put to death. Exod. 31:15.

They found a man that gathered sticks upon the sabbath day. . . . And all the congregation brought him without the camp, and stoned him with stones, and he died; as the LORD commanded Moses. Num. 15:32, 36.

Jesus broke the sabbath and justified the act.

Therefore did the Jews persecute Jesus, and sought to slay him, because he had done these things on the sabbath day. John 5:16.

At that time Jesus went on the sabbath day through the corn; and his disciples were an hungred, and began to pluck the ears of corn, and to eat. But when the Pharisees saw it, they said unto him, "Behold, thy disciples do that which is not lawful to do upon the sabbath day." But he said unto them, . . . "Have ye not read in the law, how that on the sabbath days the priests in the temple profane the sabbath, and are blameless?" Matt. 12:1, 2, 3, 5.

Baptism commanded.

Go ye therefore, and teach all nations, baptizing them in the name of the Father, and of the Son, and of the Holy Ghost. Matt. 28:19.

Baptism not commanded.

I thank God that I baptized none of you, but Crispus and Gaius. . . . For Christ sent me not to baptize, but to preach the gospel. 1 Cor. 1:14, 17.

Every kind of animal allowed for food.

Every moving thing that liveth shall be meat for you. Gen. 9:3.

Whatsoever is sold in the shambles, that eat. . . . 1 Cor. 10:25.

There is nothing unclean of itself. Rom. 14:14.

Certain kinds of animals prohibited for food.

Nevertheless these shall ye not eat of them that chew the cud, or of them that divide the cloven hoof; as the camel, and the hare, and the coney: for they chew the cud, but divide not the hoof; therefore, they are unclean unto you. And the swine, because it divideth the hoof, yet cheweth not the cud, it is unclean unto you: ye shall not eat of their flesh, nor touch their dead carcase. Deut. 14:7, 8.

Taking of oaths sanctioned.

If a man vow a vow unto the LORD, or swear an oath to bind his soul with a bond; he shall not break his word, he shall do according to all that proceedeth out of his mouth. Num. 30:2.

He that sweareth in the earth shall swear by the God of truth. Isa. 65:16.

Now therefore swear unto me here by God. . . . And Abraham said, "I will swear. . . ." There they sware both of them. Gen. 21:23, 24, 31.

Because he [God] could swear by no greater, he sware by himself. Heb. 6:13.

And I . . . made them swear by God. . . . Neh. 13:25.

Taking of oaths forbidden.

But I say unto you, Swear not at all; neither by heaven; for it is God's throne. Matt. 6:34.

Marriage approved and sanctioned.

And the LORD God said, "It is not good that the man should be alone; I will make him an help meet for him." Gen. 2:18.

And God said unto them, "Be fruitful, and multiply, and replenish the earth. . . ." Gen. 1:28.

For this cause shall a man leave father and mother, and shall cleave to his wife. Matt. 19:5.

Marriage is honourable in all. . . . Heb. 13:4.

Marriage disapproved.

It is good for a man not to touch a woman. . . . For I [Paul] would that all men were even as I myself. . . . It is good for them if they abide even as I. 1 Cor. 7:1, 7, 8.

Freedom of divorce permitted.

When a man hath taken a wife, and married her, and it come to pass that she find no favour in his eyes, . . . then let him write her a bill of divorcement, and give it in her hand, and send her out of his house. Deut. 24:1.

When thou goest out to war against thine enemies, and the LORD thy God hath delivered them into thine hands, and thou hast taken them captive, And seest among the captives a beautiful woman, and hast a desire unto her . . . then thou shalt bring her home to thy house; . . . and after that thou shalt go in unto her, and be her husband, and she shall be thy wife. And it shall be, if thou have no delight in her, then thou shalt let her go whither she will; but thou shalt not sell her at all for money, thou shalt not make merchandise of her. . . . Deut. 21:10-14.

Adultery sanctioned.

But all the women children, that have not known a man by lying with him, keep alive for yourselves. Num. 31:18.

And the LORD said unto Hosea, "Go, take thee a wife of whoredoms. . . ." Then said the LORD unto me, "Go yet, love a woman beloved of her friend, yet an adulteress. . . ." So I bought her . . . and I said unto her, "Thou shalt abide for me many days; thou shalt not play the harlot, and thou shalt not be for another man: so will I also be for thee." Hos. 1:2; 3:1-3.

Divorce restricted.

But I say unto you, That whosoever shall put away his wife, saving for the cause of fornication, causeth her to commit adultery. Matt. 5:32.

Adultery forbidden.

Thou shalt not commit adultery. Exod: 20:14.

Whoremongers and adulterers God will judge. Heb. 13:4.

Marriage or cohabitation with a sister denounced.

Cursed be he that lieth with his sister, the daughter of his father, or the daughter of his mother. Deut. 27:22.

And if a man shall take his sister, his father's daughter, or his mother's daughter, . . . it is a wicked thing. Lev. 20:17.

A man may marry his brother's widow.

If brethren dwell together, and one of them die, and have no child, the wife of the dead shall not marry without unto a stranger: her husband's brother shall go in unto her, and take her to him to wife. . . . Deut. 25:5.

Hatred to kindred enjoined.

If any man come to me, and hate not his father, and mother, and wife, and children, and brethren, and sisters, yea, and his own life also, he cannot be my disciple. Luke 14:26.

Intoxicating beverages recommended.

Give strong drink unto him that is ready to perish, and wine unto those that be of heavy hearts. Let him drink and forget his poverty, and remember his misery no more. Prov. 31:6, 7.

Drink no longer water, but use a little wine for thy stomach's sake and thine often infirmities. 1 Tim. 5:23.

Abraham married his sister, and God blessed the union.

And Abraham said, . . . "She is my sister; she is the daughter of my father, but not the daughter of my mother; and she became my wife." Gen. 20:11, 12.

And God said unto Abraham, "As for Sarai, thy wife, . . . I will bless her, and give thee a son also of her." Gen. 17:15, 16.

A man may not marry his brother's widow.

If a man shall take his brother's wife, it is an unclean thing. . . ; they shall be childless. Lev. 20:21.

Hatred to kindred condemned.

Honour thy father and mother. Eph. 6:2.

Husbands, love your wives. . . . For no man ever yet hated his own flesh. Eph. 5:25, 29.

Intoxicating beverages discountenanced.

Wine is a mocker, strong drink is raging: and whosoever is deceived thereby is not wise. Prov. 20:1.

Wine that maketh glad the heart of man. Ps. 104:15.

Wine, which cheereth God and man. . . . Judg. 9:13.

It is our duty to obey rulers, who are God's ministers and punish evildoers only.

Let every soul be subject unto the higher powers. For there is no power but of God: the powers that be are ordained of God. Whosoever therefore resisteth the power, resisteth the ordinance of God: and they that resist shall receive to themselves damnation. For rulers are not a terror to good works, but to evil. . . . For for this cause pay ye tribute also: for they are God's ministers, attending continually upon this very thing. Rom. 13:1-3, 6.

The scribes and Pharisees sit in Moses' seat: all therefore whatsoever they bid you observe, that observe and do. Matt. 23:2, 3.

Submit yourselves to every ordinance of man for the Lord's sake: whether it be to the king, as supreme; Or unto governors, as unto them that are sent by him for the punishment of evildoers. . . . 1 Pet. 2:13, 14.

I counsel thee to keep the king's commandment. . . . Whoso keepeth the commandment shall feel no evil thing. Eccles. 8:2, 5.

It is not our duty to obey rulers who sometimes punish the good, and receive damnation therefore.

But the midwives feared God, and did not as the king of Egypt commanded them. . . . Therefore God dealt well with the midwives. Exod. 1:17, 20.

Shadrach, Meshach, and Abednego, answered and said, . . . "Be it known unto thee, O king, that we will not serve thy gods, nor worship the golden image which thou hast set up." Dan. 3:16, 18.

Wherefore king Darius signed the writing and the decree [that whosoever shall ask a petition of any God or man for thirty days, . . . he shall be cast into the den of lions]. . . . Now, when Daniel knew that the writing was signed, he went into his house; and . . . kneeled upon his knees three times a day and prayed, . . . as he did aforetime. Dan. 6:9, 7, 10.

And the rulers were gathered together against the Lord, and against his Christ. For of a truth against thy holy child Jesus, whom thou hast anointed, both Herod, and Pontius Pilate, with the Gentiles, and the people of Israel, were gathered together. . . . Acts 4:26, 27.

Beware of the scribes, which love to go in long clothing, and love salutations in the market-places, And the chief seats in the synagogues. . . . These shall receive greater damnation. Mark 12:38-40.

And Herod with his men of war set him at naught, and mocked him, and arrayed him in a gorgeous robe, and sent him again to Pilate. . . . And Pilate gave sentence. . . . And when they were come to the place, which is called Calvary, there they crucified him. . . . And the people stood by beholding. And the *rulers* also with them derided him. . . . Luke 23:11, 24, 33, 35.

Woman's rights denied.

And thy desire shall be to thy husband, and he shall rule over thee. Gen. 3:16.

I suffer not a woman to teach, nor to usurp authority over the man, but to be in silence. I Tim. 2:12.

They are commanded to be under obedience, as also saith the law. 1 Cor. 14:34.

Even as Sara obeyed Abraham, calling him lord. 1 Pet. 3:6.

Woman's rights affirmed.

And Deborah, a prophetess, . . . judged Israel at this time. . . . And Deborah said unto Barak, "Up, for this is the day in which the LORD hath delivered Sisera into thine hand." And the LORD discomfited Sisera, and all his chariots, and all his host, with the edge of the sword before Barak. Judg. 4:4, 14, 15.

The inhabitants of the villages ceased, they ceased in Israel, until that I Deborah arose, that I arose a mother in Israel. Judg. 5:7.

And on my handmaidens I will pour out in those days my Spirit; and they shall prophesy. Acts 2:18.

And the same man had four daughters, virgins, which did prophesy. Acts 21:9.

Obedience to masters enjoined.

Servants, obey in all things your masters according to the flesh. . . . And whatsoever ye do, do it heartily, as to the Lord. . . . Col. 3:22, 23.

Servants, be subject to your masters with all fear; not only to the good and gentle, but also to the froward. 1 Pet. 2:18.

Obedience due to God only.

Thou shalt worship the Lord thy God, and him only shalt thou serve. Matt. 4:10.

Be not ye servants of men. 1 Cor. 7:23.

Neither be ye called masters: for one is your Master, even Christ. Matt. 23:10.

HISTORICAL FACTS

God hardened Pharaoh's heart.

But I will harden his heart, that he shall not let the people go. Exod. 4:21.

And the LORD hardened the heart of Pharaoh. . . . Exod. 9:12.

Pharaoh hardened his own heart.

But when Pharaoh saw that there was respite, he hardened his heart, and hearkened not unto them. Exod. 8:15.

Abraham departed to go into Canaan.

And Abram took Sarai his wife, and Lot his brother's son . . . ; and they went forth to go into the land of Canaan; and into the land of Canaan they came. Gen. 12:5.

Abraham went not knowing where.

By faith Abraham, when he was called to go out into a place which he should after receive for an inheritance, obeyed; and he went out, not knowing whither he went. Heb. 11:8.

Abraham begat a son when he was a hundred years old, by the interposition of providence.

Sarah conceived, and bare Abraham a son in his old age, at the set time of which God had spoken to him. Gen. 21:2.

And being not weak in faith, he considered not his own body now dead, when he was about an hundred years old. . . . Rom. 4:19.

Therefore sprang there even of one, and him as good as dead, so many as the stars of the sky. . . . Heb. 11:12.

Abraham begat six children more after he was a hundred years old, without any interposition of providence.

Then again Abraham took a wife, and her name was Keturah. And she bare him Zimran, and Jokshan, and Medan, and Midian, and Ishbak, and Shuah. Gen. 25:1, 2.

Jacob bought a sepulcher of the sons of Hamor.

And the bones of Joseph . . . buried they in Shechem, in a par-

Abraham bought it of the sons of Emmor.

In the sepulchre that Abraham bought for a sum of money of the

cel of ground which Jacob bought of the sons of Hamor the father of Shechem. . . . Josh. 24:32.

sons of Emmor the father of Sychem. Acts 7:16.

Ahaziah was the youngest son of Jehoram.

And the inhabitants of Jerusalem made Ahaziah, his [Jehoram's] youngest son king in his stead: for the band of men that came with the Arabians to the camp had slain all the eldest. 2 Chron. 22:1.

Ahaziah was not the youngest son of Jehoram.

The LORD stirred up against Jehoram the spirit of the Philistines, and of the Arabians, . . . and they came up into Judah . . . and carried away all the substance that was found in the king's house, and his sons also, and his wives; so that there was never a son left him, save Jehoahaz, the youngest of his sons. 2 Chron. 21:16, 17.

David sinned in numbering the people.

And David's heart smote him after that he had numbered the people. And David said unto the LORD, "I have sinned greatly in that I have done." 2 Sam. 24:10.

David never sinned except in the matter of Uriah.

David did that which was right in the eyes of the LORD, and turned not aside from any thing that he commanded him all the days of his life, save only in the matter of Uriah the Hittite. 1 Kings 15:5.

John the Baptist recognized Jesus as the Messiah.

The next day John seeth Jesus coming unto him, and saith, "Behold the Lamb of God, which taketh away the sin of the world. . . . And I saw, and bare record that this is the Son of God." John 1:29, 34.

John the Baptist did not recognize Jesus as the Messiah.

Now when John had heard in the prison the works of Christ, he sent two of his disciples, And said unto him, "Art thou he that should come, or do we look for another?" Matt. 11:2, 3.

John the Baptist was Elias.

This is Elias, which was for to come. Matt. 11:14.

John the Baptist was not Elias.

And they asked him, "What then? Art thou Elias?" And he saith, "I am not." John 1:21.

The infant Jesus was taken into Egypt.

He took the young child and his mother by night, and departed into Egypt: And was there until the death of Herod. . . . But when Herod was dead . . . he arose, and took the young child and his mother, and came . . . and dwelt in a city called Nazareth. Matt. 2:14, 15, 19, 21, 23.

Jesus preached his first sermon sitting on the mount.

And seeing the multitudes, he went up into a *mountain*: and when he was set, his disciples came unto him: And he opened his mouth, and taught them, saying. . . . Matt. 5:1, 2.

John was in prison when Jesus went into Galilee.

Now after that John was put in prison, Jesus came into Galilee, preaching the gospel of the kingdom of God. . . . Mark 1:14.

Vinegar mingled with gall was offered to Jesus.

They gave him vinegar to drink mingled with gall. Matt. 27:34.

Judas returned the pieces of silver.

Then Judas . . . brought again the thirty pieces of silver to the

The infant Jesus was not taken into Egypt.

And when the days of her purification according to the law of Moses were accomplished, they brought him to Jerusalem, to present him to the Lord. . . . And when they had performed all things according to the law of the Lord, they returned . . . to their own city Nazareth. Luke 2:22, 39.

He preached his first sermon standing in the plain.

And he came down with them, and stood in the *plain*, and the company of his disciples, and a great multitude of people . . . came to hear him. . . . And he lifted up his eyes on his disciples, and said . . . . Luke 6:17, 20.

John was not in prison when Jesus went into Galilee.

Again the next day after John stood, and two of his disciples; And looking upon Jesus as he walked, he saith, "Behold the Lamb of God!" . . . The day following Jesus would go forth into Galilee. . . . John 1:35, 36, 43.

Wine mingled with myrrh was offered to him.

And they gave him to drink wine mingled with myrrh. Mark 15:23.

Judas did not return the pieces of silver.

Now this man purchased a field with the reward of iniquity. . . .

chief priests and elders. . . . Matt. 27:3.

Acts 1:18.

But one woman came to the sepulcher.
The first day of the week cometh Mary Magdalene early when it was yet dark, unto the sepulchre. John 20:1.

Two women came to the sepulcher.
In the end of the sabbath, as it began to dawn toward the first day of the week, came Mary Magdalene and the *other Mary* to see the sepulchre. Matt. 28:1.

Three women came to the sepulcher.
And when the sabbath was past, Mary Magdalene, and Mary the mother of James, and Salome, had brought sweet spices, that they might come and anoint him. Mark 16:1.

More than three women came to the sepulcher.
It was Mary Magdalene, and Joanna, and Mary the mother of James, and *other women* that were with them. . . . Luke 24:10.

It was at sunrise when they came to the sepulcher.
And very early in the morning the first day of the week, they came unto the sepulchre at the rising of the sun. Mark 16: 2.

It was some time before sunrise when they came.
The first day of the week cometh Mary Magdalene early while it was *yet dark*, unto the sepulchre . . . . John 20:1.

Two angels were seen at the sepulcher, standing up.
And it came to pass, as they were much perplexed thereabout, behold, two men *stood* by them in *shining garments*. Luke 24:4.

But one angel was seen, and he was sitting down.
For the angel of the LORD descended from heaven, and came and rolled back the stone from the door, and sat upon it. . . . And *the angel* answered and said unto the women, "Fear not. . . ." Matt. 28:2, 5.

Two angels were seen within the sepulcher.
And as she wept, she stooped down and looked into the sepulchre, And seeth two angels in white. . . . John 20:11, 12.

But one angel was seen within the sepulcher.
And entering into the sepulchre, they saw a young man sitting on the right side, clothed in a long white garment. Mark 16:5.

The one angel seen was without the sepulcher.

The angel . . . rolled back the stone from the door, and sat upon it. Matt. 28:2.

The women went and told the disciples of Christ's resurrection.

And they departed quickly from the sepulchre with fear and great joy; and did run to bring his disciples word. Matt. 28:8.

And returned from the sepulchre, and told all these things unto the eleven. . . . Luke 24:9.

The women did not go and tell the disciples.

And they went out quickly, and fled from the sepulchre; for they trembled and were amazed: neither said they any thing to any man. Mark 16:8.

The angels appeared after Peter and John visited the sepulcher.

Peter therefore went forth, and that other disciple, [whom Jesus loved], and came to the sepulchre, . . . and went into the sepulchre, and seeth the linen clothes. . . . Then the disciples went away again. . . . But Mary stood without at the sepulchre, weeping: and as she wept she stooped down and looked into the sepulchre, And seeth two angels in white. . . . John 20:3, 6, 10-12.

The angels appeared before Peter alone visited the sepulcher.

Behold, two men stood by them [the women] in shining garments. . . . And they . . . returned from the sepulchre, and told all these things unto the eleven. . . . Then arose Peter, and ran unto the sepulchre; and stooping down, he beheld the linen clothes laid by themselves, and departed wondering. . . . Luke 24:4, 8, 9, 12.

Jesus appeared first to Mary Magdalene.

Now, when Jesus was risen early, the first day of the week, he appeared first to Mary Magdalene . . . . Mark 16:9.

And when she had thus said, she turned herself back and saw Jesus standing, and knew not that it was Jesus. John 20:14.

He appeared to neither of the Marys.

Now upon the first day of the week, very early in the morning, they came unto the sepulchre, bringing the spices which they had prepared, and certain others with them. And they found the stone rolled away from the sepulchre. And they entered in, and found

283

Jesus appeared first to the two Marys.

And as they (Mary Magdalene and the other Mary) went to tell his disciples, behold Jesus met them, saying, "All hail." Matt. 28:9.

not the body of the LORD Jesus. And it came to pass, as they were much perplexed thereabout, behold, two men stood by them in shining garments: And as they were afraid, and bowed down their faces to the earth, they said unto them, "Why seek ye the living among the dead? He is not here, but is risen: remember how he spake unto you when he was yet in Galilee, Saying, 'The Son of man must be delivered into the hands of sinful men, and be crucified, and the third day rise again.'" And they remembered his words, And returned from the sepulchre, and told all these things unto the eleven, and to all the rest. It was Mary Magdalene, and Joanna, and Mary the mother of James, and other women that were with them, which told these things unto the apostles. Luke 24:1-11.

Jesus was to be three days and three nights in the grave.

So shall the Son of man be three days and three nights in the heart of the earth. Matt. 12:40.

He was but two days and two nights in the grave.

And it was the third hour, and they crucified him. . . . It was the preparation, that is, the *day before the sabbath.* . . . And Pilate . . . gave the body to Joseph. And he . . . laid him in a sepulchre. . . . Now, when Jesus was risen early the *first day of the week*, he appeared first to Mary Magdalene. Mark 15:25, 42, 44-46; and 16:9.

The Holy Ghost was bestowed at Pentecost.

And when the day of Pentecost

The Holy Ghost was bestowed before Pentecost.

And when he said this, he

284

was fully come, they were all with one accord in one place. . . . And they were all filled with the Holy Ghost. . . . Acts 2:1, 4.

breathed on them, and saith unto them, "Receive ye the Holy Ghost." John 20:22.

Jesus first appeared to the eleven disciples in a room at Jerusalem.

And they rose up the same hour, and returned to Jerusalem, and found the eleven gathered together. . . . And as they thus spake, Jesus himself stood in the midst of them. . . . But they were terrified and affrighted, and supposed that they had seen a spirit. Luke 24:33, 36, 37.

The same day at evening, being the first day of the week, when the doors were shut where the disciples were assembled, . . . came Jesus and stood in the midst. . . . John 20:19.

He first appeared to them on a mountain in Galilee.

Then the eleven disciples went away into Galilee, into a mountain where Jesus had appointed them. And when they saw him, they worshipped him: but some doubted. Matt. 28:16, 17.

Jesus ascended from mount Olivet.

And when he had spoken these things, while they beheld, he was taken up; and a cloud received him out of their sight. . . . Then returned they unto Jerusalem from the mount called Olivet. . . . Acts 1:9, 12.

Did he ascend from either place?

Afterward he appeared unto the eleven as they *sat at meat*, and upbraided them with their unbelief. . . . So then after the Lord had spoken unto them, he was received up into heaven. . . . Mark 16:14, 19.

He ascended from Bethany.

And he led them out as far as to Bethany, and he lifted up his hands and blessed them. And it came to pass, while he blessed them, he was parted from them, and carried up into heaven. Luke 24:50, 51.

SPECULATIVE DOCTRINES

The law was superseded by the Christian dispensation.

The law and the prophets were until John: since that time the kingdom of God is preached. . . . Luke 16:16.

The law was not superseded by the Christian dispensation.

I am come not to destroy, but to fulfil. For verily I say unto you, Till heaven and earth pass, one jot or one tittle shall in no wise pass from the law till all be fulfilled. Whosoever therefore shall break one of these least commandments, and shall teach men so, he shall be called the least in the kingdom of heaven. Matt. 5:17, 18, 19.

It was lawful for the Jews to put Jesus to death.

The Jews answered him [Pilate], "We have a law, and by our law he ought to die. . . ." John 19:7.

It was not lawful for the Jews to put him to death.

The Jews therefore said unto him [Pilate], "It is not lawful for us to put any man to death." John 18:31.

Children are punished for the sins of their parents.

I the LORD thy God am a jealous God, visiting the iniquity of the fathers upon the children. . . . Exod. 20:5.

Because by this deed thou hast given great occasion to the enemies of the LORD to blaspheme, the child also that is born unto thee shall surely die. 2 Sam. 12:14.

Children are not punished for the sins of their parents.

The son shall not bear the iniquity of the father. . . . Ezek. 18:20.

Neither shall the children be put to death for the fathers. Deut. 24:16.

Man is justified by faith alone.

Knowing that a man is not justified by the works of the law, but by

Man is not justified by faith alone.

The doers of the law shall be justified. Rom. 2.13.

the faith of Jesus Christ. . . . Gal. 2:16.

The just shall live by faith. And the law is not of faith. Gal. 3:11, 12

It is impossible to fall from grace.

And I give unto them eternal life; and they shall never perish, neither shall any man pluck them out of my hand. John 10:28.

Neither death, nor life, nor angels, nor principalities, nor powers, nor things present, nor things to come, Nor height, nor depth, nor any other creature, shall be able to separate us from the love of God, which is in Christ Jesus our Lord. Rom. 8:38, 39.

It is possible to fall from grace.

But when the righteous turneth away from his righteousness, and committeth iniquity, and doeth according to all the abominations that the wicked man doeth, shall he live? All his righteousness that he hath done shall not be mentioned: in his trespass that he hath trespassed, and in his sin that he hath sinned, in them shall he die. Ezek. 18:24.

For it is impossible for those who were once enlightened, and have tasted of the heavenly gift, and were made partakers of the Holy Ghost, And have tasted the good word of God, and the powers of the world to come, If they shall fall away, to renew them again unto repentance. Heb. 6:4-6.

For if after they have escaped the pollutions of the world through the knowledge of the Lord and Saviour Jesus Christ, they are again entangled therein and overcome, the latter end is worse with them than the beginning. For it had been better for them not to have known the way of righteousness, than, after they have known it, to turn from the holy commandment delivered unto them. 2 Pet. 2:20, 21.

No man is without sin.

Who can say, I have made my

Christians are sinless.

Whosoever is born of God doth

288

heart clean, I am pure from my sin? Prov. 20:9.

There is none righteous, no, not one. Rom. 3:10.

There is to be a resurrection of the dead.

The trumpet shall sound, and the dead shall be raised. . . . 1 Cor. 15:52.

Reward and punishment to be bestowed in this world.

Behold, the righteous shall be recompensed in the earth: much more the wicked and the sinner. Prov. 11:31.

Annihilation the portion of all mankind.

Why died I not from the womb? why did I not give up the ghost when I came out of the belly . . ? For now should I have lain still and been quiet, I should have slept: then had I been at rest, With kings and counselors of the earth, which built desolate places for themselves; Or with princes that had gold, who filled their houses with silver; Or as an hidden untimely birth I had not been; as infants which never saw light. *There* the wicked cease from troubling; and there the weary be at rest. . . . The small and great are there; and the servant is free from his master. Wherefore is light given to him that is in misery, and life unto the

not commit sin; . . . he cannot sin, because he is born of God. . . . Whosoever abideth in him sinneth not. . . . He that committeth sin is of the Devil. 1 John 3:9, 6, 8.

There is to be no resurrection of the dead.

They are dead, they shall not live; they are deceased, they shall not rise. Isa. 26:14.

Reward and punishment to be bestowed in the next world.

Then he shall reward every man according to his works. Matt. 16:27.

According to that he hath done, whether it be good or bad. 2 Cor. 5:10.

Endless misery the portion of a part of mankind.

These shall go away into everlasting punishment. Matt. 25:46.

And the devil that deceived them was cast into the lake of fire and brimstone, where the beast and the false prophet are, and shall be tormented day and night for ever and ever. . . . And whosoever was not found written in the book of life was cast into the lake of fire. Rev. 20:10, 15.

And the smoke of their torment ascendeth up for ever and ever. Rev. 14:11.

And many of them that sleep in the dust shall awake, some to . . . everlasting contempt. Dan. 12:2.

bitter in soul; Which long for death, but it cometh not; . . . Which rejoice exceedingly, and are glad, when they can find the grave? Job 3:11, 13-17, 19-22.

The dead know not any thing . . . . For there is no work, nor device, nor knowledge, nor wisdom, in the grave, whither thou goest. Eccles. 9:5, 10.

For that which befalleth the sons of men befalleth beasts, even one thing befalleth them: as the one dieth, so dieth the other; yea, they have all one breath; so that a man hath no pre-eminence above a beast. . . . All go unto one place. Eccles. 3:19, 20.

The earth is to be destroyed.

And I saw a great white throne, and him that sat on it, from whose face the earth and the heaven fled away; and there was found no place for them. Rev. 20:11.

No evil shall happen to the godly.

There shall no evil happen to the just. Prov. 12:21.

Who is he that will harm you, if ye be followers of that which is good? 1 Pet. 3:13.

Worldly good and prosperity the lot of the godly.

For the LORD loveth judgment, and forsaketh not his saints; they are preserved forever. . . . The

The earth is never to be destroyed.

Who laid the foundations of the earth, that it should not be removed for ever. Ps. 104:5.

Evil does happen to the godly.

And the LORD said unto Satan, "Hast thou considered my servant Job, that there is none like him in the earth, a perfect and an upright man?" . . . So went Satan forth . . . and smote Job with sore boils from the sole of his foot unto his crown. Job 2:3, 7.

Worldly misery and destitution the lot of the godly.

For the time would fail me to tell of Gedeon, and of Barak, and of Samson, and of Jephthae; of

290

wicked watcheth the righteous, and seeketh to slay him. The LORD will not leave him in his hand, nor condemn him when he is judged. . . . Mark the perfect man, and behold the upright: for the end of that man is peace. Ps. 37:28, 32, 33, 37.

Blessed is the man that walketh not in the counsel of the ungodly. . . . Whatsoever he doeth shall prosper. Ps. 1:1, 3.

And the LORD was with Joseph, and he was a prosperous man. Gen. 39:2.

So the LORD blessed the latter end of Job more than his beginning. Job 42:12.

David also, and Samuel, and of the prophets. . . . And others had trial of cruel mockings and scourgings, yea, moreover of bonds and imprisonment: They were stoned, they were sawn asunder, were tempted, were slain with the sword: they wandered about in sheepskins and goatskins; being destitute, afflicted, tormented; . . . they wandered in deserts, and in mountains, and in dens and caves of the earth. Heb. 11:32. 36-38.

These are they which came out of great tribulation, and have washed their robes, and made them white in the blood of the Lamb. Rev. 7:14.

Yea, and all that will live godly in Christ Jesus shall suffer persecution. 2 Tim. 3:12.

And ye shall be hated of all men for my name's sake. Luke 21:17.

Worldly prosperity a blessing and a reward of righteousness.

There is no man that hath left house, or brethren, or sisters, or father, or mother, or wife, or children, or lands, for my sake and the gospel's, But he shall receive an hundredfold now in this time, houses, and brethren, and sisters, and mothers, and children, and lands. . . . Mark 10:29, 30.

I have been young, and now am old; yet have I not seen the righteous forsaken, nor his seed begging bread. Ps. 37:25.

If thou return unto the Almighty, thou shalt be built up. . . . Then

Worldly prosperity a curse and a bar to future reward.

Blessed be ye poor. Luke 6:20.

Lay not up for yourselves treasures upon earth. . . . For where your treasure is, there will your heart be also. Matt. 6:19, 21.

And it came to pass, that the *beggar* died, and was carried by the angels into Abraham's bosom. Luke 16:22.

It is easier for a camel to go through the eye of a needle, than for a rich man to enter into the kingdom of God. Matt. 19:24.

Woe unto you that are rich! for ye have received your consola-

shalt thou lay up gold as dust. . . . Job 22:23, 24.

In the house of the righteous is much treasure. Prov. 15:6.

The Christian yoke is easy.

Come unto me, all ye that labour and are heavy laden, and I will give you rest. Take my yoke upon you. . . . For my yoke is easy, and my burden is light. Matt. 11:28-30.

Who is he that will harm you, if ye be followers of that which is good? 1 Pet. 3:13.

The fruit of God's spirit is love and gentleness.

The fruit of the Spirit is love, joy, peace, longsuffering, gentleness, goodness. . . . Gal. 5:22.

Prosperity and longevity enjoyed by the wicked.

They [men of the world] are full of children, and leave the rest of their substance to their babes. Ps. 17:14.

There is a wicked man that prolongeth his life in his wickedness. Eccles. 7:15.

tion. Luke 6:24.

The Christian yoke is not easy.

In the world ye shall have tribulation. John 16:33.

Yea, and all that will live godly in Christ Jesus shall suffer persecution. 2 Tim. 3:12.

Whom the Lord loveth he chasteneth, and scourgeth every son whom he receiveth. . . . But if ye be without chastisement, whereof all are partakers, then are ye bastards, and not sons. Heb. 12:6, 8.

The fruit of God's spirit is vengeance and fury.

And the Spirit of the LORD came mightily upon him. . . . And he . . . slew a thousand men. . . . Jud. 15:14, 15.

And it came to pass on the morrow, that the evil spirit from God came upon Saul . . . and there was a javelin in Saul's hand. And Saul cast the javelin; for he said, "I will smite David even to the wall with it." 1 Sam. 18:10, 11.

Prosperity and longevity denied to the wicked.

But it shall not be well with the wicked, neither shall he prolong his days. . . . Eccles. 8:13.

They [the hypocrites] die in youth. . . . Job 36:14.

Be not over much wicked, neither be foolish: why shouldst thou

Wherefore doth the way of the wicked prosper? wherefore are all they happy that deal very treacherously? Jer. 12:1.

Riches a blessing.

The rich man's wealth is his strong city, but the destruction of the poor is their poverty. Prov. 10:15.

If thou return to the Almighty then thou shalt be built up. . . . Then shalt thou lay up gold as dust. Job 22:23, 24.

So the LORD blessed the latter end of Job more than his beginning: for he had fourteen thousand sheep, and six thousand camels, and a thousand yoke of oxen, and a thousand she asses. Job 42:12.

A good name a blessing.

A good name is better than precious ointment. Eccles. 7:1.

A good name is rather to be chosen than great riches. . . . Prov. 22:1.

Laughter commended.

To every thing there is a season, and a time. . . . A time to weep, and a time to laugh. Eccles. 3:1, 4.

Then I commended mirth, because a man hath no better thing under the sun, than to eat, and to drink, and to be merry. Eccles. 8:15.

A merry heart doeth good like a medicine. Prov. 17:22.

die before thy time? Eccles. 7:17.

Poverty is a blessing.

Blessed be ye poor. . . . Woe unto you that are rich! Luke 6:20, 24.

Hath not God chosen the poor of this world rich in faith, and heirs of the kingdom . . .? James 2:5.

Neither poverty nor riches a blessing.

Give me neither poverty nor riches; feed me with food convenient for me: Lest I be full, and deny thee, and say, "Who is the LORD?" or lest I be poor, and steal, and take the name of my God in vain. Prov. 30:8, 9.

A good name is a curse.

Woe unto you, when all men shall speak well of you! Luke 6:26.

Laughter condemned.

Woe unto you that laugh now! Luke 6:25.

Sorrow is better than laughter: for by the sadness of the countenance the heart is made better. The heart of the wise is in the house of mourning; but the heart of fools is in the house of mirth. Eccles. 7:3, 4.

The rod of corrections a remedy for foolishness.

Foolishness is bound in the heart of a child; but the rod of correction shall drive it far from him. Prov. 22:15.

Prophecy is sure.

We have also a more sure word of prophecy; whereunto ye do well that ye take heed, as unto a light that shineth in a dark place. . . . 2 Pet. 1:19.

There is no remedy for foolishness.

Though thou shouldst bray a fool in a mortar, . . . yet will not his foolishness depart from him. Prov. 27:22.

Prophecy is not sure.

At what instant I shall speak concerning a nation, and concerning a kingdom, to pluck up, and to pull down, and to destroy it; If that nation, against whom I have pronounced, turn from their evil, I will repent of the evil that I thought to do unto them. And at what instant I shall speak concerning a nation, and concerning a kingdom, to build and to plant it; If it do evil in my sight, that it obey not my voice, then I will repent of the good, wherewith I said I would benefit them. Jer. 18:7-10.

The prophets prophesy falsely, and the priests bear rule by their means. . . . From the prophet even unto the priest every one dealeth falsely. Jer. 5:31; 6:13.

Man's life was to be one hundred and twenty years.

His days shall be an hundred and twenty years. Gen. 6:3.

Man's life is but seventy years.

The days of our years are threescore years and ten. Ps. 90:10.

Miracles a proof of divine mission.

Now, when John had heard in the prison the works of Christ, he sent two of his disciples, And said unto him, "Art thou he that should come, or do we look for another?" Jesus answered and said unto

Miracles not a proof of divine mission.

And Aaron cast down his rod before Pharaoh, and before his servants, and it became a serpent. Then Pharaoh also called the wise men and the sorcerers: now, the

294

them, "Go and shew John again those things which ye do hear and see: The blind receive their sight, and the lame walk, the lepers are cleansed, and the deaf hear, the dead are raised. . . ." Matt. 11:2-5.

Rabbi [Jesus], we know that thou art a teacher come from God: for no man can do these miracles that thou doest, except God be with him. John 3:2.

And Israel saw that great work which the LORD did upon the Egyptians: and the people feared the LORD and believed the LORD and his servant Moses. Exod. 14:31.

magicians of Egypt, they also did in like manner with their enchantments. For they cast down every man his rod, and they became serpents. Exod. 7:10-12.

If there arise among you a prophet, or a dreamer of dreams, and giveth thee a sign or wonder, And the sign or the wonder come to pass, whereof he spake unto thee, saying, "Let us go after other gods, which thou hast not known, and let us serve them"; Thou shalt not hearken unto the words of that prophet, or that dreamer of dreams. Deut. 13:1-3.

If I [Jesus] by Beelzebub cast out devils, by whom do your sons cast them out? Luke 11:19.

All scripture is inspired.

All scripture is given by inspiration of God. . . . 2 Tim. 3:16.

Some scripture is not inspired.

But I speak this by permission, and not by commandment. . . . But to the rest speak I, not the Lord. 1 Cor. 7:6, 12.

That which I speak, I speak it not after the Lord. . . . 2 Cor. 11:17.

ADDENDA

Hatred to the Edomite sanctioned.
And he [Amaziah] did that which was right in the sight of the LORD, yet not like David his father: he did according to all things as Joash his father did. . . . He slew of Edom in the valley of salt ten thousand, and took Selah by war, and called the name of it Joktheel unto this day. 2 Kings 14:3, 7.

Hatred to the Edomite forbidden.
Thou shalt not abhor an Edomite; for he is thy brother. Deut. 23:7.

Moses feared Pharaoh.
And he said, "Who made thee a prince and a judge over us? intendest thou to kill me, as thou killedst the Egyptian?" And Moses feared, and said, "Surely this thing is known." Now when Pharaoh heard this thing, he sought to slay Moses. But Moses fled from the face of Pharaoh. . . . Exod. 2:14.

Moses did not fear Pharaoh.
By faith he forsook Egypt, not fearing the wrath of the king: for he endured, as seeing him who is invisible. Heb. 11:27.

There were fourteen generations from Abraham to David, and fourteen from the Babylonish captivity to Christ.
So all the generations from Abraham to David are fourteen generations; and from David until the carrying away into Babylon are fourteen generations; and from the carrying away into Babylon unto Christ are fourteen generations. Matt. 1:17.

There were thirteen generations.
Abraham begat Isaac; and Isaac begat Jacob; and Jacob begat Judas and his brethren; And Judas begat Phares and Zara of Thamar; and Phares begat Esrom; and Esrom begat Aram; And Aram begat Aminadab; and Aminadab begat Naason; and Naason begat Salmon; and Salmon begat Booz of Rachab; and Booz begat Obed of Ruth; and Obed begat Jesse; And Jesse begat David. . . . And after they were brought to Baby-

297

lon, Jechonias begat Salathiel; and Salathiel begat Zorobabel; And Zorobabel begat Abiud; and Abiud begat Eliakim; and Eliakim begat Azor; And Azor begat Sadoc; and Sadoc begat Achim; and Achim begat Eliud; And Eliud begat Eleazar; and Eleazar begat Matthan; and Matthan begat Jacob; And Jacob begat Joseph the husband of Mary, of whom was born Jesus . . . . Matt. 1:2-6, 12-16.

A woman of Canaan besought Jesus.

Then Jesus went thence, and departed into the coasts of Tyre and Sidon. And, behold, a woman of Canaan came out of the same coasts, and cried unto him, saying, "Have mercy on me, O Lord, thou son of David; my daughter is grievously vexed with a devil." Matt. 15:21, 22.

A Greek woman besought Jesus.

And from thence he arose, and went into the borders of Tyre and Sidon, and entered into an house, and would have no man know it: but he could not be hid. For a certain woman, whose young daughter had an unclean spirit, heard of him, and came and fell at his feet: The woman was a Greek, a Syrophenician by nation; and she besought him that he would cast forth the devil out of her daughter. Mark 7:24-26.

Ahaziah began to reign in the twelfth year of Joram.

In the twelfth year of Joram the son of Ahab king of Israel did Ahaziah the son of Jehoram king of Judah begin to reign. 2 Kings 8:25.

Ahaziah began to reign in the eleventh year.

And in the eleventh year of Joram the son of Ahab began Ahaziah to reign over Judah. 2 Kings 9:29.

Christ laid down his life for his friends.

This is my commandment, That ye love one another, as I have loved you. Greater love hath no

Christ laid down his life for his enemies.

For if, when we were enemies, we were reconciled to God by the death of his Son, much more,

man than this, that a man lay down his life for his friends. John 15:12,13.

A fool should be answered according to his folly.
Answer a fool according to his folly, lest he be wise in his own conceit. Prov. 26:5.

The fear of man was to be upon every beast.
And the fear of you and the dread of you shall be upon every beast of the earth, and upon every fowl of the air, upon all that moveth upon the earth, and upon all the fishes of the sea; into your hand are they delivered. Gen. 9:2.

being reconciled, we shall be saved by his life. Rom. 5:10.

A fool should not be answered according to his folly.
Answer not a fool according to his folly, lest thou also be like unto him. Prov. 26:4.

The fear of man is not upon the lion.
A lion which is strongest among beasts, and turneth not away for any. Prov. 30:30.

Very many more contradictions, especially historical, may be found in the Bible, besides those embraced under the 144 propositions; but some are comparatively trivial, others are not apparent from mere citation without comment, and others are only cumulative proofs of propositions already abundantly supported.

As an instance of discrepancy of statement, take the inscription set over the head of Jesus at the Crucifixion:

THE KING OF THE JEWS. — Mark 15:26.
THIS IS THE KING OF THE JEWS. — Luke 23:38.
THIS IS JESUS THE KING OF THE JEWS. — Matt. 27:37.
JESUS OF NAZARETH THE KING OF THE JEWS. — John 19:19.

As a remarkable instance of discrepancy of names and numbers, take the two chapters, Ezra 2 and Nehemiah 7. They are almost exactly alike, the whole of the former being repeated in the latter, with slight variations. Both give the names of the families that returned from Babylon to Jerusalem, and the number of each. They agree in making the whole number 42,360, besides 7,337 servants; but on casting up the separate numbers, the whole sum in Ezra is 29,818, and in Nehemiah 31,089. And in comparing the two chapters verse by verse we find twenty-seven discrepancies in figures and thirty in names.

[American Atheists here provides you with the chapters from Ezra (2:1-70) and Nehemiah (7:6-73) which were not provided in the original. They are placed next to each other to facilitate comparison by the reader. Corresponding verses are placed next to each other to match. In a few cases this required a minor reversal of order of the verses, but nothing has been omitted.]

EZRA	NEHEMIAH
1. Now these are the children of the province that went up out of the captivity, of those which had been carried away, whom Nebuchadnezzar the King of Babylon had carried away unto Babylon, and came again unto Jerusalem and Judah, every one unto his city;	6. These are the children of the province, that went up out of the captivity of those that had been carried away, whom Nebuchadnezzar the King of Babylon had carried away, and came again to Jerusalem and to Judah, every one unto his city;
2. Which came with Zerubbabel: Jeshua, Nehemiah, *Seraiah, Reelaiah*, Mordecai, Bilshan, *Mizpar*, Bigvai, *Rehum*, Baanah. The number of the men of the people of Israel:	7. Who came with Zerubbabel, Jeshua, Nehemiah, *Azariah, Raamiah, Nahamani*, Mordecai, Bilshan, *Mispereth*, Bigvai, *Nehum*, Baanah. The number, I say, of the men of the people of Israel was this;
3. The children of Parosh, two thousand an hundred seventy and two.	8. The children of Parosh, two thousand an hundred seventy and two.
4. The children of Shephatiah, three hundred seventy and two.	9. The children of Shephatiah, three hundred seventy and two.
5. The children of Arah, *seven hundred seventy and five*.	10. The children of Arah, *six hundred fifty and two*.
6. The children of Pahathmoab, of the children of Jeshua and Joab, two thousand eight hundred and *twelve*.	11. The children of Pahathmoab, of the children of Jeshua and Joab, two thousand and eight hundred and *eighteen*.
7. The children of Elam, a thousand two hundred fifty and four.	12. The children of Elam, a thousand two hundred fifty and four.
8. The children of Zattu, *nine* hundred forty and five.	13. The children of Zattu, *eight* hundred forty and five.

9. The children of Zaccai, seven hundred and threescore.
10. The children of *Bani*, six hundred forty and *two*.
11. The children of Bebai, six hundred twenty and *three*.
12. The children of Azgad, *a thousand two hundred* twenty and two.
13. The children of Adonikam, six hundred sixty and *six*.
14. The children of Bigvai, two thousand *fifty and six*.
15. The children of Adin, *four hundred fifty and four*.
16. The children of Ater of Hezekiah, ninety and eight.
17. The children of Bezai, three hundred twenty and *three*.
18. The children of *Jorah*, an hundred and twelve.
19. The children of Hashum, *two hundred twenty and three*.
20. The children of *Gibbar*, ninety and five.
21. The children of Bethlehem, an hundred *twenty and three*.
22. The men of Netophah, *fifty and six*.
23. The men of Anathoth, an hundred twenty and eight.
24. The children of *Azmaveth*, forty and two.
25. The children of *Kirjatharim*, Chephirah, and Beeroth, seven hundred and forty and three.
26. The children of Ramah and Gaba, six hundred twenty and one.
27. The men of Michmas, an hundred twenty and two.

14. The children of Zaccai, seven hundred and threescore.
15. The children of *Binnui*, six hundred forty and *eight*.
16. The children of Bebai, six hundred twenty and *eight*.
17. The children of Azgad, *two thousand three hundred* twenty and two.
18. The children of Adonikam, six hundred threescore and *seven*.
19. The children of Bigvai, two thousand *threescore and seven*.
20. The children of Adin, *six hundred fifty and five*.
21. The children of Ater of Hezekiah, ninety and eight.
23. The children of Bezai, three hundred twenty and *four*.
24. The children of *Hariph*, an hundred and twelve.
22. The children of Hashum, *three hundred twenty and eight*.
25. The children of *Gibeon*, ninety and five.
26. The men of Bethlehem and Netophah, an hundred *fourscore and eight*.
27. The men of Anathoth, an hundred twenty and eight.
28. The men of *Beth*-azmeveth, forty and two.
29. The men of *Kirjathjearim*, Chephirah, and Beeroth, seven hundred forty and three.
30. The men of Ramah and Gaba, six hundred twenty and one.
31. The men of Michmas, an hundred and twenty and two.

28. The men of Bethel and Ai, *two hundred* twenty and three.
29. The children of Nebo, fifty and two.
30. *The children of Magbish, an hundred fifty and six.*
31. The children of the other Elam, a thousand two hundred fifty and four.
32. The children of Harim, three hundred and twenty.
33. The children of Lod, Hadid, and Ono, seven hundred twenty and *five.*
34. The children of Jericho, three hundred forty and five.
35. The children of Senaah, three thousand and *six hundred* and thirty.
36. The priests: the children of Jedaiah, of the house of Jeshua, nine hundred seventy and three.
37. The children of Immer, a thousand fifty and two.
38. The children of Pashur, a thousand two hundred forty and seven.
39. The children of Harim, a thousand and seventeen.
40.The Levites: the children of Jeshua and Kadmiel, of the children of *Hodaviah,* seventy and four.
41. The singers: the children of Asaph, an hundred *twenty* and eight.
42. The children of the porters: the children of Shallum, the children of Ater, the children of Talmon, the children of Akkub, the children of Hatita, the children of

32. The men of Bethel and Ai, *an hundred* twenty and three.
33. The men of the other Nebo, fifty and two.

34. The children of the other Elam, a thousand two hundred fifty and four.
35. The children of Harim, three hundred and twenty.
37. The children of Lod, Hadid, and Ono, seven hundred twenty and *one.*
36. The children of Jericho, three hundred forty and five.
38. The children of Senaah, three thousand *nine hundred* and thirty.
39. The priests: the children of Jedaiah, of the house of Jeshua, nine hundred seventy and three.
40. The children of Immer, a thousand fifty and two.
41. The children of Pashur, a thousand two hundred forty and seven.
42. The children of Harim, a thousand and seventeen.
43. The Levites: the children of Jeshua, of Kadmiel, and of the children of *Hodevah,* seventy and four.
44. The singers: the children of Asaph, an hundred *forty* and eight.

45. The porters: the children of Shallum, the children of Ater, the children of Talmon, the children of Akkub, the children of Hatita, the children of Shobai, an hundred

Shobai, in all an hundred thirty and *nine*.

43. The Nethinims: the children of Ziha, the children of Hasupha, the children of Tabbaoth,

44. The children of Keros, the children of *Siaha*, the children of Padon,

45. The children of *Lebanah*, the children of *Hagabah*, the children of *Akkub*,

46. The children of *Hagab*, the children of Shalmai, the children of Hanan,

47. The children of Giddel, the children of Gahar, the children of Reaiah,

48. The children of Rezin, the children of Nekoda, the children of Gazzam,

49. The children of Uzza, the children of *Paseah*, the children of Besai,

50. The children of *Asnah, the children of Mehunim*, the children of *Nephusim*,

51. The children of Bakbuk, the children of Hakupha, the children of Harhur,

52. The children of *Bazluth*, the children of Mehida, the children of Harsha,

53. The children of Barkos, the children of Sisera, the children of *Thamah*,

54. The children of Neziah, the children of Hatipha.

55. The children of Solomon's servants: the children of Sotai, the children of Sophereth, the children of *Peruda*,

thirty and *eight*.

46. The Nethinims: the children of Ziha, the children of Hashupha, the children of Tabbaoth,

47. The children of Keros, the children of *Sia*, the children of Padon,

48. The children of *Lebana*, the children of *Hagaba*, the children of Shalmai,

49. The children of Hanan, the children of Giddel, the children of Gahar,

50. The children of Reaiah, the children of Rezin, the children of Nekoda,

51. The children of Gazzam, the children of Uzza, the children of *Phaseah*,

52. The children of Besai, the children of *Meunim*, the children of *Nephishesim*,

53. The children of Bakbuk, the children of Hakupha, the children of Harhur,

54. The children of *Bazlith*, the children of Mehida, the children of Harsha,

55. The children of Barkos, the children of Sisera, the children of *Tamah*,

56. The children of Neziah, the children of Hatipha,

57. The children of Solomon's servants: the children of Sotai, the children of Sophereth, the children of *Perida*,

56. The children of Jaalah, the children of Darkon, the children of Giddel,

57. The children of Shephatiah, the children of Hattil, the children of Pochereth of Zebaim, the children of Ami.

58. All the Nethinims, and the children of Solomon's servants, were three hundred ninety and two.

59. And these were they which went up from Telmelah, *Telharsa*, Cherub, *Addan*, and Immer: but they could not shew their father's house, and their seed, whether they were of Israel:

60. The children of Delaiah, the children of Tobiah, the children of Nekoda, six hundred *fifty* and two.

61. And of the children of the priests: the children of Habaiah, the children of Koz, the children of Barzillai: which took a wife of the daughters of Barzillai the Gileadite, and was called after their name:

62. These sought their register among those that were reckoned by genealogy, but they were not found: therefore were they, as polluted, put from the priesthood.

63. And the Tirshatha said unto them, that they should not eat of the most holy things, till there stood up a priest with Urim and with Thummim.

64. The whole congregation together was forty and two thousand three hundred and threescore.

58. The children of Jaala, the children of Darkon, the children of Giddel,

59. The children of Shephatiah, the children of Hattil, the children of Pochereth of Zebaim, the children of *Amon*.

60. All the Nethinims, and the children of Solomon's servants, were three hundred ninety and two.

61. And these were they which went up also from Telmelah, *Telharesha*, Cherub, *Addon*, and Immer: but they could not shew their father's house, nor their seed, whether they were of Israel.

62. The children of Delaiah, the children of Tobiah, the children of Nekoda, six hundred *forty* and two.

63. And of the priests: the children of Habaiah, the children of Koz, the children of Barzillai, which took one of the daughters of Barzillai the Gileadite to wife, and was called after their name.

64. These sought their register among those that were reckoned by genealogy, but it was not found: therefore were they, as polluted, put from the priesthood.

65. And the Tirshatha said unto them, that they should not eat of the most holy things, till there stood up a priest with Urim and Thummim.

66. The whole congregation together was forty and two thousand three hundred and threescore.

65. Beside their servants and their maids, of whom there were seven thousand three hundred thirty and seven: and there were among them *two hundred* singing men and singing women.

66. Their horses were seven hundred thirty and six; their mules, two hundred forty and five;

67. Their camels, four hundred thirty and five; their asses, six thousand seven hundred and twenty.

68. And some of the chief of the fathers, when they came to the house of the LORD which is at Jerusalem, offered freely for the house of God to set it up in his place:

69. They gave after their ability unto the treasure of the work *threescore and one thousand drams of gold, and five thousand pound of silver, and one hundred priests' garments.*

70. So the priests, and the Levites, and some of the people, and the singers, and the porters, and the Nethinims, dwelt in their cities, and all Israel in their cities.

67. Beside their manservants and their maidservants, of whom there were seven thousand three hundred thirty and seven: and they had two hundred *forty and five* singing men and singing women.

68. Their horses, seven hundred thirty and six: their mules, two hundred forty and five:

69. Their camels, four hundred thirty and five: six thousand seven hundred and twenty asses.

70. And some of the chief of the fathers gave unto the work. The Tirshatha gave to the treasure *a thousand drams of gold, fifty basons, five hundred and thirty priests' garments.*

71. And some of the chief of the fathers gave to the treasure of the work *twenty thousand drams of gold, and two thousand and two hundred pound of silver.*

72. And that which the rest of the people gave was *twenty thousand drams of gold, and two thousand pound of silver, and threescore and seven priests' garments.*

73. So the priests, and the Levites, and the porters, and the singers, and some of the people, and the Nethinims, and all Israel, dwelt in their cities; *and when the seventh month came,* the children of Israel were in their cities.

[American Atheist Ed. — Thus, in comparing the two chapters verse by verse, we find twenty-seven discrepancies in figures and twenty-six in names.]

All of this careful numbering was forbidden if Jahweh himself did not command it. When David, who was "perfect" in Jahweh's eye, took a census, he was immediately punished. See 1 Chron. 21:2, 7, 8:

> And David said to Joab and to the rulers of the people, "Go: number Israel from Beersheba even to Dan; and bring the number of them to me, that I may know it." . . . And God was displeased with this thing; therefore he smote Israel. And David said unto God, "I have sinned greatly, because I have done this thing: but now, I beseech thee, do away the iniquity of thy servant; for I have done very foolishly."]

THE BIBLE
CONTRADICTS ITSELF

[American Atheist Ed. — Included in this compiled *Bible Handbook* is a short offering first published in Australia in 1968. At that time the World Wide Church of God was a phenomenon proliferating via radio throughout the world. At the time of the current publication that church has been rent with ideological schism and is fast disappearing from the world scene.]

AUTHOR'S PREFACE

To Christians of the fundamentalist ilk the Bible is a fetish — an object of blind devotion and superstitious veneration.

By means of radio broadcasts and the distribution of large quantities of literature these pious folk seek to convince the world that "Holy Writ" contains the solution to all worldly problems. (One must, of course, accept the particular brand of bibliolatry purveyed by the sect concerned; and there is a considerable difference of opinion as to which is the "correct" brand.)

Prominent in these fields of activity is an organization styling itself "The Radio Church of God," which in addition to distributing printed matter, literally by the ton, broadcasts nightly from some 300 radio stations, covering every continent — except Antarctica!

The founder and chief propagandist of this church is one Herbert W. Armstrong, who lets it be known that he has "more knowledge and understanding of the Bible than anyone (else) on earth." Mr. Armstrong insists that the Bible is veritably the word of God and that everything contained in it is absolute truth. With heavy emphasis he says, "Either ALL the bible is TRUE or all of it is FALSE,"* and he declares that the only reason people reject the Bible is because they "secretly want to serve their own lusts."

Sects such as the Adventists, Jehovah's Witnesses, and the Christadelphians are not far behind in their efforts to direct world thinking "aright." All express their conviction that the Bible is wholly inspired and inerrant. In a pamphlet recently issued by the last-named sect and entitled "How to Read The Bible" its author insists that there is nothing disharmonious in that collection of writings. "Though the writers were divided by class, by age, by country, by disposition, there is wonderful harmony in all they wrote. Some wrote in the center of city life, others in the wilderness; some were free men, others were slaves; some wrote in exile, others in the midst of comfort. But there is no contradiction, no

---

*It is difficult to imagine anything more nonsensical than this pronouncement. Atheist students of the Bible fully recognize that amid a mass of myth, legend, folklore, and pseudohistory there can be found much authentic history in the so-called book of books.

disagreement. Whence came this wonderful unity. From God! They all wrote under divine inspiration. They were God's agents, proclaiming his message unto men. . . ."

The contents of *The Bible Contradicts Itself* will provide a sufficient answer to such extravagant and wholly untrue claims. A good deal of the matter contained therein has been culled from *The Bible Handbook*.

JOHN BOWDEN
Sydney, N.S.W. Australia
January 1968

[American Atheist Ed. — Herbert W. Armstrong, the founder of the Worldwide Church of God, died at his home in Pasadena, California, on January 17, 1986, at age ninety-three.]

310

THE OLD TESTAMENT

The entire earth covered with water.

And the earth was without form, and void; and darkness was upon the face of the deep. And the Spirit of God moved upon the face of the waters. . . . And God made the firmament, and divided the waters which were under the firmament from the waters which were above the firmament: and it was so. . . . And God said, "Let the waters under the heaven be gathered together unto one place, and let the dry land appear:" and it was so. And God called the dry land Earth; and the gathering together of the waters called he Seas: and God saw that it was good. Gen. 1:2, 7, 9-10.

Trees brought forth before man created.

And God said, "Let the earth bring forth grass, the herb yielding seed, and the fruit tree yielding fruit after his kind, whose seed is in itself, upon the earth:" and it was so. And the earth brought forth grass, and herb yielding seed after his kind, and the tree yielding fruit, whose seed was in itself, after his kind: and God saw that it was good. . . . So God created man in his own image, in the image of God created he him; male and

Very little water; a mist went up from the face of the earth and "watered the whole face of the ground."

And every plant of the field before it was in the earth, and every herb of the field before it grew: for the LORD God had not caused it to rain upon the earth, and there was not a man to till the ground. But there went up a mist from the earth, and watered the whole face of the ground. Gen. 2:5, 6.

Trees are made after man formed.

And the LORD God formed man of the dust of the ground, and breathed into his nostrils the breath of life; and man became a living soul. And the LORD God planted a garden eastward in Eden; and there he put the man whom he had formed. And out of the ground made the LORD God to grow every tree that is pleasant to the sight, and good for food; the tree of life also in the midst of the garden, and the tree of knowledge of good and evil. Gen. 2:7-9.

311

female created he them. Gen.
1:11, 12, 27.

[There are in Genesis two distinct and divergent accounts of
creation. The first, Gen. 1:1. — Gen. 2:4., has affinities with the
Babylonian creation myth, the chief difference being that the Babylonian
writer, with a more acute perception and a greater logic, has the
creation of the heavenly bodies precede the formation of the earth, thus
avoiding the absurdity of having three "evenings and mornings" — the
division of day from night — before there was a sun in the sky.

The second creation story is an adaptation of a second Babylonian
legend which was inscribed in Sumerian characters and is therefore
much older than the first version. In this account man is created before
the beasts, as in the second genesaic narrative. This variant myth was
published by its discoverer, Dr. Theo. Pinches.

The stylistic and linguistic differences in the two genesaic accounts
stand out. In the first account we find characteristic phrases, oft
repeated. "And God [Elohim] said, 'Let there be. . .' "; "and it was so";
"and God saw that it was good"; "and the evening and the morning
were." We read of "creeping things." Not one of these distinctive
phrases can be found in the second story, with its freely flowing
narrative style which is in such marked contrast to the formal,
grandiloquent style of the first account. The two accounts are further
distinguished by their designation of the Deity. In the first account it is
Elohim (translated "God") who brings into being the universe and all
that therein is; in the second account it is Jahweh Elohim (translated
"LORD God") who does things. Never once does Elohim in the second
narrative appear without the accompanying Jahweh; never once in the
first narrative does it appear *with* the name Jahweh.

When these facts are considered together with the contradictions set
out above there is little room for doubt that in the opening chapters of
Genesis we have two distinct and irreconcilable accounts of creation.]

Noah perfect in his generations.	*Noah falls into a drunken stupor.*
These are the generations of Noah: Noah was a just man and perfect in his generations, and Noah walked with God. Gen. 6:9.	And he [Noah] drank of the wine, and was drunken; and he was uncovered within his tent. Gen. 9:21.

312

Fowls of every kind taken into the ark by pairs.

Of fowls after their kind, and of cattle after their kind, of every creeping thing of the earth after his kind, two of every sort shall come unto thee, to keep them alive. Gen. 6:20.

The fowls of the air go in by sevens.

And the LORD said unto Noah ". . . Of every clean beast thou shalt take to thee by sevens, . . . Of fowls also of the air by sevens, the male and the female; to keep seed alive upon the face of all the earth." Gen. 7:3.

[In the account of the Noachian deluge two originally distinct and independent narratives have been merged. Note that Noah and his family twice enter the ark in readiness for the "take off" (Compare Gen. 7:7 ["And Noah went in, and his sons, and his wife, and his sons' wives with him, into the ark, because of the waters of the flood."] with Gen. 7:13 ["In the selfsame day entered Noah, and Shem, and Ham, and Japheth, the sons of Noah, and Noah's wife, and the three wives of his sons with them, into the ark."].) Compare verses 13 and 14 of chapter eight ("And it came to pass in the six hundredth and first year, in the first month, the first day of the month, the waters were dried up from off the earth: and Noah removed the covering of the ark, and looked, and, behold, the face of the ground was dry. And in the second month, on the seven and twentieth day of the month, was the earth dried. And God spake unto Noah, saying, "Go forth of the ark, thou, and thy wife, and thy sons, and thy sons' wives with thee."). If these verses be regarded as part of a single, continuous story, it follows that Noah and his family and the menagerie remained in the odoriferous ark unnecessarily for fifty-six days!].

There were Nephilim (Revised Standard Version, translated "giants" in the Authorized Version) in the earth before the commencement of the Flood which is said to have drowned all living things except the occupants of the ark.

The Nephilim were on the earth in those days; and also afterward, when the sons of God came in to the daughters of men, and they

The Nephilim somehow managed to survive!

And there we saw the Nephilim (the sons of Anak, who come from the Nephilim); and we seemed to ourselves like grasshoppers, and so we seemed to them. Num. 13:33.

bore children to them, the same became mighty men which were of old, men of renown. Gen. 4:4.

The whole earth of one language and one speech.
And the whole earth was of one language, and of one speech. Gen. 11:1.

The whole earth was not of one language and one speech.
By these were the isles of the Gentiles divided in their lands; every one after his tongue, after their families, in their nations. . . . These are the sons of Ham, after their families, after their tongues, in their countries, and in their nations. . . . These are the sons of Shem, after their families, after their tongues, in their lands, after their nations. Gen. 10:5, 20, 31.

Lot is Abram's nephew.
And they took Lot, Abram's brother's son, who dwelt in Sodom, and his goods, and departed. Gen. 14:12.

Lot is Abram's brother.
And when Abram heard that his brother was taken captive, he armed his trained servants, born in his own house, three hundred and eighteen, and pursued them unto Dan. . . . And he brought back all the goods, and also brought again his brother Lot, and his goods, and the women also, and the people. Gen. 14:14, 16.

Chedorlaomer and his allies smite all the country of the Amalekites.
And in the fourteenth year came Chedorlaomer, and the kings that were with him, and smote the Rephaims in Ashteroth Karnaim, and the Zuzims in Ham, and the Emims in Shaveh Kiriathaim, And the Horites in their mount Seir, unto Elparan, which is by the wilderness. And they returned,

There were then no Amalekites; they figure as descendants of Abram's grandson Esau.
And Timna was concubine to Eliphaz Esau's son; and she bare to Eliphaz Amalek: these were the sons of Adah Esau's wife. Gen. 36:12.

Amalek is later described as "the first of nations."

and came to Enmishpat, which is Kadesh, and smote all the country of the Amalekites, and also the Amorites, that dwelt in Hazezontamar. Gen. 14:5-7.

And when he looked on Amalek, he took up his parable, and said, "Amalek was the first of the nations; but his latter end shall be that he perish for ever." Num. 24:20.

God was known to Abraham (Abram) by the name "Jahweh."

And Abraham called the name of that place Jehovahjireh: as it is said to this day, "In the mount of the LORD it shall be seen." Gen. 22:14.

God was not known by the name "Jahweh" by any of the patriarchs.

And I appeared unto Abraham, unto Isaac, and unto Jacob, by the name of God Almighty, but by my name JEHOVAH was I not known to them. Exod. 6:3.

[Josh. 24:2, 14-15: And Joshua said unto all the people, "Thus saith the LORD God of Israel, 'Your fathers dwelt on the other side of the flood in old time, even Terah, the father of Abraham, and the father of Nachor: and they served other gods. . . .' Now therefore fear the LORD, and serve him in sincerity and in truth: and put away the gods which your fathers served on the other side of the flood, and in Egypt; and serve ye the LORD. And if it seem evil unto you to serve the LORD, choose you this day whom ye will serve; whether the gods which your fathers served that were on the other side of the flood, or the gods of the Amorites, in whose land ye dwell: but as for me and my house, we will serve the LORD." supports this.

Yet we are told in Gen. 4:26 that when Enos was born then began men to call upon the name of Jahweh." It has to be borne in mind that the word "LORD" printed in small capitals equals Jahweh; and according to Genesis the god was known to and venerated by all the patriarchs under that name. This is further evidence that the book of Genesis was not completed until after the time of Moses.]

Beersheba was given its name by Abraham.

And he said, "For these seven ewe lambs shalt thou take of my hand, that they may be a witness unto me, that I have digged this well." Wherefore he called that place Beersheba; because there

The name was bestowed by Isaac.

And it came to pass the same day, that Isaac's servants came, and told him concerning the well which they had digged, and said unto him, "We have found water." And he called it Shebah: therefore the name of the city is Beersheba

315

they sware both of them. Gen. 21:30-31.

unto this day. Gen. 26:32-33.

Jacob changes the name Luz to "Bethel" when he was on his way to Padan-aram.

And he called the name of that place Bethel: but the name of that city was called Luz at the first. Gen. 28:19.

He effects the change of name when returning home from Padan-aram twenty years later.

So Jacob came to Luz, which is in the land of Canaan, that is, Bethel, he and all the people that were with him. And he built there an altar, and called the place El-bethel: because there God appeared unto him, when he fled from the face of his brother. . . . And Jacob called the name of the place where God spake with him, Bethel. Gen. 35:6-7, 15.

[When we turn back to Gen. 12:5, 8 (And Abram took Sarai his wife .. . and they went forth to go into the land of Canaan; and into the land of Canaan they came. . . . And he removed from thence unto a mountain on the east of Bethel, and pitched his tent, having Bethel on the west, and Hai on the east: and there he builded an altar unto the LORD, and called upon the name of the LORD.) and Gen. 13:3 (And he went on his journeys from the south even to Bethel, unto the place where his tent had been at the beginning, between Bethel and Hai.), we find that Bethel was known by that name to Abraham!]

Jacob's name was changed to Israel on the bank of the river Jabbok.

And he rose up that night, and took his two wives, and his two womenservants, and his eleven sons, and passed over the ford Jabbok. . . . And he said, "Thy name shall be called no more Jacob, but Israel: for as a prince hast thou power with God and with men, and hast prevailed." Gen. 32:22, 28.

[The Jabbok runs into the Jordan from the east.]

His name was changed to Israel at Bethel (or el-Bethel).

And God said unto him, "Thy name is Jacob: thy name shall not be called any more Jacob, but Israel shall be thy name": and he called his name Israel. Gen. 35:10.

[Bethel was on the west side of Jordan and north of Jerusalem.]

Joseph is sold into Egypt by Midianites.

And the Midianites sold him into Egypt unto Potiphar, an officer of Pharaoh's, and captain of the guard. Gen. 37:36.

At a wayside inn on their way home from Egypt each of Joseph's brothers finds money hidden in his sack.

And as one of them opened his sack to give his ass provender in the inn, he espied his money; for, behold, it was in his sack's mouth. And he said unto his brethren, "My money is restored; and, lo, it is even in my sack:" and their heart failed them, and they were afraid, saying one to another, "What is this that God hath done unto us?" Gen. 42:27-28.

[The brothers speaking to Joseph] "And it came to pass, when we came to the inn, that we opened our sacks, and, behold, every man's money was in the mouth of his sack, our money in full weight: and we have brought it again in our hand." Gen. 43:21.

He is sold into Egypt by Ismaelites.

Then there passed by Midianites merchantmen; and they drew and lifted up Joseph out of the pit, and sold Joseph to the Ishmeelites for twenty pieces of silver: and they brought Joseph into Egypt. Gen. 37:28.

And Joseph was brought down to Egypt; and Potiphar, an officer of Pharaoh, captain of the guard, an Egyptian, bought him of the hands of the Ismeelites, which had brought him down thither. Gen. 39:1.

The money was not discovered until the brothers reached home.

And they came unto Jacob their father unto the land of Canaan, and told him all that befell unto them. . . . And it came to pass as they emptied their sacks, that, behold, every man's bundle of money was in his sack: and when both they and and their father saw the bundles of money, they were afraid. Gen. 42:29, 35.

317

Benjamin a "little one," a "lad," the apple of his father's eye.

And we [Joseph's brothers] said unto my lord, "We have a father, an old man, and a child of his old age, a little one; and his brother is dead, and he alone is left of his mother, and his father loveth him. ... The lad cannot leave his father: for if he should leave his father, his father would die." Gen. 44:20, 22.

When the Jacob clan migrated to Egypt shortly afterwards, Benjamin was a grown man with ten sons! He had more sons than any of his brothers.

And these are the names of the children of Israel, which came into Egypt, ... And the sons of Benjamin were Belah, and Becher, and Ashbel, Gera, and Naaman, Ehi, and Rosh, Muppim, and Huppim, and Ard. Gen. 46:8, 21.

[The genealogical details given in Num. 26:38-40 (The sons of Benjamin after their families: of Bela, ... of Ashbel, ... of Ahiram, ... of Shupham, ... of Hupham, ... And the sons of Bela were Ard and Naaman.) give but seven names; two of these, Ard and Naaman, are said to be grandchildren — not children (as according to the Genesaic writer) — of Benjamin; another two, Ahiram and Shupham, were unknown to the Genesaic writer. The chronicler gives two different genealogies (The sons of Benjamin; Bela, and Becher, and Jediael, three. — 1 Chron. 7:6; Now Benjamin begat Bela his firstborn, Ashbel the second, and Aharah the third, Nohah the fourth, and Rapha the fifth. — 1 Chron. 8:1-2.); one gives three and the other five names. Thus there are four conflicting genealogies with only two names, Bela and Ashbel, common to all four.]

Jahweh to write the words of the law on the tables of stone.

And the LORD said unto Moses, "Hew thee two tables of stone like unto the first: and I will write upon these tables the words that were in the first tables, which thou brakest." Exod. 34:1.

Jahweh instructs Moses to write the words, and Moses does so.

And the LORD said unto Moses, "Write thou these words: for after the tenor of these words I have made a covenant with thee and with Israel." And he was there with the LORD forty days and forty nights; he did neither eat bread, nor drink water. And he wrote upon the tables the words of the covenant, the ten commandments. Exod. 34:27-28.

318

Mosera is but two stopping places from Sinai (or Horeb).

And the children of Israel took their journey from Beeroth of the children of Jaakan to Mosera: there Aaron died, and there he was buried, and Eleazar his son ministered in the priest's office in his stead. Deut. 10:6.

Mosera is the fourteenth stopping place.

And they removed from the desert of Sinai, and pitched at Kibrothhattaavah. And they departed from Kibrothhattaavah, and encamped at Hazeroth. And they departed from Hazeroth, and pitched in Rithmah. And they departed from Rithmah, and pitched at Rimmonparez. And they departed from Rimmonparez, and pitched in Libnah. And they removed from Libnah, and pitched at Rissah. And they journeyed from Rissah, and pitched in Kehelathah. And they went from Kehelathah, and pitched in mount Shapher. And they removed from mount Shapher, and encamped in Haradah. And they removed from Haradah, and pitched in Makheloth. And they removed from Makheloth, and encamped at Tahath. And they departed from Tahath, and pitched at Tarah. And they removed from Tarah, and pitched in Mithcah. And they went from Mithcah, and pitched in Hashmonah. And they departed from Hashmonah, and encamped at Moseroth. Num. 33: 16-30.

After leaving Mosera (Moseroth) the children of Israel proceed to Benejaakan; thence to Horhagidgad, and then on to Jotbathah.

And they departed from Moseroth, and pitched in Benejaakan. And they removed from Benejaakan, and encamped at Horhagid-

Benejaakan did not follow, it preceded Mosera. After leaving Mosera the Israelites proceeded to Gudogah, thence to Jotbath.

And the children of Israel took their journey from Beeroth of the children of Jaakan to Mosera: there Aaron died, and there he

gad. And they went from Horha-gidgad, and pitched in Jotbathah. Num. 33:31-33.

was buried, and Eleazar his son ministered in the priest's office in his stead. From thence they journeyed unto Gudgodah; and from Gudgodah to Jotbath, a land of rivers of waters. Deut. 10:6-7.

The Levites' service to commence at the age of thirty.

From thirty years old and upward even unto fifty years old shalt thou number them, every one that entereth into the service, to do the work of the tabernacle of the congregation. Num. 4:30.

The Levites' service is to commence at the age of twenty-five.

This is it that belongeth unto the Levites: from twenty and five years old and upward they shall go in to wait upon the service of the tabernacle of the congregation. Num. 8:24.

The Edomites spurned the Israelites when the starving people sought sustenance and a right of way.

And [the king of] Edom said unto him, "Thou shalt not pass by me, lest I come out against thee with the sword." And the children of Israel said unto him, "We will go by the high way: and if I and my cattle drink of thy water, then I will pay for it: I will only, without doing any thing else, go through on my feet." And he said, "Thou shalt not go through." And Edom came out against him with much people, and with a strong hand. Thus Edom refused to give Israel passage through his border: wherefore Israel turned away from him. Num. 20:18-21.

The Edomites (children of Esau) allowed the wanderers to pass through their territory and provided them with food and drink.

Thus dwelt Esau in mount Seir: Esau is Edom. Gen. 36:8.

Thou shalt sell me meat for money, that I may eat; and give me water for money, that I may drink: only I will pass through on my feet; (As the children of Esau which dwell in Seir, and the Moabites which dwell in Ar, did unto me;) until I shall pass over Jordan into the land which the LORD our God giveth us. Deut. 2:28-29.

The Moabites refused aid to the wanderers.

An Ammonite or Moabite shall

The Moabites did render aid.

Thou shalt sell me meat for money, that I may eat; and give me

320

not enter into the congregation of the LORD; even to their tenth generation shall they not enter into the congregation of the LORD for ever: Because they met you not with bread and with water in the way, when ye came forth out of Egypt. . . . Deut. 23:3-4.

The whole of the house of Korah was swallowed up when the earth opened.

And the earth opened her mouth, and swallowed them up, and their houses, and all the men that appertained unto Korah, and all their goods. Num. 16:32.

Joshua set up twelve stones in the midst of Jordan where they remained.

And Joshua set up twelve stones in the midst of Jordan, in the place where the feet of the priests which bare the ark of the covenant stood: and they are there unto this day. Josh. 4:9.

The whole of Canaan conquered and its inhabitants utterly destroyed by Joshua.

And Joshua returned, and all Israel with him, to Debir; and fought against it: And he took it, and the king thereof, and all the cities thereof; and they smote them with the edge of the sword, and utterly destroyed all the souls that were therein; he left none remaining: as he had done to Hebron, so he did to Debir, and to

water for money, that I may drink: only I will pass through on my feet; (As the children of Esau which dwell in Seir, and the Moabites which dwell in Ar, did unto me;) until I shall pass over Jordan into the land which the LORD our God giveth us. Deut. 2:28-29.

They did not all perish; the children survived.

Notwithstanding the children of Korah died not. Num. 26:11.

The stones were removed from the Jordan.

And those twelve stones, which they took out of Jordan, did Joshua pitch in Gilgal. Josh. 4:20.

Canaan not entirely subdued even after the death of Joshua.

Now after the death of Joshua . . . Judah went up; and the LORD delivered the Canaanites and the Perizzites into their hand: and they slew of them in Bezek ten thousand men. And they found Adonibezek in Bezek; and they fought against him, and they slew the Canaanites and the Perizzites. . . . Now the children of Judah had fought against Jerusalem, and had

the king thereof; as he had done also to Libnah, and to her king. So Joshua smote all the country of the hills, and of the south, and of the vale, and of the springs, and all their kings: he left none remaining, but utterly destroyed all that breathed, as the LORD God of Israel commanded. And Joshua smote them from Kadeshbarnea even unto Gaza, and all the country of Goshen, even unto Gibeon. Josh. 10:38-41.

And it came to pass, when Jabin king of Hazor had heard those things, that he sent to Jobab king of Madon, and to the king of Shimron, and to the king of Achshaph, And to the kings that were on the north of the mountains, and of the plains south of Chinneroth [Galilee], and in the valley, and in the borders of Dor on the west, And to the Canaanite on the east and on the west, and to the Amorite, and the Hittite, and the Perizzite, and the Jebusite in the mountains, and to the Hivite under Hermon in the land of Mizpeh. And they went out, they and all their hosts with them, much people, even as the sand that is upon the sea shore in multitude, with horses and chariots very many. . . . And the LORD delivered them into the hand of Israel, who smote them, and chased them unto great Zidon, and unto Misrephothmaim, and unto the valley of Mizpeh eastward; and they smote them, until they left them none remaining. . . .

taken it, and smitten it with the edge of the sword, and set the city on fire. And afterward the children of Judah went down to fight against the Canaanites, that dwelt in the mountain, and in the south, and in the valley. And Judah went against the Canaanites that dwelt in Hebron: . . . And from thence he went against the inhabitants of Debir: . . . And Othniel the son of Kenaz, Caleb's younger brother, took it: . . . And Judah went with Simeon his brother, and they slew the Canaanites that inhabited Zephath, and utterly destroyed it. And the name of the city was called Hormah. Also Judah took Gaza with the coast thereof, and Askelon with the coast thereof, and Ekron with the coast thereof. And the LORD was with Judah; and he drave out the inhabitants of the mountain; but could not drive out the inhabitants of the valley, because they had chariots of iron. And they gave Hebron unto Caleb, as Moses said: and he expelled thence the three sons of Anak. And the children of Benjamin did not drive out the Jebusites that inhabited Jerusalem; but the Jebusites dwell with the children of Benjamin in Jerusalem unto this day. And the house of Joseph, they also went up against Bethel: and the LORD was with them. And the house of Joseph sent to descry Bethel. . . . And . . . they smote the city with the edge of the sword; . . . Neither did Manasseh drive out

And Joshua at that time turned back, and took Hazor, and smote the king thereof with the sword: for Hazor beforetime was the head of all those kingdoms. And they smote all the souls that were therein with the edge of the sword, utterly destroying them: there was not any left to breathe: and he burnt Hazor with fire. . . . So Joshua took all that land, the hills, and all the south country, and all the land of Goshen, and the valley, and the plain, and the mountain of Israel, and the valley of the same; Even from the mount Halak, that goeth up to Seir, even unto Baalgad in the valley of Lebanon under mount Hermon: and all their kings he took, and smote them, and slew them. Josh. 11: 1-4, 8, 10-11, 16-17.

And these are the kings of the country which Joshua and the children of Israel smote on this side Jordan on the west, from Baalgad in the valley of Lebanon even unto the mount Halak, that goeth up to Seir; which Joshua gave unto the tribes of Israel for a possession according to their divisions; In the mountains, and in the valleys, and in the plains, and in the springs, and in the wilderness, and in the south country; the Hittites, the Amorites, and the Canaanites, the Perizzites, the Hivites, and the Jebusites. . . . The king of Jerusalem, one; the king of Hebron, one; . . . The king of Debir, one; . . . The king of Hormah, one; the king of Megiddo, one; The king of Dor the inhabitants of Bethshean and her towns, nor Taanach and her towns, nor the inhabitants of Dor and her towns, nor the inhabitants of Ibleam and her towns, nor the inhabitants of Megiddo and her towns: but the Canaanites would dwell in that land. And it came to pass, when Israel was strong, that they put the Canaanites to tribute, and did not utterly drive them out. Neither did Ephraim drive out the Canaanites that dwelt in Gezer; but the Canaanites dwelt in Gezer among them. Neither did Zebulun drive out the inhabitants of Kitron, nor the inhabitants of Nahalol; but the Canaanites dwelt among them, and became tributaries. Neither did Asher drive out the inhabitants of Accho, nor the inhabitants of Zidon, nor of Ahlab, nor of Achzib, nor of Helbah, nor of Aphik, nor of Rehob: But the Asherites dwelt among the Canaanites, the inhabitants of the land: for they did not drive them out. Neither did Naphtali drive out the inhabitants of Bethshemesh, nor the inhabitants of Bethanath; but he dwelt among the Canaanites, the inhabitants of the land: nevertheless the inhabitants of Bethshemesh and of Bethanath became tributaries unto them. And the Amorites forced the children of Dan into the mountain: for they would not suffer them to come down to the valley: But the Amorites would dwell in mount Heres in Aijalon, and in Shaalbim:

in the coast of Dor, one; . . . The king of Tirzah, one; and all the kings thirty and one. Josh. 12:7, 8, 10, 13, 14, 21, 24.

yet the hand of the house of Joseph prevailed, so that they became tributaries. And the coast of the Amorites was from the going up to Akrabbim, from the rock, and upward. Judg. 1:1, 4-5, 8-11, 13, 17-23, 25, 27-36.

Hebron was given to and occupied by Caleb before the death of Joshua.

Hebron therefore became the inheritance of Caleb the son of Jephunneh the Kenezite unto this day, because that he wholly followed the LORD God of Israel. Josh. 14:14.

And unto Caleb the son of Jephunneh he gave a part among the children of Judah, according to the commandment of the LORD to Joshua, even the city of Arba the father of Anak, which city is Hebron. Josh. 15:13.

Judah takes Hebron after the death of Joshua.

And Judah went against the Canaanites that dwelt in Hebron: (now the name of Hebron before was Kirjatharba:) and they slew Sheshai and Ahiman, and Talmai. Judg. 1:10.

Othniel takes Debir before the death of Joshua.

And he went up thence to the inhabitants of Debir: and the name of Debir before was Kirjathsepher. And Caleb said, "He that smiteth Kirjathsepher, and taketh it, to him will I give Achsah my daughter to wife." And Othniel the son of Kenaz, the brother of Caleb, took it: and he gave him Achsah his daughter to wife. Josh. 15:15-17.

The city is taken by Othniel after the death of Joshua.

And from thence he went against the inhabitants of Debir: and the name of Debir before was Kirjathsepher: And Caleb said, "He that smiteth Kirjathsepher, and taketh it, to him will I give Achsah my daughter to wife." And Othniel the son of Kenaz, Caleb's younger brother, took it: and he gave him Achsah his daughter to wife. Jud. 1:11-13.

The Canaanites to be driven out of Bethshean.

The Canaanites not driven out.

And the LORD was with Judah;

324

And the children of Joseph said, "The hill is not enough for us: and all the Canaanites that dwell in the land of the valley have chariots of iron, both they who are of Bethshean and her towns, and they who are of the valley of Jezreel." And Joshua spake unto the house of Joseph, even to Ephraim and to Manasseh, saying, "Thou art a great people, and hast great power: thou shalt not have one lot only: But the mountain shall be thine; for it is a wood, and thou shalt cut it down: and the outgoings of it shall be thine: for thou shalt drive out the Canaanites, though they have iron chariots, and though they be strong." Josh. 17:16-18.

and he drave out the inhabitants of the mountain; but could not drive out the inhabitants of the valley, because they had chariots of iron. . . . Neither did Manasseh drive out the inhabitants of Bethshean and her towns, nor Taanach and her towns, nor the inhabitants of Ibleam and her towns, nor the inhabitants of Megiddo and her towns: but the Canaanites would dwell in that land. And it came to pass, when Israel was strong, that they put the Canaanites to tribute, and did not utterly drive them out. Judg. 1:19, 27-28.

Jael drives a nail into Sisera's temple whilst he was asleep.

Then Jael Heber's wife took a nail of the tent, and took an hammer in her hand, and went softly unto him, and smote the nail into his temples, and fastened it into the ground: for he was fast asleep and weary. So he died. Judg. 4:21.

The nail was driven into Sisera's head whilst he stood upright.

She put her hand to the nail, and her right hand to the workmen's hammer; and with the hammer she smote Sisera, she smote off his head, when she had pierced and stricken through his temples. At her feet he bowed, he fell, he lay down: at her feet he bowed, he fell: where he bowed, there he fell down dead. Judg. 5:26-27.

The spirit of Jahweh came upon Samson, so he slew thirty Philistines.

And the spirit of the LORD came upon him, and he went down to Ashkelon, and slew thirty men of them, and took their spoil,

But the fruit of the Spirit is love.

But the fruit of the Spirit is love, joy, peace, longsuffering, gentleness, goodness, faith, Meekness, temperance: against such there is no law. Gal. 5:22-23.

and gave change of garments unto them which expounded the riddle. Judg. 14:19.

The Philistines subdued all the days of Samuel.

So the Philistines were subdued, and they came no more into the coast of Israel: and the hand of the LORD was against the Philistines all the days of Samuel. 1 Sam. 7:13.

The Philistines later invade Israel.

And the Philistines gathered themselves together to fight with Israel, thirty thousand chariots, and six thousand horsemen, and people as the sand which is on the sea shore in multitude: and they came up, and pitched in Michmash, eastward from Bethaven .... behold, Samuel came. 1 Sam. 13:5, 10.

A saying about Saul "explained."

And it came to pass, when all that knew him beforetime saw that, behold, he prophesied among the prophets, then the people said one to another, "What is this that is come unto the son of Kish? Is Saul also among the prophets?" And one of the same place answered and said, "But who is their father?" Therefore it became a proverb, "Is Saul also among the prophets?" 1 Sam. 10:11-12.

A different "explanation" is given.

And he stripped off his clothes also, and prophesied before Samuel in like manner, and lay down naked all that day and all that night. Wherefore they say, "Is Saul also among the prophets?" 1 Sam. 19:24.

Saul inquired of Jahweh before consulting a familiar spirit.

And when Saul enquired of the LORD, the LORD answered him not, neither by dreams, nor by Urim, nor by prophets. Then said Saul unto his servants, "Seek me a woman that hath a familiar spirit, that I may go to her, and enquire of her." 1 Sam. 28:6, 7.

Saul inquired not of Jahweh.

So Saul died for his transgression which he committed against the LORD, even against the word of the LORD, which he kept not, and also for asking counsel of one that had a familiar spirit, to enquire of it; And enquired not of the LORD: therefore he slew him, and turned the kingdom unto David the son of Jesse. 1 Chron. 10:13-14.

326

Saul died by his own hand.

Then said Saul unto his armour-bearer, "Draw thy sword, and thrust me through therewith; lest these uncircumcised come and thrust me through, and abuse me." But his armourbearer would not; for he was sore afraid. Therefore Saul took a sword and fell upon it. And when his armourbearer saw that Saul was dead, he fell likewise upon his sword, and died with him. 1 Sam. 31:4.

He was killed by an Amalekite.

And the young man that told him said, "As I happened by the chance upon mount Gilboa, behold, Saul leaned upon his spear; and, lo, the chariots and horsemen followed hard after him. And when he looked behind him, he saw me, and called unto me. And I answered, 'Here am I.' And he said unto me, 'Who art thou?' And I answered him, 'I am an Amalekite.' He said unto me again, 'Stand, I pray thee, upon me, and slay me: for anguish is come upon me, because my life is yet whole in me.' So I stood upon him, and slew him, because I was sure that he could not live after that he was fallen: and I took the crown that was upon his head, and the bracelet that was on his arm, and have brought them hither unto my lord." 2 Sam. 1:6-10.

Saul was slain by the Philistines.

And David went and took the bones of Saul and the bones of Jonathan his son from the men of Jabeshgilead, which had stolen them from the street of Bethshan, where the Philistines had hanged them, when the Philistines had slain Saul in Gilboa. 2 Sam. 21:12.

David a man of war before he fought Goliath.

Then answered one of the servants, and said, "Behold, I have seen a son of Jesse the Bethlehemite, that is cunning in playing,

David not a man of war then.

And Saul said to David, "Thou art not able to go against this Philistine to fight with him: for thou art but a youth, and he a man of war from his youth." . . . And Saul

and a mighty valiant man, and a man of war, and prudent in matters, and a comely person, and the LORD is with him." 1 Sam. 16:18.

armed David with his armour, and he put an helmet of brass upon his head; also he armed him with a coat of mail. And David girded his sword upon his armour, and he assayed to go; for he had not proved it. And David said unto Saul, "I cannot go with these; for I have not proved them." And David put them off. 1 Sam. 27:33, 38-39.

The sure mercies of David extolled.

And as concerning that he raised him up from the dead, now no more to return to corruption, he said on this wise, "I will give you the sure mercies of David." Acts 13:34.

The sure mercies are not very evident.

But the king took the two sons of Rizpah the daughter of Aiah, whom she bore to Saul, Armoni and Mephibosheth; and the five sons of Michal the daughter of Saul, whom she brought up for Adriel the son of Barzillai the Meholathite: and he delivered them into the hands of the Gibeonites, and they hanged them in the hill before the LORD: and they fell all seven together, and were put to death in the days of harvest, in the first days, in the beginning of barley harvest. 2 Sam. 21:8-9.

Solomon was David's second son by Bathsheba.

And the LORD struck the child that Uriah's wife bare unto David, and it was very sick.... And David comforted Bathsheba his wife, and went in unto her, and lay with her: and she bare a son, and he called his name Solomon: and the LORD loved him. 2 Sam. 12:15, 24.

He was David's fourth son by Bathsheba.

And these were born unto him in Jerusalem; Shimea, and Shobab, and Nathan, and Solomon, four, of Bathshua the daughter of Ammiel: 1 Chron. 3:5.

328

God gave Solomon exceeding wisdom.

And God gave Solomon wisdom and understanding exceedingly much, and largeness of heart, even as the sand that is on the sea shore. 1 Kings 4:29.

The temple artisan's mother was from the tribe of Naphtali.

He was a widow's son of the tribe of Naphtali, and his father was a man of Tyre, a worker in brass: and he was filled with wisdom, and understanding, and cunning to work all works in brass. And he came to king Solomon, and wrought all his work. 1 Kings 7:14.

Solomon's payment to Tyre was wheat and oil.

And Solomon gave Hiram twenty thousand measures of wheat for food to his household, and twenty measures of pure oil: thus gave Solomon to Hiram year by year. 1 Kings 5:11.

Hiram sends Solomon 420 talents of gold.

And Hiram sent in the navy his servants, shipmen that had knowledge of the sea, with the servants

A pious peasant's wisdom (by religious standards) is greater. Thus God was very foolish.

For it came to pass, when Solomon was old, that his wives turned away his heart after other gods: and his heart was not perfect with the LORD his God, as was the heart of David his father. 1 Kings 11:4.

She was from the tribe of Dan.

The son of a woman of the daughters of Dan, and his father was a man of Tyre, skilful to work in gold, and in silver, in brass, in iron, in stone, and in timber, in purple, in blue, and in fine linen, and in crimson; also to grave any manner of graving, and to find out every device which shall be put to him, with thy cunning men, and with the cunning men of my lord David thy father. 2 Chron. 2:14.

His payment was wheat, barley, wine, and oil.

And, behold, I will give to thy servants, the hewers that cut timber, twenty thousand measures of beaten wheat, and twenty thousand measures of barley, and twenty thousand baths of wine, and twenty thousand baths of oil. 2 Chron. 2:10.

He sends him 450 talents of gold.

And Hiram sent him by the hands of his servants ships, and servants that had knowledge of the sea; and they went with the

of Solomon. And they came to Ophir, and fetched from thence gold, four hundred and twenty talents, and brought it to king Solomon. 1 Kings 9:27, 28.

3,300 temple overseers.

Beside the chief of Solomon's officers which were over the work, three thousand and three hundred, which ruled over the people that wrought in the work. 1 Kings 5:16.

Officers that bare rule numbered 550.

These were the chief of the officers that were over Solomon's work, five hundred and fifty, which bare rule over the people that wrought in the work. 1 Kings 9:23.

Asa took away the high places.

And Asa did that which was good and right in the eyes of the LORD his god: For he took away the altars of the strange gods, and the high places, and brake down the images, and cut down the groves: 2 Chron. 14:2-3.

Jehosophat took away the high places.

Therefore the LORD stablished the kingdom in his hand; and all Judah brought to Jehosophat presents; and he had riches and honour in abundance. And his heart

servants of Solomon to Ophir, and took thence four hundred and fifty talents of gold, and brought them to king Solomon. 2 Chron. 8:18.

3,600 temple overseers.

And he set threescore and ten thousand of them to be bearers of burdens, and fourscore thousand to be hewers in the mountains, and three thousand and six hundred overseers to set the people a work. 2 Chron. 2:18.

The number of officers was 250.

And these were the chief of king Solomon's officers, even two hundred and fifty, that bare rule over the people. 2 Chron. 8:10.

Asa never took away the high places.

But the high places were not removed: nevertheless Asa's heart was perfect with the LORD all his days. 1 Kings 15:14.

But the high places were not taken away out of Israel: nevertheless the heart of Asa was perfect all his days. 2 Chron. 15:17.

Jehosophat did not take away the high places.

Howbeit the high places were not taken away: for as yet the people had not prepared their hearts unto the God of their fathers. Now the rest of the acts of

was lifted up in the ways of the LORD: moreover he took away the high places and groves out of Judah. 2 Chron. 17:5-6.

Joash buried with his fathers.

And his servants arose, and made a conspiracy, and slew Joash in the house of Millo, which goeth down to Silla. For Jozachar the son of Shimeath, and Jehozabad the son of Shomer, his servants, smote him, and he died; and they buried him with his fathers in the city of David: and Amaziah his son reigned in his stead. 2 Kings 12:20-21.

Josiah destroys Baalism in the eighteenth year of his reign.

And it came to pass in the eighteenth year of king Josiah, that the king sent Shaphan the son of Azaliah, the son of Meshullam, the scribe, to the house of the LORD, . . . And Hilkiah the high priest said unto Shaphan the scribe, "I have found the book of the law in the house of the LORD." And Hilkiah gave the book to Shaphan, and he read it. . . . And the King commanded Hilkiah the high priest, and the priests of the second order, and the keepers of the door, to bring forth out of the temple of the LORD all the vessels that were made for Baal, and for the grove, and for all the host of heaven: and he burned them without Jerusalem in the fields of Kidron, and carried out the ashes of them unto

Jehosophat, first and last, behold, they are written in the book of Jehu. . . . 2 Chron. 20:33-34.

Joash not buried with his fathers.

So they executed judgment against Joash. And when they were departed from him, (for they left him in great diseases,) his own servants conspired against him for the blood of the sons of Jehoiada the priest, and slew him on his bed, and he died: and they buried him in the city of David, but they buried him not in the sepulchres of the kings. 2 Chron. 24:24-25.

Josiah destroys Baalism in the twelfth year of his reign before the book of the law discovered.

For in the eighth year of his reign, while he was yet young, he began to seek after the God of David his father: and in the twelfth year he began to purge Judah and Jerusalem from the high places, and the groves, and the carved images, and the molten images. And they brake down the altars of Baalim in his presence; and the images, that were on high above them, he cut down; and the groves, and the carved images, and the molten images, he brake in pieces, and made dust of them, and strowed it upon the graves of them that had sacrificed unto them. And he burnt the bones of the priests upon their altars, and cleansed Judah and Jerusalem. And so did

331

Bethel. And he put down the idolatrous priests, whom the kings of Judah had ordained to burn incense in the high places in the cities of Judah, and in the places round about Jerusalem; them also that burned incense unto Baal, to the sun, and to the moon, and to the planets, and to all the host of heaven. And he brought out the grove from the house of the LORD, without Jerusalem, unto the brook Kidron, and burned it at the brook Kidron, and stamped it small to powder, and cast the powder thereof upon the graves of the children of the people. And he brake down the houses of the sodomites, that were by the house of the LORD, where the women wove hangings for the grove. And he brought all the priests out of the cities of Judah, and defiled the high places where the priests had burned incense, from Geba to Beersheba, and brake down the high places of the gates that in the entering in of the gate of Joshua the governor of the city, which were on a man's left hand at the gate of the city . . . . And he defiled Topheth, which is in the valley of the children of Hinnom, that no man might make his son or his daughter to pass through the fire to Molech. And he took away the horses that the kings of Judah had given to the sun, at the entering in of the house of the LORD, by the chamber of Nathanmelech, the chamberlain, which was in the suburbs, and

he in the cities of Manasseh, and Ephraim, and Simeon, even unto Naphtali, with their mattocks round about. And when he had broken down the altars and the groves, and had beaten the graven images into powder, and cut down all the idols throughout all the land of Israel, he returned to Jerusalem. Now in the eighteenth year of his reign, when he had purged the land, and the house, he sent Shaphan the son of Azaliah, and Maaseiah the governor of the city, and Joah the son of Joahaz the recorder, to repair the house of the LORD his God. . . . And Hilkiah answered and said to Shaphan the scribe, "I have found the book of the law in the house of the LORD." And Hilkiah delivered the book to Shaphan. 2 Chron. 34:3-8, 15.

burned the chariots of the sun with fire. And the altars that were on the top of the upper chamber of Ahaz, which the kings of Judah had made, and the altars which Manasseh had made in the two courts of the house of the LORD, did the king beat down, and brake them down from thence, and cast the dust of them into the brook Kidron. And the high places that were before Jerusalem, which were on the right hand of the mount of corruption, which Solomon the king of Israel had builded for Ashtoreth the abomination of the Zidonians, and for Chemosh the abomination of the Moabites, and for Milcom the abomination of the children of Ammon, did the king defile. And he brake in pieces the images, and cut down the groves, and filled their places with the bones of men. Moreover the altar that was at Bethel, and the high place which Jeroboam the son of Nebat, who made Israel to sin, had made, both that altar and the high place he brake down, and burned the high place, and stamped it small to powder, and burned the grove. And as Josiah turned himself, he spied the sepulchres that were there in the mount, and sent, and took the bones out of the sepulchres, and burned them upon the altar, and polluted it, according to the word of the LORD which the man of God proclaimed, who proclaimed these words. Then he said, "What title is that that I see?"

And the men of the city told him, "It is the sepulchre of the man of God, which came from Judah, and proclaimed these things that thou hast done against the altar of Bethel." And he said, "Let him alone; let no man move his bones." So they let his bones alone, with the bones of the prophet that came out of Samaria. And all the houses also of the high places that were in the cities of Samaria, which the kings of Israel had made to provoke the LORD to anger, Josiah took away, and did to them according to all the acts that he had done in Bethel. And he slew all the priests of the high places that were there upon the altars, and burned men's bones upon them, and returned to Jerusalem. 2 Kings 22:3, 8; 23:4-8, 10-20.

Jehoiakin's three month and ten day old reign began at age eight.

Jehoiachin was eight years old when he began to reign, and he reigned three months and ten days in Jerusalem: and he did that which was evil in the sight of the LORD. 2 Chron. 36:9.

Zedekiah was Jehoiakin's uncle.

And Jehoiachin the king of Judah went out to the king of Babylon, he, and his mother, and his servants, and his princes, and his officers: and the king of Babylon took him in the eighth year of his reign. . . . And the king of Babylon made Mattaniah his father's bro-

Jehoiakin's three-month old reign began at age eighteen.

Jehoiachin was eighteen years old when he began to reign, and he reigned in Jerusalem three months. And his mother's name was Nehushta, the daughter of Elnathan of Jerusalem. 2 Kings 24:8.

Zedekiah was Jehoiakin's brother.

Jehoiachin was eight years old when he began to reign, and he reigned three months and ten days in Jerusalem: and he did that which was evil in the sight of the LORD. And when the year was expired, king Nebuchadnezzar sent, and brought him to Babylon, with

ther king in his stead, and changed his name to Zedekiah. 2 Kings 24:12, 17.

Nebuchadnezzar carries off at least 18,000 captives.

And Jehoiachin the king of Judah went out to the king of Babylon, he, and his mother, and his servants, and his princes, and his officers: and the king of Babylon took him in the eighth year of his reign. . . . And he carried away all Jerusalem, and all the princes, and all the mighty men of valour, even ten thousand captives, and all the craftsmen and smiths: none remained, save the poorest sort of the people of the land. . . . And all the men of might, even seven thousand, and craftsmen and smiths a thousand, all that were strong and apt for war, even them the king of Babylon brought captive to Babylon. 2 Kings 24:12, 14, 16.

And in the fifth month, on the seventh day of the month, which is the nineteenth year of king Nebuchadnezzar king of Babylon, came Nebuzaradan, captain of the guard, a servant of the king of Babylon, unto Jerusalem. . . . Now the rest of the people that were left in the city, and the fugitives that fell away to the king of Babylon, with the remnant of the multitude, did Nebuzaradan the captain of the guard carry away. 2 Kings 25:8, 11.

the goodly vessels of the house of the LORD, and made Zedekiah his brother king over Judah and Jerusalem. 2 Chron. 36:9-10.

Nebuchadnezzar carries off 4,600 captives.

This is the people whom Nebuchadnezzar carried away captive: in the seventh year three thousand Jews and three and twenty: In the eighteenth year of Nebuchadnezzar he carried away captive from Jerusalem eight hundred thirty and two persons: In the three and twentieth year of Nebuchadnezzar Nebuzaradan the captain of the guard carried away captive of the Jews seven hundred forty and five persons: all the persons were four thousand and six hundred. Jer. 52:28-30.

Elijah casts his mantle on Elisha when he first meets him.

So he departed thence, and found Elisha the son of Shaphat, who was plowing with twelve yoke of oxen before him, and he with the twelfth: and Elijah passed by him, and cast his mantle upon him. 1 Kings 19:19.

Elisha's deputy anoints Jehu, grandson of Himshi. Elijah did not crown Hazael.

And Hazael said, "But what, is thy servant a dog, that he should do this great thing?" And Elisha answered, "The LORD hath shewed me that thou shalt be king over Syria" 2 Kings 8:13.

And Elisha the prophet called one of the children of the prophets, and said unto him, "Gird up thy loins, and take this box of oil in thine hand, and go to Ramoth-gilead: And when thou comest thither, look out there Jehu the son of Jehoshaphat the son of Nimshi, and go in, and make him arise up from among his brethren, and carry him to an inner chamber; then take the box of oil, and pour it on his head, and say, Thus saith the Lord, I have anointed thee king over Israel.' Then open the door, and flee, and tarry not." 2 Kings 9:1-3.

Elisha picks up the mantle after Elijah's departure.

And it came to pass, as they still went on, and talked, that, behold, there appeared a chariot of fire, and horses of fire, and parted them both asunder; and Elijah went up by a whirlwind into heaven. And Elisha saw it, . . . He took up also the mantle of Elijah that fell from him, and went back and stood by the bank of Jordan. 2 Kings 2:11-13.

The task of anointing Hazael and Jehu had been delegated to Elijah by Jahweh. Jehu was the son of Nimshi.

And the LORD said unto him, "Go, return on thy way to the wilderness of Damascus: and when thou comest, anoint Hazael to be king over Syria: And Jehu the son of Nimshi shalt thou anoint to be king over Israel: and Elisha the son of Shaphat of Abelmeholah shalt thou anoint to be prophet in thy room." 1 Kings 19:15-16.

All Jewish people who went to Egypt were to die there.

And now therefore hear the word of the LORD, ye remnant of Judah; Thus saith the LORD of hosts, the God of Israel; "If ye wholly set your faces to enter into Egypt, and go to sojourn there; Then it shall come to pass, that the sword, which ye feared, shall overtake you there in the land of Egypt, and the famine, whereof ye were afraid, shall follow close after you there in Egypt; and there ye shall die. So shall it be with all the men that set their faces to go into Egypt to sojourn there; they shall die by the sword, by the famine, and by the pestilence: and none of them shall remain or escape from the evil that I will bring upon them." Jer. 42:15-17.

Because of their sins, the Jews are to return to Egypt.

Because Ephraim hath made many altars to sin, altars shall be unto him to sin. . . . They sacrifice flesh for the sacrifices of mine offerings, and eat it; but the LORD accepteth them not; now will he remember their iniquity, and visit their sins: they shall return to Egypt. Hos. 8:11, 13.

Jahweh to have mercy upon the house of Judah.

But I will have mercy upon the house of Judah, and will save them by the LORD their God, and will not save them by bow, nor by

Some were to escape.

Yet a small number that escape the sword shall return out of the land of Egypt into the land of Judah, and all the remnant of Judah, that are gone into the land of Egypt to sojourn there, shall know whose words shall stand, mine, or theirs. Jer. 44:28.

I will bring them again also out of the land of Egypt, and gather them out of Assyria; and I will bring them into the land of Gilead and Lebanon; and place shall not be found for them. Zech. 10:10.

According to the same prophet, the Jews are not to return to Egypt.

I taught Ephraim also to go, taking them by their arms; but they knew not that I healed them. . . . He shall not return into the land of Egypt, but the Assyrian shall be his king, because they refused to return. Hos. 11:3, 5.

Jahweh decides that Judah shall "fall" with Ephraim.

And the pride of Israel doth testify to his face: therefore shall Israel and Ephraim fall in their iniquity; Judah also shall fall with

sword, nor by battle, by horses, nor by horsemen. Hos. 1:7.

After changing his mind once (see right), Jahweh, who "changes not" (Mal. 3:6. — "For I am the LORD, I change not; therefore ye sons of Jacob are not consumed."), again changes his mind in favor of mercy for Ephraim.

I will not execute the fierceness of mine anger, I will not return to destroy Ephraim: for I am God, and not man; the Holy One in the midst of thee: and I will not enter into the city. Hos. 11:9.

them. They shall go with their flocks and with their herds to seek the LORD; but they shall not find him; he hath withdrawn himself from them. They have dealt treacherously against the LORD: for they have begotten strange children: now shall a mouth devour them with their portions. . . . Ephraim shall be desolate in the day of rebuke: among the tribes of Israel have I made known that which shall surely be. . . . For I will be unto Ephraim as a lion, and as a young lion to the house of Judah: I, even I, will tear and go away; I will take away, and none shall rescue him. Hos. 5:5-7, 9, 14.

Jahweh to let the Jews go on a rampage among all the Gentiles.

In that day will I make Jerusalem a burdensome stone for all people: all that burden themselves with it shall be cut in pieces, though all the people of the earth be gathered together against it. . . . In that day will I make the governors of Judah like an hearth of fire among the wood, and like a torch of fire in a sheaf; and they shall devour all the people round about, on the right hand and on the left: and Jerusalem shall be inhabited again in her own place, even in Jerusalem. . . . And it shall come to pass in that day, that I will seek to destroy all the nations that come against Jerusalem. Zech. 12:3, 6, 9.

Some Gentiles to be humble. Only the obdurate to be "wasted."

Thus saith the Lord GOD, "Behold I will lift up mine hand to the Gentiles, and set up my standard to the people: and they shall bring thy sons in their arms, and thy daughters shall be carried upon their shoulders. And kings shall be thy nursing fathers, and their queens thy nursing mothers: they shall bow down to thee with their face toward the earth, and lick up the dust of thy feet; and thou shalt know that I am the LORD: for they shall not be ashamed that wait for me." Isa. 49:22-23.

Therefore thy gates shall be open continually; they shall not be shut day nor night; that men may bring unto thee the forces of the

Gentiles, and that their kings may be brought. For the nation and kingdom that will not serve thee shall perish; yea, those nations shall be utterly wasted. Isa. 60:11-12.

"In that day" *Jahweh is to make Jerusalem* "a burdensome stone for all [Gentile] people: all that burden themselves with it shall be cut to pieces, though all the people of the earth be gathered together against it" (Zech. 12:3, 9). *We learn that it is Jahweh himself who will gather all nations against Jerusalem to battle. But before he decides to "go forth" against these nations he will see to it that the city is taken, its houses rifled, and its a women ravished. Half the city's defenders are to go into captivity.* ("For I will gather all nations against Jerusalem to battle; and the city shall be taken, and the houses rifled, and the women ravished; and half of the city shall go forth into captivity, and the residue of the people shall not be cut off from the city." — Zech. 14:2.) *It is then and only then that the god will deal it out to the people he himself had brought against his "holy city;" they are to be smitten with a plague: "Their flesh will consume away while they stand upon their feet, and their eyes shall consume away in their holes, and their tongue will consume away in their mouth" (Zech. 14:12). See also Zeph 3:6, 8* ("I have cut off the nations: their towers are desolate; I made their streets waste, that none passeth by: their cities are destroyed, so that there is no man, that there is none inhabitant. . . . Therefore wait ye upon me, . . . until the day that I rise up to the prey: for my determination is to gather the kingdoms, to pour upon them mine indignation, even all my fierce anger: for all the earth shall be devoured with the fire of my jealousy.").

The statement that Jahweh is to permit Jerusalem to be taken, its women ravished, etc. does not quite square with an earlier promise (Zech. 12:8) that "In that day shall the LORD defend the inhabitants of Jerusalem; and he that is feeble among them in that day shall be as David; and the house of David shall be as God, as the angel of the LORD before them"!

But it appears that, after all, some of the stricken gentiles will survive ("And it shall come to pass, that every one that is left of all the nations which came against Jerusalem shall even go up from year to year to worship the King, the LORD of hosts, and to keep the feast of tabernacles" — Zech. 14:16.).

"In those days it shall come to pass, that ten men shall take hold out of all the languages of the nations, even shall take hold of the skirt of him that is a Jew, saying, 'We will go with you: for we have heard that God is with you.' " (Zech. 8:23) *Micah, however, insists that* "all people will walk every one in the name of his god," *while* "we [the Jews] will walk in the name of the LORD our God for ever and ever." (Mic. 4:5)

(A scribal redactor sought to neutralise this flat negation of the belief cherished by Jewish patriots that in the very near future their god would force their oppressors to acknowledge his supremacy and submit to Jewish domination. He interpolated a passage from Isaiah. Compare Micah 4:1-3 ("But in the last days it shall come to pass, that the mountain of the house of the LORD shall be established in the top of the mountains, and it shall be exalted above the hills; and people shall flow unto it. And many nations shall come, and say, 'Come, and let us go up to the mountain of the LORD, and to the house of the God of Jacob; and he will teach us of his ways, and we will walk in his paths:' for the law shall go forth of Zion, and the word of the LORD from Jerusalem. And he shall judge among many people, and rebuke strong nations afar off; and they shall beat their swords into plowshares, and their spears into pruning-hooks: nation shall not lift up a sword against nation, neither shall they learn war any more.") *with Isaiah 2:2-4* ("And it shall come to pass in the last days, that the mountain of the LORD's house shall be established in the top of the mountains, and shall be exalted above the hills; and all nations shall flow unto it. And many people shall go and say, 'Come ye, and let us go up to the mountain of the LORD, to the house of the God of Jacob; and he will teach us of his ways, and we will walk in his paths:' for out of Zion shall go forth the law, and the word of the LORD from Jerusalem. And he shall judge among the nations, and shall rebuke many people: and they shall beat their sword into plowshares, and their spears into pruninghooks: nation shall not lift up sword against nation, neither shall they learn war any more.) *The redactor was probably deterred by superstitious dread from striking out the non-conforming words.]*

"And it shall come to pass in that day, that the light shall not be clear, nor dark: But it shall be one day which shall be known to the LORD, not day, nor night: but it shall come to pass, that at evening time it shall be light." — Zech. 14:6-7.

Joel, however, insists "The earth shall quake before them; the heavens shall tremble: the sun and the moon shall be dark, and the stars shall withdraw their shining." (Joel 2:10). *Amos also declares* "Shall not the day of the LORD be darkness, and not light? even very dark, and no

340

brightness in it?" (Amos 5:20).

Isaiah speaks with two voices. In 13:10 ("For the stars of heaven and the constellations thereof shall not give their light: the sun shall be darkened in his going forth, and the moon shall not cause her light to shine.") *He agrees with Joel, but in 30:26. he states* ("Moreover the light of the moon shall be as the light of the sun, and the light of the sun shall be sevenfold, as the light of seven days, in the day that the LORD bindeth up the breach of his people, and healeth the stroke of their wound.").

THE FATE OF BABYLON. *Isaiah implies and Jeremiah definitely states that the whole land of Babylon was to be destroyed;* ("And I will render unto Babylon and to all the inhabitants of Chaldea all their evil that they have done in Zion in your sight, saith the LORD. Behold, I am against thee, O destroying mountain, saith the LORD, which destroyeth all the earth: and I will stretch out mine hand upon thee, and roll thee down from the rocks, and will make thee a burnt mountain. And they shall not take of thee a stone for a corner, nor a stone for foundations; but thou shalt be desolate for ever, saith the LORD. . . . Prepare against her the nations with the kings of the Medes, the captains thereof, and all the rulers thereof, and all the land of his dominion. And the land shall tremble and sorrow: for every purpose of the LORD shall be performed against Babylon, to make the land of Babylon a desolation without an inhabitant. . . . Therefore thus saith the LORD; Behold, I will plead thy cause, and take vengeance for thee; and I will *dry up her sea, and make her springs dry*. . . . As Babylon hath caused the slain of Israel to fall, so at Babylon shall fall the slain of all the earth." — Jer. 51:24-26, 28-29, 36, 49). *But according to Isaiah 14:22-23,* "For I will rise up against them, saith the LORD of hosts, and cut off from Babylon the name, and remnant, and son, and nephew, saith the LORD. I will also make it a possession for the bittern, and *pools of water*: and I will sweep it with the besom of destruction, saith the LORD of hosts."

Our prophecy "experts" are fully aware that the threatened destruction of the land of Babylon never came to pass, and they discreetly omit mention of Jeremiah in this connection. Our attention is directed to the threat to the city of Babylon, which we are told was carried out to the letter. But it wasn't!

According to Jeremiah 51:11 ("Make bright the arrows; gather the shields: the LORD hath raised up the spirit of the kings of the Medes: for his device is against Babylon, to destroy it; because it is the vengeance

341

of the LORD, the vengeance of his temple."), *Jahweh had moved the Medes to destroy Babylon (see also Isa. 13:17-19* — "Behold, I will stir up the Medes against them, which shall not regard silver; and as for gold, they shall not delight in it. Their bows also shall dash the young men to pieces; and they shall have no pity on the fruit of the womb; their eye shall not spare children. And Babylon, the glory of kingdoms, the beauty of the Chaldees' excellency, shall be as when God overthrew Sodom and Gomorrah."). *But not even the book of Daniel, which states (falsely) that the Medes captured Babylon, says that they destroyed it* ("In that night was Belshazzar the king of the Chaldeans slain. And Darius the Median took the kingdom, being about threescore and two years old. It pleased Darius to set over the kingdom an hundred and twenty princes, which should be over the whole kingdom." — Dan. 5:30-31; 6:1).

Here in brief is a summary of events relating to Babylon: the city was completely destroyed in 689 B.C. by the Assyrian king Sennacherib, who slaughtered its inhabitants. On the death of Sennacherib, Babylon was rebuilt by his son and successor Esarhaddon. After Esarhaddon's death the city revolted against the Assyrians. It was recaptured by Esarhaddon's successor, Assurbanipul (668-626 B.C.). But Assurbanipul did not revenge himself upon the rebels; he simply "moved in and ruled." Shortly after this monarch's death the Assyrian Empire was destroyed by the Scythians and its history came to an end.

After the extinction of Assyria as a nation the throne of Babylon was seized by the Chaldean general Nabopolassar. Under his son Nebuchadnezzar the city became a showplace. It was this city of Nebuchadnezzar which, according to Jeremiah, was, together with the rest of the country, to be made "wholly desolate" as a punishment for the carrying off the Jews. (Let us note in passing that it had been ordained by Jahweh himself that Nebuchadnezzar should scourge the Jewish people. For doing what he was divinely impelled to do, not only Nebuchadnezzar, but the whole of his people were to suffer!)

But, as already intimated, the threatened destruction never came to pass.

The history of the city after the captivity is as follows:

In 538 Babylon fell to the Persians under Cyrus' general Gobryas (NOT to the Medes under Darius, who was not a Mede but a Persian — second in succession to Cyrus, third if we include the usurper Smerdis or Bardis, who called himself Nebuchadnezzar the third). The city later revolted against Persian domination. It is then that Darius came into the picture; he recaptured the city, during the assault destroying most of the outworks. But the city itself suffered little damage.

Some 200 years later Babylon was captured by Alexander the Great, who also spared the city and its inhabitants. Under the Selucidae, who were heirs to Alexander's Asian conquests, Babylon rapidly declined in importance. Most of its inhabitants were transferred to the new city of Selucia; and it was after this that the city of Babylon commenced to decay.

Among those who remained in Babylon were the descendants of the Jews of the captivity, who elected to remain where they were instead of returning to Judea with their compatriots. Jews inhabited the city right up to the second century A.D. and it was there that the Babylonian recension of the Talmud was compiled.

There is a reference to Babylon at the end of the first epistle of Peter ("Peter, an apostle of Jesus Christ, to the strangers scattered throughout Pontus, Galatia, Cappadocia, Asia, and Bithynia. . . . The church that is at Babylon, elected together with you, saluteth you; and so doth Marcus my son." — 1 Pet. 1:1; 5:13). *Christians wish us to believe that the Babylon there mentioned was Rome, as in the book of Revelation; but it is clear that it is the Chaldean city that was meant.*

Babylon was finally abandoned and became a ruin shortly after the second century A.D. The canals which had been constructed by the Babylonian kings and which had drained the swamps silted up, and the region became unhealthy.

Much of the ancient city has been restored by archeologists, and it has become a tourist attraction. None of these archeologists, it may be mentioned, has encountered the dragons, satyrs, and other "doleful creatures" which it was said would infest the place ("But wild beasts of the desert shall lie there; and their houses shall be full of doleful creatures; and owls shall dwell there, and satyrs shall dance there." — Isa. 13:21; "And Babylon shall become heaps, a dwellingplace for dragons, an astonishment, and an hissing, without an inhabitant." — Jer. 51:37.).

Let it be emphasised: no sudden catastrophe overwhelmed Babylon; the decay was gradual. And apart from the inconvenience they suffered by their transference to Selucia, the native inhabitants of the city of that time suffered no harm. In any case it is utterly ridiculous to suggest that any disabilities they experienced were the result of an offence committed several centuries previously.

THE NEW TESTAMENT

Andrew and Peter called to be disciples before Jesus commenced his ministry and before John the Baptist had been cast into prison.

Again the next day after John stood, and two of his disciples; And looking upon Jesus as he walked, he saith, "Behold the Lamb of God!" . . . One of the two which heard John speak, and followed him, was Andrew, Simon Peter's brother. He first findeth his own brother Simon, and saith unto him, "We have found the Messias," which is, being interpreted, the Christ. And he brought him to Jesus. And when Jesus beheld him, he said, "Thou art Simon the son of Jona: thou shalt be called Cephas," Which is by interpretation, A stone. John 1:35-36, 40-42.

Christhood not revealed to Peter through flesh and blood.

And Simon Peter answered and said, "Thou art the Christ, the Son of the living God." And Jesus answered and said unto him, "Blessed art thou, Simon Barjona: for flesh and blood hath not

Jesus commenced preaching before summoning Andrew and Peter, and after John the Baptist was in prison.

Now when Jesus had heard that John was cast into prison, he departed into Galilee; . . . And Jesus walking by the sea of Galilee, saw two brethren, Simon called Peter, and Andrew his brother, casting a net into the sea: for they were fishers. And he saith unto them, "Follow me, and I will make you fishers of men." Matt. 4:12, 18-19.

Now after that John was put in prison, Jesus came into Galilee, preaching the gospel of the kingdom of God. . . . Now as he walked by the sea of Galilee, he saw Simon and Andrew his brother casting a net into the sea: for they were fishers. And Jesus said unto them, "Come ye after me, and I will make you fishers of men." Mark 1:14, 16-17.

Christhood is revealed to Peter through flesh and blood.

One of the two which heard John speak, and followed him, was Andrew, Simon Peter's brother. He first findeth his own brother Simon, and saith unto him, "We have found the Messias," which is,

revealed it unto thee, but my Father which is in heaven." Matt. 16:16-17.

The devil "tempts" Jesus at the temple, then on the mountain.

Then the devil taketh him up into the holy city, and setteth him on a pinnacle of the temple. . . . Again, the devil taketh him up into an exceeding high mountain, and sheweth him all the kingdoms of the world, and the glory of them; And saith unto him, "All these things will I give thee, if thou wilt fall down and worship me." Matt. 4:5, 8-9.

Relations with mammon advised.

And I say unto you, Make to yourselves friends of the mammon of unrighteousness; that, when ye fail, they may receive you into everlasting habitations. Luke 16:9.

Peter's faith not to fail.

And the Lord said, "Simon, Simon, behold, Satan hath desired to have you, that he may sift you as wheat: But I have prayed for thee, that thy faith fail not: and when thou art converted, strengthen thy brethren." Luke 22:31-32.

Jesus heals the leper before entering Peter's house.

When he was come down from the mountain, great multitudes followed him. And, behold, there came a leper and worshipped him,

being interpreted, the Christ. John 1:40-41.

The devil "tempts" Jesus on the mountain, then at the temple.

And the devil, taking him up into an high mountain, shewed unto him all the kingdoms of the world in a moment of time. . . . If thou therefore wilt worship me, all shall be thine. . . . And he brought him to Jerusalem, and set him on a pinnacle of the temple, and said unto him, "If thou be the Son of God, cast thyself down from hence." Luke 4:5, 7, 9.

Relations with mammon discouraged.

No servant can serve two masters: for either he will hate the one, and love the other; or else he will hold to the one, and despise the other. Ye cannot serve God and mammon. Luke 16:13.

Peter's faith to fail.

And he said. "I tell thee, Peter, the cock shall not crow this day, before that thou shalt thrice deny that thou knowest me." Luke 22:34.

Jesus heals the leper after departing Peter's house.

And forthwith, when they were come out of the synagogue, they entered into the house of Simon and Andrew, with James and John.

saying, "Lord, if thou wilt, thou canst make me clean." And Jesus put forth his hand, and touched him, saying, "I will; be thou clean." And immediately his leprosy was cleansed.... And when Jesus was come into Peter's house, he saw his wife's mother laid, and sick of a fever. Matt. 8:1-3, 14.

But Simon's wife's mother lay sick of a fever, and anon they tell him of her.... And there came a leper to him, beseeching him, and kneeling down to him, and saying unto him, "If thou wilt, thou canst make me clean." And Jesus, moved with compassion, put forth his hand, and touched him, and saith unto him, I will; be thou clean." And as soon as he had spoken, immediately the leprosy departed from him, and he was cleansed. Mark 1:29-30, 40-42.

Salvation gained with only belief.

For God so loved the world, that he gave his only begotten son, that whosoever believeth in him should not perish, but have everlasting life. John 3:16.

And they said, "Believe on the Lord Jesus Christ, and thou shalt be saved, and thy house[!]." Acts 16:31.

Salvation secured through good work.

And when he was gone forth into the way, there came one running, and kneeled to him, and asked him, "Good master, what shall I do that I may inherit eternal life?" And Jesus said unto him, ... "Thou knowest the commandments, Do not commit adultery, Do not kill, Do not steal, Do not bear false witness, Defraud not, Honour thy father and mother." And he answered and said unto him, "Master, all these have I observed from my youth." Then Jesus beholding him loved him, and said unto him, "One thing thou lackest: go thy way, sell whatsoever thou hast, and give to the poor, and thou shalt have treasure in heaven: and come, take up the cross, and follow me." Mark 10:17-20.

Pure religion and undefiled before God and the Father is this, To

Jesus was sent only for Jews.

These twelve Jesus sent forth, and commanded them, saying, "Go not into the way of the Gentiles, and into any city of the Samaritans enter ye not: But go rather to the lost sheep of the house of Israel." Matt. 10:5-6.

But he answered and said, "I am not sent but unto the lost sheep of the house of Israel." Matt. 15:24.

The cursed fig tree immediately withered.

And seeing a fig tree by the wayside he went to it, and found nothing on it but leaves only. And he said to it, "May no fruit ever come from you again!" And the fig tree withered at once. When the disciples saw it they marveled, saying, "How did the fig tree wither at once?" Matt. 21:19. (RSV)

Jesus is meek and gentle.

Now I Paul myself beseech you by the meekness and gentleness of Christ. . . . 2 Cor. 10:1.

Take my yoke upon you, and learn of me; for I am meek and lowly in heart: and ye shall find rest unto your souls. Matt. 11:29.

visit the fatherless and widows in their affliction, and to keep himself unspotted from the world. James 1:27.

Jesus was sent for the whole world.

Go ye therefore, and teach all nations, baptising them in the name of the Father, and of the Son, and of the Holy Ghost. Matt. 28:19.

And he said unto them, "Go ye into all the world, and preach the gospel to every creature." Mark 16:15.

The cursed fig tree did not immediately wither.

And when even was come, he went out of the city. And in the morning, as they passed by, they saw the fig tree dried up from the roots. And Peter calling to remembrance saith unto him, "Master, behold, the fig tree which thou cursedst is withered away." Mark 11:19-21.

Jesus is not meek and gentle.

And the Lord said unto him, "Now do ye Pharisees make clean the outside of the cup and the platter; but your inward part is full of ravening and wickedness. Ye fools, did not he that made that which is without make that which is within also? But rather give alms of such things as ye have; and, behold, all things are clean unto you. But woe unto you, Pharisees!

for ye tithe mint and rue and all manner of herbs, and pass over judgment and the love of God: these ought ye to have done, and not to leave the other undone. Woe unto you, Pharisees! for ye love the uppermost seats in the synagogues, and greetings in the markets. Woe unto you, scribes and Pharisees, hypocrites! for ye are as graves which appear not, and the men that walk over them are not aware of them." ... And he said, "Woe unto you also, ye lawyers! for ye lade men with burdens grievous to be borne, and ye yourselves touch not the burdens with one of your fingers. Woe unto you! for ye build the sepulchres of the prophets, and your fathers killed them. . . . Therefore also said the wisdom of God, I will send them prophets and apostles, and some of them they shall slay and persecute: That the blood of all the prophets, which was shed from the foundation of the world, may be required of this generation; From the blood of Abel unto the blood of Zacharias, which perished between the altar and the temple: verily I say unto you, It shall be required of this generation. Woe unto you, lawyers! for ye have taken away the key of knowledge: ye entered not in yourselves, and them that were entering in ye hindered." Luke 11:39-44, 46-47, 49-52.

The scourging of the money-changers occurred at the commencement of Jesus' ministry.

This beginning of miracles did Jesus in Cana of Galilee, and manifested forth his glory; and his disciples believed on him. After this he went down to Capernaum, he, and his mother, and his brethren, and his disciples: and they continued there not many days. And the Jews' passover was at hand, and Jesus went up to Jerusalem, And found in the temple those that sold oxen and sheep and doves, and the changers of money sitting: And when he had made a scourge of small cords, he drove them all out of the temple, and the sheep, and the oxen; and poured out the changers' money, and overthrew the tables; . . . After these things came Jesus and his disciples into the land of Judea; and there he tarried with them, and baptized. And John also was baptizing in Aenon near to Salim, because there was much water there: and they came, and were baptized. For John was not yet cast into prison. John 2:11-15; 3:22-24.

The scourging occurred near the end of Jesus' ministry.

And the disciples went, and did as Jesus commanded them, And brought the ass, and the colt, and put on them their clothes, and they set him thereon. And a very great multitude spread their garments in the way; others cut down branches from the trees, and strawed them in the way. . . . And Jesus went into the temple of God, and cast out all them that sold and bought in the temple, and overthrew the tables of the moneychangers, and the seats of them that sold doves. . . . Matt. 21:6-8, 12.

And they brought the colt to Jesus, and cast their garments on him; and he sat upon him. And many spread their garments in the way: and others cut down branches off the trees, and strawed them in the way. . . . And they come to Jerusalem: and Jesus went into the temple, and began to cast out them that sold and bought in the temple, and overthrew the tables of the moneychangers, and the seats of them that sold doves. Mark 11:7-8, 15.

And they brought him to Jesus: and they cast their garments upon the colt, and they set Jesus theron. And as he went, they spread their clothes in the way. . . . And he went into the temple, and began to cast out them that sold therein, and them that bought. Luke 19:35-36, 45.

Jesus shows no fear before his betrayal.

Therefore, when he [Judas] was gone out, Jesus said, "Now is the Son of man glorified, and God is glorified in him." John 13:31.

Father, I will that they also, whom thou hast given me, be with me where I am; that they may behold my glory, which thou hast given me: for thou lovedst me before the foundation of the world. John 17:24.

Judas then, having received a band of men and officers from the chief priests and Pharisees, cometh thither with lanterns and torches and weapons. Jesus therefore, knowing all things that should come upon him, went forth, and said unto them, "Whom seek ye?" John 18:3-4.

Jesus shows agony before his betrayal.

And he was withdrawn from them about a stone's cast, and kneeled down, and prayed, Saying, "Father, if thou be willing, remove this cup from me: nevertheless not my will, but thine, be done." And there appeared an angel unto him from heaven, strengthening him. And being in an agony he prayed more earnestly: and his sweat was as it were great drops of blood falling down to the ground. And when he rose up from prayer, and was come to his disciples, he found them sleeping for sorrow, And said unto them, "Why sleep ye? rise and pray, lest ye enter into temptation." And while he yet spake, behold a multitude, and he that was called Judas, one of the twelve, went before them, and drew near unto Jesus to kiss him. Luke 22:41-47.

Jesus is betrayed by a kiss.

Now he that betrayed him gave them a sign, saying, "Whomsoever I shall kiss, that same is he: hold him fast." And forthwith he came to Jesus, and said, "Hail, master;" and kissed him. Matt. 26:48-49.

And he that betrayed him had given them a token, saying, "Whomsoever I shall kiss, that same is he; take him, and lead him away safely." And as soon as he was come, he goeth straightway

Jesus averts a kiss.

Judas then, having received a band of men and officers from the chief priests and Pharisees, cometh thither with lanterns and torches and weapons. Jesus therefore, knowing all things that should come upon him, went forth, and said unto them, "Whom seek ye?" They answered him, "Jesus of Nazareth." Jesus saith unto them, "I am he." And Judas also, which betrayed him, stood with them. As

to him, and saith, "Master, master;" and kissed him. Mark 14:44-45.

soon then as he had said unto them, "I am he," they went backward, and fell to the ground. Then asked he them again, "Whom seek ye?" And they said, "Jesus of Nazareth." Jesus answered, "I have told you that I am he: if therefore ye seek me, let these go their way:" . . . Then the band and the captain and officers of the Jews took Jesus, and bound him. John 18:3-8, 12.

(It is not explained why it was necessary for Judas to identify a man who had only recently made a triumphal entry into the capital city and received the plaudits of the crowd; who had several encounters with Jewish leaders, and who had frequently drawn attention to himself by his "mighty works." Judas would never have dared betray the man who had manifested such great powers.)

Jesus does not carry his cross.

And as they came out, they found a man of Cyrene, Simon by name: him they compelled to bear his cross. Matt. 27:32.

And they compel [sic] one Simon a Cyrenian, who passed by, coming out of the country, the father of Alexander and Rufus, to bear his cross. Mark 15:21.

And as they led him away, they laid hold upon one Simon, a Cyrenian, coming out of the country, and on him they laid the cross, that he might bear it after Jesus. Luke 23:26.

Jesus crucified on a cross.

And he bearing his cross went

Jesus bears his cross.

Then delivered he him therefore unto them to be crucified. And they took Jesus, and led him away. And he bearing his cross went forth into a place called the place of a skull, which is called in the Hebrew Golgotha. John 19: 16-17.

Jesus hanged on a tree.

The God of our fathers raised

352

forth into a place called the place of a skull, which is called in the Hebrew Golgotha: Where they crucified him, and two other with him, on either side one, and Jesus in the midst. John 19:17-18.

up Jesus, whom ye slew and hanged on a tree. Acts 5:30.

And we are witnesses of all things which he did both in the land of the Jews, and in Jerusalem; whom they slew and hanged on a tree. Acts 10:39.

And when they had fulfilled all that was written of him, they took him down from the tree, and laid him in a sepulchre. Acts 13:29.

Jesus' last words.

And about the ninth hour Jesus cried with a loud voice, saying, "*Eli, eli, lama sabachthani?*" that is to say, "My God, my God, why hast thou forsaken me?" . . . Jesus, when he had cried again with a loud voice, yielded up the ghost. Matt. 27:46, 50.

And when Jesus had cried with a loud voice, he said, "Father, unto thy hands I commend my spirit:" and having said thus, he gave up the ghost. Luke 23:46.

When Jesus therefore had received the vinegar, he said, "It is finished:" and he bowed his head, and gave up the ghost. John 19:30.

Joseph of Arimathea and Nicodemus bury Jesus' body with myrrh and aloes.

And after this Joseph of Arimathea, being a disciple of Jesus, but secretly for fear of the Jews, besought Pilate that he might take away the body of Jesus: and Pilate gave him leave. He came therefore, and took the body of Jesus. And there came also Nicodemus, which at the first came to Jesus by night and brought a mixture of myrrh and aloes, about an hundred pound weight. Then took they the body of Jesus, and wound it in linen clothes with the spices, as the manner of the Jews is to bury.

Joseph, alone, buries the body without myrrh and aloes.

And when he [Pilate] knew it of the centurion, he gave the body to Joseph. And he bought fine linen, and took him down, and wrapped him in the linen, and laid him in a sepulchre which was hewn out of a rock, and rolled a stone unto the door of the sepulchre. Mark 15:45-56.

And, behold, there was a man named Joseph, a counsellor; and he was a good man, and a just: . . . This man went unto Pilate, and begged the body of Jesus. And he took it down, and wrapped it in linen, and laid it in a sepulchre that

Now in the place where he was crucified there was a garden; and in the garden a new sepulchre, wherein was never man yet laid. There laid they Jesus therefore because of the Jews' preparation day; for the sepulchre was nigh at hand. John 19:38-42.

was hewn in stone, wherein never man before was laid. Luke 23:50, 52-53.

Jesus' death accompanied by an earthquake. The centurion believes because of it. Dead people rise from graves to say hello to strangers, never to be heard from again.

Jesus, when he had cried again with a loud voice, yielded up the ghost. And, behold, the veil of the temple was rent in twain from the top to the bottom; and the earth did quake, and the rocks rent; And the graves were opened; and many bodies of the saints which slept arose, And came out of the graves after his resurrection, and went into the holy city, and appeared unto many. Now when the centurion, and they that were with him, watching Jesus, saw the earthquake, and those things that were done, they feared greatly, saying. "Truly this was the Son of God." And many women were there beholding afar off, which followed Jesus from Galilee, ministering unto him. Matt. 27:50-55.

No earthquake. The centurion believes because of Jesus' cries. Nobody notices open graves with awakening dead men.

And Jesus cried with a loud voice, and gave up the ghost. And the veil of the temple was rent in twain from the top to the bottom. And when the centurion, which stood over against him, saw that he so cried out, and gave up the ghost, he said, "Truly this man was the Son of God." There were also women looking on afar off.

And when Jesus had cried with a loud voice, he said, "Father, into thy hands I commend my spirit:" and having said thus, he gave up the ghost. Now when the centurion saw what was done, he glorified God, saying, "Certainly this was a righteous man." And all the people that came together to that sight, beholding the things which were done, smote their breasts, and returned. And all his acquaintance, and the women that followed him from Galilee, stood afar off, beholding these things. Luke 23:46-49.

When Jesus therefore had received the vinegar, he said, "It is finished:" and he bowed his head and gave up the ghost. The Jews therefore, because it was the preparation, that the bodies should not remain upon the cross on the sabbath day, (for that sabbath day was an high day,) besought Pilate that their legs might be broken, and that they might be taken away. John 19:30-31.

The women prepared spices after the sabbath to anoint the body of Jesus (which according to John had been embalmed!).

And when the sabbath was past, Mary Magdalene, and Mary the mother of James, and Salome, bought sweet spices, so that they might go and anoint him. Mark 16:1 (Revised Standard Version).

(The Authorized Version translators thoughtfully inserted the word "had" to make it appear that the women had previously bought and prepared the spices.)

The messengers at the sepulchre were standing.

And it came to pass, as they were much perplexed thereabout, behold, two men stood by them in shining garments. Luke 24:4.

The women prepared the spices before the sabbath.

And that day was the preparation, and the sabbath drew on. And the women also, which came with him from Galilee, followed after, and beheld the sepulchre, and how his body was laid. And they returned, and prepared spices and ointments; and rested the sabbath day according to the commandment. Luke 23:54-56.

They were sitting.

And, behold, there was a great earthquake: for the angel of the Lord descended from heaven, and came and rolled back the stone from the door, and sat upon it. Matt. 28:2.

And entering into the sepulchre, they saw a young man sitting on the right side, clothed in a long white garment; and they were affrighted. Mark 16:5.

And seeth two angels in white sitting, the one at the head, and the other at the feet, where the body of Jesus had lain. John 20:12.

355

Mary Magdalene did not observe the messengers when she first arrived at the sepulchre.

The first day of the week cometh Mary Magdalene early, when it was yet dark, unto the sepulchre, and seeth the stone taken away from the sepulchre. Then she runneth, and cometh to Simon Peter, and to the other disciple, whom Jesus loved, and saith unto them, "They have taken away the Lord out of the sepulchre, and we know not where they have laid him." Peter therefore went forth, and that other disciple, and came to the sepulchre. . . . Then the disciples went away again unto their own home. But Mary stood without at the sepulchre weeping: and as she wept, she stooped down, and looked into the sepulchre, And seeth two angels in white sitting, the one at the head, and the other at the feet, where the body of Jesus had lain. John 20:1-3, 10-12.

The women see Jesus.

And they departed quickly from the sepulchre with fear and great joy; and did run to bring his disciples word. And as they went to tell his disciples, behold, Jesus met them, saying, "All hail." And they came and held him by the feet, and worshipped him. Matt. 28:8-9.

She observed them on her first visit.

And the angel answered and said unto the women, "Fear not ye: for I know that ye seek Jesus, which was crucified." . . . And they departed quickly from the sepulchre with fear and great joy; and did run to bring his disciples word. Matt. 28:5, 8.

And he saith unto them, "Be not affrighted: Ye seek Jesus of Nazareth, which was crucified: he is risen; he is not here: behold the place where they laid him. But go your way, tell his disciples and Peter that he goeth before you into Galilee: there shall ye see him, as he said unto you." Mark 16:6-7.

And as they were afraid, and bowed down their faces to the earth, they said unto them, "Why seek ye the living among the dead?" . . . And they remembered his words, And returned from the sepulchre and told all these things unto the eleven, and to all the rest. Luke 24:5, 8-9.

The women do not see Jesus.

And they remembered his words, And returned from the sepulchre, and told all these things unto the eleven, and to all the rest. It was Mary Magdalene, and Joanna, and Mary the mother of James, and other women that were with them, which told these things unto the apostles. And their words seemed to them as idle tales, and they believed them not. Then a-

356

rose Peter, and ran unto the sepulchre; and stooping down, he beheld the linen clothes laid by themselves, and departed, wondering in himself at that which was come to pass. And, behold, two of them went that same day to a village called Emmaus, which was from Jerusalem about threescore furlongs. And they talked together of all these things which had happened. And it came to pass, that, while they communed together and reasoned, Jesus himself drew near, and went with them. Luke 24:8-14.

Mary Magdalene recognized Jesus.
And as they went to tell his disciples, behold, Jesus met them, saying, "All hail." And they came and held him by the feet, and worshipped him. Matt. 28:9.

Mary Magdalene did not recognize Jesus.
And when she had thus said, she turned herself back, and saw Jesus standing, and knew not that it was Jesus. John 20:14.

Not all the disciples were finally convinced of the resurrection.
Then the eleven disciples went away into Galilee, into a mountain where Jesus had appointed them. And when they saw him, they worshipped him: but some doubted. Matt. 28:16-17.

All the disciples were convinced.
After these things Jesus shewed himself again to the disciples at the sea of Tiberias; and on this wise shewed he himself. . . . Jesus saith unto them, "Come and dine." And none of the disciples durst ask him, "Who art thou?" knowing that it was the Lord. John 21:1, 12.

The disciples were glad to see Jesus.
And when he had so said, he shewed unto them his hands and his side. Then were the disciples glad, when they saw the Lord. John 20:20.

The disciples were affrighted.
And as they thus spake, Jesus himself stood in the midst of them, and saith unto them, "Peace be unto you." But they were terrified and affrighted, and supposed that they had seen a spirit. Luke 24:36-37.

357

THE GENEALOGY OF JESUS

The book of the generation of Jesus Christ, the son of David, the son of Abraham. Abraham begat Isaac; and Isaac begat Jacob; and Jacob begat Judas and his brethren; And Judas begat Phares and Zara of Thamar; and Phares begat Esrom; and Esrom begat Aram; And Aram begat Aminadab; and Aminadab begat Naasson; and Naasson begat Salmon; And Salmon begat Booz of Rachab; and Booz begat Obed of Ruth; and Obed begat Jesse; And Jesse begat David the king; and David the king begat Solomon of her that had been the wife of Urias; And Solomon begat Roboam; and Roboam begat Abia; and Abia begat Asa; And Asa begat Josaphat; and Josaphat begat Joram; and Joram begat Ozias; And Ozias begat Joatham; and Joatham begat Achaz; and Achaz begat Ezekias; And Ezekias begat Manasses; and Manasses begat Amon; and Amon begat Josias; And Josias begat Jechonias and his brethren, about the time they were carried away to Babylon: And after they were brought to Babylon, Jechonias begat Salathiel; and Salathiel begat Zorobabel; And Zorobabel begat Abiud; and Abiud begat Eliakim; and Eliakim begat Azor; And Azor begat Sadoc; and Sadoc begat Achim; and Achim begat Eliud; And Eliud begat Eleazar; and Eleazar begat Matthan; and Matthan begat Jacob; And Jacob begat

And Jesus himself began to be about thirty years of age, being (as was supposed) the son of Joseph which was the son of Heli, Which was the son of Matthat, which was the son of Levi, which was the son of Melchi, which was the son of Janna, which was the son of Joseph, Which was the son of Mattathias, which was the son of Amos, which was the son of Naum, which was the son of Esli, which was the son of Nagge, Which was the son of Maath, which was the son of Mattathias, which was the son of Semei, which was the son of Joseph, which was the son of Juda, Which was the son of Joanna, which was the son of Rhesa, which was the son of Zorobabel, which was the son of Salathiel, which was the son of Neri, Which was the son of Melchi, which was the son of Addi, which was the son of Cosam, which was the son of Elmodam, which was the son of Er, Which was the son of Jose, which was the son of Eliezer, which was the son of Jorim, which was the son of Matthat, which was the son of Levi, which was the son of Simeon, which was the son of Juda, which was the son of Joseph, which was the son of Jonan, which was the son of Eliakim, Which was the son of Melea, which was the son of Menan, which was the son of Mattatha, which was the son of Nathan, which was the son of David, Which was the son of Jesse,

Joseph the husband of Mary, of whom was born Jesus, who is called Christ. Matt. 1:1-16.

which was the son of Obed, which was the son of Booz, which was the son of Salmon, which was the son of Naasson, Which was the son of Aminadab, which was the son of Aram, which was the son of Esrom, which was the son of Phares, which was the son of Juda, Which was the son of Jacob, which was the son of Isaac, which was the son of Abraham, which was the son of Thara, which was the son of Nachor, Which was the son of Saruch, which was son of Ragau, which was the son of Phalec, which was the son of Heber, which was the son of Sala, Which was the son of Cainan, which was the son of Arphaxad, which was the son of Sem, which was the son of Noe, which was the son of Lamech, Which was the son of Mathusala, which was the son of Enoch, which was the son of Jared, which was the son of Maleleel, which was the son of Cainan, which was the son of Enos, which was the son of Seth, which was the son of Adam, which was the son of God. Luke 3:23-38.

The genealogy of Jesus as given by Matthew is hopelessly at variance with that furnished by Luke.

In Matt. 1:17 the writer sums up the genealogy thus: "So all the generations from Abraham to David are fourteen generations; and from David until the carrying away into Babylon are fourteen generations; and from the carrying away into Babylon unto Christ are fourteen generations."

There are thirteen, not fourteen generations in the third series; and the number fourteen is obtained in the second series only by the deliberate omission of four names — Ahaziah, Joash, and Amaziah between Joram and Azariah (Ozias); and Jehoiakim between Josiah *and Jeconiah.* Compare *1 Chron. 3:11-12, 15-16* ("Joram his son, Ahaziah, his son, Joash his son, Amaziah his son, Azariah his son, Jotham his son.") *with Matt. 1:8-9, 11.*

We find that whereas in 1 Chron. 3:17-19 ("And the sons of Jeconiah; Assir, Salathiel his son, Malchiram also, and Pedaiah, and Shenazar, Jecamiah, Hoshama, and Nedabiah. And the sons of Pedaiah were Zerubbabel, and Shimei") *Zerubbabel is the son of Pedaiah and the nephew of Salathiel; in both Matthew and Luke he is the son of Salathiel.*

In both Chronicles and Matthew, Salathiel is the son of Jeconias. But in Luke he is the son of Neri.

In Matthew, Abuid is the son of Zorobabbel (Zerubabbel). In Luke Zerubbabel's son is Rhesa. According to the chronicler (I Chron. 3:19-20 — "And the sons of Pedaiah were Zerubbabel, and Shimei: and the sons of Zerubbabel; Meshullam, and Hananiah, and Shelomith their sister: And Hashubah, and Ohel, and Berechiah, and Hasadiah, Jushabhesed, five"), *Zerubbabel had seven sons; but neither Matthew's Abuid nor Luke's Rhesa is among them.*

Apart from Joseph there are only two names common to the lists as given by Matthew and Luke — Salathiel and Zerubbabel; and both of these two names certainly have no business in Luke's list. Matthew follows the line of Solomon, while Luke lists that of Nathan, both of whom were sons of David.

Whereas Matthew has it that there were twenty-six generations from David to Jesus, Luke makes it forty-one — a difference of some 400 years!

Finally, if Jesus was born of a virgin, Joseph was not his father and he was not descended from David. By introducing the story of the virgin birth both writers have stultified themselves. Mary was not of the Davidic line; she was the cousin of Elizabeth, who belonged to the tribe of Levi. (Luke 1:5, 34-36 — "There was in the days of Herod, the king of Judea, a certain priest named Zacharias, of the course of Abia: and his wife was of the daughters of Aaron, and her name was Elisabeth. . . . Then said Mary unto the angel, 'How shall this be, seeing I know not a man?' And the angel answered and said unto her, '. . . And, behold, thy cousin Elisabeth she hath also conceived a son in her old age: and this is the sixth month with her, who was called barren.' ").

The story of the miraculous birth of Jesus was an adaptation of similar stories of pagan gods. Christians could not allow that these gods had a status superior to that of Jesus. If they were virgin born, so was Jesus!

In Mark, generally regarded as the earliest gospel, there is not so much as a hint of a virgin birth, whilst in John it is ruled out entirely, as also is the Davidic descent. Here we have a Jesus who was the word "made flesh" existing from the beginning and without parentage. With utter disregard for consistency John, in 6:42, records without comment the remark of "the Jews" that Jesus was the son of Joseph ("And they said, 'Is not this Jesus, the son of Joseph, whose father and mother we know? how is it then that he saith, "I came down from heaven"? ' ").

As already noted Paul affirmed the Davidic ancestry of Jesus, but declared that the birth was "according to the flesh" (Rom. 1:3 — "Concerning his son Jesus Christ our Lord, which was made of the seed of David according to the flesh.").

Paul sees no reason to keep the law.

Knowing that a man is not justified by the works of the law, but by the faith of Jesus Christ, even we have believed in Jesus Christ, that we might be justified by the faith of Christ, and not by the works of the law: for by the works of the law shall no flesh be justified. Gal. 2:16.

Christ hath redeemed us from the curse of the law, being made a curse for us: for it is written, "Cursed is every one that hangeth on a tree." Gal. 3:13.

Paul keeps the law when it is convenient.

And the day following Paul went in with us unto James; and all the elders were present.... And when they heard it, they glorified the Lord, and said unto him, "Thou seest, brother, how many thousands of Jews there are which believe; and they are all zealous of the law: ... Do therefore this that we say to thee: We have four men which have a vow on them; Them take, and purify thyself with them, and be at charges with them, that they may shave their heads: and all may know that those things, whereof they were informed concerning thee, are nothing; but that thou thyself also walkest orderly, and keepest the law." . . . Then Paul took the men, and the next day purifying himself with them entered into the temple, to signify the accomplishment of the days of purification, until that an offering should be offered for every one of them. Acts 21:18, 20, 23-24, 26.

Speaking in tongues is understandable by men.

And they were all filled with the Holy Ghost, and began to speak with other tongues, as the Spirit gave them utterance. And there were dwelling at Jerusalem Jews, devout men, out of every nation under heaven. Now when this was noised abroad, the multitude came together, and were confounded, because that every man heard them speak in his own language. And they were all amazed and marvelled, saying one to another, "behold, are not all these which speak Galileans? And how hear we every man in our own tongue, wherein we were born?" Acts 2:4-9.

Speaking in tongues is not understandable by men.

For he that speaketh in an unknown tongue speaketh not unto men, but unto God: for no man understandeth him; howbeit in the spirit he speaketh mysteries. But he that prophesieth speaketh unto men to edification, and exhortation, and comfort. He that speaketh in an unknown tongue edifieth himself; but he that prophesieth edifieth the church. 1 Cor. 14:2-4.

AMERICAN ATHEIST ADDENDA

ABSURDITIES & CONTRADICTIONS
OLD TESTAMENT

Sons of God ravish daughters of men, then God blames men for being "wicked."

And it came to pass, when men began to multiply on the face of the earth, and daughters were born unto them, That the sons of God saw the daughters of men that they were fair; and they took them wives of all which they chose. And the LORD said, "My spirit shall not always strive with man, for that he also is flesh: yet his days shall be an hundred and twenty years." There were giants in the earth in those days; and also after that, when the sons of God came in unto the daughters of men, and they bare children to them, the same became mighty men which were of old, men of renown. Gen. 6:1-4.

There is a striking similarity here to ancient Greek mythology. There can be little doubt that both this, the Greek, and other similar myths originated from the same source or sources.

The entire earth covered with 22½ feet of water.

And the waters prevailed exceedingly upon the earth; and all the high hills, that were under the whole heaven, were covered. Fifteen cubits upward did the waters prevail; and the mountains were covered. Gen. 7:19-20.

Christians might try to "explain" this by saying the water sloped with the land instead of going to the lowest level.

Sex is blessed.

And God blessed them, and God said unto them, "Be fruitful, and multiply, and replenish the earth, and subdue it: and have dominion over the fish of the sea, and over the fowl of the air, and over every living thing that moveth upon the earth." Gen. 1:28.

Noah was a just man and perfect in his generations, and Noah walked with God. And Noah begat

Sex is condemned.

That the sons of God saw the daughters of men that they were fair; and they took them wives of all which they chose. And the LORD said, "My spirit shall not always strive with man, for that he also is flesh: yet his days shall be an hundred and twenty years." Gen. 6:2-3.

three sons, Shem, Ham and Japheth. Gen. 6:9-10.

God condemns violence.

And God said unto Noah, "The end of all flesh is come before me; for the earth is filled with violence through them; and, behold, I will destroy them with the earth." *Gen. 6:13.* (It cannot be ignored that God destroyed the earth with violence, when his alleged omnipotent power should have been able to peacefully change the ways of men.)

God commends violence.

But Sihon king of Heshbon would not let us pass by him: for the LORD thy God hardened his spirit, and made his heart obstinate, that he might deliver him into thy hand, as appeareth this day. . . . And we took all his cities at that time, and utterly destroyed the men, and the women, and the little ones, of every city, we left none to remain. Deut. 2:30, 34.

There were but three generations in the house of Reuben during the 215 years (see page 3), and those three generations became 43,730 people.

And the sons of Reuben; Hanoch, and Phallu, and Hezron, and Carmi. Gen. 46:9.

Reuben, the eldest son of Israel: the children of Reuben; Hanoch, of whom cometh the family of the Hanochites: of Pallu, the family of the Palluites. . . . These are the families of the Reubenites: and they that were numbered of them were forty and three thousand and seven hundred and thirty. And the sons of Pallu; Eliab. And the sons of Eliab; Nemuel, and Dathan, and Abiram. This is that Dathan and Abiram, which were famous in the congregation, who strove against Moses and against Aaron in the company of Korah, when they strove against the LORD. Num. 26:5, 7-9.

Joshua drives out the Anakim from Hebron.

And at that time came Joshua, and cut off the Anakims from the mountains, from Hebron, from Debir, from Anab, and from all the mountains of Judah, and from all the mountains of Israel: Joshua destroyed them utterly with their cities. Josh. 11:21.

Caleb drives out the Anakim from Hebron.

And unto Caleb the son of Jephunneh he gave a part among the children of Judah, according to the commandment of the LORD to Joshua, even the city of Arba the father of Anak, which city is Hebron. And Caleb drove thence the three sons of Anak, Sheshai, and

Ahiman, and Talmai, the children of Anak. Josh. 15:13-14.

To further confuse matters Judah drives them out again after the death of Joshua ["Now after the death of Joshua it came to pass ... And Judah went against the Canaanites that dwelt in Hebron: (now the name of Hebron before was Kirjatharba:) and they slew Sheshai, and Ahiman, and Talmai." — Judg. 1:1, 10.].

Debir taken by Joshua.	*Debir taken by Othniel.*
And Joshua returned, and all Israel with him, to Debir; and fought against it. And he took it, and the king thereof, and all the cities thereof; and they smote them with the edge of the sword, and utterly destroyed all the souls that were therein; he left none remaining: as he had done to Hebron, so he did to Debir, and to the king thereof; as he had done also to Libnah, and to her king. Josh. 10:38-39.	And he went up thence to the inhabitants of Debir: and the name of Debir before was Kirjathsepher .... And Othniel the son of Kenaz, the brother of Caleb, took it: and he gave him Achsah his daughter to wife. Josh. 15:15, 17.

To further complicate matters Othniel took Debir after the death of Joshua ("Now after the death of Joshua it came to pass ... And from thence he went against the inhabitants of Debir: and the name of Debir before was Kirjathsepher: ... And Othniel the son of Kenaz, Caleb's younger brother, took it: and he gave him Achsah his daughter to wife." — Judg. 1:1, 11, 13.).

Joshua utterly destroys Hazor and kills its King Jabin.	*The same king is fought and killed 120 years after the death of Joshua.*
And it came to pass, when Jabin king of Hazor had heard those things, that he sent to Jobab king of Madon, and to the king of Shimron, and to the king of Achshaph. ... And Joshua at that time turned back, and took Hazor, and smote the king thereof with the	Now after the death of Joshua it came to pass ... And the land had rest forty years. And Othniel the son of Kenaz died. . ... So Moab was subdued that day under the hand of Israel. And the land had rest fourscore years. ... And the LORD sold them into the hand of

367

sword: for Hazor beforetime was the head of all those kingdoms. And they smote all the souls that were therein with the edge of the sword, utterly destroying them: there was not any left to breathe: and he burnt Hazor with fire. Josh. 11:1, 10-11.

Jabin king of Canaan, that reigned in Hazor; the captain of whose host was Sisera, which dwelt in Harosheth of the Gentiles. . . . And the hand of the children of Israel prospered, and prevailed against Jabin the King of Canaan, until they had destroyed Jabin king of Canaan. Judg. 1:1; 3:11, 30; 4:2, 24.

God does not repent.

God is not a man that he should lie; neither the son of man that he should repent. Num. 23:19.

God repents of his evil.

And when the angel stretched out his hand upon Jerusalem to destroy it, the LORD repented him of the evil. . . . 2 Sam. 24:16.

NEW TESTAMENT

Jesus names Simon "the rock" in the middle of his ministry.

And Jesus answered and said unto him, "Blessed art thou, Simon Bar-jona: for flesh and blood hath not revealed it unto thee, but my Father which is in heaven. And I say also unto thee, That thou art Peter, and upon this rock I will build my church; and the gates of hell shall not prevail against it." Matt. 16:7-18. (*"Peter"* is the latin word for "stone." *"Bar"* is Hebrew for "son of.")

Jesus names Simon "the rock" at the start of his ministry.

One of the two which heard John speak, and followed him, was Andrew, Simon Peter's brother. . . . And he brought him to Jesus. And when Jesus beheld him, he said, "Thou art Simon the son of Jona: thou shalt be called Cephas," which is by interpretation, A stone. John 1:40, 42.

Jesus curses the fig tree after making a scene at the temple.

And Jesus went into the temple of God, and cast out all them that sold and bought in the temple, and overthrew the tables of the money-changers, and the seats of them that sold doves. . . . And he left them, and went out of the city into Bethany; and he lodged there. Now in the morning as he returned into the city, he hungered. And when he saw a fig tree in the way, he came to it, and found nothing thereon, but leaves only, and said unto it, "Let no fruit grow on thee henceforward for ever." And presently the fig tree withered away. Matt. 21:12, 17-19.

Jesus curses the fig tree before making a scene at the temple.

And seeing a fig tree afar off having leaves, he came, if haply he might find any thing thereon: and when he came to it, he found nothing but leaves; for the time of figs was not yet. And Jesus answered [?] and said unto it, "No man eat fruit of thee hereafter for ever." And his disciples heard it. And they come to Jerusalem: and Jesus went into the temple, and began to cast out them that sold and bought in the temple, and overthrew the tables of the money-changers, and the seats of them that sold doves. Mark 11:13-15.

369

The devils sought to not go out of the country. And he asked him, "What is thy name?" And he answered, saying, "My name is Legion: for we are many." And he besought him much that he would not send them away out of the country. Mark 5: 9-10.	The devils sought to not go into the deep. And Jesus asked him, saying, "What is thy name?" And he said, "Legion:" because many devils were entered into him. And they besought him that he would not command them to go out into the deep. Luke 8:30-31.

This was followed by the devils going "into the deep" anyway. ("Then went the devils out of the man, and entered into the swine: and the herd ran violently down a steep place into the lake, and were choked." — Luke 8:33.) Why did not Jesus in his "infinite goodness" spare the swines' lives? Why did he cause the loss of much property for the swines' owner? Why did he not just send the devils into the sea by themselves?

Jesus did not know he was being betrayed by Judas. And forthwith he came to Jesus, and said, "Hail, master;" and kissed him. And Jesus said unto him, "Friend, wherefore art thou come?" Then came they, and laid hands on Jesus, and took him. Matt. 26:49-50.	Jesus knew he was being betrayed by Judas. And he that was called Judas, one of the twelve, went before them, and drew near unto Jesus to kiss him. But Jesus said unto him, "Judas, betrayest thou the Son of man with a kiss?" Luke 22:47-48.

The women are told outside the sepulchre that Jesus was risen. In the end of the sabbath, as it began to dawn toward the first day of the week, came Mary Magdalene and the other Mary to see the sepulchre. And, behold, there was a great earthquake: for the angel of the Lord descended from heaven, and came and rolled back the stone from the door, and sat upon it. . . . And the angel answered and said unto the women,	The women go into the tomb and are perplexed. Now upon the first day of the week, very early in the morning, they came unto the sepulchre, bringing the spices which they had prepared, and certain others with them. And they found the stone rolled away from the sepulchre. And they entered in, and found not the body of the Lord Jesus. And it came to pass, as they were much perplexed thereabout, be-

"Fear not ye: for I know that ye seek Jesus, which was crucified. He is not here: for he is risen, as he said. Come, see the place where the Lord lay." Matt. 28:-2, 5-6.

hold, two men stood by them in shining garments. Luke 24:1-4.

Jesus showed himself to the disciples at a mountain in Galilee, and they knew him.

Then the eleven disciples went away into Galilee, into a mountain where Jesus had appointed them. And when they saw him, they worshipped him: but some doubted. Matt. 28:16-17.

Jesus showed himself to the disciples on the shore of Galilee, and they did not know him.

After these things Jesus shewed himself again to the disciples at the sea of Tiberias [Galilee]; and on this wise shewed he himself. . . . But when the morning was now come, Jesus stood on the shore: but the disciples knew not that it was Jesus. John 21:1, 4.

The destruction of Rome was supposed to have occurred during the reign of the eighth emperor of Rome.

And there came one of the seven angels which had the seven vials, and talked with me, saying unto me, "Come hither; I will shew unto thee the judgment of the great whore that sitteth upon many waters: With whom the kings of the earth have committed fornication, and the inhabitants of the earth have been made drunk with the wine of her fornication." So he carried me away in the spirit into the wilderness: and I saw a woman sit upon a scarlet coloured beast, full of names of blasphemy, having seven heads and ten horns. And the woman was arrayed in purple and scarlet colour, and decked with gold and precious stones and pearls, having a golden cup in her hand full of abominations and filthiness of her fornication: And upon her forehead was a name written, MYSTERY, BABYLON THE GREAT, THE MOTHER OF HARLOTS AND ABOMINATIONS OF THE EARTH. And I saw the woman drunken with the blood of the saints, and with the blood of the martyrs of Jesus: and when I saw her, I wondered with great admiration. And the angel said unto me, "Wherefore didst thou marvel? I will tell thee the mystery of the woman, and of the beast that carrieth her, which hath the seven heads and ten horns. The beast that thou sawest was, and is not; and shall ascend out of the bottomless pit, and go into perdition: and they that dwell on the earth shall wonder, whose names were not written in

371

the book of life from the foundation of the world, when they behold the beast that was, and is not, and yet is. And here is the mind which hath wisdom. The seven heads are seven mountains, on which the woman sitteth. And there are seven kings: five are fallen, and one is, and the other is not yet come; and when he cometh, he must continue a short space. And the beast that was, and is not, even he is the eighth, and is of the seven, and goeth into perdition. And the ten horns which thou sawest are ten kings, which have received no kingdom as yet; but receive power as kings one hour with the beast. These have one mind, and shall give their power and strength unto the beast. These shall make war with the Lamb, and the Lamb shall overcome them: for he is Lord of lords, and King of kings: and they that are with him are called, and chosen, and faithful." And he saith unto me, "The waters which thou sawest, where the whore sitteth, are peoples, and multitudes, and nations, and tongues. And the ten horns which thou sawest upon the beast, these shall hate the whore, and shall make her desolate and naked, and shall eat her flesh, and burn her with fire. For God hath put in their hearts to fulfil his will, and to agree, and give their wisdom unto the beast, until the words of God shall be fulfilled. And the woman which thou sawest is that great city, which reigneth over the kings of the earth." *Rev. 17:1-18.*

Rome was universally recognized as the "city of seven hills." This chapter refers to the sixth king (emperor) as reigning at the time of its writing. The seventh was to come and reign only "a short space" before the eighth, the beast, was to appear. Thus at this time, sometime in the first century A.D., the kingdom of God was supposed to come and destroy Rome.

History records that there was no such event.

Don't Miss The
American Atheist

Founded by the first lady of Atheism, Dr. Madalyn O'Hair, the *American Atheist* is the magazine of the modern Atheist.

From the latest deeds of Atheist activists to the last antics of the religious right, its articles run the gamut of issues important to Atheists. Skirmishes in the state/church separation battle, the life-style and history of Atheism, religious criticism, current events are all included in the focus of this journal. The nation's hottest topics — school prayer, abortion, creationism — are all covered in its pages from the Atheist's viewpoint.

This magazine's writers bring readers a unique spectrum of viewpoints from literally all over the world. Examples? One columnist offers glimpses into the religions of India. Another highlights the pain of women in the Arab world. Jon Murray, president of American Atheists, spotlights the progress of Atheism (and religion) in the United States.

So why miss any more of this fascinating magazine? Though it is free to members of American Atheists, it is also available to nonmembers on a yearly subscription basis. Go ahead: Check off a box below and head into the wonderful world of Atheism.

☐ Regular subscription, $25   ☐ Sustaining subscription, $50
☐ Foreign subscription, $35   (tax-deductible)
☐ Sample copy, $2

Last name ————————— First name ——————————

Address ——————————————————————————

City/State/Zip ——————————————————————

☐ I am enclosing a check or money order for $ ——————— payable to American Atheists.

☐ Please charge my credit card for $ ———————. ☐ Visa or ☐ MasterCard

Card # ————————————————————————————

Bank Name ———————————————————————

Expiration date ——————————————————————

Signature ——————————————————————

Return form to:
American Atheists, Inc., P. O. Box 140195, Austin, TX 78714-0195

"AIMS AND PURPOSES"

(as recorded in documents of incorporation)

AMERICAN ATHEISTS ARE ORGANIZED:

(1) to stimulate and promote freedom of thought and inquiry concerning religious beliefs, creeds, dogmas, tenets, rituals, and practices;

(2) to collect and disseminate information, data, and literature on all religions and promote a more thorough understanding of them, their origins, and their histories;

(3) to advocate, labor for, and promote in all lawful ways the complete and absolute separation of state and church;

(4) to advocate, labor for, and promote in all lawful ways the establishment and maintenance of a thoroughly secular system of education available to all;

(5) to encourage the development and public acceptance of a humane ethical system, stressing the mutual sympathy, understanding, and interdependence of all people and the corresponding responsibility of each individual in relation to society;

(6) to develop and propagate a social philosophy in which man is the central figure, who alone must be the source of strength, progress, and ideals for the well-being and happiness of humanity;

(7) to promote the study of the arts and sciences and of all problems affecting the maintenance, perpetuation, and enrichment of human (and other) life; and

(8) to engage in such social, educational, legal, and cultural activity as will be useful and beneficial to members of American Atheists and to society as a whole.

"DEFINITIONS"

Atheism is the *Weltanschauung* (comprehensive conception of the world and of total human life value systems) of persons who are *free* from theism — *i.e., free from* religion. It is predicated on ancient Greek Materialism.

American Atheism may be defined as the mental attitude that unreservedly accepts the supremacy of reason and aims at establishing a life-style and ethical outlook verifiable by experience and the scientific method, independent of all arbitrary assumptions of authority or creeds.

Materialism declares that the cosmos is devoid of immanent conscious purpose; that it is governed by its own inherent, immutable, and impersonal laws; that there is no supernatural interference in human life; that man — finding his resources within himself — can and must create his own destiny. Materialism restores to man his dignity and his intellectual integrity. It teaches that we must prize our life on earth and strive always to improve it. It holds that man is capable of creating a social system based on reason and justice. Materialism's "faith" is in man and man's ability to transform the world culture by his own efforts. This is a commitment which is in every essence life-asserting. It considers the struggle for progress as a moral obligation and impossible without noble ideas that inspire man to struggle and bold creative works. Materialism holds that humankind's potential for good and for an outreach to more fulfilling cultural development is, for all practical purposes, unlimited.

American Atheists is a nonpolitical, nonprofit, educational organization. Another of its functions is to act as a "watchdog" to challenge any attempted breach of what Thomas Jefferson called "the wall of separation between state and church," upon which principle our nation was founded.

Membership is open only to those who are in accord with the "Aims and Purposes" indicated above and who are Atheist Materialists. Membership in the national organization is a prerequisite for membership in state, county, city, or local chapters. Membership fee categories are reflected on the reverse side of this sheet (American Atheists Membership Application form).

American Atheists, Inc.
P. O. Box 140195
Austin, TX 78714-0195

Membership Application For American Atheists

Last name _____ First name _____

Companion's name (if family or couple membership)

Last name _____ First name _____

Address _____

City/State/Zip _____

This is to certify that I am/we are in agreement with the "Aims and Purposes" and the "Definitions" of American Atheists. I/We consider myself/ourselves to be Materialist or Non-theist (*i.e.*, A-theist) and I/we have, therefore, a particular interest in the separation of state and church and American Atheists' efforts on behalf of that principle.

I/We usually identify myself/ourselves for public purposes as (check one):

☐ Atheist ☐ Objectivist ☐ Agnostic
☐ Freethinker ☐ Ethical Culturist ☐ Realist
☐ Humanist ☐ Unitarian ☐ I/We evade any re-
☐ Rationalist ☐ Secularist ply to a query
☐ Other: _____

I am/We are, however, an Atheist(s) and I/we hereby make application for membership in American Atheists. Both dues and contributions are to a tax-exempt organization and I/we may claim these amounts as tax deductions on my/our income tax return(s). *(This application must be dated and signed by the applicant[s] to be accepted.)*

Signature _____ Date _____

Signature _____ Date _____

Membership in American Atheists includes a subscription to the monthly journal *American Atheist* and the monthly *Insider's Newsletter* as well as all the other rights and privileges of membership. Please indicate your choice of membership dues:

☐ Life, $750
☐ Couple Life, $1,000 (Please give both names above.)
☐ Sustaining, $150/year
☐ Couple/Family, $75/year (Please give all names above.)

☐ Individual, $50/year
☐ Age 65 or over, $25/year (Photocopy of ID required.)
☐ Student, $20/year (Photocopy of ID required.)

Upon your acceptance into membership, you will receive a handsome gold embossed membership card, a membership certificate personally signed by Jon G. Murray, president of American Atheists, our special monthly *Insider's Newsletter* to keep you informed of the activities of American Atheists, and a subscription to *American Atheist*. Life members receive a specially embossed pen and pencil set; sustaining members receive a commemorative pen. Your name will be sent to the Chapter in your local area if there currently is one, and you will be contacted so you may become a part of the many local activities. Memberships and subscriptions are nonrefundable.

☐ I am/We are enclosing a check or money order for $ _____ payable to American Atheists

☐ Please charge my/our charge card for $ _____ . ☐ Visa or ☐ MasterCard

Card # _____

Bank Name _____

Expiration date _____

Signature _____

Return form to:
American Atheists, Inc., P. O. Box 140195, Austin, TX 78714-0195